AF271451

ADVANCE PRAISE FOR DARREN WALKER'S
THE IDEA OF AMERICA

Darren Walker is driven by a deep conviction that the idea of America can be realized if we work together—and his book will make believers out of readers, too. It beautifully captures the spirit of optimism, creativity, and compassion that has made him one of the most influential leaders of the twenty-first century and a force for change on so many important issues.

—**Michael Bloomberg**

Darren Walker's collection of essays, speeches, and reflections is a testimony from one of the most powerful voices in modern philanthropy. *The Idea of America* explores how rediscovering our common principles can illuminate a united path forward, at a time when we need it most.

—**Amal Clooney and George Clooney**

Darren Walker reaches into the marrow of who we are now—and who we might still become. Through a stunning chronicle of his life and learnings, Darren offers not just a reflection, but a reckoning: He shares his vision while reminding us that justice and dignity are not merely ideals of the past, but tasks of the present. Darren is dynamic, propulsive, intentional. His influence is a sprawl—from emerging artists to the world's most high-profile leaders. *The Idea of America* speaks to that reach, and, more importantly, to the rare and generous spirit that fuels it. In this beautiful book, Darren Walker's unshakable purpose becomes our rallying call.

—**Ava DuVernay**

With the values of pluralism, inclusion, and social justice under assault, we need to reassert how our historic, shared ideals should unite Americans rather than pull us apart. In these bracing essays, Darren Walker summons us, on the 250th anniversary of our founding, to remember our higher calling as a nation.

—**Walter Isaacson**

Darren Walker ushered in a new era in the history of American philanthropy, dedicated to closing the inequality gap, centering human dignity, and advancing social justice. In his valedictory book, he curates years of brilliant reflections, seminal essays, and beautifully crafted speeches. Readers witness his remarkable rise, his inquisitive and fertile mind, the clarity of his strategic vision, and the courage of his convictions. Through his visionary leadership, he has rallied us to the enduring creed of forging a more perfect union for all, especially our most disadvantaged fellow citizens. Darren Walker is a singular leader and a unique historical figure, and this collection is both a deeply moving record of his theory and practice of philanthropy, as well as an invaluable resource for those seeking inspiration in these challenging times, eager to build on his legacy by imagining and pursuing a more just and hopeful future.
—**Henry Louis Gates, Jr.**

THE
IDEA
OF
AMERICA

THE IDEA OF AMERICA

REFLECTIONS ON INEQUALITY, DEMOCRACY, AND THE VALUES WE SHARE

DARREN WALKER

WILEY

Library of Congress Cataloging-in-Publication Data is Available:

ISBN 9781394353828 (Cloth)
ISBN 9781394353842 (ePDF)
ISBN 9781394353835 (ePub)

Cover Design: Wiley
Author Photo: © Annie Leibovitz

SKY10124234_081425

To all who serve the idea of America: That out of many, we are one—created equal with inalienable rights—united by our fidelity to the democratic values we hold self-evident even still.

CONTENTS

**PART II
UPROOTING INEQUALITY AND MOVING
THE FORD FOUNDATION FORWARD**

Contents

PART IV
THE ART OF DEMOCRACY

**PART V
DEMOCRATIC CAPITALISM:
ECONOMIC OPPORTUNITY AND SHARED PROSPERITY**

PART VI
THE COVID-19 CRISIS: EXTRAORDINARY TIMES, EXTRAORDINARY MEASURES

PART VII
FROM AN AMERICAN CENTURY
TO INCLUSIVE GLOBAL ENGAGEMENT

PART VIII
OUT OF MANY, ONE:
WHY DIFFERENCE NEED NOT YIELD DIVISION

Contents

PART IX
THE PROMISE OF AMERICA

Contents

PART X
IN CELEBRATION:
PROFILES IN LOVE AND LEADERSHIP

PART XI
A CALL FOR COURAGEOUS, MORAL LEADERSHIP

Contents

FOREWORD

President Bill Clinton

You never know who you'll run into walking the halls at the Clinton Global Initiative's Annual Meeting—from young social entrepreneurs, activists, athletes, and academics to CEOs of big companies and founders of small ones they hope will grow; from heads of state and government officials to leaders of small and large NGOs working on every kind of issue; from Hollywood royalty to actual royalty.

In the twenty years since we started holding the meetings, there's always a buzz when Darren Walker enters the room. The explanation for this is simple: In the universe of people working to do social good, few voices are as respected and few track records are as accomplished as his. His leadership of the Ford Foundation has not only transformed a storied institution, but reimagined philanthropy and changed America and the world. When he speaks, this crowd listens.

Darren's journey has been as improbable as it has been uniquely American. Born in a charity hospital in Louisiana and raised in a shotgun house in rural Texas, the trajectory of his life changed forever when his mother enrolled him in the first class of Head Start in 1965. Supported by his family, teachers, and community, he thrived in school. He went on to attend The University of Texas with the help of a Pell grant, earning both his bachelor's and law degrees there.

After working in law and finance for several years, Darren made the transition from the private to the nonprofit sector in the 1990s through his tireless efforts to revitalize Harlem with the Abyssinian Development Corporation. Among his greatest accomplishments was bringing the first supermarket to 125th Street, serving as an anchor to the stretch of boulevard where I would open my post-presidential office just two years later. He then moved to the Rockefeller Foundation, where among other initiatives, he spearheaded the organization's Hurricane Katrina recovery efforts. In 2010, he joined the Ford Foundation, becoming its president in 2013.

In 2015, Darren and Ford announced a bold effort to refocus the foundation's work to solely address the issue of inequality, in all its forms—"in influence, access, agency, resources, and respect." Inequality, he argued, underlies nearly all other challenges facing the world. Addressing it could strengthen and fundamentally change our political, economic, and cultural systems to ensure full participation and afford the dignity that accompanies it for all people, everywhere. This would change how and for what Ford provided funding, and how it operated and invested as an institution.

Darren's announcement was soon followed by his landmark essay, "Toward a New Gospel of Wealth," in which he argued that the nineteenth-century model of charity was no longer suited to our increasingly interdependent world. He urged us to move from generosity to justice—not just treating the symptoms of inequality, but dismantling the systems that perpetuate it. That meant listening to more voices and perspectives, especially those who had been left out and left behind for too long and who are closest to the problems we need to solve. And it meant asking hard questions about ourselves and our positions within the power structures that cause inequality in the first place.

In Darren's leadership at Ford since then, he's proved his words were not hollow. He's overseen more than $7 billion in grantmaking to groundbreaking individuals and organizations who are addressing the root causes of poverty and injustice. He's launched an initiative to invest $1 billion of Ford's endowment in mission-oriented areas like affordable housing and biotech, generating a return of both purpose and profit. During the COVID-19 crisis, he pioneered Ford's issuance of the first-ever social bond by a foundation, with the proceeds providing unrestricted support to Ford's nonprofit partners. And in 2021, he announced that Ford would no longer invest in fossil fuels. Every one of these actions encouraged other foundations large and small to follow in Ford's footsteps.

In these pages, you will meet the essential Darren Walker through his most essential speeches and writings, extolling the promise of America and of pluralist democracy all around the world. This is a collection that looks forward, not backward. It doesn't just memorialize Darren's leadership, though it does that. It's also a roadmap for how we move forward together, informed by our shared values.

Throughout the collection, you'll see Darren's prescience. From the very beginning of his tenure in 2013 (and before), he foresaw how inequality of all kinds was tearing apart America's social fabric—and, in turn, tearing apart our culture and politics at the seams. It's only grown worse as the years have progressed, as polarization and the zero-sum politics of resentment become more entrenched and our information ecosystem becomes more broken. Darren captures the sweep of these troubling trends masterfully in his 2024 address at Cooper Union.

But as he has said many times, including in that speech, what makes America great is not the fact of our perfection but our efforts to become more perfect—the mission our founders set for us nearly 250 years ago.

What makes America strong is that at key moments, we've been courageous enough to acknowledge our flaws and missteps—and then bold enough to turn wrong into right.

Dr. Martin Luther King Jr. summarized America's journey well when he said, "The arc of the moral universe is long, but it bends toward justice." Winston Churchill took a slightly more pessimistic approach when he is said to have quipped, "America always does the right thing after exhausting every other option." So far, they've both been right, though Dr. King might have said less poetically that we zig and zag toward justice.

In times like this, when we are moving dangerously backward, it is important to remember that there are very few permanent victories or defeats in human affairs. It may be that we are in a period of two steps back before we'll take three steps forward again. After all, as Darren says, "Hope is the oxygen of democracy." If we truly believe in the promise of America, we can't give up.

The unfinished work ahead, for all of us, is to embrace Darren's call as our own—to build an economy that works for everyone, a society worthy of our noblest aspirations, and a politics that appeals to our better angels. If we all do our part, as Darren has done for twelve years at the Ford Foundation, we can build a future we are truly proud to share.

THE
IDEA
OF
AMERICA

What makes America great is not the fact of our perfection but our act of becoming more perfect. What makes the American people exceptional is that we have the strength to acknowledge our failings—moral, structural, personal—and the courage to make wrong into right.

Let's step away from the extremes and from the edge, away from the sanctimony and certitude. Let's build longer bridges, not higher walls. The cost of the alternative is greater than any of us can bear.

Let's resolve to listen with humility, curiosity, and empathy— with open hearts and minds. Let's resolve to extend the presumption of grace and the benefit of the doubt.

The road to enduring justice runs through reconciliation, and the road to reconciliation runs through truth.

One of our hard truths is that, as the poet says, America has never been America. Another truth is that it can be still, and it must be, and it will be—if we renew our fidelity to the values that bind us, both despite and because of our differences.

The New York Times
July 4, 2022

PART I

MY AMERICAN STORY AND OUR AMERICAN JOURNEY

As we approach the 250th anniversary of our founding, we must redeclare that we all are created equal, endowed with equally inalienable rights, and recommit ourselves to realizing these values. We must rededicate ourselves to what President Abraham Lincoln called "the unfinished work" of building the pluralist democracy to which we all aspire.

I believe fiercely in the promise of America. My love for this nation is unyielding and unwavering.

As Americans, we have a charge to keep, a beacon to keep alight, especially now, as minoritarian tyranny has taken hold of our institutions. It is systematically dismantling the scaffolding from which we built our democracy, without any clear sense of what will replace it. For some, perhaps, the objective is not to replace it at all.

In this new era of deconstruction, we must summon renewed fortitude, resilience, and vigilance, with reverence for those who came before us and resolve for those who follow. This will require patriotic defiance, with respect for the rule of law but with fidelity to the ideals that precede it.

With hope, let us rejoin and rebuild, until America is America and the unfinished is complete.

The New York Times
June 30, 2023

FINDING MY WAY HOME

Statement upon Appointment as President of the Ford Foundation
New York, New York
July 25, 2013

I am humbled by the trust you have placed in me. I pledge to work with energy and integrity; to lead while listening and learning; to give my everything in service of our mission to build a world that is fairer and more just.

It's been said that our journeys are neither marathons nor sprints, but relays. In that spirit, I have the honor of taking up the baton carried by my venerable predecessors, legends in the field of philanthropy.

To Franklin Thomas, a trailblazer, a visionary, and a mentor to me and so many: Thank you. It is not possible to overstate the influence you've had on me—and on this singular institution. Your voice still echoes in the halls here, and your shadow looms large over our ways of being and our ways of seeing.

To Susan Berresford: Thank you for your decades of good works, strong leadership, and great example. During my years at the Rockefeller Foundation, I always admired you from afar—and found great inspiration in your decency and integrity. I must say that, today, I appreciate your counsel and your friendship more than ever.

To Luis Ubiñas: Thank you for so much—for supporting me, for encouraging me, and for bringing me here. I, quite literally, would not be here had you not called and invited me to talk on a beautiful spring day in 2010.

And, of course, to my colleagues in this building and around the world: I cannot express the depth of my appreciation and admiration for each of you. You have nurtured me, inspired me, sometimes indulged me, and always cheered me on. Our friends and colleagues in Delhi, Cairo, Nairobi, and Johannesburg were particularly generous and welcoming on my recent visits with them.

I must say, the first time I walked into our iconic headquarters as an employee of the Ford Foundation, I not only knew that my life had changed; I knew that I had found my way home.

Almost fifty years ago, my mother was raising my sister Renee and me in the rural, East Texas town of Ames, population 1,800. We lived in a narrow, shotgun house. We had just enough, but not a lot.

Sometime around my fifth birthday, a clipboard-carrying young woman knocked on our door—and began a conversation with my mom on our porch. As it turned out, this woman worked for a brand-new education program—the leading edge of President Johnson's War on Poverty—and she asked my mother if she would enroll me.

My mother said yes, of course. And not long thereafter, I began attending a makeshift preschool at a church not far from our home. It was not until years later that I learned that the idea for this particular program was funded with an investment from the Ford Foundation.

The program was called Head Start. And it gave me mine.

During the years and decades that followed, the Ford Foundation indirectly—and sometimes directly—altered my life's course.

I often remind people that I've never attended a day of private school in my life. I attended the Goose Creek, Texas, public schools—and the Ford Foundation has been, and remains, a passionate advocate for public education.

I'm also a proud alum of The University of Texas, where I went to college and law school, and because my family was low-income, my education was financed in part by a Pell grant, another Ford Foundation policy innovation.

During and after school, I benefited, I'm certain, from affirmative action and diversity policies—policies that the Ford Foundation's courageous grantees like the NAACP Legal Defense and Educational Fund and Mexican American Legal Defense and Education Fund have championed for a half century. Given my background, there were gaps in my college readiness no doubt, but my potential was recognized, and I think most who look at my record in college would agree that it was a successful one.

I started my career in New York, working at a Wall Street law firm and investment bank, where I learned countless, invaluable lessons. But I knew a job in finance wasn't my fate. And after a decade, there it was again—the Ford Foundation was back in my life.

First, in 1994, I met Reverend Calvin Butts and Karen Phillips, the dynamic duo who had founded the Abyssinian Development Corporation, one of many community development corporations across the country, as you know, brought to us all by the Ford Foundation.

People in Harlem didn't appreciate the media's repeated references to Harlem as a "ghetto." So Calvin Butts, Karen Phillips, and other community residents decided that they should begin the heavy lifting of rebuilding their historic neighborhood and restoring its reputation.

But at the time, ADC was just getting going—and it needed funding. Fortunately, Ford had created the Local Initiatives Support Corporation or LISC. With the support of LISC's energetic leader Paul Grogan, it awarded ADC with a sizeable grant, more than enough to hire a younger, slimmer Darren Walker. And not long thereafter, we secured our first Ford Foundation grant—an imprimatur of excellence—courtesy of Ford's Melvin Oliver and Fred Davie.

And thus began an unexpected adventure that later brought me to the Rockefeller Foundation. To the world of philanthropy, about which, quite frankly, I knew absolutely nothing. And eventually to my role with Judith Rodin, a brilliant agent of innovation and change. The rest, as they say, is history.

The point of all this is both simple and profound: In so many ways, my life's story is inseparable from the Ford Foundation's story. I am of this place. I am because of it.

And I share my story not because it somehow makes me unique. I share it because my story is not unique.

Around the world, the Ford Foundation has touched and transformed the lives of millions of young boys and girls who have hopes and dreams, aspirations that they have the right to pursue.

Around the globe, we and our grantees measure our accomplishments in wars for social justice won—and in battles for social justice we're still waging. We are builders at the Ford Foundation. We build lasting institutions, human capital and capacity, transformative ideas.

So our work remains as relevant as ever, perhaps more so. And that is precisely because what philanthropy can—and must—do has never been more important. This is why we are called to be here—all of us.

I'm reminded, in fact, of a message to philanthropists written by Dr. Martin Luther King Jr., exactly fifty years ago, as he and so many others prepared for the Birmingham Campaign.

"Philanthropy is commendable," he wrote. "But"—and I'm quoting here—"it must not cause the philanthropist to overlook the circumstances of economic injustice which make philanthropy necessary."

Think about that. These words still challenge us today. They challenge us not to be smug in our privilege—nor comfortable in our abundance.

Maybe the way we should see it is that our most important job is to work ourselves out of a job—to toil against injustice until there is justice; to even out inequality until there is equality.

That means we will never be content to merely wait for "the long arc of history" to "bend toward justice." Rather, we find and support those who are doing the bending—our valiant grantees.

And, finally, in everything we do, we cannot lose sight of the imperative for social innovation. We have to honestly ask and assess: As an institution that has been on front lines of social innovation for seventy-five years, how do we most effectively reimagine, reinvent, and retool today—to advance not only development, but justice?

In the days and weeks ahead, I'm excited to spend as much time with as many of you as possible. I'll ask this question and others, like, how can we better cooperate and collaborate and cocreate with our peer and partner institutions?

I pledge to listen—and I promise to learn.

Most of all, I give you my word: I will not forget where we started—where I started—and what we all stand for, and what we work for. The fight for human dignity wherever we are in the world. The unfettered expansion of human rights. The unrelenting pursuit of social justice. The conviction that all children—like those two kids on the stoop in East Texas—deserve a fair start in life, no matter where or how we begin.

For me, the board's decision to appoint me as the Ford Foundation's tenth president is the thrill of my life. As I said, I'm deeply humbled in so many ways.

But the greatest honor and privilege of all is that I can continue serving with you, my colleagues—from New Delhi to New York; from Jakarta to Johannesburg; from Cairo to Beijing; from Lagos to Rio de Janeiro, Santiago, and Mexico City. You are the foundation of this foundation. I will always, always remember that.

And so let's embrace our future. Boldly. With ambition and humility. Mindful of our legacy. With the conviction of our ideals and values. But, most of all, together.

BUILD A BRIDGE TO A BETTER WORLD

Address to The University of Texas at Austin Class of 2015
Austin, Texas
May 23, 2015

Thank you, President Powers, for your generous words, for so warmly welcoming me back to the Forty Acres, and—much more importantly—for your almost forty years of service to The University of Texas.

Through decades of progress, and a few moments of adversity, your unwavering courage has set a powerful example for generations—and your boundless love for this institution has remained a stalwart inspiration to me, and to alumni around the world.

To you, President Powers; to our distinguished regents; to President-Elect Fenves; esteemed deans; members of the faculty and staff; honored guests; family and friends of the graduates; and, most importantly to the Class of 2015: Congratulations!

This is a momentous evening—a monumental rite of passage—one of those special, fleeting moments that will radiate in your memories for the rest of your lives.

Take it from me. I can vividly recall almost everything about my commencement day. The pride. The joy. The uncertainty. The relief.

I also remember when I first set foot on this campus in 1978; I was a clueless, naive, skinny version of myself. There I was, walking past new kinds of people (I had never seen hippies before); walking on the Drag and into this weird, funky, hole-in-the-wall grocery store (a place called Whole Foods).

I always knew I wanted to be a part of the UT community—and, though I've traveled far and wide, I've never been apart from it.

My first semester here, I believe I responded to every sign-up sheet I saw on the West Mall. During my time on this magical campus, I drank UT life from a firehose. Every drop. In many ways, it was only when I arrived here that my life finally started.

Now, to understand what I mean, you have to understand where I was coming from.

I was born to a single mother in a charity hospital, and we lived in a small, segregated, Louisiana town. But my mother realized that this community was not a place of opportunity for my sister and me, and so we moved to Texas, where we had family—specifically to a town called Ames, population 1,800, in Liberty County.

My mom studied to become a nurse's assistant, a job she worked—with pride and dignity—for decades. I attended public schools.

We didn't have a lot. But we had enough. And these were my beginnings.

Class of 2015: I tell you all this for two reasons. First, your name is on the degree, but it doesn't belong only to you. The second reason I tell you this story is because my story is your story.

The story of a boy who started life in a little shotgun house in Ames, Texas; the story of a young man who made his way up the ladder in a new city, who has the great privilege of leading an institution committed to ending poverty and injustice in the world—this is a Texas story. This is an American story.

It's a story about transcending and overcoming; about the pathway out and forward. In short, it's a story about bridges. About crossing them. Building them. Being them.

You see, my mother crossed a bridge to take my sister and me into Texas. I'll never forget crossing the bridge over the Colorado River on my first visit to Austin. I crossed a bridge into New York when I took my University of Texas education out into the world.

In fact, every major turning point in my life—every figurative bridge—has been accompanied by a literal one.

Yet, the most important crossings in our lives are not always made of cables and concrete and steel. The bridges in our lives take many forms.

On my journey, there was my mother—a bridge from poverty into possibility. But there also were public policies that reflected the generosity of America, the country we love—the only country in the world where my story could even be possible.

A program called Head Start was my bridge between being unready for life and prepared for school.

Private scholarships from Texas philanthropists and Pell grants were my bridge between lower expectations and higher education.

And during my formative years, I always knew—with every fiber of my being—that Texas had my back. That Texas was cheering me on.

In Austin, I had mentors like my English professor, John Trimble, who told me that you don't come to college to get a job; you come to college to get an education. I had champions—women and men who, through their kindness, offered me a bridge to a world I could not have imagined on my own. Without them, I wouldn't be here. Period.

Graduates: Just like me, you're the product of a community that has prepared you to prosper and to thrive.

In New York, I inhabit a world of prep school grads and Ivy League alums. The tiny island of Manhattan is densely packed with some of the most talented, ambitious people on the planet. But my UT education—my public-school education—prepared me to compete, to succeed, and, ultimately, to lead. And it has prepared you, too.

This is the privilege of Texas bigheartedness—the promise of Texas bridges.

My bridges were Black, white, gay, straight, rich, poor, and everything in between. And like all bridges, they don't discriminate. They join people and places of all creeds and colors, of all communities and categories. They take us on a journey, together—hopefully, somewhere better. And this is something of which I was reminded only a few months ago, on a very special bridge in Selma, Alabama.

As many of you know, this year marks the fiftieth anniversary of the Civil Rights Movement's Bloody Sunday, a defining moment in American history. I was honored to attend the celebration back in March. It was incredibly, profoundly moving.

I traveled to Selma with one of my personal heroes, Congressman John Lewis, who marched on the Edmund Pettus Bridge a half century ago. When John boldly led the group of marchers forward in 1965, he was a twenty-five-year-old kid, more or less, your age. He not only yearned for a better world; he was willing to give everything for it.

Meanwhile, a few hundred miles away, I was just five years old, and I had no idea what John Lewis was doing for me. He and the others on the bridge marched into men on horses with clubs—straight into a swift and certain beating—so that I wouldn't have to. Indeed, I am here today because John Lewis, and countless others, put their lives on the line, and made sacrifices for what they believed in.

And yet, there is more that we must do together.

We must continue to bridge gaps of inequality—in our culture, in our economy, in our discourse, and in our politics. Because the truth is, we see inequality virtually everywhere—in studies and statistics; in schoolhouses and courthouses and jailhouses; and, yes, on the streets of Baltimore and Ferguson and elsewhere.

To me, the challenges of our system are intensely personal. My childhood friends were cousins—boys with talents and passions and potential no different from my own.

As I mentioned, my mother moved my sister and me from Louisiana to Texas. But what happened to my cousins who stayed behind? They found themselves in the same cycle of despair that has caught too many young Black men. By my count, five of them have spent significant time in prison.

It's hard to know why, for some of us, life unfolds in one way—and, for others, completely differently. But, in my case, I think bridges made the difference. People had my back, and institutions kept me moving forward. I had bridges built in Texas, and beyond. I had bridges to hope.

And so, I choose to be hopeful—radically hopeful—because there is hope in the progress we have seen, which affirms that more progress is possible. My story is all the evidence you need: A Black kid from a working-class, rural, Texas town, now president of one of our nation's flagship institutions.

I am proof of what happens when people set aside differences, and build bridges instead. And I've made my life's story into my life's passion—and my life's passion into my life's project: Ensuring that every boy and girl in this country and around the world can cross the same bridges that I did.

This is not a new aspiration. These are not new ideas.

America always has been about people choosing to bind themselves together. Actively choosing.

We are "we, the people." We are *e pluribus unum*—out of many, one. We are the hope of mothers and fathers of every origin crossing an ocean—or a river. We are the transcontinental railroad and transatlantic flights and the interstate highway system and the Internet. We are Ellis Island and the Edmund Pettus Bridge.

I know each of you has your own bridges to build, and to traverse. The bridge between graduation and getting a job. The bridge between an environment in peril and ecosystems back in balance. The bridge between communities desperate with need and those rich in abundance.

And so, tonight, as you cross the figurative bridge that is your commencement day—as you cross that bridge over the Colorado River and leave the Forty Acres behind; as your journey unfolds before your very eyes—think about how you can build a bridge to a better world.

You know, my office at the Ford Foundation is overflowing with mementos and memories from my unlikely journey—artifacts from global megacities and rural villages alike.

I traveled more than one hundred thousand miles last year—from boardrooms to battered slums; from Detroit to Delhi; from the United Nations to the most impoverished of countries. Everywhere I visit, I try to bring something back, even if it's just an idea.

Among the many important things I keep are two sticky notes, affixed to my computer monitor. On them are written a pair of personal mottos. One says "pressure is a privilege." The other, "You rest, you rust."

No doubt, bridges endure a lot of pressure. Bridges corrode, and crumble. They rust. Being a bridge is the work of a lifetime.

But you're prepared. Privileged, but poised to change the world.

Yes, a banker can be a bridge. A teacher can be a bridge. A social worker or a scientist, a doctor or a diplomat, a police officer or a computer programmer can be a bridge. And for you law-school grads and hopefuls out there: Even a lawyer can be a bridge.

So, every time you feel pressure, embrace the privilege. Every time you feel tempted to rest on your laurels, make that day matter. Because, yes, "what starts here changes the world," but in order to change the world, what starts here cannot stop here.

As I've traveled the globe, I've seen how Texas has prepared me for every challenge, to cross every bridge, to build bridges where they didn't yet exist. And everywhere I go, I know that the world needs a little more of that Texas spirit.

Class of 2015: Your future is here. I cannot wait to see what bridges you cross, what bridges you build, and who you bring together on your journey.

Oh, and one last thing: Hook 'em Horns!

THE POWER OF THE MIGHTY SUNFLOWER

Address to The University of Texas at Austin
Law School Class of 2016
Austin, Texas
May 21, 2016

It is wonderful to be back on the Forty Acres. I spent seven of the most glorious years of my life, formative years, on this great campus. And while I live in New York City, returning to Austin always feels like coming home.

As I remember it, law school was the best, hardest experience of my life. I felt so proud to walk up the steps of Townes Hall each morning. I was inspired and challenged by the great faculty. And I made friends and built relationships that remain with me today.

Today, as someone who travels in circles outside Texas, I can say one thing with certainty: Far beyond the borders of this state, this degree—and this institution—has a reputation for excellence, and for producing excellent lawyers. When I think about this outstanding law school, and its impact on my life, one simple word always comes to mind: Prepared.

Now this might seem like a pretty boring, unimpressive word. But there's a big idea in it. So let me tell you what I mean.

For most of the twentieth century, a law degree prepared you to be a lawyer. In the twenty-first century, a law degree prepares you to be anything you want. And no matter where I've worked—from the law firm to the trading floor, from the streets of Harlem to the halls of the Ford Foundation—I have always found that Texas Law prepared me for the task at hand. And I have come to more fully understand why the sunflower is our distinctive insignia.

The words in your program explain it this way: *The sunflower belongs to a family with worldwide distribution. So, also, do lawyers. And as the sunflower always keeps its face turned to the sun, the lawyer turns to the light of justice.*

These words have borne themselves out in my life, because of the way Texas Law prepared me. Texas Law prepared me to be a global citizen—a member of that family with worldwide distribution. Texas Law prepared me to work at the intersection of power, politics, and justice. And Texas Law prepared me to turn to the light of justice—and to fight for that justice.

After graduation, I went to New York to work at Cleary Gottlieb. Leaving Texas for New York was a big risk, but I knew that something extraordinary was in store. Like the title character in Lin-Manuel Miranda's hit Broadway musical *Hamilton*, as I went to New York in the summer of 1986 I thought: "In New York, you can be a new man."

So I joined Cleary Gottlieb where I was surrounded by lawyers from all over the world, from every top school. They were among the best, anywhere. But Texas had prepared me. Texas equipped me to succeed, to be a global citizen.

Graduates: You, too, are world-class lawyers and global citizens. Because Texas Law produces more than just Texas lawyers, or Texas leaders. It produces lawyers and leaders who can change the world. And, today, the world desperately needs you.

After my time at Cleary Gottlieb, I went to work at the investment bank UBS. It was a big change. But, again, I was prepared—but not satisfied. Because while Texas Law had prepared me to succeed, it also imparted to me a desire to contribute to society—to turn to the light of justice.

That's when I saw the most startling thing in the early 1990s: The cover of *The Economist* magazine. Over a photo of a little boy, who looked like me when I was young, the cover line said: *America's Wasted Blacks*.

As the article made clear, this young boy in Harlem—for a variety of reasons—didn't enjoy the same opportunities I had, be they Head Start, or Pell grants, or an incredible public education at a place like University of Texas. That article was a defining moment in my life.

I started volunteering for an organization called the Children's Storefront school. And when I realized that community development was my calling, I went at it with gusto.

I went to work for the Abyssinian Development Corporation in Harlem. It was the early 1990s—and Harlem was a very different place.

It was the height of the crack epidemic. Back then, you would walk through Harlem and see brownstones boarded up. You could see crack vials on the sidewalk and stoops. You could walk into the bodega and see mostly expired food. And more than the burned-out buildings, I saw the interplay of power, politics, and justice.

So I moved from my nice penthouse apartment in midtown to 120th Street. I saw how entrenched systems and structures continued to disenfranchise and disadvantage the people of Harlem. And I understood, more than ever, how advantaged I was because I had a law degree.

I understood the laws, and the levers of power. And I had a set of skills that most did not. These skills gave me—as they give you—the capacity to negotiate change, because as lawyers we can navigate the system.

So I put those skills to work, and started listening to the community to see what we could accomplish together. And with community input we did something pretty basic but desperately needed: We built Harlem's first full-service supermarket.

Getting the supermarket built was a major challenge, and is just one example of what lawyers are uniquely equipped to do at the intersection of power, politics, and justice—and how we can bring justice to those long denied it. Because while your degree may make you a doctor of laws, your Texas education makes you a seeker of justice.

My Texas education has also prepared me to be president of the Ford Foundation, where turning toward the light of justice means shining a spotlight on inequality in all of its forms.

But you can turn toward the light of justice in many other ways. Whether you are advocating in courtrooms or around conference tables, you can fight for justice. Whether you are on the ground floor of a start-up venture, or at a major NGO standing up for the rights of others, you can fight for justice.

You can fight for children in the slums of Brazil or the poor wards of Houston and Dallas. You can make justice a part of whatever you do—even if it's just giving free legal advice to your friends and family.

Because while this work for justice can happen anywhere—it is needed everywhere. And you, Texas law graduates—you are prepared to go wherever you are needed.

By now, you may have realized, I'm slightly obsessed with the musical *Hamilton*. I've seen it six times, including on opening night. My friends and partner are fatigued by my constant references, but I can't help myself.

I've been inspired by this young Alexander Hamilton, an ambitious immigrant who refuses to let opportunity slip away. And at a critical point, early in the musical, he says that he's not "throwing away his shot."

It reminds me of how I felt when I was your age, and I'm sure it's how you feel today. Because for Hamilton the man, a major turning point in his life was when he became Hamilton the lawyer.

It prepared him for the trials and triumphs to come. It was his pathway to public service. And it is through the lens of the law that we see Hamilton's participation at the Constitutional Convention, his authorship of the Federalist Papers, his time at the Treasury Department.

And the lens of the law will serve you well, too—no matter what your calling may be. Texas Law has prepared you for anything.

So graduates: Do not stop. Do not throw away your shot; your shot at contributing to a world that's counting on you; your shot at working within systems of power to change them; your shot at delivering justice for those who need it most.

Congratulations, fellow UT alumni, on this moment filled with promise—a moment for which you've spent your lives preparing; a moment that signals your preparation for life.

Keep turning to that beautiful light of justice, wherever you find it shining.

ACTIVISM IS OUR RENT

Address to the Sarah Lawrence College Class of 2018
Bronxville, New York
May 21, 2018

I'm honored to join you this morning, as we mark this momentous occasion, and celebrate your tremendous accomplishment. Today, you join a prestigious group: Graduates of Sarah Lawrence College, and there's no telling what your future might hold.

You might write chart-topping songs like Carly Simon, or shatter an industry's glass ceilings like Barbara Walters. You might upend the fashion industry like Vera Wang, or follow in the footsteps of J.J. Abrams and direct *Star Wars* episodes thirty-seven through thirty-nine.

Like all the great artists, innovators, and pioneers that have walked this campus before you, you've all come a long way to get here today. You've produced hundreds of pages of writing, uncovered troves of research, and created works of art. You've put in countless late nights chasing elusive answers, and countless more searching for the right questions.

You've worked hard—but you haven't worked alone.

In a moment, you will walk across this stage, and claim your degrees. But as you do, I hope you'll pause to remember the people who have walked with you, the ones smiling up at you from the stands, cheering and calling out your name, and the ones here with you in spirit.

You're surrounded today by friends and family, teachers and mentors, collaborators and partners who have made this journey with you; people who have worked hard to open doors of opportunity for you, and stood behind you as you stepped through them. Their names may not appear on your diploma, but this day belongs as much to them as it does to you.

Please join me in applauding them today.

It's important that we take time to recognize the people who helped us along the way—because often we're encouraged to forget them.

There's a story that we Americans like to tell ourselves: The story of the self-made man. It's the story of the entrepreneur who founds a start-up in his garage—or the minimum-wage worker who pulls himself up by his bootstraps.

But graduates: That story is pure fiction.

Reflect for just a moment on your own life story. I guarantee you wouldn't have made it very far without the help of others.

I wouldn't be here today if not for my mother, who moved us out of the small, segregated, Louisiana town where I was born. Or without the young woman with a clipboard who knocked on our door one day, asking to sign me up for a brand-new program called Head Start. I wouldn't be here without the public-school teachers who encouraged me to learn and excel. Or without the philanthropists and Pell grants that let me pursue a college education.

The particulars of our personal stories may differ, but each of us has various people and factors in our lives that have contributed to—and even paved the way for—our success. If we take a moment, we can all remember people who have helped get us where we are today.

I share this because it's often easy to forget that our success is not only our own. We live in a society that glorifies individual achievement—where selfishness is incentivized, competition is encouraged, and cooperation is too often viewed as weakness.

It's that sense of individualism—of self-concern—that has produced the greatest wealth inequality in the world. I mean, think about this: The three richest individuals in America control as much wealth as the poorest 160 million.

And yet, no person is an island, and no human achievement was ever accomplished alone.

In college, you've seen this principle at work, every day. You've gotten this far thanks to the professors who spent countless hours with you on conference work, and the dons who helped you chart your academic course. Thanks to the staff who served you lunch at Bates, and the baristas at Heimbold who kept you caffeinated during your all-nighters, and, of course, thanks to the guardians, mentors, and friends who were with you every step along the way.

But when you leave this beautiful campus and move out into the world—whether it's to Williamsburg, Crown Heights, Bed-Stuy, or Bushwick, or somewhere besides Brooklyn—you might find that your incentives and priorities start to change.

Suddenly, the built-in community that has supported you will be gone. The hundreds of friends and fellow students that surrounded you every day might dwindle to a handful of roommates.

Suddenly, the things that once mattered most—friends, community, exploring new ideas—are replaced by material concerns, like getting a job and paying rent.

Of course, there will be fresh joys, too: New places to explore, challenges to meet, friends to make. But it can be tempting sometimes, as busy adults in our individualistic society, to retreat inward. To focus on ourselves: Our work, our wants, our personal worlds.

It's an attitude that reaches even the highest offices in our country.

I don't think it's controversial to say that our leaders today are beholden to a broken set of incentives, or that many of the systems and structures that our society was built on reinforce inequities, and discourage moral leadership.

We live in a society in which our elected leaders are encouraged to spend more time courting donors than working for their constituents; our CEOs are forced to care more about their bottom line than their consumers; and in my own sector, philanthropists are tempted to avoid controversy rather than take a stand against injustice.

The result is a vacuum of moral leadership that has made the world you are about to enter a more frightening, more selfish, and, sometimes, a more violent place.

And yet, in recent years, we have started to see that vacuum filled by what some would consider an unlikely source of moral leadership: The young women and men of your generation.

A few short months ago, I remember watching in awe, as I'm sure many of you did, as the students of Marjorie Stoneman Douglas High School—survivors of an unspeakable tragedy, still fresh in their minds—led millions of young people from every major city in the US in the March For Our Lives.

I've been inspired to see college students around the country, including at Sarah Lawrence, protesting against campus sexual assault, fighting to protect campus workers, leading divestment campaigns, securing resources for their local communities, and resisting white supremacists and other champions of hate.

A 2016 UCLA study found that this generation of college students—your generation—is more committed to protest, activism, and civic engagement than at any previous point in history.

Of course, political activism and civic engagement are nothing new to Sarah Lawrence students. It was the poet and Sarah Lawrence alumna Alice Walker who said, "Activism is my rent for living on the planet."

Think about that: Activism is our rent for living on the planet.

Soon, you will leave the supportive community that Sarah Lawrence has built for you, where it has been part of your everyday life, to engage with other people and ideas. After today, you will begin the hard work of building community outside this place, and you will be tempted by all those incentives that keep so many of our leaders from acting courageously and compassionately.

My hope—my wish—for you: Resist. Be active. Use your privilege.

As graduates of an elite university, there's no denying that you are the beneficiaries of incredible privilege. All of us here today are.

So wherever you go from here—whether it is to Brooklyn or to Burbank, back to your hometown or halfway across the world—I hope you find ways to repay our society for the privileges it has extended you, and contribute to the health of our democracy.

In other words, I hope you find ways to pay your moral rent.

Now this rent will look different for different people. It might look like activism on campus or acting on behalf of others. It might mean getting involved in your local community or building a more connected global community. It might mean raising your voice or lifting up the voices of others who haven't been heard. It might be your day job or something you do on the weekends or on the side.

Because it doesn't matter what you do to pay your actual rent—whether you're an artist or an activist, a doctor or a lawyer, a professor or a program officer at a foundation, or anything else you can imagine. Whatever you do, you must find opportunities to pay your moral rent.

And while the form it takes will be different—the impact of it must be the same: To build bridges, rather than drive people apart. To inspire empathy and compassion, rather than division and disdain. To champion the values of this democracy, equality and justice, rather than be complacent about inequality or injustice. To give others hope in the face of fear, and to lead by example when others lose their way.

This is just as important as anything else you will do, because if you neglect your personal rent, you risk getting evicted. But if you neglect your moral rent, the world will never know the contributions you—and only you—can make.

Graduates, I leave you with this: In 1949, a Sarah Lawrence literature professor—a gentleman named Joseph Campbell—set out to diagram the hero's journey. And he learned all great stories share the same step: The call to action. It's a charge every hero receives—to leave their place of comfort and begin a new adventure.

So, Class of 2018, this graduation day, I offer you a call to moral action. As you embark on the next great adventure of your lives, never forget the people making this journey by your side, the people who've opened doors and lit the way for you. And no matter what path you take, become that person for someone else.

A PROUD SON OF THE AMERICAN SOUTH

June 28, 2021

I am a proud son of the American South. To paraphrase Richard Wright, I always knew that I could never leave it.

I could never leave the dusty roads of rural Louisiana and East Texas where I grew up, or the shotgun houses, like my mother's, that still signal "safeness," as Kiese Laymon wrote. I could never forget my breathtaking first glimpse of Austin—my intoxicating first visit to the Houston Museum of Fine Arts.

I carry the South with me, everywhere I go—in the dignity I see in the labor of others, the inspiration I draw from neighbors helping neighbors, the empathy with which I try to lead my own life.

Above all, the South taught me how to make sense of America's—and humanity's—most profound contradictions.

Those of us raised in the South's sticky summers and wide-open skies are well-acquainted with its tensions—tensions between the ideals to which we aspire and the injustices that we, for too long, have accepted.

As Clint Smith poignantly wrote in his extraordinary *How the Word is Passed*, the region is home to places that mean profoundly different things to different people—old plantations, haunted with the brutal violence of chattel slavery, that now serve as wedding locations; beautiful performing arts centers and museums down the street from county jails; children, full of hope for the future, graduating from high schools named for men who would have seen them as property.

Indeed, I inherited these contradictions and ironies as my own birthright. My hometown, Ames, was the Black community; the white town down the road was called Liberty.

And yet, I also inherited something beautiful and powerful from the South: A sense of pride and purpose that comes from a long legacy of raising "good trouble"; from a long history that affirms—inch by inch and acre by acre, ballot by ballot and law by law—we, the people, can narrow the gap between the perniciousness of inequality and the power of our values.

I inherited the American patriotism of the Women's Political Council in Alabama, who were instrumental in the Montgomery bus boycott, and of four college students in Greensboro, North Carolina, who sat at a lunch counter until they were served and sparked a sit-in movement that spread to thirteen states.

Throughout US history, the South has been shaped by waves of movements for justice, transforming its face—and the face of our nation at large. And it's happening once again. As my friend and fellow Louisianian, Charles Blow, posits in his book, *The Devil You Know*, a new South is on the horizon, one that recognizes that "our trauma history is not our total history."

From every walk of life, Southerners are ushering in a Third Reconstruction, fueled by a coalition fighting for justice, from voting rights to fair wages. The American South today is Black, white, Indigenous, Latino, Arab, Middle Eastern and Asian; it is rural and urban; it is disabled; it is interfaith and unbeliever; it is queer, transgender, and nonbinary—all coming together in community to erase hard edges and build bridges toward a more perfect union. They are modeling how multiracial, multi-ethnic, pluralist democracy not only endures, but flourishes.

They know—as I have always known—that the tensions of identity and inheritance need not tear us asunder. In fact, just the opposite: Our history makes us stronger. The legacy we steward teaches us to create meaning from discord, to march forever forward, so we *shall* overcome, together, at last.

At the Ford Foundation, we believe in the promise of the South to continue to ignite change around the nation. That's why we're announcing over $75 million in funding from our historic social bond to support organizations across the region. This commitment will bolster and fortify the work of tireless advocates building and advancing movements toward a more just South. From Reverend William Barber and his revival of the Poor People's Campaign to the small but mighty Women with a Vision who have taken their call for reproductive justice from Louisiana to the Supreme Court, these brilliant voices offer a fuller, more nuanced story.

They show us that the story of the South is not singular, nor even terribly unique. It is transcendent—the story of America. It is our story, about learning to reconcile the injustices that persist with our abiding hope for the future.

HEALING AND SERVING THE WORLD

Sermon to Church of the Heavenly Rest
New York, New York
October 23, 2022

Good morning, everyone. To my dear friend Rector Reverend Matt Heyd: Thank you for the invitation and for the inspiration. To the congregation: I rise with humility today, moved by your welcome and your works; awed by how—and how fully—you answer our shared calling to love.

Our faith challenges us "to do good" and "seek justice." To "rebuke the oppressor" and "relieve the oppressed." To "love your neighbor as yourself." For the way we treat "the least among us"—the immigrant, the poor, the vulnerable—that is the way we treat the greatest.

Our faith teaches us that righteousness in *our hearts* is necessary, but not sufficient. That we must use *our hands*, tired and calloused, to build "a bigger table"—to bend the universe's moral arc, with all the might we can muster. It teaches that, in the end, "three things remain: Faith, and hope, and love." But "the greatest of these is love."

At the heart of my faith, then, is the promise of that greatest love—dignity. At the heart of my faith is the dignity that all people deserve, because we all are worthy; because we all are brothers and sisters in the eyes of the creator. At the heart of my faith is the dignity that we must demand for—and deliver to—all of our neighbors, because we all are tied up in that single garment of destiny; because my liberation is bound up with yours, as yours is with mine.

And yet, friends: Look across our community. Look around our country and our world. We have sown the wind and we reap the whirlwind.

One pandemic may be on the retreat, at least in some places—but the other pandemics remain all too clear and all too present. We suffer from pandemics of racism and authoritarianism, resentment and grievance, mendacity and impunity—a nihilism that poisons our land.

We suffer from cancers on our democracy and market system—from a diseased climate that is pushing our life-sustaining ecosystems to the brink of collapse.

And, in turn, the supply of human dignity remains far too low. The demand far too high.

Yes, we *all* are endowed with an inalienable right to dignity. From our sacred and civic faith, *this much* should be self-evident.

But our history teaches that self-evident is not the same as self-actualizing—that inalienable is not inevitable.

At the turn of the last century, it was a Chicago muckraker journalist and humorist—a different kind of apostle—who coined that most illustrative phrase: "Comfort the afflicted and afflict the comfortable."

On this beautiful autumn morning—in this sacred place—I ask you to reflect on this: *Comfort the afflicted and afflict the comfortable.* I ask you to reflect on the difference—the distance, even—between the two.

You see, comforting the afflicted is about our generosity. Our kindness. Our grace. Our most magnanimous virtues.

But afflicting the comfortable is about "the greatest of these": Love.

Afflicting the comfortable is about recognizing the inequalities that make generosity both necessary and possible: White supremacy. Caste. Decades of Ayn Rand, Milton Friedman, greed-is-good excess and exploitation. The conscious choices that aggregate into a conscienceless capitalism.

Afflicting the comfortable is about reckoning with the ways in which we, ourselves—right here, right now—benefit from the very systems and structures that prey on our neighbors. Reckoning with vast disparities in access and agency, in resources and respect, in voice and value.

And afflicting the comfortable is about rectifying the deep inequalities that can deceive us into ignoring how and why we put ourselves first and others second: Reparation and repair. Restorative justice. Resetting the cycles of privilege built into our laws and customs and behaviors—our tax code and our legacy admissions and our entitlement to that place at the front of every line, and far beyond.

Recognizing, reckoning with, rectifying inequality—these ideas have special resonance here.

Three decades ago, I entered the doors at Church of the Heavenly Rest for the first time. I was a young professional, new to New York. And on Monday nights, after work, I would volunteer with the outreach ministry. Alongside many wonderful members of this congregation, I helped care for a few dozen men without homes of their own, who found food and shelter inside these doors.

That I remember those nights so clearly all these years later is a testament to your tradition of service—which has inspired so many of us to serve our neighbors in, and through, that greatest love.

When your neighbors are hungry, you feed them with shelf-stable "grace to go" meals. When the incarcerated return from paying their debt to society, you greet them with open arms, providing job training and hospitality. When city kids head back to school each fall, you prepare backpacks full of supplies so that a lack of resources is just a little less of a barrier to their academic success.

I also feel another, more complicated connection to this place and its history—because of the ground beneath our feet, literally.

We worship this morning just across the street from the opulent home of the American industrialist Andrew Carnegie—now Cooper Hewitt—and on land that Carnegie's wife, Louise Whitfield, sold to this church's forebearers nearly a century ago.

I don't have to tell this congregation that while charity has its genesis in our rituals of faith, modern philanthropy traces its beginnings to 1889, the height of the Gilded Age, when Carnegie penned what we know as "The Gospel of Wealth."

Informed by his Presbyterian tradition, and in the face of rampant inequality, Carnegie proposed a bold idea: The wealthy, he argued, should freely give from their gains to aid "the masses."

Throughout the twentieth century, the field of institutional philanthropy emerged and flourished in the pattern of Carnegie's mold.

Iconic American families—from Rockefeller, Ford, and Mellon to Gates and Buffett—endowed and expanded an extraordinary array of organizations that lifted lives and livelihoods around the world. By and large, their work—which has become my life's work—has been a force for good; our collective impact, meaningful. At the same time, though, something about the old narrative arc should make us uneasy. Something about that old gospel should make us uncomfortable, especially as people of faith.

As I see it, we cannot hide from the central contradiction built into our giving. We are creatures of our market system's unequal benefits—and yet, charged with addressing its unequal prejudice.

This tension may be particularly pronounced in our new Gilded Age—but to paraphrase a former American president, it is a moral issue as old as the Scriptures and as clear as the Constitution.

It was exactly six decades ago—between the summer of 1962 and the spring of 1963—that a thirty-something-year-old pastor in Atlanta, Reverend Dr. Martin Luther King Jr., prepared a series of sermons that would become his seminal work.

Before the boycotts and bombings in Birmingham, before the March on Washington, before Freedom Summer or Bloody Sunday, Dr. King first articulated many of his most enduring calls to conscience in a manuscript called *Strength to Love*. He actually drafted much of it during long evenings in Alabama and Georgia jails. This was Dr. King at his most prodigious.

In these pages, he declared "hate cannot drive out hate" because "only love can do that." He insisted that we "are caught in an inescapable network of mutuality." That "the ultimate measure of a man is not where he stands in moments of comfort and convenience, but where he stands at times of … controversy." And among these reflections, Dr. King challenged the origins and objectives of philanthropy.

He wrote then, and I quote: "Philanthropy is commendable, but it must not cause the philanthropist to overlook the circumstances of economic injustice that make philanthropy necessary."

This passage rattles me every single time I read it.

Because Dr. King is saying that philanthropy, kindness, "comforting the afflicted"—all of this is well and good. But good is not good enough—not to guarantee dignity for all. To ensure dignity, we also must "afflict the comfortable"—including and especially ourselves.

You see, the subject of my generosity is me. But the object of justice is the interests and needs of others.

Generosity is about giving something back. Justice is about giving something up.

At the Church of the Heavenly Rest, you know this, too—intuitively—because, yes, you house the homeless and feed the hungry. But you also fight for public policy to ensure that everyone can live and work with dignity—and, moreover, for the right of all people to vote for elected representatives who will (heaven forbid) tax the privileged so we can invest in public goods.

Yes, you provide housing and job training to the formerly incarcerated. But you also shine a light on the suffocating racism built into our criminal justice system—and, furthermore, the ways that police practices can harm people in poor neighborhoods while helping people in wealthy ones.

Yes, you give backpacks full of school supplies. But you also advocate for the kind of education that teaches our full history, the paradox of our pain and our privilege.

And your leadership in this regard, and so many others, points to a common set of obligations.

You show us that answering the call to love requires improving the systems and structures that shaped us—that we embrace a new gospel, defined by timeless terms and tenets.

Answering the call to love requires that we engage with the root causes of our most urgent crises, not just the immediate consequences—even when those root causes implicate us. That we trust the people and communities most proximate to problems to shape the most effective solutions. That we value their lived experience just as much as established expertise.

Answering the call to love requires moral leadership and moral courage: That we fix our eyes over the horizon, beyond the next earnings report or the Tuesday after next, and toward a long-term vision for a more inclusive, equitable society.

And, yes, answering the call to love requires that we step away from the extremes and from the edge, away from the sanctimony and certitude. That we listen with curiosity, and openness, and empathy—with tolerance. That we extend the presumption of grace and the benefit of the doubt.

Like on that steep, seventeen-mile road from Jericho to Jerusalem, the path to transcendence is an uphill climb—an ascent from truth to forgiveness, to reconciliation.

During the final days of Dr. King's life, he penned what he called a "testament of hope."

Written during a season of doubt, this was an epistle that he could not have known would be among his last.

He observed then, and I quote: "It is not easy to describe [crises] so profound that [they have] caused the most powerful nation in the world to stagger in confusion and bewilderment."

I think we can identify.

These days, one could be forgiven for feeling confusion and bewilderment—for feeling like we're staggering along, suffering blow after blow. But in that reflection, Dr. King also reminded us that human beings have "the capacity to do right as well as wrong"—that "history is a path upward, not downward." And this, he said, "is why I remain an optimist."

Reverend, community, friends: Let us give our own testament of hope.

Like all faith, our faith is tested; it will be tested again. Faith: "The substance of things hoped for, the evidence of things unseen." But let us embrace the *radical* optimism that we can overcome. That we shall overcome. That through our triumphs and our defeats—two steps forward, one step back—we will continue our ascent up that road. From Jericho to Jerusalem. From the inequalities that deny and diminish and divide and disenfranchise toward the fullest measure of justice—absolute equality for all people.

Let us work with ambition, but humility. With righteousness, not self-righteousness. With moral leadership that affords space for nuance and complexity and compromise. To comfort the afflicted, *and* to afflict the comfortable.

And in all things, let us "do good" and "seek justice"; "rebuke the oppressor" and "relieve the oppressed." Let us answer that call to love, with dignity for all.

And let us say, Amen.

REPEAL OF AFFIRMATIVE ACTION IS ONLY THE BEGINNING

The New York Times
June 30, 2023

Let's be honest about the painful reality: America has functioned as a full democracy—guaranteeing the franchise to all—for less than one human lifetime. In practice, our democracy is younger than me.

I was born in 1959, into an America riven by apartheid. When I was a child, the adults in my life could not vote in the Louisiana and Texas towns where I grew up.

During the first two decades of my life, the American people finally acknowledged this truth and, to borrow a phrase, acted affirmatively to address it. A new generation of American founders mobilized into a great, multiracial movement, challenged our nation to live up to its ideals, and initiated a national construction project on the foundation of the Constitution's Fourteenth Amendment (which was violated with impunity for an entire century after the nation ratified it).

In *SSFA v. Harvard's* majority opinion, Chief Justice John Roberts held that "eliminating racial discrimination means eliminating all of it"—a new version of his old affront that "the way to stop discrimination on the basis of race is to stop discriminating on the basis of race."

This glib framing, and the school of thinking it represents, established a pernicious, false moral equivalence. Those who preserved and protected Jim Crow—the institution that defended America's old racial hierarchy—were and are something altogether different from those who fought and who continue fighting for a more just America.

For me, this is no abstraction. I attended small-town Texas schools roiled by desegregation.

In grade school, I saw the vestiges of Jim Crow firsthand: The dilapidated old Negro facilities, the hanging tree adjacent to the courthouse, the swimming pool closed and filled with concrete in response to court-ordered desegregation.

And then, throughout my childhood, government and other institutions acted affirmatively to change. They began to redress the hypocrisy and harm, reckoning with the countless ways that they had protected power and privilege for some at the expense of others. From the wreckage of a lost century, they began building with laws and policies a more *American* United States.

I was a beneficiary when President Lyndon Johnson and his administration created a program called Head Start; when he signed the Civil Rights Act into law the July Fourth weekend before my fifth birthday; when he signed the Voting Rights Act into law a year later, enabling my mother and millions of people like her to vote for the first time in their lives.

I was a beneficiary when The University of Texas, my alma mater, also acted affirmatively to recruit, admit, and retain Black and Latino students, whereas it previously excluded us for the entirety of the institution's existence.

I was a beneficiary because the firms and foundations that shaped my career embraced this obligation, to make right what their predecessors had done wrong, to open doors they had closed.

Those uprooting affirmative action seem content to leave intact systems that compound privilege, exacerbating inequality—like legacy admissions policies that disproportionately favor wealthy, white applicants—resulting in lower-income students and families of all races losing out.

The court's decision also opens the door to numerous legal challenges of diversity programs across government, business, and civil society—programs explicitly designed to mitigate what Justice Thurgood Marshall called a "legacy of discrimination" beyond the college campus.

I find it regrettable that, over forty years ago, Justice Lewis Powell introduced the American public to the imperative of diversity in the shallow manner that he did.

I was a freshman in college when his seminal opinion in *Regents of the University of California v. Bakke* (1978) invited some to equate the benefits of diversity with unfairness. Since then, I have heard the recriminations of Justice Powell's argument in cloaked conversations—in the idea that necessary diversity initiatives are somehow reverse discrimination or that they correlate with lower standards or lesser outcomes.

The data suggests exactly the opposite. Study after study demonstrates that, across organizations, diversity enhances critical thinking, creativity, and collaboration, as well as productivity, profitability, and performance. It is a national tragedy that diversity is now a contested issue rather than a common interest.

And we should tell the truth about why diversity is now controversial: Opponents of diversity are opponents of any racial consciousness. They want to prevent us from understanding the ways that the past informs the present, from wrestling with the fullness and richness and complexity of our history.

Indeed, they wish to impose an ahistoric mythology on the American people that makes it harder, if not outright impossible, to address the many ways that Black and white still live in separate and unequal Americas.

We still live in an increasingly segregated society—and we see it in our classrooms and our neighborhoods and our workplaces and our criminal justice system. Statistic after statistic maintains the same burning truth.

The America that I know is better than this. We are bigger than this. We are stronger than this.

America is still courageous enough to acknowledge our failings and the reasons for our failings. And we still can be united enough to address them—to act affirmatively, once again, to extend the blessings of freedom and opportunity and justice to all.

For our part in philanthropy, we cannot be dissuaded or deterred. We must remain steadfast in our missions to narrow inequalities, to defend human dignity and human rights, and to promote democratic values and institutions at home and abroad.

And for all of us, as Americans, we must fulfill our responsibilities as well. As we approach the 250th anniversary of our founding, we must redeclare that we all are created equal, endowed with equally inalienable rights, and recommit ourselves to realizing these values. We must rededicate ourselves to what President Abraham Lincoln called "the unfinished work" of building the pluralist democracy to which we all aspire.

I believe fiercely in the promise of America. My love for this nation is unyielding and unwavering.

As Americans, we have a charge to keep, a beacon to keep alight, especially now, as minoritarian tyranny has taken hold of our institutions. It is systematically dismantling the scaffolding from which we built our democracy, without any clear sense of what will replace it. For some, perhaps, the objective is not to replace it at all.

In this new era of deconstruction, we must summon renewed fortitude, resilience, and vigilance, with reverence for those who came before us and resolve for those who follow. This will require patriotic defiance, with respect for the rule of law but with fidelity to the ideals that precede it.

With hope, let us rejoin and rebuild, until America is America and the unfinished is complete.

PART II

UPROOTING INEQUALITY AND MOVING THE FORD FOUNDATION FORWARD

Inequality and injustice persist. But they are no match for the human spirit. In the complicated, sometimes confounding, times in which we live, FordForward embodies faithful hopefulness in the future. Together, we will rise to the challenge of tackling inequality and its consequences—just as our predecessors met and mastered the challenges that defined their own times.

Moving the Ford Foundation Forward
November 8, 2015

ENDURING MISSION, NEW VISION

Inaugural Address to the Ford Foundation Community
New York, New York
September 9, 2013

Thank you all for joining in this important conversation—which, I hope, marks something of a new beginning, not just for your new president, but for each of us.

As you can imagine, I've been doing a lot of listening during the last forty-some days—and mostly, and most importantly, I've been listening to you.

I've been completely overwhelmed by your generous words, well wishes, and warm embrace. But beyond that, I've been taken with the quality and depth of your ideas and suggestions.

So I hope you recognize, in what I am about to say, many of the things you've said to me—about our work together, about how we work together, and about the culture we want to build together.

Here at Ford, we are all about building—or, more accurately put, we are all about helping others to build. Through the decades, we've helped visionaries, as we call them, to draw the blueprints of social justice; hammer together the framing and floorboards of social progress; and lift the world's social conscience. And we have supported this process of building in three very distinct ways—ways that have become deeply associated with Ford.

First, working alongside countless partners and grantees, we've laid intellectual bricks and mortar for lasting institutions—policy centers, think tanks, and on-the-ground social-justice organizations. Our own "alphabet soup" sums it up: MALDEF, PRLDEF, LISC, MDRC, OTI, and the acronyms go on. Institution building has been—and will remain—a signature element of our comparative advantage.

As will a second area: Building human capital and human capacity.

I was reminded of this just a few weeks ago. While visiting our Beijing office, I learned that the foundation supported legal training in the US of dozens of Chinese lawyers in the 1980s. Today, many of those lawyers occupy top positions across the country's judiciary, and are among China's most influential lawyers.

We can point to countless similar examples wherever the Ford Foundation has planted its flag, in fields ranging from the hard sciences to the creative arts, in policy and advocacy, in community development and social change.

And this leads to the third category of building that constitutes our comparative advantage: Investments in social innovation. From building the field of area studies to the transitional justice movement to the creation of program-related investing, we trade in the currency of ideas and social innovation.

And so, I put a fundamental question to you: What should we help to build next?

What kind of institutions? They may not necessarily be big, infrastructure-heavy NGOs, as the twenty-first century may demand a different modality.

What kind of human capacity? We may need to work beyond the lines of traditional examples like IFP.

What kind of social innovations? We need to explore how we build on current innovation—how we remain open to new ideas that we have yet to hear about but could provide a breakthrough social-justice solution.

I don't have the answers. But I do know a couple of things for certain: One, we definitely need to be asking these questions.

And two, I absolutely know that whatever we help the social-justice visionaries of this generation to build next—at its foundation will be you. Will be us. Because we are passionate about this place and its mission, and the enduring legacy we leave.

In this way, one of the indispensable elements of our culture is stewardship across generations. We're not just stewards of what we've helped build—whether institutions, capacity, or ideas. We're also stewards of the assets that we use to build.

I call these assets Ford's Bedrock Bs.

Our first asset, and most important, is our collective brainpower. You all bring tremendous knowledge, expertise, and lived experiences. Our grantees have enormous knowledge and a unique vantage, and we can and must learn from them. And we are lucky to have a diverse board, comprised of remarkable people, who are eager to contribute their knowledge and skills, too.

Second, our brand. Around the globe, we are renowned for touching and transforming the lives of millions of people, not only to accelerate development, but also to expand social justice.

Third, our billions. We are entrusted with patient capital. Our intergenerational resources allow us to address problems that are deep and complex. Thanks to the wisdom of my predecessors and our current board, we are privileged with the freedom and flexibility to take the long view.

Fourth, our building. We may work here. But our iconic home—an architectural and community treasure—is not ours exclusively; 320 East 43rd stands as a beacon for social-justice convening and collaboration.

And fifth, our boldness. We don't just have the capacity—and, arguably, the obligation—to take on unpopular fights. For decades we have had the courage to do so.

So these Ford Foundation assets—the five Bs—help distinguish us and enable us to be who we are. But there is something else that distinguishes us, and that is our culture.

Our culture is assembled from a wide array of shared ideas, shared values, shared experiences, even some shared myths. We share, for example, a sense of deep frustration about the injustice and inequality that persist in the world.

And what's more, the culture we share is not just a thing around us, but a thing that emerges from us. It's an accumulation of an infinite number of small gestures committed by each one of us.

Therefore, our culture also is something that we define. That we have power over. That we each are responsible for improving where it needs improving; for affirming where it needs affirmation; and for expressing to everyone with whom we work and partner.

I believe—and believe deeply—that in order to fulfill our mission, we need to be conscious and deliberate about our culture. Because as one of our smart trustees recently reminded me, culture eats strategy for breakfast.

Strategy matters. But we have to build our strategy on—and consistent with—our culture. This is how we become an institution that is ambitious, but humble. That seeks to inspire, not to impress. That values collaboration, not credit. That is righteous, not self-righteous. Bold, but not reckless.

And, at the end of the day, we don't stand a chance of tackling the world's most serious obstacles to social justice if we're also tussling with each other.

Now it's absolutely true that every large foundation struggles with organizational silos that artificially divide staff. Program over here; operations, investment, and administration over there. But while we need well-defined functions and lines of accountability, there is a balkanization of the mind that too often results. I believe it's both unnecessary and harmful.

So it's important for us to reaffirm that each one of us is here for a reason—a specific functional reason, of course, but also to be part of something greater than ourselves. Each of us has a role to play in fulfilling our mission, no matter how tangential that role may seem to the heart of our work.

Every grant that goes out the door? We all stand behind everyone. We all have a stake in every grantee we support. And every role should compel and demand us to explore, interrogate, analyze, and assess.

So—and here's a big priority for me—I want this to be a place that's equal parts rigorous and curious, exacting and inquisitive. I want our culture to marry these virtues—to foster an environment in which we operate at the intersection of rigor and curiosity; an environment in which we're never afraid to challenge each other's ideas without impugning each other's motives.

We all know this organization is very polite—which I appreciate. But, sometimes, we allow politeness to obfuscate the truth—and to inhibit the openness that is necessary to uncover it.

So, let's change that. And let's start by assuming a new posture. Let's replace politeness with respectful openness—openness predicated on the idea that everyone here operates from a place of good intentions. Because we do.

What does this mean, in practice? It means that when someone forgets to invite us to a meeting or include us on an email chain, we don't automatically assume it's because they're trying to exclude us.

We've all been there. But you know what? I think it's within our ability to always, always assume the best intentions of others.

And if we do, then we can nurture a culture of trust—a culture in which we are safe to transparently share and honestly debate and disagree, even with the president; but also a culture in which we on the tenth floor empower and incentivize the best in all of you.

As your president, I want to—and will—give you the freedom of flexibility; the freedom to expose and discover, to experiment and create, to unleash the power of serendipity. And, in return, I ask that you take responsibility for being part of a community that values constructive criticism.

And all of this—appreciating that we're each here for a reason, marrying rigor and curiosity, always assuming the best in one another, and starting every conversation from a place of trust—all of this points to a final, fundamental aspiration: We need to be a learning organization.

Many organizations today say they're learning organizations. But we need to mean it. So, let's commit to becoming one.

Let's become an institution excited about—and driven by—ideas. Let's agree that we want to use learning to continually improve. Let's interrogate assumptions—and challenge normative thinking. And let's place just as much value on questions as we do on answers.

For my part, I have a number of questions. I suspect you do, too.

So, let's ask: How can we best contribute to reducing the world's appalling level of inequality? I know some of our work addresses it. But I don't know that we're where we really need to be on this challenge—which, to me, is the most important social-justice issue of our time.

Let's ask: How can we accelerate the spread of human rights? How can we most effectively take advantage of urbanization and shifting demographics?

How do we, in an era of globalization, address global labor dynamics to support better outcomes for poor and vulnerable workers? How can we help more people, in more places, to access the technologies to learn, to create, and to express themselves?

How do we act on our commitment to international relations and mutual understanding during a time of conflict and extremism in much of the world?

These issues—and many others—have been preying on my mind, as I'm sure they have been on yours.

Part of the Ford Foundation's mission is to bring ideas that advance social justice to the world in real time. And so we—as a learning organization—should welcome outside experts in. We should carry our inside expertise out. And we should open our eyes and minds to a world of ideas to which we may not currently be paying attention.

To begin with, I want to hear your ideas and your questions—and we'll have ample time for that in a moment. But I understand that one of the major topics on your mind is, are things around here going to change?

It's a fair question. And the answer is yes, some things will change.

After all, the Ford Foundation has always evolved—and continues to evolve—not just to respond to external change that's already happened, but also to anticipate the external changes that are yet to come. We need to be a dynamic organization—neither complacent in our thinking nor unquestioning of our programing. The way I see it: We rest? We rust.

Now, this doesn't mean that we're just, arbitrarily, going to turn off the ignition of everything we're doing. Nothing is stopping. Any changes that we put into place will be deliberative and thoughtful.

But, at the same time, I don't want to be disingenuous. Every leader of this foundation has brought a particular perspective. And I, too, have very strong points of view—for example about the role of cultural practices as barriers to justice, especially for women, the poor, and excluded groups.

We will develop new programs, over time, to address new manifestations of injustice and inequality. And this has to be ongoing. We don't start and then finish—we continue.

Which brings me back to where I started—to the conversation we begin today. This is only the first of many opportunities for us to ask and explore, collectively; to interrogate assumptions and answers, constructively; and, ultimately, to learn from and with one another, collaboratively.

Together, we'll get started. Right here, right now. With us. For us. By us. And among us.

Thank you all, again, for this new beginning—for me, and for us.

TAKING STOCK, LOOKING AHEAD

2014 Annual Message
September 2, 2014

During the twelve months since I accepted the honor of serving as president of the Ford Foundation, I have traveled more than 125,000 miles. I wanted to get to the front lines of social change. I wanted to listen to and learn from you. And I must say, it has been the most inspiring, uplifting journey of my life.

On a trip to Beijing, I was reminded of the foundation's pioneering program that helped train an entire generation of Chinese jurists. In Jakarta and in Java's rural areas, I admired the early success of civil society in transforming the world's largest Muslim democracy and setting a powerful example for others to follow.

In the Makoko slum of Lagos, I was struck by the community's perseverance and determination in the face of a development effort that sought to uproot, dislocate, and exclude thousands of poor people. In Johannesburg, on the twentieth anniversary of South Africa's first free elections, we commemorated Ford's 1953 grant to study the effects of apartheid. We also visited organizations we support in the Khayelitsha township, and elsewhere, who still are working to disentangle apartheid's knotty inheritance.

In Detroit, I experienced the gathering resurgence of an iconic American community, and joined a partnership with fourteen other foundations to help the city navigate an unprecedented bankruptcy—demonstrating, along the way, that philanthropies can break free of their traditional constraints and rise to address complicated challenges in real time.

And in Colombia's Pacific region, I visited Quibdó, a primarily Afro-Colombian city along the Atrato River. As I walked the streets, I saw a community desperately poor in wealth, but rich in leadership. I encountered the remarkable Paula Moreno, working valiantly to advocate for Afro-Colombians who face discrimination in most facets of life. Paula made such an impression on us that we later asked her to join the foundation's board of trustees, becoming our first board member from Latin America of African descent.

A TWELVE-MONTH AWAKENING

Getting close to the work we support through travel in the US and internationally—and through hundreds of meetings at our headquarters in New York—is not just thrilling for me, personally; it really is the only way to become fully conscious of the important role the Ford Foundation and other philanthropies play in an elaborate ecosystem of human aspiration and action. Through these interactions, my unwavering belief in the foundation's core social-justice vision has been affirmed, as has my resolve to ensure that we rise to the challenges posed by a changing world.

Indeed, for me, these last twelve months have been an awakening—energizing and emboldening in a way that I never expected after the better part of two decades in philanthropy. I have learned a great deal about the demands that our mission and history place upon us. And I have been humbled.

Chief among these lessons was just how unready I was to begin a job for which one might assume I had been preparing for years. Easy as foundation work may look from some vantage points, the truth is that it is hard. Hard because you want more than anything to get it right. Hard because you want to earn the joyful privilege with which we have been entrusted. And hard because you know for sure that in at least a few cases you will get it wrong.

And while a reflection like this could be seen as characteristic of our sector's navel gazing and self-regard, I share it out of an opposite instinct: As an effort at transparency and mutual understanding.

In fact, the biggest challenge I have encountered this year stems from the contradictions inherent in what this foundation actually does, in the very rudiments of what it exists to do: We give money away for urgent work now; we steward it for the years ahead. We strive to be ambitious in what we support; we strive to be pragmatic. We aim to take risks; we aim to avoid unbridled bravado. We serve a venerable legacy; we serve a bold vision of human dignity and social justice.

Balancing these multiple vested interests means making tough choices—choices that are unlikely to satisfy the many stakeholders who care about our mission or rely on us to support theirs. I can assure you, however, that the decisions the foundation trustees and I will make in the months and years to come—about the direction of our programs, about how we apportion our funds—represent purposeful resolution of competing and equally compelling extremes.

I also assure you that I will continue to be as candid and open in the months ahead as I have tried to be throughout my first year. I am working to build a foundation culture where this sort of openness is held in as high regard as our intellectual curiosity, our rigor, and our commitment to the values we share.

REFLECTING ON WHAT'S NEXT

So let me tell you where we are and what to expect.

Like so many others, we are working to understand the changes underway in our world and to anticipate the changes yet to come. Simply put, the greater the challenge, the greater our determination to meet it.

To this end, my colleagues and I have spent the last six months identifying and analyzing significant trends that are having—and will continue to have—a major impact on the pursuit of social justice around the world.

Foremost among these trends are the rapid rise of disparities during a time of declining global poverty (what we call the *inequality dilemma*); the increasing dominance of market ideology (what we call the *consolidation of capitalism*); and the failure of many democratically elected governments to deliver on their promise (what we call the *democracy quandary*).

We also are exploring fast-moving transformations such as disruptive technology, growing extremism, threats to free expression, changing patterns of international cooperation and conflict, climate and natural resources crises, new patterns of migration and urbanization, the youth bulge and demographic shifts, and the heightened urgency for women's and girls' agency.

To be clear, these trends do not signify the areas our work will address in the years ahead. They do signify our effort to step back from grantmaking to consider, from different perspectives, the status of human dignity and the shape of social justice in the world today, and to ensure that our contribution to advancing both is in step with the changes around us.

Given the scope and pace of those changes—and the change in leadership at this institution—ambiguity and anxiety are likely in the air. I understand. I am working to strike a balance between taking the time we need to reset our compass and the urgency of marching ahead without delay.

(Xavier de Souza Briggs cites a Peruvian proverb that says the world can only be changed by those with burning patience. I am trying to work out exactly what that would feel like.)

A PERSONAL REQUEST

At the Ford Foundation, transition is complicated by a deep history. Not a day goes by without me hearing "the Ford Foundation gave us our first grant" or "the Ford Foundation's support is critical, it needs to continue." And yet we also know that the trends shaping our world require us to support new ideas, new institutions, and new forms of organizing and movement-building.

We always have been about building. The operative question now is what should we help to build next? This is the issue we are interrogating among ourselves, in conversation with you, with help from experts, friends, and kitchen cabinets. We are reading, listening, and reflecting.

From this process we expect to identify, by this November, the four to six key themes that speak to the social-justice issues of our era—themes that will organize our grantmaking during the years ahead. I urge you to anticipate evolution, not revolution. Our mission remains unyielding and tied to core principles of justice, opportunity, and understanding. I am excited about the direction in which we are headed.

At the same time, it would be disingenuous for me to suggest that everything we now support will continue or that everyone will be content. Wherever we land, I can assure you that, while hard, the choices we make will be based on thorough exploration, consultation, and reflection. And that the work we support into the future will reflect, as it always has, the vision of courageous, creative people on the front lines of social change.

So I have a favor to ask, and it is a big one. I know how hard it is to speak candidly to a foundation president—I have faced that uncomfortable moment enough times over the last twenty years, both as a grantee and a staff member. And we all know why it is hard—the power dynamics, the stakes, the personality variables. But from my vantage point, nothing could be more valuable. In truth, my single greatest fear is that I am not hearing enough constructive criticism. It is essential to our work together, and I need your input and feedback.

Ultimately, whether you agree or disagree with the choices we make, you will see a Ford Foundation that is as dynamic as the times in which we operate—that reflects our deep, abiding optimism that, with burning patience, we can help seed and spread justice around the world.

Every single day, I am privileged to come to work in a place—and with an exceptional group of trustees, colleagues, grantees, and partners—that so fully embodies this ideal. We have much yet to learn, much yet to do, and I could not be prouder of the new beginning we have made together.

WORK IN DETROIT DOESN'T END WITH GRAND BARGAIN

Detroit Free Press
November 19, 2014

This past June, I found myself sitting, awestruck, in the Rivera Court of the Detroit Institute of Arts. The court is named after Rivera for his breathtaking *Detroit Industry* frescoes that line the walls—a gift from Edsel Ford to the people of Detroit back in 1932.

The twenty-seven-panel masterpiece remains a monument to human endeavor and hard work. Eight decades after Rivera put down the paintbrush, it was still the perfect backdrop for the event I was attending.

That afternoon, I watched as the Detroit Three auto companies—Ford, Chrysler, and GM—committed $26 million toward Detroit's nearly $900 million Grand Bargain. Leaders and emissaries from government, philanthropy, and business proudly looked on. A sense of joy and relief filled the air.

Yet, what moved me most was neither the actions of the power brokers nor the timelessness of the paintings. It was two city retirees who, unaffected by the fanfare, sat quietly and with dignity at the front of the room. Their names were not printed in the program, but their life's work—and the hard work of so many others who were there—was what inspired the idea of the Grand Bargain.

Shirley Lightsey and Don Taylor are advocates for the city and its residents. They and thousands of their colleagues faced the tough choices on which the Grand Bargain hinged. And they made those tough choices. These city-makers—quiet but indefatigable leaders—were what the Grand Bargain was all about. And, for Detroit's sake, we must never forget that.

Shirley and Don represent the people who made Detroit one of the world's greatest centers of industry and art, and who stuck with it during unimaginably hard times. They are the firefighters, the police officers, and the civil servants who, once again, showed up for duty and delivered. They are the retirees who came to the table and negotiated in good faith—even, frankly, when it seemed that every option was a bad one—because it was simply the best thing for Detroit.

People with character like this are the whirring, humming engines of the Motor City. It is the toil and sacrifice of these humblest of heroes—not government or business or philanthropy—that have laid the groundwork for Detroit's renewal.

Now, as Detroit's emergency-management process draws to a close, it is precisely this example that stands as a powerful challenge to the rest of us. Detroit's elected officials must demonstrate the same commitment and resolve that has been shown so nobly by its residents. It is encouraging to already hear Mayor Mike Duggan and other city leaders talk about a culture of inclusion, transparency, and management excellence as essential to the city's future.

For foundations like the one I serve, what's important is not just what we did this year, but also what we do in the years ahead. We will bring attention to the need to fund grassroots, community-led efforts to revitalize the city from the ground up. And, in doing so, we'll strive to meet the standard of integrity, heart, and leadership shown by Detroiters like Shirley and Don, and captured in Rivera's frescoes.

There is much work to do. Hard work. But Detroit, as ever, is a city full of women and men who know how to get the job done. We stand with them—not just in the Grand Bargain, but in an even grander future.

WHAT'S NEXT FOR THE FORD FOUNDATION: A BLUEPRINT FOR SOCIAL-JUSTICE PHILANTHROPY

June 11, 2015

Last fall, when I wrote about my first year on the job, I asked you all to do something that would be very helpful to me: Tell me the truth.

That simple request drew more than two thousand emails to my inbox. Some of them were profound and insightful. Others, lighthearted. But all of them were truthful. And I couldn't be more grateful.

In reading and reflecting on each and every response, I have become more aware of the ways in which we can improve our institution, and serve our mission. Indeed, these last twenty-some months have been a transformative journey. Throughout, I have been challenged and humbled. In some cases, my beliefs were affirmed. In others, my assumptions were completely upended. In every instance, your constructive, and sometimes provocative, ideas have stirred, stimulated, and inspired.

Now it's my turn to be candid with you, and to share what we've learned, where we've landed, and how my colleagues and I hope to lead the way forward.

WHAT WE'VE LEARNED

Many have fairly pointed out that the culture of the Ford Foundation is unnecessarily hierarchical and bureaucratic, and our decision-making slow and opaque.

Many more of you told me that, taken together, the Ford Foundation's work has become too fragmented and diffuse—the whole is not greater than the sum of its parts. And in my view, it must be.

But the majority of the feedback I received was not about what we fund. It was about how we fund. Time and again, the organizations we support have said that our prioritizing project support, as opposed to general operating support, tends to stifle their work, forcing them to focus on incremental outputs rather than long-term organizational strategy and effectiveness.

In addition, while Ford has long worked around the world, we recognize that in a time of evolving global dynamics we must be better listeners and more avid learners. Our success as a philanthropy that is focused on human dignity for all people requires us to adapt our mission to a world in which the governments, institutions, and ideas of multiple nations are rising to global prominence and leadership.

And yet, amid all that was said about how we must improve, I was repeatedly reminded of our deep and established strengths. I was reminded that, in many ways, the history of the foundation reflects the history of social progress over the past six decades—whether in the movement for civil rights in the United States, the fight against apartheid in South Africa, or the quest for gender equality around the globe today.

Throughout our history, the Ford Foundation's approach has been characterized by a continuous emphasis on building institutions; investing in individuals, human capital, and leadership; and supporting new ideas. I think of these as our *three Is.*

We have helped to launch institutions like Human Rights Watch, the Public Broadcasting Service, and South Africa's Legal Resources Centre. We have stood behind thousands of extraordinary individuals, ranging from James Baldwin to Gloria Steinem, Muhammad Yunus to Ai-jen Poo. Nearly fifty Nobel laureates were Ford Foundation grantees—before they won their prizes. And we've invested in the ideas, insights, and research that have seeded pioneering movements like microfinance, financial services for the poor, and Internet rights.

While the specifics of our grants have evolved over the years, these three Is—institutions, individuals, and ideas—have remained constant, reflecting our belief that human dignity is best served by those working closest to the problems and by a diverse community of actors that together can catalyze meaningful change.

The question before us now, therefore, is this: How do we identify the institutions, individuals, and ideas that will lead the next era of progress toward human dignity for all?

ADDRESSING GLOBAL INEQUALITY

I've written previously about the global trends we studied last year in our effort to understand the state of human dignity in the world today, trends such as the pervasiveness of short-term thinking in markets, the growth of extremism, the accumulating consequences of climate change, and the struggle of democracy to fulfill its promise.

Among these many trends, the one we returned to again and again was the growth of inequality in our world. Not just the economic disparities that have emerged in global debates these past few years but also inequality in politics and participation; in culture and creative expression; in education and economic opportunity; and in the prejudicial ways that institutions and systems marginalize low-income people, women, ethnic minorities, Indigenous peoples, and people of color.

We are talking about inequality in all its forms—in influence, access, agency, resources, and respect. We would argue that inequality, in one form or another, is coded into just about every one of our social ills. Research demonstrates that extreme inequality weakens economic growth and undermines the social cohesion of societies.

So how do we program to address inequality? After consulting with thought leaders and practitioners worldwide and reviewing the available research, we asked the teams in our eleven offices to offer a region-by-region analysis—based on evidence and their own experience—of the manifestations of inequality in each regional context, as well as an assessment of the underlying drivers of that inequality.

Remarkably, although manifestations varied by region, the assessment of underlying drivers was strikingly constant across the world. Broadly stated, we found five factors that consistently contribute to inequality:

- Cultural narratives that undermine fairness, tolerance, and inclusion
- Unequal access to government decision-making and resources
- Persistent prejudice and discrimination against women as well as racial, ethnic, and caste minorities
- Rules of the economy that magnify unequal opportunity and outcomes
- The failure to invest in and protect vital public goods, such as education and natural resources

WHERE WE'RE GOING

To address and respond to these drivers of inequality, we will be working in six program areas, very much reflective of the five drivers. They are:

- Civic Engagement and Government
- Creativity and Free Expression

- Gender, Ethnic, and Racial Justice
- Inclusive Economies
- Internet Freedom
- Youth Opportunity and Learning

These six thematic areas will not be silos, each unto itself. They are ingredients that each of our offices—depending on local context and the priorities set by local partners—will combine in creative ways to disrupt the drivers of inequality. We suspect that in many cases the most dynamic front lines of social change will be found not within these six areas, but at the intersections where they connect. And our commitment to human rights and human dignity will be at the center of all of them.

In any case, our work in these areas will not attempt to cover the waterfront. These program areas may be stated broadly for now, but they will become more concrete and specific as we continue to refine our thinking and learn and adapt through our grantmaking.

BUILDING HEALTHY ORGANIZATIONS

Our thought process has not dealt solely on the themes we intend to program around. We've also been rethinking how we support the institutions, individuals, and ideas that address inequality.

According to Nonprofit Finance Fund's most recent *State of the Nonprofit Sector Survey*, the single greatest challenge facing organizations today is "achieving long-term financial sustainability." So much of the feedback we've received echoes that sentiment.

In light of this, we have decided to invest in organizations as partners—and to give them the kind of trust, flexibility, and additional supports they need to do their best work. As incubators for both individuals and ideas, organizations are essential to developing a robust ecosystem of actors addressing inequality around the world.

For this reason, we are aiming to double our commitment to supporting key anchor organizations in our six program areas. Over the next five years—from 2016 to 2020—our trustees have authorized us to allocate up to $1 billion for a concerted effort to support stronger, more sustainable, and more durable organizations.

In some cases, this may mean larger, longer-term grants that can be used more flexibly. In other cases, it may mean support for wraparound services that help an organization develop, adapt to change, or even merge with others. Whatever form it takes—depending on context and the needs of each organization—our aim is to ask not, "How do we make this grant successful?" but rather, "How do we help make this organization successful?"

In arriving at this point I have been inspired by my colleagues in the sector who are already undertaking important work to redress the lack of general-support funding in philanthropy: Larry Kramer at the William and Flora Hewlett Foundation, Chris Stone at the Open Society Foundations, Nancy Roob at the Edna McConnell Clark Foundation, Sigrid Rausing of the Rausing Trust, Herb Sandler at the Sandler Foundation, Carol Larson of the David and Lucile Packard Foundation, Kathleen Cravero-Kristoffersson at Oak Foundation, and Paul Shoemaker of Social Venture Partners. Their advice has been invaluable and offered in the spirit of authentic collaboration and partnership.

WHAT THIS MEANS

These changes are not without implications. Almost certainly, providing deeper, more intensive support will result in fewer grants and, most likely, fewer grant recipients.

There are also internal implications, including how we structure teams and work together to think about our program areas, not as individual silos, but as an integrated system. This means that if your field of work is not explicitly mentioned among our programs, it does not necessarily signal an end to our support in that field. It means the way we program is evolving to reflect how problems are best defined and addressed in a changing world.

Alongside these changes, we will continue to evolve our internal culture to be more responsive and solutions oriented, ambitious but humble, bold and transparent.

In its entirety, I call our evolving strategy Ford*Forward*. It is our blueprint for the foundation's future—how we envision a social-justice philanthropy for the twenty-first century. And as a blueprint, it is far from complete. We still are refining each of the thematic areas, designing teams and regional programs that will reflect this larger thinking.

In the next few weeks, you will be hearing more from us as we refine our thinking about how to address inequality most effectively in the diversity of contexts within which we work.

Which brings me back to you. While we are making some big changes at the foundation, what will not change is our commitment to supporting those closest to the problems, engaging collaboratively with every sector, and pursuing the cause of justice and dignity for all people, everywhere.

Today is not a new beginning. It is a next step in a quest begun eight decades ago. For over half that time, I have benefited from or been connected to the Ford Foundation. But I have never been more excited or optimistic about its future—about our ability to deliver on the promise of our mission and the purpose of our work. I look forward to continuing our journey forward, together.

ALL IN ON DETROIT

with Kofi Appenteng
Detroit Free Press
June 15, 2015

This week, the trustees of the Ford Foundation are meeting in Detroit, the city in which we were established, for the first time since moving to New York in 1946.

Why now? Because we are radically optimistic about the future of Detroit. Because we want to better understand, and learn from, the city's ascent. Because we owe a debt of gratitude to the Ford family and Ford Motor for the mission that continues to guide us. And because we want to reaffirm our commitment to this unique and important place.

Decades ago, Henry Ford II transformed the Ford Foundation into a leading global institution, charging it to tackle the most significant challenges facing humankind. On issues from civil rights in the US to empowering women around the world, we have supported visionary and courageous people working for opportunity and fairness all around the world.

Today, our focus is on inequality, which is the defining issue of our era. Inequality is more than an economic divide between the super-wealthy and the vast majority of people who struggle to make ends meet. It's also about imbalances in political, social, and cultural power that favor the few over the many.

It is why, for instance, when Detroit entered Chapter 9 bankruptcy, it was not the powerful or wealthy who were asked to sacrifice, but those already most vulnerable. Retirees saw their pensions up for grabs; residents' voices were eclipsed by unelected officials; low-income people had to fight for access to water; and irreplaceable public treasures owned by all were considered disposable. Our contribution to the Grand Bargain was a direct acknowledgment of the urgency and scale of the issues that were gripping the city and undermining its future—issues tied to inequality in how resources were collected, accounted for, and distributed. The largest single grant we've ever made in the US, it built upon a decade of investment in the region seeking to overcome inequality.

But it also built on the idea that if Detroit could get back in the starting blocks, its hardworking, resourceful, and committed residents could lead its long-term renewal. Because Detroit's remarkable, resilient people are its greatest asset.

To fulfill the promise of the Grand Bargain, all of us who care about the future of the city must understand inequality—in all its forms—as the challenge to be rooted out. From unequal educational and economic opportunities to a broken criminal justice system to an unequal distribution of public resources and services, there is much to be addressed.

We cannot tackle these issues one by one. The best investments in Detroit's new future are those that support the development of diverse civic and community leadership, back innovative ideas, and build bridges among the city's many constituencies so that the momentum established by the Grand Bargain can be harnessed and built upon.

This is the Ford Foundation's future in Detroit: Supporting civic leaders to strengthen local voices and broaden participation in decision-making, investing in neighborhood innovations that demonstrate the vast potential for vitality at community level, and lending strength to economic revitalization that is already underway.

Just as our histories are intertwined, so are our futures. Our course is your course; your challenges are our challenges. We are here for the long haul, and pledge to work tirelessly to tackle inequality and lift up the progress that Detroiters lead.

Decades ago, Detroit paved the way for American industry and ingenuity. Today, it can point the way for American prosperity and inclusion. Together, we can make that future—an even grander future—a reality.

MOVING THE FORD FOUNDATION FORWARD

November 8, 2015

Today, I'm excited to announce that the Ford Foundation's two-year transition is over. Together we are implementing Ford*Forward*—our blueprint for changes in our culture, our programs, and our assets.

Back in June, I shared the news that we would focus on combating inequality and that we had landed on a set of thematic areas aimed at addressing what we have identified globally as the five key drivers of inequality.

The rationale underlying this focus on inequality is simple and powerful: Inequality, in all its forms, represents the greatest impediment to just, fair, and peaceful societies that offer opportunity for all.

This is because inequality, in its broadest sense, can be found at the root of nearly every injustice. It stacks the rules of our systems to favor the privileged and, in that way, it compounds itself.

Addressing inequality requires a more nuanced understanding of how it operates. We are continuously striving to see its workings as both global and local, immediate and long-term, affecting people's lives as well as distorting the systems it infects.

We also are striving to be as inclusive as possible, because no one entity—not government or the private sector or civil society or philanthropy—can meaningfully address inequality on its own.

What does this mean for our work? It means we must concentrate our efforts in ways that build on our deep and established strengths, while optimizing and consolidating for impact.

CONSOLIDATING FOR IMPACT

Before today, we had thirty-five initiatives. As of this writing, we instead have fifteen lines of work. Throughout the rigorous process of reorganizing and consolidating our work, we were ever mindful of why we're changing—of why we must change.

With respect and admiration for all of the foundation's past work, we need more integration. Thus, we're breaking down silos so that program officers join interdisciplinary teams with flexible assignments. You can also expect more collaboration in the spirit of the Detroit Grand Bargain, NetGain, and our new impact investing partnerships. And you can count on a genuine institutional commitment to learning and adapting.

We will be pushing forward with a more coherent and interconnected grantmaking program—one that seeks to do fewer things better, rather than more at less than our best.

Each of our new lines of work represents our commitment to directing resources toward where we can make positive inroads. Each reflects our commitment to ensuring that the whole is greater than the sum of its parts. Each takes place at the intersection of disciplines.

While these lines of work target specific drivers of inequality, they have also been designed to have collective impact. We hope that, together, they will set in motion a multiplier effect.

MAKING DIFFICULT CHOICES

One of the realities of our new strategy is that we've had to make difficult choices. Candidly, there are several areas in which the foundation will no longer be supporting important work. This means that some outstanding organizations and fields will be receiving final grants. I recognize that, for some of you, this is difficult news to hear.

For my colleagues and me, it is of course difficult news to deliver, particularly to such worthy and deserving partners. Our decision making, however, remains grounded in specific criteria. In every piece of our portfolio, we looked at the centrality of the work to addressing inequality, the progress made toward each partner's goals, and the other philanthropic resources that are available.

As you can imagine, some of the areas from which we are stepping back have seen measurable progress or are benefiting from a new cadre of donors that have arrived since the Ford Foundation first started funding.

For example, organizations working on LGBT issues in the United States have experienced impressive gains in recent years. As a gay man, I am acutely aware that there is much more work to do on LGBT rights in the United States—and I hope that changes at Ford do not send the signal that victory can be declared in this country. That said, outside the US, the LGBT community desperately needs resources and allies, and so, as a global foundation, we're adapting and recalibrating our focus where the greatest need exists.

We have also decided to wind down our work in other fields, some of them deeply embedded in our history. These include conditional cash transfers in Latin America, microfinance, and, in the US, our initiatives extending the school day, building arts spaces, engaging religion in the public sphere, and more.

Given this, it would be disingenuous to pretend that Ford*Forward* brings welcome news to everyone. In fact, in addition to explaining that we will be leaving certain areas of work, I need to be equally clear that our new strategy means that we will be making fewer grants as well.

In recent years, the foundation has averaged over four thousand active grants annually in our portfolio. As we transition away from some areas, we expect that, during the next two years, we are likely to reduce that number by up to 20 percent.

While this new reality may be challenging in the short term, we believe that in the long run these choices—like the decisions made by my predecessors—will strengthen us. They will increase our ability to have impact in the twenty-first century and enable us to fulfill our ongoing mission in pursuit of social justice.

RECOGNIZING THAT INSTITUTIONS MATTER

At the center of the history of the Ford Foundation has been our investing in what I think of as the *three Is*—groundbreaking ideas, leading individuals, and institutions and networks.

We remain committed to all three, but, for starters, we're leaning into the importance of institutions and networks. Building durable institutions and networks will be among our highest priorities because, as we've seen throughout our history, they represent the infrastructure on which movements for change are built.

Institutions are hubs for gathering and aggregating talent; they provide the platforms that help accelerate and sustain social change. Networks are fulcrums for creativity and dissent, beacons of stability, scaffolding for aspiring change makers, and connectors for social innovators.

This is why we're excited to reaffirm that, over the next five years, we will dedicate $1 billion for building institutions and networks through our BUILD program. This program will be fully integrated into the grantmaking of our seven thematic areas, operating both within the areas and across them.

ADDRESSING THE OVERHEAD FICTION

At the same time, even outside the BUILD portfolio of grantees, we are rededicating ourselves to strengthening the partners and grantees that are recipients of our project support.

All of us in the nonprofit ecosystem are party to a charade with terrible consequences—what we might call the "overhead fiction." Simply put, because of this fiction, foundations, governments, and donors force nonprofits to submit proposals that do not include the actual costs of the projects we're funding.

I recently learned of one local government request for proposals that gave extra points to applicants that submitted proposals with lower overhead, resulting in the winning groups receiving overhead payments of 5 percent—an absurd and self-defeating outcome.

The overhead fiction also results from well-intended metrics developed by nonprofit watchdog groups that have equated lower overhead with organizational effectiveness when, in fact, the opposite may be true.

At Ford, we have been willing participants in this charade. Our policy of 10 percent overhead on project grants in no way allows for covering the actual costs to administer a project. And to be honest, we've known it.

This number does not reflect what it takes to actually manage a project, nor does it help those we support to effectively run robust organizations capable of executing projects. Thus, beginning January 1, we will double our overhead rate on project grants to 20 percent. We hope to encourage more honest dialogue about the actual operating costs of nonprofit organizations working in the US and internationally.

CONFRONTING THE ENDOWMENT QUESTION

I am mindful of another elephant in the room at most large foundations, one that represents a major opportunity for impact: The investment policy for our endowments.

Reflecting common practice at most large legacy foundations, the Ford Foundation has maintained the position that our policy is to maximize endowment returns, except in our screening out certain industries. This position, that we maximize returns, has been a source of questioning, discontent, and frustration among those we support, as well as among staff at Ford.

My own view on this subject has evolved, and I no longer find it defensible to say that our investment strategy is only to maximize the value of our endowment—just as it's no longer defensible for a corporation to say its only responsibility is to maximize shareholder value. There is growing evidence that it is possible to find impact-investing opportunities that deliver financial and social, double bottom-line returns.

In light of new regulations from the Obama administration, which encourage mission-related investment, now is an opportune time for foundation boards to confront the endowment question. For our part, the trustees and I are interested in taking up this question responsibly, thoughtfully, and based on evidence. We expect to promulgate a specific impact investing policy in the coming months.

We are grateful to learn from the path being blazed by Clara Miller of the F.B. Heron Foundation, Rip Rapson of the Kresge Foundation, Stephen Heintz of Rockefeller Brothers Fund, and others who are already exercising bold leadership in the sector to demonstrate successful approaches to impact investing.

RISK, REINVENTION, AND RENEWAL

When I shared my thoughts on a new gospel of wealth, I offered a few reflections on the history—and the promise—of philanthropy. It will likely come as no surprise, then, that I have been thinking a great deal about the role our institution has played in this larger story, and about the privilege of supporting so many courageous visionaries in the vanguard of the fight for social justice.

When I look back on the ways this foundation has contributed to change and changed itself over the past eight decades, I am struck by a number of moments: Moments of risk, reinvention, renewal, and reward.

The first came as a result of the Gaither Study Committee, whose extraordinary 1950 report created the modern Ford Foundation.

In the years that followed, Henry Ford II implemented that blueprint, moving the foundation to New York, commissioning the historic building we've occupied since 1968, and transforming a local family foundation into an international institution.

Through the 1960s and 1970s, McGeorge Bundy led another fruitful shift. The foundation seeded dozens of influential institutions across the world and funded the work of leading changemakers like Dr. Martin Luther King Jr., Gloria Steinem, Muhammad Yunus, and so many others.

When Franklin Thomas assumed the presidency, he inherited an institution in need of reform. To save the foundation from financial ruin, Frank took bold and courageous action, which positioned the foundation for a quarter century of remarkable achievement, including critical leadership on the issue of apartheid.

Susan Berresford took the helm of Ford and provided vital leadership on women's issues (playing a seminal role in the much-heralded 1995 World Conference on Women in Beijing), the arts (creating United States Artists), and education (launching Ford's International Fellows Program, which has provided advanced degrees to more than 4,500 social-justice leaders from the Global South).

Luis Ubiñas's arrival coincided with the financial crisis of 2008 and an unprecedented loss of value in our endowment. The foundation benefited from his expert knowledge of management practice, which resulted in major improvements in investment operations and administration, as well as in streamlined and strengthened programs.

WITH THANKS

Which brings us to this moment—a new and urgent moment for risk, reinvention, and renewal. Two years ago, I was honored and humbled when the foundation's board entrusted me with leadership of this institution. I want to be clear that the changes manifest in Ford*Forward* would not be possible without the stewardship of our chair, Kofi Appenteng, and our dedicated, passionate, and energetic trustees. I am enormously grateful to them for encouraging us to be ambitious and take risks, and for their willingness to engage in candid, honest, and sometimes uncomfortable conversations.

The trustees are committed to Ford being a learning organization and so while they are gratified to hear about where we have succeeded, they are equally—if not more—interested in learning about where and why we've faltered. And they believe steadfastly that the foundation must take the long view of social change, knowing that short-termism is cancerous for philanthropy.

I am also immensely grateful to Ford's remarkable staff around the world, whose commitment moves the foundation forward every day. Across our organization, my colleagues bring fierce intelligence, good humor, and a sense of urgency to their work, and they participated in our two-year transition with the same spirit. Their contributions and questions have been essential to this process and will continue to guide the next generation of our work.

MOVING FORWARD

On a cold, snowy, winter day last year, I visited the Eastern Correctional Facility, a prison in rural Ulster County, New York. There, I experienced a most astonishing and inspiring phenomenon: Incarcerated men studying Latin, debating Aristotle, and speaking fluent Mandarin. They recited the poetry of Langston Hughes and the essays of James Baldwin.

These men looked just like me—they were mostly Black and Brown, from underserved and disadvantaged backgrounds. But they had determination and hope in their faces—a look of authentic confidence that follows only from hard-earned achievement.

They were participants in the Bard Prison Initiative, the brainchild of Bard College's brilliant president, Leon Botstein, and led by the courageous Max Kenner. It is a pioneering degree-granting program for incarcerated women and men and has been the recipient of Ford Foundation support for many years.

As I visited with these men—as I spoke with them about their wrenching accounts of bad luck, bad choices, and a criminal justice system that seems designed to rob them of their humanity—I felt heartbroken but also inspired.

In their stories, I was reminded of why our support for visionaries working on the front lines of social change matters so profoundly: Yes, inequality and injustice persist. But they are no match for the human spirit.

In the complicated, sometimes confounding times in which we live, Ford*Forward* embodies faithful hopefulness in the future. Together, we will rise to the challenge of tackling inequality and its consequences—just as our predecessors met and mastered the challenges that defined their own times.

PUTTING FORD*FORWARD* INTO ACTION

June 30, 2016

It's hard to believe that just one year ago my Ford Foundation colleagues and I announced we would address inequality as the centerpiece of our new organizational strategy: Ford*Forward*.

Who could have predicted all the ways inequality and injustice would be felt in the months since: In the growing disparity of wealth; in anti-migration movements around the world; in the mass shooting at a gay nightclub in Orlando, Florida; in a political discourse that, in so many places, divides people along racial, ethnic, and religious lines.

Injustices of this kind are why we recognized inequality as the central challenge of our era and as the essential issue we must address across all our work. So, a year in, I want to offer you an update on our efforts to combat inequality in its many forms and give you a sense of what Ford*Forward* feels like in practice.

As I've said, we're not just looking at one piece of the inequality puzzle. We're working to see the whole picture, and understand how the pieces fit together. Whether it's tackling cultural narratives that breed prejudice and exclusion or addressing the structures that create unequal access to natural resources, our aim is to disrupt the underlying drivers of inequality. Those drivers take many forms, and so must our strategy.

So here's what Ford*Forward* looks like now:

TAKING AN INTEGRATED APPROACH

Inequality is not an independent concept, though it is often talked about that way. The divide we call inequality is really a set of business and cultural practices, government policies and laws, established systems and received wisdom that have the effect of generating very different opportunities and outcomes for different people. Put simply, inequality is driven by a variety of interdependent forces, and these must be understood and addressed in combination. At its core, therefore, Ford*Forward* reflects an integrated approach to addressing inequality in all its forms.

This means our support to organizations fighting inequality must look across issues, borders, and populations to find and address common root causes. Here are three examples of how we're doing that under Ford*Forward*.

Our team in Mexico and Central America is focusing its efforts around the overwhelming issue of impunity across the region, where profound violence and an underlying state of lawlessness drives inequality and threatens the lives and opportunities of all people, especially youth and the poor. Young people under the age of twenty-five, for instance, make up 70 percent of disappearances in Mexico and El Salvador. Perpetrators are rarely prosecuted, much less stopped, and their continued impunity has become one of the central social-justice challenges facing the region.

That's why we're supporting a range of organizations and leaders as they sharpen their shared analysis of impunity and tackle entrenched threats like extrajudicial killings, torture, and forced disappearances. Quite intentionally, we're working with partners who integrate distinct and diverse approaches to the issue: From pressing for greater government accountability to creating powerful works of journalism and art, to amplifying the voices of victims and their families and strengthening their rights.

Of course, dismantling this culture of impunity will not happen quickly. But with a shared vision and shared action, we are helping organizations in the region lay the groundwork for lasting change.

Globally, you can also see this integrated approach at work in the ways we are addressing inequalities that arise from extractive industries such as mining, oil, and gas. The foundation has worked on extractives for nearly a decade, supporting a range of efforts to ensure that local people benefit from these resources. Yet the work has been ad hoc. While one of our programs focused on Indigenous villagers losing their land, another looked at taxes and accountability in government, and there was little overlap in strategies.

Under Ford*Forward*, we are coordinating approaches that connect the global and the local. Today this work involves two programs (Equitable Development and Civic Engagement and Government) and multiple regional offices that work collaboratively, link the organizations they support, and share knowledge across regions. Through this more connected approach, local voices can better shape global priorities, and global platforms can foster ideas, evidence, and solidarity that help empower frontline advocates. This integrated approach helps our partners work more effectively across government, civil society, and business to find lasting solutions to make resources and global tax regimes more fair, open, and well-governed.

If our work on extractives shows the Ford*Forward* approach working across two programs and multiple offices, then our investment in public interest technology is taking that premise one step further.

As the foundation did in the 1960s with the nascent field of public interest law, today we are committed to helping establish this emerging field—in part because we know technology increasingly impacts every area of society and can help us everywhere we work. Through the NetGain partnership, we're making substantial investments in efforts to develop the tech capacities of a new generation, and to connect new technologists with opportunities in the public sector and civil society. We hope these investments are the start of a career path that enables and encourages them to use their valuable skills to advance justice and equity.

We are also supporting new leaders in their fight for social justice and, through tech-fellowship programs, infusing desperately needed tech talent into organizations on the front lines of that fight. These visionaries will help us understand the technological systems and protections needed to challenge inequality in all its forms—whether that means designing new online security protocols or transforming how civic groups communicate and engage with government leaders. We believe the learning and solutions advanced by these public interest technologists will benefit work across the social sector for years to come.

INVESTING IN ORGANIZATIONS

While these three examples touch on just a few of our newly defined strategies, one significant shift across all of our programs and regions is our emphasis on building stronger, more durable institutions. We know that institutions are essential to the fight against inequality. They develop individual leaders and incubate ideas; they outlive any one person, and their impact can be felt far beyond any one grant. A strong organization expands the time horizon of a particular mission or strategy, and establishes an outpost on the front lines of social change.

Yet these civil-society organizations are under threat around the world. With every gain they make, our partners face considerable backlash. We see this clearly, for example, in repeated attempts to limit women's access to sexual and reproductive health services, which persist even in the face of other progress in women's rights. The ongoing struggle of civil society is a necessary reminder about the state of social justice in our world: The struggle never ends and the fight never stops.

We need to build more resilient institutions to ensure their work for justice never stops, either. As part of Ford*Forward*, we're prioritizing the core health of the organizations we support in three key ways:

- We're increasing general operating support grants across all our programs and regional offices. In fact, we aim to make this our default grant whenever possible.
- We're doubling our overhead rate on project grants to 20 percent, to more adequately fund what it costs for an organization to implement a project.
- We're dedicating $1 billion over the next five years to a focused effort on institutional strengthening.

These changes are the culmination of decades of experience at the Ford Foundation, as well as what we've heard repeatedly from our partners over the nearly three years of my tenure. But for all that experience has taught us about the importance of institutions, there is still much we don't know about how best to support and strengthen them.

LEARNING ABOUT STRENGTHENING INSTITUTIONS

We want to add to existing philanthropic knowledge about what it takes to build strong civil-society organizations, and we want to do so meaningfully. In particular, we seek to better understand the kinds and levels of support that will make a critical difference to an organization's overall health and resiliency, and at what stages in its life cycle.

We are inviting a diverse mix of partners to join us on this journey of learning, beginning with 130 organizations and networks. As with all of the organizations we support, these groups are doing essential and innovative work to reduce inequality. Some are emerging organizations or networks; others are well-established field leaders. More than half of them are based or work in the Global South, while others work on domestic issues in the United States. More than half are led by women and people of color.

As a cohort, they cover a wide range of functions and capabilities—from grassroots mobilizing to policy analysis to legal services.

As part of this relationship, we are asking these organizations to commit to working more closely with us over the coming years—in sometimes unprecedented, and potentially uncomfortable, ways. Right now, we're having conversations with each organization during which we will listen, ask questions, and learn a great deal before any grant is made. We'll ask questions like: What operational issues have gone unaddressed for lack of resources? What finance and fundraising issues have been underemphasized in our funding relationships? What innovative program shifts, growth, or experiments have been left by the wayside in favor of more urgent needs and priorities?

These conversations will determine the overall look, feel, and funding level of these grants. And just as no two institutions are the same, no two of these relationships will look the same. While we're at it, we're learning to put the organizations we support in the driver's seat, and letting them take the lead in shaping a plan that best meets their organizational needs.

So while I'm sure many of you are eager to learn more and anxious to know what these grants will look like, our best answer right now is: It will depend on the unique needs and aspirations of each organization. As soon as we have a clearer sense of the specifics of each of these grants and relationships, we will make the details available on our website—both within the strategy pages for each program and region, and within the searchable grants database.

A LARGER OBJECTIVE

Though our grantmaking strategies and institution-building efforts will vary from place to place, responding to local context, custom, and needs, our larger objective remains the same. With *every* grant we make, we're asking ourselves both how our support can help disrupt inequality *and* how our support can help make an organization stronger.

As we look at what's happening around us—whether it is the global economic fallout of the Brexit vote, the unpredictable direction of our politics, the continued emergence of extremism, or the real impacts of climate change—the institutions of civil society are a source of abiding hope and inspiration for me. They breathe life into our democratic values, engage citizens in the hard work of holding governments to account, and challenge orthodoxies with fresh thinking and innovation. They also support groundbreaking individual leaders, cultivate new ideas, and create space for creativity and free expression to flourish. In short, institutions do the things that our societies deeply need and desire, and they stand alongside private enterprise and government as an essential component of vibrant, stable, and healthy societies.

I am proud that through Ford*Forward* we are doing everything we can to support these institutions and networks so they can continue to do the remarkable and inspiring work that is so necessary in our world today. We hope to strengthen a flourishing and vibrant civil society, and ensure that the courageous people within it have what they need to fight for a more just and equitable world.

IGNORANCE IS THE ENEMY WITHIN

2016 Annual Message
September 12, 2016

I was a sophomore in college when I first encountered the writing of James Baldwin. His courageous spirit, his clarion voice, and his moral imagination expanded my consciousness of what it meant to be Black in America. It helped me make sense of my own experience growing up in the rural South during the 1960s.

This past year, as I have traveled across the country and around the world, Baldwin's clear-eyed understanding of our human frailties—as well as our potential for transformation—has traveled with me. It has given me reasons for hope.

Certainly, the events of this year have tested any commitment to hope, and to the belief that equality can triumph over indifference and injustice. We are witnessing alarming levels of racism and bigotry in the West. We feel anguished and powerless over the plight of refugees from war-torn regions in the Middle East and Africa. The world over, continued violence against women and girls, ethnic minorities, LGBTQ communities, and other vulnerable people reminds us that inequality can exact deadly consequences.

In the United States, we find ourselves grieving far too often. We despair over the innocent African Americans killed by police *and* over the killings of innocent officers in Dallas and Baton Rouge. As we try to measure the incalculable costs of this violence—and the trauma it expands and extends—we are called to work with greater urgency to connect the reality we see with the solutions we seek.

As we continue to confront, and be confronted by, entrenched inequality of all kinds—as we search for ways to understand and address it—I have returned repeatedly to one of Baldwin's insights in particular: "Ignorance, allied with power," he wrote in 1972, "is the most ferocious enemy justice can have."

These words resonate powerfully today. That is in large part because they compel us to confront our responsibility. They demand that we look closely at our own ignorance and our own power. And as I discovered for myself, these two acts are not easy for any of us.

CONFRONTING POWER, PRIVILEGE, AND IGNORANCE

When Baldwin crafted his critique, *power* was held almost exclusively by wealthy white men and their institutions, including some of the very institutions whose exercise of power we still scrutinize.

Since his writing, however, our definition of the power that allies with ignorance has expanded to include *privilege*: The unearned advantages or preferential treatment from which we all benefit in different ways— whether due to our place of origin, our citizenship status, our parents, our education, our ability, our gender identity, our place in a hierarchy.

The paradox of privilege is that it shields us from fully experiencing or acknowledging inequality, even while giving us more power to do something about it. So, privilege allied with ignorance has become an equally pernicious, and perhaps more pervasive, *enemy* to justice. And just as each of us holds some form of power or privilege we can challenge in ourselves, we each hold some form of ignorance, too.

Typically, in conversations about race, the word *ignorance* is associated with outright bigotry—and no doubt the two can be related. Yet in my experience, ignorance remains such a ferocious enemy because of its silent, constant, unacknowledged presence.

I am a Black, gay man, so some might assume that I'm especially sensitive to these issues and dynamics. But during the past year I have had to confront my own ignorance and power, and come to terms with the ways I was inadvertently fueling injustice.

Last June, my colleagues and I announced that Ford*Forward* would focus on disrupting inequality. During the weeks that followed, I received more than 1,500 emails in response, mostly congratulatory. And then something happened: I was confronted with feedback that highlighted my own obliviousness.

My friend Micki Edelsohn, founder of a remarkable organization called Homes for Life in Wilmington, Delaware, was the first to note that Ford*Forward* made no mention of a huge community: The more than one billion people around the world who live with one form of disability or another, some 80 percent of them in developing countries. "I applaud you for taking on inequality," she said. "But when you talk about inequality, how can you not acknowledge people with disabilities?"

Many others reiterated her unsettling message, from former governor Tom Ridge and Carol Glazer, chairman and president, respectively, of the National Organization on Disability to Jennifer Laszlo Mizrahi, the president of RespectAbility. As a matter of fact, it was Jennifer—now among our most constructive, valued partners—who, in a rather scorching email, called me a hypocrite. I deserved it.

Indeed, those who courageously—and correctly—raised this complicated set of issues pointed out that the Ford Foundation does not have a person with visible disabilities on our leadership team; takes no affirmative effort to hire people with disabilities; does not consider them in our strategy; and does not even provide those with physical disabilities with adequate access to our website, events, social media, or building. Our fifty-year-old headquarters is currently not compliant with the Americans with Disabilities Act (ADA)—landmark legislation that celebrated its twenty-sixth anniversary this summer. It should go without saying: All of this is at odds with our mission.

DISABILITY, INEQUALITY, MISSED OPPORTUNITIES

Several thousand Georgia residents with intellectual and physical disabilities and disability rights advocates gathered outside the Georgia statehouse for 2016 Disability Day, celebrating twenty-five years of the federal Americans with Disabilities Act.

The fact is, people with disabilities—whether visible or invisible—face harsh inequalities. People with physical, sensory, intellectual, or mental health disabilities do not benefit from the same opportunities as those without. This inequality is pervasive, and it regularly intersects with other forms of inequality we already address in our work.

For instance, RespectAbility found that more than 750,000 people in our jails and prisons have a disability. How many times have I thought, talked, or written about the imperative of criminal justice reform in the past year, I wonder, without thinking about this aspect of the crisis at all?

And so, for me and for the foundation, my first question was: *How had this happened—how could we possibly miss this?* The answer, simply put, is power, privilege, and ignorance—each of which multiplies the prejudicial effects of the other.

I am personally privileged in countless ways—not least of which is that I am able-bodied, without immediate family members who have a disability. In my own life, I have not been forced to consider whether or not there were ramps before entering a building or whether a website could be used by people who were hearing or visually impaired.

In the same way that I have asked my white friends to step outside their own privileged experience to consider the inequalities endured by people of color, I was being held accountable to do the same thing for a group of people I had not fully considered. Moreover, by recognizing my *individual* privilege and ignorance, I began to more clearly perceive the Ford Foundation's *institutional* privilege and ignorance as well.

Some of my colleagues have raised the issue of disability rights in informal, individual conversations. Others have personal experience with disability, or have cared for friends and family who do. Yet over the eighteen months that we meticulously crafted Ford*Forward*—an extensive, exhaustive process—we did not meaningfully consider people with disabilities in our broader conversations about inequality.

Thinking back, I had believed that our institution—all our people, all our processes—would serve as a check and balance against individual biases. I assumed, without really stopping to acknowledge my assumption, that issues I might overlook, or be ignorant of, would be raised by someone else—and that the space was there to raise them. It is clear to me now that this was a manifestation of the very inequality we were seeking to dismantle, and I am deeply embarrassed by it.

Yet the experience has kindled a learning moment for me—and for all of us at Ford—precisely because it affirms something important about how most institutions work, or fail to, and how we can make them work better for more people.

This is not to say this system of checks and balances does not already exist. The diversity of perspectives within our organization and our board is perhaps one of our greatest strengths. Still, as some have pointed out, this diversity does have gaps. As an organization composed of individuals with different inherent biases, we are not immune to ignorance. While checking each other's ignorance in one area, we may simultaneously—and unconsciously—reinforce and even ratify it in another. In this way, an absent voice or constituency may not merely be unconsidered; it may as well not exist.

This kind of institutional ignorance is wide ranging. We see it when companies and organizations offer unpaid internships, and in the lack of diversity on the boards of cultural institutions. We see it in the false choices between pro-victim and pro–law enforcement policy imperatives, and in responses to institutionalized racism more broadly. I think it's fair to say that this same narrow-mindedness undercuts all of us in philanthropy— and given our charge, it is unconscionable. Despite our best intentions, when we fail to address ignorance within our organizations, we are complicit in allowing inequality to persist.

The good news is: We can change. And we are changing. Among all the many challenges facing our world and our work, the solution to this one is entirely within our control. In order to make our organizations more effective, we must consciously, deliberately lead them to become less ignorant.

FROM IGNORANCE TO ENLIGHTENMENT

So how do we do this? How do we move from unwitting ignorance to enlightened action?

For my colleagues and me, the transformation starts with acknowledging our own fallibility and deficiencies. We are becoming more comfortable with uncomfortable feedback. Rather than adopting a defensive posture by default, we are opening ourselves to dialogue and learning. As we know, change takes time, and we may not succeed fully right away. But we are committed to doing better, and we hope that continual feedback will keep us honest.

In this particular case, we have sought out the counsel of numerous people with disabilities, as well as disability rights advocates—including visionary leaders like Judy Heumann and former Senator Tom Harkin, and our colleagues at the Open Society Foundations and Wellspring Advisors, who were pioneering funders in this area more than a decade ago. These conversations have offered us tremendous insight into how we can—and will—include people with all types of disabilities in our work.

To be clear, we will not initiate a new program on disabilities. Rather, we will integrate an inclusive perspective across all of our grantmaking. As I've come to learn, the mantra of the disability community is "nothing about us, without us"—words that ring true across our work. After all, we make better decisions when we hear and heed the important contributions of all humankind. And I am confident that by adding and applying this additional lens across our efforts—by asking the extra question, are we mindful of the needs of people with disabilities?—we will see new opportunities we otherwise might have missed.

We also are taking immediate, practical action. For starters, we revisited our plans for the renovation of our headquarters to ensure that we go beyond the requirements of the ADA, so people with and without disabilities have the same quality of experience in the Ford Foundation building. We are also addressing our hiring practices. And soon we will ask all potential vendors and grantees to disclose their commitments to people with disabilities in the context of their efforts on diversity and inclusion.

This is an example of how the Ford Foundation is striving to redress an issue we didn't get right. But more than that, it is a call to reflect on our personal and collective ignorance—and to work more conscientiously to combat that ignorance, no matter what shape it takes.

For some, this might mean reconsidering the makeup of a board or leadership team—or reexamining recruiting and hiring practices that may unintentionally exclude certain people. For others, it might mean reassessing a program based on the context that surrounds it, or reflecting on the language we use when we talk about the people we work with. Or it might mean asking for uncomfortable comments and criticism, and seizing them as an opportunity for growth.

DEMANDING MORE OF OURSELVES, DELIVERING MORE FOR OTHERS

We simply cannot and will not defeat the enemies of justice—or dispel ignorance—without taking time to reflect on our own lives, and without asking difficult questions: *Who am I forgetting? Which of my assumptions are flawed? Which of my beliefs are misbegotten?*

To do this, we need to put aside our pride. We need to open our eyes, ears, minds, and hearts in order to embrace a complete and intersectional view of inequality. Only when we permit ourselves to be equal parts vigilant and vulnerable can we model the kind of honest self-reflection we hope to see across our society.

If "ignorance allied with power" is, in fact, the greatest enemy of justice—and the greatest fuel for inequality—then empathy and humility must be among justice's greatest allies. This will be the work of our year ahead and beyond. It is the work of engaging directly with the root causes and circumstances of injustice that make philanthropy both possible and necessary.

For my part, I am hopeful. By demanding and expecting more of ourselves and our institutions, we can deliver more for others. By listening more to each other, we can continue to forge a more just way forward, together.

UNLEASHING THE POWER OF ENDOWMENTS: THE NEXT GREAT CHALLENGE FOR PHILANTHROPY

Stanford Social Innovation Review
April 5, 2017

For the better part of two decades, the world of philanthropy has been engaged in an important, sometimes contested conversation about "impact"—both how we measure it and how we deliver it. More recently, this discussion—in the Ford Foundation's halls and throughout our sector—has focused on how to create impact through the capital markets, specifically through impact investing.

As with most foundations, our own impact-related work—our support for individuals, institutions, and ideas—has remained almost entirely separate from the way we steward our endowment. While most of our work is grant-making, the vast majority of our assets are actually financial investments.

Since 1969, US tax law has mandated that foundations pay out a minimum of 5 percent of their total assets each year. For the Ford Foundation, in recent years, meeting (and often exceeding) this requirement has translated to an annual grantmaking budget of around $500 million to $550 million. Meanwhile, we put the other 95 percent of our assets to work in the investment market, with the goal of earning financial returns that sustain the grantmaking power of our endowment over time. This, I hasten to add, is no easy task.

I believe the time is right for us to look at this paradigm with fresh eyes—to consider how we might start to bridge the gap between philanthropic impact and investments. Indeed, as I wrote last year in "Moving the Ford Foundation Forward," we have come to believe that if we expect to overcome the forces of injustice and inequality, we need to expand our imaginations and our arsenals. In short, we must begin to more deliberately leverage the power of our endowment.

And so I am pleased that after many months of analysis and planning, the Ford Foundation's Board of Trustees has authorized the allocation of up to $1 billion of our endowment, to be phased in over ten years, for mission-related investments (MRIs). While this field is still emerging, we are making this commitment because we believe MRIs are the next great tool for social transformation, in philanthropy and beyond.

If philanthropy's past half century was about optimizing the 5 percent, its next half century will be about beginning to harness the 95 percent as well, carefully and creatively.

OUR HISTORY IN IMPACT INVESTING: PROGRAM-RELATED INVESTMENTS

This decision was a long time coming, and would not be possible if not for the hard work of so many pioneers and visionaries in the impact investing community. Indeed, it represents the next step in a long march that stretches back to the very beginnings of impact investing.

Fifty years ago, in April 1967, Ford Foundation staff presented a report to trustees titled *Program-Directed Investments*. It argued that philanthropy was about more than grantmaking.

Our predecessors believed that philanthropy "should be viewed as a continuum of contractual options with the outright grant placed at one extreme, something close to a market investment at the other, and in between a series of alternatives representing ascending degrees of gifting." The following year, the foundation sought and received a ruling from the IRS that allowed us to create a new investment vehicle called program-related investments, or PRIs.

By law, PRIs are charitable investments. They take the form of loans, guarantees, and equity. These investments are directly aligned with a foundation's programmatic commitments and must meet legal charitable standards, as well.

Like grants, PRIs generally come out of a foundation's program budget and count toward the 5 percent foundations are required to pay out every year. Unlike grants, PRIs are expected to be repaid. They are not, however, expected to provide a return at competitive, risk-adjusted market rates. PRIs often allow for both higher levels of risk and lower levels of financial return than conventional financial investments.

We have found PRIs to be one of the most effective arrows in our quiver. Since 1968, the foundation has directed more than $670 million to PRIs, supporting social entrepreneurs and community development institutions around the world in their efforts to, among other things, preserve affordable housing, improve access to financial services and markets, create quality jobs, and advance arts and culture. And, as expected, our PRI fund has broken even—or better—over time, while making catalytic investments. PRIs allow us to take risks consistent with our mission in ways that much larger investors, such as banks and pension funds, often cannot or will not.

Our predecessors of fifty years ago understood that philanthropy is a spectrum with a host of options—options that have continued to grow and mature over the decades. While PRIs have allowed foundations like ours to tap the power of our grantmaking budgets in novel ways, today, our mission compels us to explore how we might mobilize our most significant financial resource: Our endowments.

THE NEXT STEP: MISSION-RELATED INVESTMENTS

At its most basic level, philanthropy always has been about directing financial capital to solve social problems. And foundations always have had a unique relationship to our capitalist system, a relationship I explored two years ago in my essay "Toward a New Gospel of Wealth."

I am often reminded of how Henry Ford II urged our forebearers to "examine the question of our obligations to our economic systems." He asked that we consider how philanthropy, "as one of the [market] system's most prominent offspring, might act most wisely to strengthen and improve its progenitor."

This obligation has become more pronounced in recent years. As a global foundation committed to fighting injustice, it is not lost on my colleagues and me that the very same systems that produce inequality also created our endowment, which, wisely invested, continues to fund our fight *against* inequality.

Since our mission has been funded by returns on our endowment, we have come to believe, firmly, that we have a special responsibility—and unique opportunity—to help influence the very markets that allow us to operate.

Clearly, one way we can do this is by taking a measured and carefully considered step to experiment with new kinds of investments that enlarge the meaning of the word *returns*.

This is not a new consideration. Concerns about socially responsible investing go back to the founding of modern stock markets centuries ago—and debates about reconciling the gains in "sin stocks" with ethical standards and religious values.

Since the 1980s, divestment movements around the world have asked institutional investors, in particular, to consider how their investments are related to the wider world. Whether they were demanding divestment from tobacco, fossil fuels, or apartheid South Africa, these movements reminded us that our investments are part of a broad ecosystem of consequences, intended and unintended—consequences that we realized we could not ignore.

Today, we have an opportunity to build on this proud, powerful legacy. Previous divestment movements tried to prevent investors from harming society; now, institutional investors can begin to move from "do no harm" to exploring how to "do more good."

That brings us to mission-related investments, or MRIs. Through this new tool, we will leverage the power of our endowment, and start to unlock the potential of the 95 percent to create impact through the market. MRIs seek to achieve attractive financial returns while also advancing the foundation's mission. Unlike PRIs, MRIs can bring to bear large amounts of capital in the service of multiple bottom lines.

WHY NOW: THE CHANGING LANDSCAPE

The Ford Foundation is not the first to commit a portion of its endowment to MRIs. We follow in the footsteps of—and are learning from—those foundations that pioneered the use of this tool. They include the early signatories to the More for Mission movement, as well as a number of other foundations that have announced new and significant initiatives in recent years, including the Rockefeller Brothers Fund, Kellogg Foundation, John D. and Catherine T. MacArthur Foundation, Kresge Foundation, McKnight Foundation, F.B. Heron Foundation, Wallace Global Fund, Surdna Foundation, Bill & Melinda Gates Foundation, and Open Society Foundations. While these institutions have taken a variety of approaches, their commitment demonstrates leadership and courage. Their initial steps should inspire all of us to consider how we might leverage the power of our endowments to promote dignity, equality, and justice for people around the world.

Significant changes in the capital markets have also made this step much easier for us to explore, and hopefully for others to consider, too. All manner of financial institutions, from private wealth advisers to large asset owners, are now deploying investment products to meet the rapid increase in investor demands for sustainable investments.

In the past, there have been three main reasons why most American foundations have not invested any portion of their endowments into MRIs.

First, legal uncertainty served as a barrier. Until recently, it was not clear whether MRIs could meet the prudent investor standards that government sets for how foundations can invest their endowments. But last year, the United States Treasury clarified its position, establishing the legality of MRIs as part of a larger effort to encourage them.

Second, there have been legitimate questions about whether there is enough evidence to prove that mission-related investments yield desirable financial or social returns.

We've come to realize that if we hope to answer this second question, it is our responsibility to put more of our money where our mouths are. For this promising sector to continue to grow and mature it needs more data, which requires a greater depth of experience and a greater measure of leadership. While the Ford Foundation has previously been willing to commit grant dollars, we are now excited to take the next step and commit endowment dollars, too.

The experience of others has given us reason to be optimistic, as has the continued growth of the field. For example, over the past few years the tools available to measure social impact have become increasingly precise, thanks in large part to the work of several leading institutions:

- The Sustainability Accounting Standards Board (SASB), an independent council, has worked to standardize corporate reporting of material nonfinancial data in areas like employment, environmental sustainability, and governance.

- An initiative of the Global Impact Investing Network, IRIS (Impact Reporting and Investment Standards) is a catalog of accepted performance metrics that helps guide investors who want to consider their social and environmental impact.
- The Global Impact Investing Ratings System (GIIRS) rates companies and funds based on their environmental and social impact, in a manner similar to Standard & Poor's credit risk ratings. GIIRS is hosted by B Lab.
- The Mission Investors Exchange is the leading network of foundations committed to collective learning and mobilizing their assets in ways that align with their mission.

Third and finally, when it comes to investment management, the boards of most foundations (ours included) are focused on maintaining the grantmaking power of endowments over time. Boards are the faithful stewards of our portfolios, with the duty to ensure that foundations make only rock solid, reliable investments. And rightly so: Hanging in the balance is the continuation of all the important work and organizations that foundations support.

Yet I believe that our posture can and should gradually evolve, that we can responsibly steward our assets while finding a path toward more transformational impact. While we recognize that MRI funds are newer—and therefore less tested and trusted—they nonetheless present a clear opportunity for exactly this type of evolution.

OUR DECISION

And so, for our part, the Ford Foundation has decided to gradually and prudently invest up to $1 billion of our endowment in MRI funds, to be phased in over the next ten years.

This decision is a natural extension of our history of PRI investing, which will continue to play an important role in our approach to impact. It is deeply rooted in our ongoing program work to build more inclusive economies, help mature the impact investing sector, and fulfill our special obligation to help move market-based economies toward the "high road"—squaring the dynamism of markets with society's highest values, especially fairness and human dignity.

This work represents a new frontier for us, and will require new people with new skills. So, we will build a special team of dedicated, veteran investment professionals to manage our MRIs. Unlike our excellent, existing investment team, this group of financial analysts and advisers focused on MRIs will report to our program leadership, and be held accountable for social and financial returns that contribute to our mission and, over time, to our annual programmatic payout as well.

As for the objective of our MRIs, our early efforts will target areas that have long been central to our mission of disrupting inequality in all its forms. In the United States, we'll start by examining investments that make housing more affordable and inclusive. And in developing countries, we'll look at how MRIs could expand access to vital financial services, particularly for low-income and other underserved communities.

Not only will *what* we invest in reflect our values—*how* we make these investments and report on them will be informed by our mission, as well. We hope to make diversity, equity, and inclusion bywords of this investment movement, paying attention to the makeup of investment teams, as well as where they invest and with what values. We join a growing number of committed pension funds, universities, foundations, and other institutional investors in not only considering diversity and inclusion but also recognizing how it can be a powerful contributor to performance and impact. And we will make our financial and impact performance completely transparent, to help move the wider marketplace forward.

In every way possible, we will work to ensure that these MRIs complement the work we are already doing through our grantmaking and PRIs, and contribute to our larger vision for a more equal, more just world. And to be clear: This careful, gradual allocation of some endowment resources to MRIs will have little to no impact on our grantmaking budget.

We believe we can achieve attractive financial returns while also contributing to meaningful social progress by following a steady, deliberative approach, building in strong oversight and risk management by our board of trustees, and working fully with partners in the private, public, and non-profit sectors. Throughout this process, we will learn as we go and share as we learn.

THE NEXT GREAT CHALLENGE FOR PHILANTHROPY

Of course, while I am profoundly pleased that the Ford trustees have made a significant commitment to MRIs, we know that a billion dollars—despite being a lot of money—is not nearly enough to grow and prove this space.

One of my former colleagues, Antony Bugg-Levine, a founder of the impact investing movement, has framed the problem presciently. He often says that our social challenges and social capital form a kind of ledger, with liabilities on one side and assets on another. The fact is, we face trillions of dollars in risks and liabilities—whether from environmental degradation, disease burden, lack of affordable housing, persistent joblessness, the impact of structural and systemic racism and gender bias, or so many other drivers and consequences of inequality—compared with only a few billion dollars of philanthropic assets. With the gap so wide and the stakes so high, we cannot afford to leave any option unexplored.

My conviction is that this moment offers us an opportunity to help capital markets become accelerators of justice. And my hope is that, before long, many more foundations, of all kinds and sizes, will find ways to tap the power of their own endowments to help contribute to multiple bottom lines. Pension funds, university endowments, sovereign wealth funds, and others can do the same in ways consistent with their respective missions, expertise, and fiduciary obligations. In time, I fervently believe, we will see a thriving, mature sector in which everyone can make impact investments that produce both sustainable financial returns and substantial social returns. Maybe it will take decades more to get there. But we'll never know if we don't make a start.

Since the birth of foundations, our endowments have been essential to our work. Going forward, I believe they will become an essential part of our work and how we continue that work into the future. This is the next great challenge in philanthropy: To find and finance more social good than we ever have before.

It is a challenge we will rise to meet together.

A $1 BILLION EXPERIMENT IN PHILANTHROPIC INVESTING

The Wall Street Journal
April 7, 2017

Since 1969, US law has mandated that foundations, like the one I lead, pay out at least 5 percent of their total assets each year to maintain their tax-exempt status. Meanwhile, we put the other 95 percent of our assets to work in the market, with the objective of earning financial returns that sustain our grantmaking capacity over the long haul. This is no easy task—which is why most philanthropic institutions maintain a wall of separation between program work and investment-management operations.

Since becoming president of the Ford Foundation three years ago, however, I've been asking what more we can do with our endowment. Why not start deploying it for both financial returns and mission-driven, philanthropic ends? Why not experiment with investing directly in projects and programs that will have a social impact?

This week, we announced that the Ford Foundation will devote up to $1 billion of its $12 billion endowment over the next decade to mission-related investments, or MRIs. Other philanthropies—such as the Heron and McKnight foundations and the Rockefeller Brothers Fund—are the pioneers in this movement, and pension funds and other institutional investors are making moves in the same direction.

The potential investment pool is enormous. The Foundation Center estimates that American grantmaking foundations hold some $865 billion in assets. The Global Impact Investing Network notes that the pool is much larger when we include other types of institutional investors, family offices, and wealthy individuals seeking double-bottom-line investments.

The push toward impact investing is viewed with valid skepticism. Many in the financial and philanthropic sectors believe that investing should focus exclusively on the financial bottom line, and MRIs have yet to prove that they can provide a reliable rate of return. It is a nascent field, and we still need large, pooled studies of varied asset classes over long time horizons.

Social returns have proved even more challenging to measure than financial returns. After all, investors can target many different kinds of impact: Creating good jobs for the disadvantaged, supporting entre-preneurs from underrepresented backgrounds, banking the unbanked, improving public health, or promoting a more sustainable environment.

Several institutions that we have supported with grants—such as the Sustainability Accounting Standards Board—have developed metrics and standards that companies and investment professionals can adopt or adapt to suit their needs. Over the next decade, we expect that the field's capacity to measure and report on social risks and returns will evolve dramatically, thanks to greater investments of intellectual and financial capital.

We have spent decades shaping and shepherding efforts to generate social impacts and measure them. As part of scaling up the microfinance industry in the developing world, for instance, we have supported the creation of social-performance standards that help donors and lenders hold themselves accountable for getting capital into the hands of the poor, not just more profitable customers.

For us, mission-related investing will demand the same hardheaded pragmatism that we bring to managing all of our endowment assets. We must ask whether the potential returns—in a diversified affordable housing preservation fund, for example, or in an equity fund for tech startups that deliver financial services to the unbanked—are compelling enough to warrant the risks. And are the financial returns attractive enough, given other ways we might invest to generate social impact?

Fortunately, the philanthropic sector isn't alone in these ambitions. Ordinary investors are also increasingly demanding options that include a social return. "Clients are telling us they want their portfolios to reflect their values and help improve the world they live in," said Andy Sieg of Merrill Lynch in 2015.

Antony Bugg-Levine, the CEO of the Nonprofit Finance Fund, helped to name and establish the impact-investment movement when we served together at the Rockefeller Foundation a decade ago. He argues that our social challenges and social capital should be seen as a kind of figurative balance sheet, with liabilities on one side and assets on the other. We face trillions of dollars in risks and liabilities—from education to infrastructure, from housing to health care—compared with mere billions of philanthropic giving. The challenge is to close that gap.

The Ford Foundation's $1 billion is not going to change the world by itself. The trillions of dollars that could follow just might.

ALIGNING OUR INVESTMENTS AND OUR VALUES

October 18, 2021

Eight years ago, the Ford Foundation's trustees appointed me president, the honor of my life. I pledged, then, that we would reimagine the way we use all of our assets, physical and financial. I've long believed that, across philanthropy, it is necessary but not sufficient to grant only the 5 percent required by the United States tax code. We also have a responsibility to use the other 95 percent, and beyond—to harness the full power of our assets in the fight for a more just and fair world.

Over the years, my colleagues and I have strived to optimize our resources in the best interest of our grantees, communities, and society at large—in a balanced but ambitious way.

Almost five years ago, this was the guiding principle behind our $1 billion commitment to mission-related investments, which are proving the potential of capital markets to deliver both a financial and social return. Last year, during the worst of the COVID-19 pandemic, the same philosophy led us to finance a $1 billion social bond, effectively doubling our payout rate and injecting a capital booster to our grantees during a period of uncertainty and peril.

Today, we are pleased to announce another major step in the same direction: Going forward, the foundation's endowment will not invest in any fossil-fuel-related industries. As with any significant decision in a dynamic organization, this choice did not come without trade-offs. One of the implicit challenges of preserving our grantmaking power in perpetuity is managing an endowment that grows ahead of inflation. As my partner on this journey Eric Doppstadt, Ford's remarkable chief investment officer, often reminds us, this is no easy endeavor.

Although just 0.3 percent of the Ford Foundation's endowment is directly invested in fossil fuel companies, we take our duties as fiduciaries seriously and we're mindful that if we put restrictions on our investments, we may forsake some amount of return for future generations.

At the same time, however, the Ford Foundation's trustees, leadership team, and I recognize a risk graver than forsaken value: There is no perpetuity without a planet.

We face profound challenges on an existential scale. Fires and floods are worsening—and on top of it all, the distortion of our market system, and the inequality it's produced, have overloaded the burden of these disasters onto the backs of the poor, the marginalized, and the vulnerable. I believe that the intersecting crises of climate change and inequality threaten to make an outmoded vision of perpetuity, at best, obsolete—and, at worst, destructive.

As a global community, our window for necessary change is closing. If we only do what we've always done, the worst may well sneak up on us while we're safeguarding some old, rosy vision of economic perpetuity.

And so, here at the Ford Foundation, we've decided our imperative must be to marshal the combined power of our resources, our policies and practices, and our position of leadership to help protect the planet from the existential threat of climate disaster. This includes renovating our headquarters in New York City to meet the LEED Gold certification standard.

With our endowment, our strategy is twofold: First, we commit to not doing harm. The consequences are too great to justify any additional investments in fossil-fuel industries.

Second, no less important, we will look for opportunities to invest in enterprises and funds that are fueling new technologies and capabilities, contributing to a renewable sector that is strong, diverse, and varied enough to sustain a green-energy economy.

This work is a crucial course correction. But in order to fully address the crises of our time, it must be paired with the generative work of investment in an alternative paradigm—a more sustainable way of life.

As a large institutional investor, the Ford Foundation can and will play a meaningful role here—by continuing to evolve our own endowment policies, thereby joining the vanguard of a wider change across our economy.

Absent change, sooner or later, our markets are sure to collapse under the weight of a poisoned planet. A system that treats environmental, social, and corporate governance targets as marketing is doomed to fail in an era of environmental, social, and governance catastrophe; as the problems we face multiply in both kind and proportion, so, too, should our solutions.

To be sure, some argue we should move further, faster. If climate catastrophe is so dangerous, one might ask, why won't you just divest all of your fossil-fuel-related assets right now?

I respect this critique. I, too, am cautious of the word "wait," which, as Dr. Martin Luther King Jr. wrote, too often means "never."

But the reality is, the relatively small segment of our endowment currently locked up in fossil fuel investments has not increased since 2017—and retreating from our limited partnerships or other positions at a loss would drain much-needed resources from our grantmaking. So, we reject the zero-sum thinking that our approach needs to be all or nothing, immediately or never. Instead, we are laying the groundwork for a forward-looking, evolving strategy—one that serves people and the planet alike.

Reaching this juncture has been made possible by colleagues at other foundations willing to generously engage with me, offering thoughtful and wise counsel, in particular Ellen Dorsey (Wallace Global Fund), Stephen Heintz (Rockefeller Brothers Fund), and Senator Tim Wirth (UN Foundation). Their courage, wisdom, and righteous impatience inspired me immensely.

Each of them helped me navigate my own personal journey toward aligning our foundation's investments and values. In addition to Eric Doppstadt, I'm enormously grateful to Tom Kempner, chair of our board investment committee, board chair Francisco Cigarroa, and all the Ford Foundation trustees who were encouraging advocates for transforming our principles into policy and action.

To address the climate crisis, we must join together with urgency and purpose. Let's continue building on this new foundation—to ensure the work of justice lives on in perpetuity, as does the planet on which our very survival depends.

HEALING THE BREACH: THE FORD FAMILY AND FORD FOUNDATION

with Edsel B. Ford II
Fortune
December 5, 2024

In the annals of American philanthropy, few dramas captivate quite like the estrangement between the Ford family and the Ford Foundation. For years, it was an object of fascination, a subject of inquiry, and even fodder for the tabloids. And in the cloistered, exclusive worlds of wealth and philanthropy, it remained something of a cautionary tale and case study —oversimplified, distorted, and mythologized as a breach, a break for generations of donors to avoid at all costs.

The real history, the archival record, is much more nuanced and complex. The story has no heroes or villains, nor a clean narrative arc. It is also inseparable from the broader epic of American history that created it and that, in turn, it helped create.

The story begins with America's preeminent industrialist Henry Ford and his son Edsel (Edsel II's grandfather). In 1936, with an initial gift of $25,000, Edsel chartered an independent philanthropy (unaffiliated with the Ford Motor Company) to further "scientific, educational, and charitable purposes, all for the public welfare."

After Edsel's untimely passing in 1943, and then Henry's subsequent passing in 1947, Edsel's son Henry II then fully endowed the independent institution with their bequests, transforming it into the largest foundation in the world.

During the eight decades since, the foundation has given some $80 billion (adjusted for inflation) to support human dignity, human rights, and human potential—opportunity, equality, and justice—all around the globe.

This is in addition to the Ford Motor Company Fund, now Ford Philanthropy, the corporate foundation that Henry II established in 1949. Funded with Ford Motor Company profits, it too has distributed billions of dollars in grants to a wide range of organizations and communities in Michigan and more than thirty countries.

In 1976, Henry II famously resigned from the Ford Foundation's board of directors, making front-page news in the major papers of the day. As the prevailing account held, he found the foundation's work and culture to be too imperious and unaccountable. (At the same time, though, he always maintained his "positive feelings" about the institution's "significant contributions" and defended its "magnificent record of achievement.") This began a forty-year pause in the relationship between the family and the independent foundation. Some might even call it a divorce.

And yet, when the City of Detroit, Michigan, faced its historic bankruptcy in 2013, the time for reengagement had long since arrived. And so, together—company, family, and foundation—we joined forces, all constituents within a wide coalition, to help resolve the crisis while protecting the community's institutions, workers, and families.

In the decade since, the Ford Foundation has fully recommitted to its hometown, its sister Ford-family institutions, and surrounding communities, providing nearly $380 million of investment. And in 2019, the foundation's board appointed Henry Ford III (Edsel II's son) as a trustee (the first Ford to serve in this capacity since Henry II's resignation), officially beginning a new chapter of this century-old story.

We are proud of our extraordinary rapprochement. Today, the past is now past, at long last. In all candor, the foundation's reputation suffered because of the saga—and some of the family felt alienated from its legacy. We cannot change any of this.

But in another sense, our shared history drives our shared vision for a shared future—for Detroit, for Michigan, for America, and for the kind of market system and democratic capitalism that the Ford name and Ford Foundation have always signified.

After all, among Henry Ford's many innovations was the American middle class—and a nation in which workers could buy the products they built. And it was Henry Ford II who challenged us all to recognize the mutuality between America's economic system and its robust philanthropic sector.

"The foundation is a creature of capitalism," Henry II argued in 1977, and thus, it must embrace its "obligations" to "strengthen and improve its progenitor." Alongside the Ford Foundation's mission to promote "the public welfare," this charge informs and inspires its work to address inequalities of all kinds to this day.

Of course, other elements of our shared story are instructive, too—especially in this volatile, uncertain, polarized period.

For one, we've proven that we can resolve differences when we affirmatively decide that the values that bring us together are more important than the old slights and grievances that divide us.

The family and foundation are no monoliths. We do not, and could not, agree on every single issue; both encompass a wide range of perspectives on the challenges and opportunities ahead. And yet, we also know, we need not agree on everything in order to forge partnership and progress where possible.

Ultimately, all of this reflects our place in—and our pride in—that broader American story: Our faith in and fidelity to this nation we love; our enduring responsibilities to the communities to which we belong; and our belief in a philanthropic pluralism that represents the diversity of America while reinforcing our democratic capitalism.

As ever, change is the one constant in life. Times change, perspectives change, priorities change. But we believe that strong families and strong institutions—and in our case, strong bonds between the two—bring steadiness amidst the swirling winds. We each are better for our renewed partnership with each other.

PART III

A NEW GOSPEL OF GIVING FOR OUR NEW GILDED AGE

As I see it, we cannot hide from the central contradiction built into our giving. We are creatures of our economic and social systems' unequal benefits—and yet, we are charged with addressing their unequal outcomes. And the tension is particularly pronounced in this, our own Gilded Age—our own era of extremes, and inequalities, and extreme inequalities. Dr. Martin Luther King Jr. … summed this up perfectly. Six decades ago, he wrote, "Philanthropy is commendable, but it must not cause the philanthropist to overlook the circumstances of economic injustice that make philanthropy necessary." In other words, we must reckon with the inequality that makes philanthropy both necessary and possible.

The Atlantic
September 9, 2024

REJECTING THE TYRANNY OF STRATEGY

Stanford Social Innovation Review
May 15, 2014

Philanthropy is at an inflection point. During the last decade, our sector has become mired in a false choice. We have been trapped in a binary discourse that categorizes grantmakers as either strategic or undisciplined, either focused or haphazard, either rigorous or sloppy.

Too many of us have bought into a polemic that fails to account for the ways in which social change transpires. Worse still, by pressing our grantees to see the process of social change in this same inauthentic light, we inadvertently undermine their efforts when we should be empowering them.

The heart of our sector's challenge is that "strategic philanthropy" too often minimizes or ignores complexity because it is difficult to understand, predict, and factor into a formula. Better, doctrine tells us, just to limit and contain it.

We look for silver bullets and simple solutions because we have convinced ourselves that if it cannot be measured, it does not matter. And in turn, we miss potential breakthroughs.

My perspective is informed by my experience as a grantmaker and—importantly—as a grantee at Harlem's Abyssinian Development Corporation. During those days, I—and many of my colleagues—sometimes felt imprisoned by logic frameworks, theories of change, and elegant PowerPoint decks that sought to oversimplify how our neighborhood revitalization programs would affect our community. To us, social change could not be diagrammed with boxes and arrows, even though the foundation initiatives that funded our work demanded we explain it within a neatly organized "strategic framework."

I believe that philanthropy is at its best when we promote and protect a marketplace of ideas. Given free, full, and transparent conversation, the best idea ought to prevail. Why should it be any different in our own approaches to our own work?

After fifteen years of experimentation and experience, we know that social change does not follow an algorithm. It is messy. It comes in fits and starts, through feats and defeats. It unfolds in different patterns, at different paces, in different places. And because change in complex systems is unpredictable—no matter how well-intentioned and well-reasoned the model behind it—the time has come for us to set aside our adherence to a prescriptive theology that constrains how philanthropy approaches solving complex challenges.

Where do we go from here? First, we should open our eyes and minds to the entire spectrum of alternatives—approaches that anticipate and embrace complexity without neglecting rigor and outcomes. We absolutely must focus on outcomes—on economic equality, environmental stewardship, and social justice. These crucial challenges are the reason for our very existence. At the same time, we should support our grantees' pursuit of these outcomes without being doctrinaire and directive about their precise technique.

Furthermore, philanthropy needs sharper tools and more inclusive frameworks that allow us, as philanthropists, to account for the considerable complexity of real-world problem solving. To date, our culture has stigmatized program work that relies more on grantees' perspectives than on grantmakers'. We should be celebrating it.

Finally, we in philanthropy need to reorient the way we see ourselves. We frequently assume that foundations are central protagonists in the story of social change when, really, we are the supporting cast.

We each must play our own role. Our institutions can seed innovations. We can help grantees identify when and how to pivot. We can spread new ideas and best practices. We can harvest and harness learning from many grantees to improve our practice. But we are not—and we should not position ourselves—at the center of the process. It is our partners and grantees who implement and execute. This fundamental recognition must inform what we do and how we do it. After all, our most important obligation is to stand with courageous and creative visionaries on the front lines of social change, not to demand that they fall in line behind us.

TOWARD A NEW GOSPEL OF WEALTH

2015 Annual Message
October 1, 2015

As I begin my third year at the Ford Foundation's helm, I am reminded of how privileged I am—and we all are—to serve this institution.

For my colleagues and me, these past fifteen months have entailed both deep introspection about this privilege and broad exploration of how we can harness and direct it to advance our mission. For us, what has unfolded is a process of discovery and renewal that has led us to reorganize our programming around the global crisis of inequality. We call this ongoing renewal Ford*Forward*.

Next month, I'll be sharing more details about our thematic areas and the specific grantmaking lines of work through which we will carry out our programming. I look forward to beginning a new phase for the foundation that builds on Ford's rich and varied history.

Since sharing the news of our focus on inequality, I've been encouraged—and, candidly, surprised—by the overwhelming response.

As the chasm of inequality widens and deepens in communities around the world, we seem to have struck a nerve.

Yet while inequality certainly merits attention and effort, some have fairly pointed out a tension—if not a contradiction—between philanthropic efforts to address inequality and the structural economic realities that make it possible for foundations to exist at all.

THE ORIGINS OF MODERN PHILANTHROPY

This tension stretches back more than a century. In 1889, the American industrialist Andrew Carnegie composed his "Gospel of Wealth," a short essay with far-reaching impact. It is, in many ways, the intellectual charter of modern philanthropy, and its basic precepts remain the underpinning of US giving and, in turn, have greatly influenced an era of burgeoning philanthropic enterprise around the world.

Carnegie articulated his philosophy at a time when inequality had reached unprecedented levels in the United States. In an age of excess, titans of industry enjoyed lives of startling opulence; ordinary people endured low wages, dangerous working conditions, and overcrowded, unhealthy living quarters. He argued—as some still do—that inequality on this scale is an unavoidable condition of the free-market system and that philanthropy is one effective means of ameliorating the conditions the market produces.

Today, in this new period of rising inequality, it is timely that we reflect on the principles of philanthropy as originally set forth in Carnegie's influential "Gospel of Wealth"—to consider to what degree they point to the realities and responsibilities of philanthropy in our time, and to openly acknowledge and confront the tension inherent in a system that perpetuates vast differences in privilege and then tasks the privileged with improving the system.

To be sure, philanthropy today is broader and more diverse than ever before. Its tens of thousands of individual practitioners around the world follow a variety of approaches, as intentional and unique as they are. As ever, there is no one-size-fits-all solution.

Moreover, philanthropy continues to advance through bold experiments with new models. From the global Giving Pledge initiated by Bill Gates and Warren Buffett to the Robin Hood Foundation in New York City to major philanthropic communities emerging in China, India, Latin America, Africa, the Gulf States, and elsewhere, a twenty-first-century style of giving back is lifting the lives and lots of millions of people around the world. It is building schools, preserving cultural and natural diversity, and generating new vaccines, agricultural innovation, and the social entrepreneurship of a millennial generation of change agents. In the sheer persistence and proliferation of the philanthropic idea, Carnegie's "Gospel" reverberates loud and clear—and I deeply admire the leadership and example of philanthropists and foundations around the world that we are honored to work with and learn from.

And yet, despite this vast ledger of undeniable public good, the tension persists. Why, in too many parts of the world, have we failed to provide employment, education, and health care, decent nutrition and sanitation? What underlying forces drive the very inequality whose manifestations we seek to ameliorate?

RETHINKING THE GOSPEL OF GIVING

My thinking on this issue has been shaped by the words of Dr. Martin Luther King Jr. and his profound statement: "Philanthropy is commendable," he wrote, "but it must not cause the philanthropist to overlook the circumstances of economic injustice which make philanthropy necessary."

I hasten to add that it is not solely economic injustice that philanthropy exists to address, and I believe Dr. King had a broader idea at heart: He challenges us still to look at underlying structures and systems, the roots of injustice, the causes of human suffering, and the sources of our own privilege.

In other words, perhaps the time has come to take the radicalism of Carnegie's nineteenth-century revolution, mesh it with the courage of Dr. King's, and make it our own. Perhaps it is time for a reimagined gospel of giving. To borrow a phrase from Carnegie's "Gospel" itself, we might recognize "the changed conditions of this age" and adopt "modes of expressing this spirit suitable to the changed conditions under which we live." We might disentangle the web of conditions that make philanthropy both possible and necessary.

If we're being honest, we might acknowledge that we are crashing into the limits of what we can do with a nineteenth-century interpretation of philanthropy's founding doctrine.

A TWENTY-FIRST-CENTURY VIEW OF INEQUALITY

First of all, no one in philanthropy has the independent resources to solve our collective problems. In his lifetime, Andrew Carnegie gave away some $350 million. Even in today's currency, this is a pittance in comparison with the world's *trillions of dollars* of needs for food and housing, education, infrastructure, and health care.

What's more, even though Carnegie understood and set out to address the notion of inequality (though he understood the problem more narrowly as "poverty"), he did so with a very different set of insights and a very different set of conditions within which to work. Compared with 125 years ago, we live in more enlightened, egalitarian, and participatory societies. In part because of what modern philanthropy helped set in motion, our polities have expanded in significant ways, making room to hear and heed more diverse voices and perspectives.

We also have technology, data, and a century of randomized controlled trials, which, together, enable us to broaden our scope and understand increasingly intricate patterns of injustice and how they persist and reproduce over time. In doing so, we are able to cast light on deep-seated, systemic problems—problems that in the absence of these insights would be attributed solely to individual failures or subject to misleading generalization.

Where Carnegie might have identified illiteracy as a source of inequality, for example, we now understand that the reverse is true—or, at the very least, that a complex symbiosis is at work. We understand, in a way he did not, that social, cultural, political, and economic inequalities set in place reinforcing conditions from the very start of life—in homes, in neighborhoods, and in schools—that create cycles of poverty, illiteracy, and lack of opportunity.

We also know that inequality is built on antecedents—preexisting conditions ranging from ingrained prejudice and historical racial, gender, and ethnic biases to regressive tax policies that cumulatively define the systems and structures that enable inequality to fester.

Because today we know more and are exposed to a diversity of views and insights, we can engage in a more thorough examination of the underlying barriers that prevent people from advancing in society. We can grapple not just with what is happening but also with *how* and *why*. And I believe that change must come in three basic forms.

THREE STEPS TOWARD REDUCING INEQUALITY

First, we need to open ourselves up to more critical, honest discussions about deeply rooted cultural norms and structures, including racial, gender, ethnic, and class biases.

We have made impressive progress on these issues, but some social and economic progress cannot blind us to the reality that far too many are left behind because of inequality's asphyxiating grip on the aspirations of people in every corner of every country.

Second, we foundations need to reject inherited, assumed, paternalist instincts—an impulse to put grantmaking rather than changemaking at the center of our worldview.

For philanthropists working globally, our efforts shouldn't be a matter of Western institutions directing NGOs in the Global South or treating our grantees as contract-project managers rather than as valued partners. Instead, we should be strands in the web—South to South, South to North—making connections and modeling the kind of equality we hope to achieve by listening and learning and lifting others up.

Furthermore, we'd be well served to recognize that the more excluded people are, the harder it is truly to hear them. We all believe that those most affected by policy ought to have a voice in creating it. So our work should lend agency—and legitimacy—to slum dwellers and rural farmers, incarcerated people and refugees, migrants pursuing a better life and families on public assistance.

Third, we need to interrogate the fundamental root causes of inequality even, and especially, when it means that we ourselves will be implicated.

It is incumbent upon each of us to dig deeper and relish the dirt beneath our fingernails; what for Carnegie was bedrock to us has become topsoil. There are obscured root causes buried deep in our history, our institutions, and our cultural practices—causes we have to unearth and evaluate in the harsh light of day.

For one example, when we talk about economic inequality, we might acknowledge an underlying, unspoken hierarchy in which we relate everything back to capital. In most areas of life, we have raised market-based, monetized thinking over all other disciplines and conceptions of value.

We might ask related questions, too.

Within legacy institutions like ours, we should ask, how does our privilege insulate us from engaging with the most difficult root causes of inequality and the poverty in which it ensnares people?

How does our work—our approach to awarding grants, our hiring and contracting policies, even our behavior toward our partners and grantees—reinforce structural inequality in our society?

Why *are* we still necessary, and what can we do to build a world where we no longer are *as* necessary?

For individual philanthropists, it may well be appropriate to ask a similar set of questions: Is the playing field on which I accumulated my wealth level and fair? Does the system privilege people like me in ways that compound my advantages?

OUR OBLIGATION TO CAPITALISM

These questions are at the heart of our collective work but also at the core of our aspiration for an economic system *that works for more people.*

As Henry Ford II, framer of the modern Ford Foundation, wrote in a 1976 letter to his fellow trustees, the foundation is "in essence, a creature of capitalism." Therefore, he suggested, we ought to "examine the question of our obligations to our economic systems and to consider how the foundation, as one of the system's most prominent offspring, might act most wisely to strengthen and improve its progenitor."

To put it more bluntly, we were established by a market system and endowed by the money of the past century's 1 percent. We are stewards of enormous resources—participants in and beneficiaries of a market system. As a result, our work is quite literally enabled by returns on capital. In turn, I believe we are obligated to strengthen and improve the system of which we are part. My conviction is no anathema to capitalism. Adam Smith himself argued that the "invisible hand" could not be blind to the condition of society, and that "no society can surely be flourishing and happy, of which the far greater part of the members are poor and miserable." This from a visionary who was not only the forefather of American capitalism but also the author of *The Theory of Moral Sentiments*, which he regarded as more important than his *The Wealth of Nations.*

Philanthropy's role is to contribute to the flourishing of the far greater part—to help foster a stronger safety net and a level playing field. With each generation, we should be guided by our legacy of support for social progress and human achievement in the spirit of the Green Revolution, advances in public health and human rights, social movement building, creative expression, cultural innovation, and so much more.

Ultimately, this reckoning with—this reimagining of—philanthropy's first principles and its relationship to our market system will not be easy, but this moment requires that we not go easy on ourselves.

Some might see this as a problem or as pressure. To me, however, it is inseparable from our privilege—because with privilege comes responsibility.

In this spirit, let us commit ourselves to proffering and preaching and practicing a new gospel—a gospel commensurate with our time.

Let us bridge the philosophies of Smith and Carnegie and King and break the scourge of inequality. For when we do, to paraphrase another of Dr. King's most powerful insights, we at last will bend the *demand curve* toward justice.

MAINTAINING THE MOBILITY ESCALATOR TOGETHER

*Statement upon Election to the
American Academy of Arts and Sciences*
Cambridge, Massachusetts
October 18, 2015

I'm humbled and honored to join you—and to accept your election to the venerated ranks of the American Academy of Arts and Sciences. I must say, this is a moment made all the more humbling by dint of the distinguished colleagues and friends with whom I share this day—my fellow inductees.

My journey to this hallowed hall began in a small, segregated, Louisiana town—fifty-some years ago—where I was born in a charity hospital to a single mother. As I got older, my mother realized that a community poisoned by poverty and prejudice was not a place of opportunity for my sister and me. So, we moved to Texas—to Ames, population 1,400—where we had family. We lived in a narrow, shotgun house. My mom studied to become a nurse's assistant, a job she worked—with pride and dignity—for decades. We didn't have a lot, but we had enough.

I was in the inaugural Head Start. I attended public schools, The University of Texas, where I received scholarships endowed by wealthy, generous Texans—along with Pell grants financed by the American people.

The entire time, I felt like everyone—my state, my country—was cheering me on. After law school, I moved to New York, where I worked at a law firm, then an investment bank. I led a community organization in Harlem. And after many years working in community development, I joined the Rockefeller Foundation, then the Ford Foundation, the institution that I now am privileged to serve.

Now, I share all of this not because I am special. I share this because it shows how America is special.

And while it is true that we have our share of problems, for much of my lifetime, America's social-mobility escalator has been moving—lifting people as high as their hard work and talent will take them.

But, today, that escalator is slowing to a crawl. For some, it's stopped completely.

What does this say about America's future?

I worry—I despair—that in the years ahead, stories like mine will be far less likely in America.

And the reason is, in a word, inequality.

Across the country and around the world, we face a crisis of inequality, what I consider the existential threat of our time. Inequality—in all its forms, economic, social, political, racial, gender—compounds upon itself. Because of widening gaps, more people are slipping through the cracks, falling further and further behind.

We've seen the manifestations of inequality all across our society— whether you're looking at overrepresented populations in our jails and prisons, or underrepresented ones in our boardrooms and C-suites. We've read about it in the opinion pages and bestselling books. We've felt its asphyxiating effect on our democracy.

I'm deeply unsettled—deeply troubled—by all of this.

I'm unsettled when leaders of institutions of higher education—which undergird our democratic society—censor themselves on justice and fairness because they are afraid of offending the privileged.

As someone who benefits from great privilege—in a room replete with people who have benefited from great privilege—I think about my obligations to earn this privilege, to interrogate my own privilege. And I ask myself, how do I use my privilege as a tool to address—rather than compound—the inequality which makes my privilege possible?

Of course, this obligation is not new.

A century and a quarter ago, the industrialist Andrew Carnegie found himself the beneficiary of the American dream. This son of poor immigrants had risen to become one of the wealthiest men in the world—and in 1889, Carnegie reflected on these things in an essay we now refer to as "The Gospel of Wealth."

He wrote, and I'm quoting here: "Rich men should be thankful for one inestimable boon. They have it in their power" to organize "benefactions from which the masses of their fellows will derive lasting advantage, and thus dignify their own lives."

Carnegie articulated his philosophy during a time when inequality had reached unprecedented levels in the United States. And in our own era of rising inequality, we must openly acknowledge—and confront—a tension inherent in our economic, political, and social systems.

This tension is plain to see: Our systems in America perpetuate vast differences in privilege, and then task the privileged—all of us—with improving the systems that benefit us.

As a foundation president, my thinking on this issue has been shaped by Dr. Martin Luther King Jr. About philanthropy, he wrote, and I quote: "Philanthropy is commendable, but it must not cause the philanthropist to overlook the circumstances of economic injustice which make philanthropy necessary."

To me, Dr. King's words are my North Star—a guiding light.

He challenges us to assess and address underlying structures and systems, to uproot the root causes of suffering and injustice, to not overlook the circumstances that make our work necessary.

But I am an optimist. I am optimistic because of institutions like the academy, which oxygenates our democracy.

We know so much more than we did 125 years ago—in part because of the work of this academy—and this knowledge compels and directs our action. All of my life, I've benefited from—and learned from—the generosity of privileged people who understood their obligations, people who understood the pressure that comes with their privilege.

It will take all of us embodying this spirit—actively working, attentively questioning—to address the fundamental barriers to opportunity for too many Americans.

It will take all of us remembering that our greatest privilege—our inestimable boon—is our opportunity to repair our nation's fabric in the service of human dignity and justice for all.

This is the work of our generation.

And I am proud to be on the journey with so many of you, members of the American Academy of Arts and Sciences.

WHY GIVING BACK ISN'T ENOUGH

The New York Times
December 18, 2015

During this season of giving, I will join millions of Americans in volunteering to feed the homeless, contributing to clothing drives, and donating to poverty-fighting charities. Yet I worry that through these acts of kindness I absolve myself of asking deeper questions about injustice and inequality. We Americans are a remarkably bighearted people, but I believe the purpose of our philanthropy must not only be generosity, but justice.

The origins of formal philanthropy date from at least 1889, when the American industrialist Andrew Carnegie composed his "Gospel of Wealth." He drafted this intellectual charter at the peak of the Gilded Age, when inequality had reached extreme levels. Carnegie argued, as many still do, that inequality on this scale is an unavoidable condition of the free-market system—and that it was even desirable, if the promise of wealth incentivized hard work. Philanthropy, he believed, would ease the pressure of rising social anxiety that followed from inequality—ameliorating the afflictions of the market without altering the market system itself.

During the twentieth century, an entire field of institutional philanthropy emerged and flourished in the pattern of Carnegie's mold. Iconic American families—Gates, Knight, MacArthur, Mellon, Rockefeller—endowed and expanded foundations that built schools and libraries, developed new vaccines, revolutionized agriculture, and advanced human freedom. My own organization, the Ford Foundation, has given billions to support everything from public television in the United States to microlending in Bangladesh.

Our work has been indisputably for the good: Millions of people around the world have access to new tools and resources with which to improve their lives. A few months ago, the World Bank estimated that, for the first time in history, fewer than one in ten human beings lives in extreme poverty. This is progress.

And yet, for all the advances made in the last century, society's challenges may have outpaced philanthropy's resources. Today, the cumulative wealth of the most generous donors seems a pittance compared with the world's trillions of dollars' worth of need. Generosity, blooming as it may be from legacies of both Carnegie's age and the newly enriched, is no longer enough.

The world may need a reimagined charter of philanthropy—a "Gospel of Wealth" for the twenty-first century—that serves not just American philanthropists, but the vast array of new donors emerging around the world.

This new gospel might begin where the previous one fell short: Addressing the underlying causes that perpetuate human suffering. In other words, philanthropy can no longer grapple simply with what is happening in the world, but also with how and why.

Feeding the hungry is among our society's most fundamental obligations, but we should also question why our neighbors are without nutritious food to eat. Housing the homeless is an imperative, but we should also question why our housing markets are so distorted. As a nation, we need more investment in education, but not without questioning educational disparities based on race, class, and geography.

Our self-awareness—our humility—shouldn't be limited to examining the problems. It should include the structures of solutions, like giving itself. As the Rev. Dr. Martin Luther King Jr. said, "Philanthropy is commendable, but it must not cause the philanthropist to overlook the circumstances of economic injustice which make philanthropy necessary." It is, after all, an offspring of the free market; it is enabled by returns on capital.

And yet, too often, we have declined to question our own circumstances: A system that produces vast differences in privilege, and then tasks the most privileged with improving the system.

Whatever our intentions, the truth is that we can inadvertently widen inequality in the course of making money, even though we claim to support equality and justice when giving it away. And while our end-of-year giving might support worthy organizations, we must also ask if these financial donations contribute to larger social change.

In other words, "giving back" is necessary, but not sufficient. We should seek to bring about lasting, systemic change, even if that change might adversely affect us. We must bend each act of generosity toward justice.

We, as foundations and individuals, should fund people, their ideas, and organizations that are capable of addressing deep-rooted injustice. We should ensure that the voices of those most affected by injustice—women, racial minorities, the poor, religious and ethnic minorities, and LGBT individuals—help decide where and what philanthropy puts money behind, not in simply receiving whatever philanthropy decides to give them.

We can wield data and technology, see through a diversity of viewpoints, and draw upon a century of philanthropy's success and failure to identify and address the barriers holding people back.

This modern giving charter should look different in different settings. At the Ford Foundation, our efforts will focus on inequality: Not just wealth disparities, but injustices in politics, culture, and society that compound inequality and limit opportunity. We will ask questions like, *are* we hearing—and heeding—those who understand the problems best? What can we do to leverage our privilege to disrupt the drivers of inequality?

Others in philanthropy will take different, but no less effective, approaches. Many already are answering King's call, working intensely toward a world that renders philanthropy unnecessary. Ultimately, we each must do our part to ensure that giving not only makes us feel better, but also makes our society more just.

PHILANTHROPY IS AN AMERICAN IDEA AND BIRTHRIGHT

TIME
June 30, 2016

Charity—humanity's most benevolent impulse—is a timeless and border-less virtue, dating at least to the dawn of religious teaching. Philanthropy as we understand it today, however, is a distinctly American phenomenon, inseparable from the nation that shaped it. From colonial leaders to modern billionaires like Buffett, Gates, and Zuckerberg, the tradition of giving is woven into our national DNA.

Like so many of our social structures, the formal practice of giving money to aid society traces its origin to a founding father. Benjamin Franklin, an icon of individual industry and frugality even in his own day, understood that with the privilege of doing well came the price of doing good. When he died in 1790, Franklin thought to future generations, leaving in trust two gifts of one thousand pounds of sterling silver—one to the city of Boston, the other to Philadelphia. Per his instruction, a portion of the money and its dividends could not be used for two hundred years.

While Franklin's gifts lay in wait, the tradition he established evolved alongside the young nation. After the Civil War, rapid industrialization concentrated unfathomable wealth in the hands of a few, creating a period of unprecedented inequality. In response, the steel magnate Andrew Carnegie pioneered scientific philanthropy, which sought to address the underlying causes of social ills, rather than their symptoms. In his lifetime, Carnegie gave away more than $350 million, the equivalent of some $9 billion today. His 1889 essay "Wealth"—now better known as Carnegie's "The Gospel of Wealth"—effectively launched modern philanthropy by creating a model that the wealthy continue to follow.

Two decades later, John D. Rockefeller endowed the Rockefeller Foundation, which soon became the largest such "benevolent trust" in the world. Prior to World War II, the Rockefeller Foundation provided more foreign aid than the entire federal government.

Other, often far less well-known men and women have played a critical role in philanthropy's evolution. One of my personal heroes is Julius Rosenwald, who made his fortune building Sears, Roebuck and Co. With his giving, Rosenwald helped construct more than 5,300 schools across the segregated South and opened classroom doors to a generation of African-American students, including Maya Angelou and Congressman John Lewis.

America's philanthropic instinct is not limited to the rich. The nation's history is rife with people like Oseola McCarty, a Mississippi washerwoman who gave away her life savings of $150,000 in 1995 to fund college scholarships for low-income students with promise.

What accounts for this culture of generosity? The answer is not solely altruistic. Incentives in the tax code, for one, encourage the well-off to give.

And philanthropy has long helped improve the public image of everyone from robber barons to the new tech elite.

More troubling, however, are the foundational problems that make philanthropy so necessary. Just before his death, Dr. Martin Luther King Jr. wrote, "Philanthropy is commendable, but it must not cause the philanthropist to overlook the circumstances of economic injustice which make philanthropy necessary."

Indeed, King illuminates a central contradiction: Philanthropy is an offspring of the market, conceived and sustained by returns on capital, yet its most important responsibility is to help address the market's imbalances and inadequacies.

Today, institutional giving is undergoing a radical transformation. Priscilla Chan and Mark Zuckerberg made headlines for committing $45 billion in Facebook stock through a limited liability corporation. They're among a host of emerging donors who are experimenting with approaches to giving away their fortunes outside the boundaries of traditional foundations.

Only twenty-six years ago, the last of Franklin's gifts were finally made available, having multiplied to $6.5 million. More than the sum, they represent a broader principle: We are custodians of a public trust, even if our capital was derived from private enterprise, and our most important obligation is ensuring that the system works more equally and more justly for more people. This belief is core to our national character.

THE COMING OF HOPE: A VISION FOR PHILANTHROPY IN THE NEW YEAR

2019 New Year's Message
January 9, 2019

For me, the holiday season often arrives and departs with the echo of Maya Angelou's wisdom ringing in my ears and rattling through my consciousness. With the pause in our individual pursuits and the joy of shared celebration, with the retrenchment of the night and the rewinding of the calendar, there visits, as Angelou wrote, "a halting of hate time." In such a moment, "We, Baptist and Buddhist, Methodist and Muslim ... We, the Jew and the Jainist, the Catholic and the Confucian ... We shout with glorious tongues at the coming of hope. All the earth's tribes loosen their voices to celebrate the promise of peace."

As we begin 2019—a year that already portends to be among the most tumultuous in memory—I certainly welcome "the coming of hope." After all, at the Ford Foundation we are in the business of hope. Our hopes for our grantees, our communities, and our world inform the work we do each and every day.

At the same time, we must set our hope in relief against the realities of a world that feels on edge and off kilter, more precarious and less predictable. The reason for all of this, in my view, should not come as a surprise: Our political and economic system continues to produce and perpetuate staggering inequalities of all kinds.

Millions of people feel frustrated with, and excluded by, an out-of-balance global economic system they are decreasingly willing to tolerate. In the United States and globally, we see the evidence and urgency mounting: Grassroots movements objecting to fundamental inequalities in our society are mobilizing, calling out for fairness and justice. They are naming causes of our current plight—among them, global capitalism that produces outsize wealth for owners and increased insecurity for workers; authoritarian leaders who foment division, discord, and dysfunction; fast-moving technological innovation, with consequences citizens are only now beginning to understand; and the long-standing evils of racism, classism, ableism, homophobia, and patriarchy. And although this is our society's truth, it—like all truth—is under constant assault as the fidelity of facts, and our faith in them, is undermined.

Make no mistake, the exploitation of our democratic-capitalist system is intentional. Too often, the powerful and privileged who might stem the callousness and corruption seem largely to ignore it, avoid it, minimize it, or, worst of all, maximize it for their own gain.

In our politics, leaders openly disdain, demean, and deconstruct vital public institutions designed to serve us and our system of self-government. Implicit in these actions is a disregard for what democratic government can do to promote equality, justice, and human dignity. The result is predictable. As the late Senator Daniel Patrick Moynihan was known to say, "If you have contempt for government, you will get contemptible government." We currently have way too much of both.

It's plain to see, there are real flaws in the systems we have created to govern our politics, our economy, and our social relations—flaws that have yielded the inequalities now pulling at the fabric of society.

AN OBLIGATION TO LISTEN AND DO BETTER

A generation ago, Henry Ford II named philanthropy "a creature of capitalism"—and called on its practitioners to contemplate how, as "one of [our] system's most prominent offspring," philanthropy might help to "strengthen and improve its progenitor." It is beyond the capacity of philanthropy to fix our economic and political systems. But as beneficiaries of the biases and flaws of these systems, I believe holders of wealth and influence today—whether individuals, corporations, or foundations—share an urgent obligation to try.

To do so, we must first recognize and reckon with the fact that philanthropy is by no means immune from the plague of inequality. If we are to be legitimate participants in the fight against it, there is urgency to our embracing this truth.

During the past year, a number of journalists, academics, and commentators have offered insightful—and sometimes incisive—critiques of philanthropy as an enterprise. While I may not agree with aspects of these assessments, in the aggregate, all raise valid, valuable, substantive concerns. Many have pointed to the ways philanthropy replicates the worst dynamics and inequalities of our broader society. A few examples:

- Anand Giridharadas's *Winners Take All* coins the term "MarketWorld" to describe a key force Giridharadas believes is driving much of philanthropy to reinforce a rigged economic system. While the book ignores countless examples of humble, social-justice philanthropy, it rightly skewers that segment of philanthropic giving that boasts of saving the world while fundamentally strengthening the economic and social structures that separate us.

- Edgar Villanueva's *Decolonizing Wealth* spotlights the history of colonialism and oppression that gave rise to our country's financial system and vast wealth—an argument that resonates in many places in the world where these forces have subjugated people and stripped away value—and reveals how structural racism continues to shape philanthropy today.
- Rob Reich's *Just Giving* scrutinizes the undemocratic nature of wealth and philanthropy, and argues for considerable changes to make giving more transparent and accountable in service of democratic values. Like Villanueva, Reich expresses belief in and admiration for the past and potential of philanthropy, while nonetheless offering a rigorous analysis of how the current system can seem to bypass democratic will.

These critiques are voices in a growing chorus that we ignore at our own peril. Rather than taking a "this too shall pass" attitude, philanthropists need to engage in repairing the very mechanisms that produce, preserve, and promote our privilege. I believe we must practice a better vision of philanthropy, one that improves itself and the societies of which we are members.

THE ARCHITECTURE OF PROGRESS

It bears repeating that the challenges inherent in our democratic-capitalist system did not arrive overnight. Creating a fairer, more just world is no small order. It requires leaders of every sector and discipline, working with new purpose. It requires engaged citizens, effective governments, capitalists (including yours truly) who promote shared prosperity, and enduring social movements.

And it requires us. To do our part in this drive for real change, philanthropists and funders of every stripe must invest in the architects and architecture of progress—the individuals, ideas, and institutions that make change happen.

My fundamental, unwavering belief in philanthropy is informed by history and my own personal journey. Philanthropy was crucial in creating the blueprint for social progress in the twentieth century that helped nations around the world eradicate disease, that lifted children like me out of poverty, and that financed the development of thousands of institutions and new capacity that expanded opportunity for billions of people around the globe. Philanthropy helped sustain the Civil Rights Movement in the United States, the anti-apartheid movement in South Africa, and the human rights movement in Latin America during the most oppressive years of military government.

Placing meaningful resources in the hands of those closest to the problems, backing their visionary efforts over time, listening and learning at every step of the journey—this is the philanthropy we need today. But to fully and honestly address the problem of inequality and the ways it is embedded in philanthropy, there is even more we must do.

For starters, let's agree that contemptible government, and contempt for government, are antithetical to the objectives of any philanthropist who cares about positive change in the world. Regardless of differences among philanthropic givers about the relative size and function of government, all philanthropic effort relies on the rule of law and functioning, effective government systems for scaling impact. No matter how independent we think our efforts are, our resources pale in comparison to public resources and the impact they have on daily life and the course of human dignity. I believe good works require good government.

To this end, there is much more we can be doing to support the health of representative government and its institutions, especially in the face of rising authoritarianism. Advancing and vigorously protecting an independent press, for one; standing behind a fair and thorough census; supporting voting rights and opposing all efforts to curtail citizen access to the ballot; advancing innovations by governments at the local and state levels that make them more efficient and responsive; protecting the rule of law for all people, including immigrants; building the public case for reform in areas of deep inequality, such as our education and criminal justice systems; placing workers and worker movements at the center of policy discussions as the economy of the future is designed; investing in research that demonstrates how our economic system can be made more equitable and sustainable; and protecting a free and open Internet, which today is our de facto public square.

No funder should consider these areas and others like them as being outside their mission. We are public trusts; we ought to show more faith in public institutions and own our accountability to them.

RECKONING WITH PRIVILEGE

But beyond what we can do to improve the unequal systems around us, we must honestly grapple with the privileges our organizations enjoy as their beneficiaries. This means interrogating our own unconscious biases, cultivating humility in ourselves and our organizations, and more clearly understanding how others experience the institutions of philanthropy—how remote we can be, how insular, how difficult to navigate. It also means investing in research and initiatives that might make us uncomfortable, and that hold us accountable, so that our actions reflect our aspirations for a more just, more equal world.

We know that the communities most proximate to the problems possess unique insight into the solutions. That is why, in everything we do, we ought to ensure that the people affected by our work are guaranteed a voice in its design and implementation. To this end, diversity must be a priority throughout our organizations—and especially at the top of them. One recent BoardSource survey suggests that the boards and leadership of foundations are remarkably homogeneous. We must work to become more heterogeneous in an increasingly diverse world or we risk cynicism and backlash from stakeholders who don't see themselves represented in our institutions.

Finally, we must trust those we fund, and fund them adequately to do what they believe is best, not what we think is best. This means putting ourselves in the shoes of prospective grantees and communities, treating them like partners rather than contractors, and entrusting organizations with long-term general support funding and project grants that provide adequate overhead. It means acknowledging the power imbalance that often makes our grantees reluctant to engage honestly and authentically.

The good news is that I see a growing movement to appreciate the criticisms of philanthropy, and to face them head-on. This is a movement of philanthropists not merely concerned with funding good works but also with improving how we fund them. I am inspired by Agnes Gund's leadership in creating Art for Justice; Oklahoma businessman George Kaiser's work to reduce the rising number of women in prisons; Jon Stryker's fight to protect LGBTQ people in difficult regions; a group of current and former CEOs who are working to promote inclusive capitalism; and a number of foundations that are working to promote more grantmaking in the American South, a region historically overlooked by national foundations. Internationally, philanthropists like Nandan and Rohini Nilekani (India) and Mo Ibrahim (Africa) are having an impact through pioneering grantmaking in regions with little history of social-justice giving.

I believe they and many other philanthropists represent a movement from generosity to justice. To me, this is the best response to philanthropy's deepest flaws and inherent contradictions.

CONFRONTING INEQUALITY IN THE YEARS AHEAD

Each December, the Merriam-Webster dictionary selects its "word of the year"—a noun that people have looked up more consistently over the course of that year than others, suggesting that it has been particularly relevant to the popular discourse.

In 2018, that word was "justice." I do not think this is a coincidence.

This past year, we have seen acts of extreme injustice around the world and across our nation—at our farthest borders and inside our most hallowed halls. And we have seen how organizations have fought for justice every step of the way, how philanthropists have incorporated it into their ways of seeing and being.

As our system falters under the inequality it has produced, as society seems increasingly strained by—and susceptible to—ever-widening gaps, those of us who have benefited from this inequality need to look in the mirror and ask why. Then we should ask how we fix it, with justice as our objective.

In this way, for all of us, the road map for 2019 is clear. Given the progress we've made, and the work ahead, we cannot turn back now. We must redouble our efforts and forge forward, boldly, courageously, joyfully. We must dedicate ourselves, anew, to the cause of justice—and "shout," in the words of the poet, "with glorious tongues at the coming of hope."

With appreciation for your partnership, I wish you a productive new year.

THE HARD WORK OF HOPE: HOW WE MOVE FORWARD

2020 New Year's Message
January 22, 2020

With the new year comes a new beginning, an opportunity for reflection and renewal. And yet, a month into this new year and decade, the promise of the New is already overwhelmed by the Old—by climate crisis and geopolitical crisis years in the making; by crises of misinformation, online and off; by crises of inequality in opportunity, voice, and progress.

Day by day, we lose ground to fire and fear, corruption and cynicism, partisanship and polarization. As authoritarianism and nationalism advance, democratic values and institutions remain in retreat.

The hits keep on coming. And while depletion, depression, and "democracy grief," as one columnist called it, are perfectly understandable reactions (I'll confess, I feel it sometimes, too), they do nothing to douse the flames or calm the fury.

This week in the United States, we honor the life and legacy of Dr. Martin Luther King Jr. and it feels fitting to heed his timeless call: The urgency of now—of our now—has never been fiercer.

To me, embracing this urgency—harnessing its power to carry us closer to justice—is the defining task of this year, and of every day and hour ahead. This is a time to step up, not check out—a time to reenlist, reengage, and reconnect, both with each other and with the deep, abiding optimism at the heart of the democratic creed.

We must ask ourselves: How do we escape the maelstrom, and elevate the makers and markers of progress? How do we move beyond the constant harm and hurt—and move toward the healing and reconciliation we crave and the real change we so desperately need?

These are not easy questions—and they defy obvious answers. No doubt, we must strive to understand the world in its fullness and complexity. But with justice as our guiding light, I remain hopeful that we can make our political and economic systems more inclusive—and, in turn, repair and rebuild our trust in one another.

I find myself reflecting, often, on one of my heroes, Congressman John Lewis, who fought for justice alongside Dr. King and is courageously facing a new fight against cancer. Five years ago, Congressman Lewis invited me and a number of leaders to join him on a pilgrimage across the Edmund Pettus Bridge in Selma, Alabama—the hallowed ground where he and thousands of others had marched directly into unimaginable violence, changing the course of America's Civil Rights Movement and democracy forever. As we commemorated the fiftieth anniversary of what we now call Bloody Sunday on that modest bridge, we affirmed a sacred conviction, in the congressman's words, that "love will conquer hate" and "hope will conquer fear."

We also recognized the tremendous power of sacrifice and struggle. As the congressman once said, we cannot "get lost in a sea of despair" because "our struggle is not the struggle of a day, a week, a month, or a year; it is the struggle of a lifetime."

Around the world today, we are seeing examples of sacrifice abound, particularly from young people, women, people with disabilities, rural and Indigenous communities, and people of color. Kynan Tegar, Greta Thunberg, Artemisa Xakriabá, and the youth who are leading movements to stop climate change, and the millions of everyday citizens in places like Chile, Haiti, Hong Kong, India, Lebanon, Mexico, and Sudan who are demanding more transparency and equality, more dignity and democracy, are proving themselves worthy heirs to the legacy of Congressman Lewis and the many courageous individuals throughout our global history who have put their safety, their bodies, and, at times, their lives on the line in the name of justice.

The truth is those who are committed to, and fighting for, social justice are no strangers to sacrifice. Many courageous champions of change have sacrificed, and will continue to sacrifice, for the most righteous of reasons.

But we must ask why those with the least tend to sacrifice the most, while those with the most power, the most resources, the most privilege, and the most potential to do good tend to resist the transformational change that would produce a world with more justice? Why are well-positioned people capable of making the changes we need so hesitant to do more? What new crisis needs to befall us before we, together, are spurred to collective action?

Too many unaffected by the inequities of our day remain at a remove, holding themselves apart, exonerating themselves for their complicity in systems in desperate need of repair. I believe to rebuild trust, the people who benefit most will need to sacrifice more—whether resources, comfort, or power.

At the end of last year, we hosted a conference on the future of philanthropy, and I was struck by the philosophy that has driven Luis Miranda Jr., longtime activist and father of Lin-Manuel Miranda, throughout his life: "If it doesn't hurt … then you're not giving enough."

This conception of sacrifice is profound: Only when it is uncomfortable, even painful to give of ourselves, only when your life makes a meaningful shift away from something you otherwise might want do you know that you are giving beyond your own benefit.

In this way, sacrifice is the expression of so much of what I've explored in *From Generosity to Justice*, which aims to push philanthropy to address the root causes, rather than merely the effects, of injustice. Sacrifice is giving selflessly, yes, but also on behalf of others—on behalf of justice.

So, if you are someone who benefits from tremendous good fortune and privilege, consider how you can contribute to your community in a way that, to use Miranda's word, "hurts."

Perhaps that means paying a higher tax rate to increase public resources to solve our collective challenges or devoting more effort toward attacking the root causes of injustice. Perhaps it means asking, honestly, which system, status, or status quo you are willing to step away from or challenge to benefit others?

This kind of sacrifice—the willingness to put the needs of others ahead of oneself—has a value beyond what is given up. Sacrifice speaks volumes. Sacrifice reminds people that we are bound together, that we share a destiny, and that we all are better served by mutual trust and respect than mutual contempt.

No doubt, the sacrifices we must make—during 2020 and beyond— will be difficult. But now is not the time to tire. Now is the time to try—and try again. Dr. King reminds us that "every step toward the goal of justice requires sacrifice, suffering, and struggle."

We need to lay a new foundation for an inclusive future with more inclusive economies. We need to marry good intentions with more meaningful actions. And we need to demand more sacrifice from our leaders—too many of whom are more eager to stay in power than use their power to address the old crises that will shape yet another new year.

In ordinary times, hope is rare. But in these extraordinary times, hope is *radical*.

And so, let us embrace a radical kind of hope. Let us inspire each other to sacrifice more. Let us commit to the hard work of hope so, even as division and discord take center stage, we can keep our eyes on justice as both our guiding light and the ultimate prize.

I hope more leaders will reduce the inequality of sacrifice, which is critical to achieving inclusion and fairness. I hope we draw from that potent combination of urgency and patience, of optimism and realism, of faith and action, and start to build a future that benefits each and every one of us.

IN SUPPORT OF PHILANTHROPIC PLURALISM

with Heather Templeton Dill, Kathleen Enright, Sam Gill,
Brian Hooks, and Elise Westhoff
The Chronicle of Philanthropy
April 13, 2023

The United States has a strong, globally respected tradition of independent philanthropy that includes and is exemplified by the nation's private foundations.

This tradition is woven into the tapestry of US democracy, which, alongside government and business, encompasses a large and diverse civil society made up of varying forms of association and collaboration—nonprofit service organizations, organized religion, community groups, civic organizations, and more. Each of these sectors—government, business, and civil society—plays a role in keeping communities healthy and vital.

Historically, the role of philanthropy in civil society has been premised on the notion that truly independent financial capital dedicated to the public good is critical to national progress. Philanthropy can focus on issues that sometimes fall off the public agenda. Philanthropy can take risks on ideas that may be overlooked. And philanthropy can support multiple—and even conflicting—ideas and solutions intended to respond to fraught, thorny, and sometimes controversial issues.

Lately, though, American politics has denigrated the value of such pluralistic approaches.

Some of the stress on pluralism is stylistic, but much is substantive. Many of the issues that divide America are real and consequential. When it comes to issues such as race, wealth, climate, and religion, the stakes are high. And as the stakes grow, so, too, do the perceived costs of engagement—or even toleration—of people, views, and ideas on the other side of ever brighter lines of division.

The result of these pressures, however meritorious and morally urgent, is that foundations and philanthropists are often expected to pledge allegiance to one or another narrow set of prescribed views.

Each of us represents foundations and individual donors with different—and strongly held—views on issues of fundamental importance to society. Yet together we recognize that philanthropy provides the greatest value when donors enable and encourage pluralism by supporting and investing in a wide and diverse range of values, missions, and interests.

Philanthropy plays an essential role in shaping the marketplace of ideas. The reasons a foundation supports a particular issue or cause often influences how a foundation distributes its funds. And these differences reflect the diverse sensibilities, beliefs, and values that make up America's pluralistic society.

During these turbulent times, diversity in philanthropic giving can help shape and inform discussions about the most important issues of the day. It is through this diversity that philanthropy can proffer, study, and test a multiplicity of ideas and approaches to confront society's greatest challenges.

AVOIDING DESTRUCTIVE DISAGREEMENTS

To do this well, philanthropy can—and should—become skilled at effectively engaging in disagreements on approaches or even outcomes. This is because, as stark and rancorous as our social divisions may be, to best serve society we must commit to productive, not destructive, negotiation.

Not all social and political agendas are morally equivalent. But every agenda includes a range of considerations that would benefit from the interplay among a wide range of ideas and sentiments. In the marketplace of ideas, the best ones may not always or inevitably rise to the top. But to at least stand a chance, they must be forged in the fire of a dynamic and open marketplace.

The history of philanthropy is a history of using private capital to supplement, not replace, other approaches to investing in and supporting a prosperous and just society. A critical way philanthropy does this is by helping to make pluralism possible. Philanthropy as a whole makes its greatest contribution to democracy when all foundations and donors engage in the unfettered pursuit of their own mission, interests, and prerogatives.

At a time when the nation's commitment to pluralism is strained, the six of us are renewing our commitment to philanthropic pluralism and encouraging our peers to do the same by embracing a truly healthy, independent philanthropic sector that:

- Demonstrates a wide range of views and perspectives on the most important issues confronting democracy and society.
- Benefits from the open and authentic contributions of its constituents.
- Encourages consensus on common values, such as respect and open inquiry, as well as disagreement on contested issues of societal significance.

We propose the following principles to help guide a rigorous and respectful discourse among philanthropies, especially those that approach issues from different perspectives:

1. We recognize and affirm the right and prerogative of foundations and philanthropists to take programmatic or public stances in accordance with their best judgment. And while it is appropriate for any donor to question or challenge another's views, we should not question the underlying legitimacy of any foundation or philanthropist holding a particular view.

2. We behave as if the foundations and individual donors who take stances with which we disagree are also committed to the betterment of society. We assume that those involved in philanthropy have the best intentions, even if they take a different approach.

3. When we challenge another's views or activities, we focus on substantive arguments and invite response. While disagreements may be profound—even fundamental—we believe that public debates should rely on reason and open conversation. We discourage practices such as personal or *ad hominem* attacks because we regard them as unhelpful to productively advancing knowledge within a pluralistic society.

4. We seek to approach disagreements with respect. Respect does not imply acceptance of a view or even commitment to a common resolution. It does recognize our common dignity. We take seriously the questions that some might raise about our perspectives, public positions, and programs. We believe critique of what we do is an opportunity for us all to learn.

5. We reject efforts by anyone to circumscribe or proscribe the programmatic prerogatives of donors or their foundations, so long as the exercise of those prerogatives conforms with the law.

Foundations exist in other nations and contexts, but they are in many ways a quintessentially American institution. At a time of unprecedented stress on our institutions, we invite our peers to join us in affirming and putting these commitments into practice as we work together to keep America's independent philanthropic tradition alive, vital, and relevant.

FINDING PHILANTHROPY'S FORGOTTEN FOUNDER

The Atlantic
September 9, 2024

For a poor, Black son of the South like me, beginning life in Jim Crow's grip, the haughty, heady world of professional philanthropy might as well have been a different planet. When I first landed at the Rockefeller Foundation, I immersed myself in the history of the institution and the field. I read about the captains of industry, famously dubbed "robber barons" by muckrakers at *The Atlantic*: Andrew Carnegie and Andrew Mellon and John Pierpont Morgan and Henry Ford, whose namesake foundation I've been privileged to serve as president for the past eleven years.

The standard line is that modern philanthropy traces its beginnings to 1889, when Carnegie wrote what we know as "The Gospel of Wealth." In the face of rampant inequality, Carnegie proposed a bold idea: The wealthy, he argued, should freely give from their gains to aid "the masses" —though not the "unworthy" poor, whom he deemed too lazy and irresponsible to merit support. In fact, Carnegie accepted that inequality was a natural, even inevitable, by-product of capitalism, and so not a condition that philanthropy (itself a "creature of capitalism," as Henry Ford II later said) bore any responsibility to address.

But here and there, I heard mentions of another name—Rosenwald—that was not included in the traditional pantheon of philanthropy's founders, which piqued my curiosity.

I began to explore. I asked the experts. Between meetings, I snuck downstairs to the in-house Rockefeller Foundation library to research.

What I discovered was a radically different approach to philanthropy—and to the capitalism that at once precedes, enables, and necessitates it. In the life and leadership of Julius Rosenwald, our first social-justice philanthropist, I found a perhaps unlikely lodestar—an inspiration for my own work and my own way of working.

I was born in August 1959, to a single mother in a Louisiana charity hospital. My mom, my sister, and I lived together in a small shotgun house—a shack, really—in rural East Texas.

Throughout my childhood, I heard the name Rosenwald. I knew of the Rosenwald Schools, almost five thousand in number, distributed across the old South. Once, they educated one out of every three Black children in the region, including Thurgood Marshall and John Lewis, Zora Neale Hurston and Maya Angelou. I knew that the schools were synonymous with opportunity, advancement, and excellence.

But the man behind the schools? I hadn't a clue who he was.

Decades later, after stints in law and finance and running a Harlem nonprofit, I found my own calling in philanthropy—and, as my fate would have it, I landed at one of the best-known philanthropies of them all, the venerable Rockefeller Foundation (established in 1913, around the time that Rosenwald started to build his schools).

And so I set out to rediscover Julius Rosenwald. He was born, I learned, in Springfield, Illinois, in 1862, a few blocks from Abraham Lincoln's residence. His German Jewish immigrant parents manufactured uniforms for

Union officers, and they raised their son in the Reform temple where his father served as president.

Together, they practiced a strand of socially conscious Judaism that emphasized the values of *tzedakah*, or "righteousness," and *tikkun olam*, "repairing the world"—informed by the charge of Deuteronomy: *Justice, justice shall you pursue.*

After an apprenticeship in Manhattan's garment district, Rosenwald settled in Chicago. There, he sold men's suits and eventually, in 1895, invested $75,000 (nearly $3 million today) in a 50 percent ownership stake in one of his distributors—a fledgling business called Sears, Roebuck and Company. (Notably, he bought out the Roebuck of Sears Roebuck.)

Rosenwald's managerial and marketing ingenuity spurred the business to prodigious success, as America's emerging middle class ordered clothing, kitchenware, and almost anything else they could imagine from the first mail-order catalog. One characteristic innovation from the young Rosenwald: Printing a thicker catalog on smaller stock, so housewives would place it at the top of their pyramid of magazines in their kitchens or living rooms.

In 1906, Congress authorized, and the post office implemented, a new rural delivery service, which ushered in a consumer-goods revolution. No longer were farmers required to trek into town for their mail. Riding the wave, Sears quickly became, in its own words, "the world's largest store"—the Amazon of its time. And in 1908, Rosenwald became the president of Sears, ultimately amassing one of American history's great fortunes.

Rosenwald charted a middle course amid the extremes of the Gilded Age, steering between the gathering provocateurs who rejected capitalism on one side and the industrialists who exploited it on the other.

His early-twentieth-century views don't align perfectly with my own—he was, for example, anti-union. But in many other ways, Rosenwald was a champion of a more inclusive capitalism—a democratic capitalism—that aspired to strengthen the growing republic by mitigating inequality.

His vision is more relevant than ever—more requisite, too—and in it, we can find seeds of our own repair and renewal.

At Sears, Rosenwald offered a pioneering employee-benefits program, including competitive compensation, paid vacation and sick days, and reliable bonuses. Even more remarkably, he experimented with an early version of employee ownership, offering veteran employees the option to purchase company stock, which later evolved into an extensive profit-sharing program.

Rosenwald attributed his success to "opportunity, enterprise, and luck," not his own guile, guts, or genius. Unlike many of his era, he did not see wealth alone as proof of virtue. And he devoted his life to extending and expanding that opportunity and luck for others—both in making his fortune and in giving it away.

As a philanthropist, Rosenwald gave significantly within his own communities—to Jewish and immigrant causes and Chicago institutions, including Jane Addams's Hull House, the University of Chicago, and the Museum of Science and Industry. But he directed most of his giving toward ensuring, as he said in 1918, that Black Americans enjoy "an equal chance with the white man to climb as high … as their individual capacity warrants."

This was an audacious objective, given the state of Black America at the time. And one struggles to imagine John D. Rockefeller or Andrew Carnegie, for instance, even contemplating such a project.

Rewind the clock to the eve of the Civil War: In 1860, the United States' Black population numbered about 4.4 million. By 1900—thirty-five years after slavery's official demise—that population had doubled. And yet, at the turn of the century, nine out of every ten African Americans lived in the South, three out of four ensnared in chattel slavery's brutal successor institution, sharecropping. By custom and law, barely half could read or write. In many places across the South, state and local bodies had banned basic education in Black communities with formal anti-literacy legislation, to say nothing of the informal enforcement via a regime of racial terror.

Against this painful, entrenched injustice, Rosenwald went to work, in close partnership with lifelong friends and colleagues such as Booker T. Washington, the founder of the Tuskegee Institute, who was perhaps his most influential mentor and adviser from 1911 onward. In the segregated South, they collaborated with Black communities to build 4,978 public schools from 1912 to 1937. And as the dream of safety, dignity, and opportunity carried millions of Black Americans to the industrializing North during the Great Migration, Rosenwald, at Washington's urging, provided for a range of organizations that would help transition the migrants into urban life—including the YMCA, the Urban League, and the NAACP.

Rosenwald's relative obscurity today reflects an almost willful collective ignorance of Jewish-American contributions to our democracy in general—and to progress for African Americans in particular—a pattern of erasure that we would be well served to acknowledge now, as new cleavages emerge between two communities that have been so essential to each other's liberation.

When I reflect on all of this, I cannot help but wonder about Rosenwald's prescient sense of the duality—the convergences and divergences—of the Jewish and Black American experiences. Both Jewish and Black Americans were rendered inferior by the codes of American caste. Both suffered—in different ways, to different extents—from racial inequality and violence, from lynchings and pogroms. Both were diaspora communities—and in the North, at least, both were migrant communities, escaping poverty and persecution with little more than the shirts on their backs and the hopes in their hearts.

Furthermore, Rosenwald discerned that as long as one community was vulnerable, so, too, was the other. And he held fast to the converse, as well: Integration and opportunity and prosperity for one would beget the same for both.

In turn, I believe, he sensed that interracial, interfaith partnership would benefit not just one group or the other, but our shared American community. Ultimately, we are all the protagonists in a bigger American story—the story of a small circle of mostly white, Protestant, property-owning men in Philadelphia that, generation by generation, continues to grow wider because of the patriotic struggle and sacrifice of the people who were once excluded: Black and Brown people, Indigenous people, Jewish people, Muslim people, women, queer people, disabled people.

As remarkable as *what* Rosenwald did to repair his broken world was *how* he did it. He invested in what I call the three Is: Individuals, their ideas, and their institutions. For two decades, he handed out open-ended fellowships to Black Americans, including the likes of Ralph Ellison, Langston Hughes, Marian Anderson, and W. E. B. Du Bois—all told, three generations of important figures in the arts and sciences, both celebrated and unsung. He also invested in research that unlocked insights about how to improve the human condition, including better agricultural practices and breakthroughs in medicine and public health. And he invested in transformational organizations—hospitals and settlement houses and an array of civil-society organizations, whose work improved not just the day-to-day conditions of the dislocated, dispossessed, and disenfranchised, but also their longer-term opportunities for inclusion in the American project.

Moreover and more broadly, Rosenwald approached his philanthropy with a set of commitments that powerfully inform my own. He sought, in his words, "permanent rather than palliative measures," to address the root causes of inequality, not merely its symptoms. He said, "What I want to do is try and cure the things that seem wrong." He didn't say ameliorate or alleviate consequences. He said "cure"—and he meant it, even if curing the disease would implicate the people and systems that were engaged in the healing. This, too, was different in kind from the giving of Rockefeller and Carnegie, men who advocated for the "scientific philanthropy" that invested in research and discovery, while accepting racial hierarchies as normative.

Rosenwald almost always invested more than dollars—finding ways to offer a full spectrum of resources and support for the people and organizations he cared about. He also insisted in many instances that his contributions be matched, not only by other philanthropists, but by the communities to which he gave (even if through nonmonetary means) so that those communities were meaningfully invested in each project's success.

And he listened to and learned from the people closest to the problems he was trying to solve—the people already putting solutions into practice—valuing lived experience as equal to established expertise.

In all of these ways and others, Rosenwald represents a different branch of philanthropy's phylogenetic tree, part of but also apart from the philosophies of philanthropy's founders—the people about whom I learned when I started on my own journey through this strange world.

Why was he forgotten? Unlike his fellow titans of industry, Rosenwald was a lifelong skeptic of endowments, as he argued in the pages of this very publication, and he insisted that his heirs spend down the assets he had directed to charity within twenty-five years of his death. The largest fund he created was dissolved in 1947. Many of his contemporaries dismissed this approach as apostasy. Rosenwald recognized, in a way that his fellow barons could not, that many endowments serve founders and funders, laundering their legacies, more effectively than the people and communities they purport to benefit.

Throughout the twentieth century, the field of institutional philanthropy flourished in Carnegie's mold, not Rosenwald's. American families—including many of today's billionaire founders—endowed and expanded an extraordinary array of organizations that delivered one hundred years of progress. By and large, their work has been a force for good; their collective impact, meaningful.

At the same time, though, I believe that something about the old narrative arc should make us uneasy. Something about the old gospel should make us uncomfortable.

As I see it, we cannot hide from the central contradiction built into our giving. We are creatures of our economic and social systems' unequal benefits—and yet, we are charged with addressing their unequal outcomes. And the tension is particularly pronounced in this, our own Gilded Age—our own era of extremes, and inequalities, and extreme inequalities.

Dr. Martin Luther King Jr.—one of relatively few Black leaders in the Civil Rights Movement's vanguard who did not attend a Rosenwald School—summed this up perfectly. Six decades ago, he wrote, "Philanthropy is commendable, but it must not cause the philanthropist to overlook the circumstances of economic injustice that make philanthropy necessary."

In other words, we must reckon with the inequality that makes philanthropy both necessary and possible: Economic inequality, social inequality, religious inequality, racial inequality. This was Rosenwald's project, as it ought to be our collective project today.

Ultimately, Rosenwald's unique story gives testament to the shared fate that binds us together. His legacy teaches us that although our atomized individual identities matter, our shared identity—our shared American values, our obligations to one another—matters most.

Someone once asked Rosenwald, this modest Jewish clothier from Springfield, why he devoted such a significant portion of his benefaction to Black Americans. He replied simply, "I do not see how America can go ahead if part of its people are left behind."

Pirkei Avot, a rabbinic text on ethics, affirms that we are not obligated to complete the work, but neither are we free to desist from it. Julius Rosenwald lived this precept to the fullest, embracing the hard work of hope. And this is why Rosenwald—the apotheosis of interracial, interfaith, interdependent solidarity—remains the indispensable philanthropist for our time, the hero hidden in plain sight all along.

PART IV

THE ART OF DEMOCRACY

Without art, there is no empathy. Without empathy, there is no justice. The arts have the power to lead us forward, to heal us, to bring us together … The arts are the key to building and rebuilding bridges in our society—between cities and rural counties; between the poor and the prosperous; between the past, the present, and the possible. And in this way, investment in the arts is an investment in moral imagination, in our capacity for empathy—an investment in the kind of greatness that comes with a deeper, richer understanding of one another and ourselves.

The Kennedy Center
Washington, DC
March 20, 2017

OPEN AND FREE: ON ARTS, DEMOCRACY, AND INEQUALITY

Address to the Association of Art Museum Directors
Mexico City, Mexico
January 26, 2015

I am delighted to be with you. As you know, for more than a half century, the Ford Foundation has been an ardent supporter of museums and galleries, of creative expression and cultural innovation.

In fact, many of your institutions have been at it for just as long—if not longer—affirming the inseparability of the creative spirit from the human spirit, of the arts from our democracies.

And, today, I'd like to reflect on exactly this: The place of the arts in my life, in our communities, and in our society—as well as the undeniable threat that inequality poses to the arts and our democracies as a whole.

MY JOURNEY IN—AND BECAUSE OF—THE ARTS

For as long as I can remember, the arts have imbued energy and meaning into my life.

As a child growing up in Ames, a little town in Southeast Texas, I pored over the glossy pages of art magazines that my grandmother, a domestic, brought me from the homes of the wealthy families for whom she worked. Page after page, hour after hour, my mind visited worlds from which I otherwise would have been excluded. My horizons—my sense of the possible—expanded far beyond the hardscrabble, East Texas landscape. In many ways, because of the arts, my economic situation never limited my expectations for myself.

As a student at The University of Texas at Austin, I first saw the Dance Theatre of Harlem and my life was changed forever.

As a young professional in New York in the 1980s, I fell in love with the city's museums and galleries, the likes of which I had never experienced before. I also fell in love with an art dealer, and was introduced to an entirely new world of collectors, curators, and critics.

I found a passion for the performing arts and theater and documentary film—becoming something of a culture vulture. My appetite for the arts was never sated.

Throughout my two decades in philanthropy, I have advocated for creative visionaries and sought new ways to support them. And when I joined the Ford Foundation from the Rockefeller Foundation, it was as the institution's vice president of, among other things, *creativity*.

Suffice it to say, I am a fervent believer in the transformational, uplifting power of artistic expression. And I'm not alone. Earlier this month you announced that more than sixty-one million people across Canada, Mexico, and the United States visited your art museums last year.

This is tremendous news, a powerful testament to the place and purpose of your institutions. Indeed, art is something that we can all share in—a theater, if you will, where all people have equality of vision and equality of voice.

And yet, from my vantage point, I have noticed a troubling trend during the last few years. Not in attendance, but in attitude.

A GATHERING CRISIS FOR THE ARTS: A MENTALITY OF INSTRUMENTALITY

Increasingly, art institutions and artists themselves are internalizing a mentality of *instrumentality*, a particular kind of defensiveness.

They justify their contributions in economic terms alone. They plead for resources and protest for relevance—defending their very existence with studies and statistics.

To be sure, the arts are an economic engine around the world. According to the United States National Endowment for the Arts and Bureau of Economic Analysis, in the US alone, the arts contribute some $500 billion a year to GDP. That's not nothing.

Yet, the global art community is—and should see itself as—much more than this. And while the arts' diminished prominence and defensive posture cannot be denied, it can be understood—and beyond the classic excuses of budget cutting and belt tightening.

WHY IS THIS CRISIS HAPPENING?

You might be wondering, why is this crisis happening? Where does this mentality of instrumentality come from?

To my mind, there are three main reasons.

For one thing, in this digital age, cultural innovators are straining to differentiate themselves—and struggling to cut through all the noise. The reason is that we are immersed in visual media—and although all art may be media, all media is certainly not art.

According to a 2010 study by our colleagues at the Kaiser Family Foundation, today's young people pack eleven hours of media content into an average of seven and a half hours in front of their devices. That means they consume a staggering 1.6 hours of media every hour. By definition, much of this consumption is passive. Empty calories.

Too often, we look at our screens without engaging in any meaningful way with what is on them.

Art, on the other hand, demands an observer's *active* participation. It moves. It provokes. It infuriates. It inspires. It elevates and equalizes. And our humanity is dependent upon it.

Second, as a result of big data's ascent, we increasingly overemphasize information at the expense of intuition.

Don't get me wrong, facts and figures—aggregations and algorithms— have their due place. We should be monitoring and measuring.

Nevertheless, we've allowed ourselves to buy into a false assumption: Our culture has bought into the idea that if something *can't* be measured, then it somehow doesn't matter. And, in turn, we've decreased our commitment to a lot of things that *do*.

No doubt, it is not easy to quantify the so-called impact of a musician, dancer, painter, or filmmaker—let alone a graffitist or video-game coder. We don't have a stock exchange that puts a price on creativity.

But, in my eyes, this is no excuse for only funding those things that deliver immediately quantifiable returns. And this is true across philanthropy; another story for another day.

But—third—the most fundamental cause of today's crisis in the arts is connected with a deeper transformation underway in our society: During these last few decades, we have raised market-oriented thinking above *all* other kinds and categories of human understanding.

Where once we treated different fields of knowledge and action with equal respect, we, today, subordinate everything under economics. In medicine, we talk about cost curves and insurance schemes—with relatively scant attention to the *care* in health care. In the US, especially, we champion the so-called STEM disciplines in our schools because our politicians tell us "that's where the jobs are!" And this intellectual inequality —thinking economically rather than holistically—this perpetuates economic inequality and social inequality and political inequality.

Indeed, all of the inequalities that jeopardize our society's wellness follow from this single manipulation—the idea that every element of our lives must be defined in relation to capital. No place is this distortion more palpable, problematic, and pernicious than in the arts.

SHORT-TERMISM INFECTS OUR DECISION-MAKING

One particular manifestation of this market-oriented thinking is the assumption that nonprofits need to behave like businesses; that the walls of our museums should function like the financial markets which too often prioritize short-term gain over long-term good.

This kind of short-termism has infected so many dimensions of our lives. It has distorted the way our society makes decisions.

This, of course, is a global challenge. But take an example from our own recent experience: The Detroit Institute of Arts.

At the Ford Foundation, we watched as billionaires circled above a bankrupt city—the very image of inequality in our time—waiting to descend, waiting to strip down and sell a museum and its masterpieces. The dismantling and selling off the art in one of America's great treasures is cause for outrage.

This may have made sense in the short term. But in the longer term, it was unacceptable.

These potential buyers simply were not invested in the Detroit of 2020, of 2030, of 2050—let alone in the people who live there.

What's more, the fact this great treasure was at risk of being sold is perhaps the greatest metaphor we have for the threat of short-termism to the arts, and to the broader society.

THIS ISN'T MERELY AN ARTS ISSUE; IT'S AN INEQUALITY ISSUE

To me, we should not need to *defend* the arts—nor to *protect* the arts.

The arts deserve celebration, not defense. They demand affirmation, not protection.

Our society's *under*valuing of the arts and *over*valuing of the market reflects and reinforces a perversion of justice—indeed, a pervasive injustice.

And this injustice goes by the name of inequality.

From Ecclesiastes to Plato's *Republic*, Western thought has been organized on the principle that everything has its place. All aspects of human intellect and achievement are part of a delicate equilibrium. In a classical sense, this is the very definition of justice.

Today, our reliance on—and reverence for—short-term, market-based justifications reveals a profound *imbalance* in the way our society is organized. An inequality of the highest order.

THE FORD FOUNDATION'S COMMITMENT: THE ARTS WILL REMAIN AT THE HEART OF EVERYTHING WE DO

And we cannot sit idly by as the imaginations of our young people are starved of the fuel to fully fire. We cannot sit idly by as their horizons are pulled in and closed off. Their dreams are curtailed. Their sense of the possible is diminished.

As democracies, we owe ourselves better. We still can be a society that celebrates art—that, literally, treasures creative expression. And must continue working to translate this aspiration into action.

Sixteen months into my presidency at the Ford Foundation, I hear friends and colleagues asking, where does the foundation stand on arts and culture today?

My answer is that, for us, they remain right where they belong—at the heart of everything we think about, invest in, and stand for.

This year, we're exploring and experimenting. We're working through, and with, arts organizations to determine how we most effectively can advance the arts—and, by extension, democracy and equality.

Because, simply put: Less art leads to more inequality. More inequality leads to less justice. And this is not something with which *any of us* should be comfortable.

OUR CALL TO ACTION

For this reason, it's up to us—up to funders and institutions alike—to restore the arts to their place of importance, and restore balance to our imbalanced way of thinking.

More than this, given the challenges we face, we all have a responsibility to go back to the basics in our communities. To support art from the community, art about the community, art for the community.

Because, ultimately, art museums are not only underwritten by communities, but are the underpinning of them. They are the fulcrum on which society's balance hinges—the forum where inequality is neutralized. And for your institutions to be essential in the community, you must engage with the community.

It's not enough to say we're open late on Thursdays or that we're free on Fridays. That's not the openness or freedom the arts require—and, for that matter, inspire. Our communities deserve something greater.

As museum directors, you struggle with this—and so much more—every day. You have donors to court, doors to keep open, budgets to balance.

And I feel for you. You were trained for a world in which you were a curator, not a community organizer; an academic, not an advocate or ambassador or architect of democracy.

But when our arts are under siege—financially, like at the DIA, or more fundamentally through this pervasive market-based thinking I've been discussing—then you should be furious. You should be appalled. Most importantly, you should be moved to action.

But I am hopeful—not just optimistic, but radically optimistic. Together, we can—we will—reimagine what we do: For the good of the arts and the good of our democracies in a time of inequality. And on every step of the journey, you'll have a full partner in us.

THE IMPERATIVE OF DIVERSITY IN ARTS AND CULTURE

*Introduction of Partnership with New York City
Department of Cultural Affairs*
New York, New York
January 27, 2015

Good morning, everyone. Welcome to the Ford Foundation.

Thank you, Mayor Bill de Blasio and Commissioner Tom Finkelpearl, for your outstanding leadership and for your ongoing commitment to building an arts and culture sector that reflects and represents the city—and country—it serves.

To me, our shared challenge of diversifying New York's arts institutions is a crucial one. It's also deeply personal—because I'm not just a proponent for them; I'm a product of them.

As a child, it was art that transported my mind from my small, Southeast Texas town to a wider world from which I otherwise would have been excluded.

As a student at The University of Texas in the early 1980s, the Dance Theatre of Harlem first mesmerized me. My life was transformed forever.

As a young professional in New York, later in the decade, I fell in love with the city's museums and galleries.

I know the difference that cultural institutions can make because I have lived it.

From my perspective, our topic today is neither an abstraction nor a distraction. It's fundamental. It's essential.

Less diversity in our arts community leads to less diversity in our arts. And less diversity in our arts does not merely make life duller, dimmer, diminished. It's a disavowal of human dignity—of social justice—to children like me; to children with imaginations starved of the fuel to fully fire; to communities with smaller senses of themselves, and all that they are capable of.

All of this, all of it, is connected to an insidious misperception of why diversity matters in the first place.

For so many institutions, diversity is often—and incorrectly—viewed in terms of sacrifice.

At colleges and universities, some claim affirmative action policies require us to sacrifice the place of a more deserving student for a less deserving one.

On many boards—particularly of institutions where development responsibilities loom large—some believe that diversity may result in the absence of millions of dollars in giving.

In these cases, and in others, diversity is seen as a deficit. As a cost. As a trade-off. Something lost, not something gained.

Well, we're here because we disagree.

Profoundly.

We're here because diversity is not a sacrifice. It's a strength. It's not about the absence of something. It's about the presence of something. It's about effectiveness. It's about excellence—organizationally and operationally.

In fact, organizational diversity and operational excellence are inseparable—inextricably intertwined.

And this is precisely because diversity contributes three of the key ingredients in the recipe for excellence. Diversity brings perspective to our institutions. It brings wider networks of advocates and audiences—new links in new webs. And in our increasingly heterogeneous nation, it adds legitimacy and credibility as well.

Let's unpack this for a moment.

First, as a nation founded on the ideal of pluralism, we must protect—and promote—our conviction that everyone has a unique perspective to share. Because when we look at problems through many eyes, and many lenses, we're more likely to see new and better solutions.

For this reason, it's not enough to have so many of our boards comprised entirely—or nearly entirely—of older, wealthier, and, yes, whiter members of a very few, very selective industries.

By limiting its demographics, we limit a board's relationship to our wider democracy. We make ourselves more susceptible to groupthink.

Of course, this cuts both ways. To organizations predominately of color: We also can't continue to have homogeneous boards exclusively for the sake of preserving an institution's identity.

In all candor, when I was at the Abyssinian Development Corporation, we struggled with this ourselves. We need to embrace diversity, too—to model it and to demonstrate its value—because in addition to added perspectives, diversity leads to expanded networks.

It leads to networks of ambassadors, networks of creative visionaries and cultural innovators, networks of leaders and managers, and, yes, networks of donors as well. During an era in which we elevate and amplify the so-called wisdom of the crowd, we need as big and broad a crowd as we can get.

And, finally, it is not lost on anyone that, looking around New York today, we see a majority-minority city: A community one-quarter Black, one-quarter Latino, one-eighth Asian.

As a result, without diversity at the top, an institution lacks legitimacy throughout. A lack of diversity undermines the credibility of institutions seeking to engage with an increasingly diverse citizenry and forces communities of color to ask: Why would we consider visiting your museum or theater—why would we expose our children to you—if you won't consider the opinions of anyone else?

In many ways, this is a question of values and of what we value. It's a question of governance, not management. In other words, it is a test for—and of—our boards.

In order to increase diversity in arts organizations, those in power—boards of trustees—have to value diversity because without diversity there is no excellence.

We need to find ways to get boards to buy in, to move beyond tokenism and to change their culture.

We need to reimagine the role of our boards—to think beyond capital campaigns to consciousness campaigns.

We need to systematize this work and help connect boards in need of diversity to ideal candidates.

And we need to talk openly about why diversity matters—in the arts and beyond.

I know this isn't easy. Actually, it's quite hard. You're under a lot of pressure, financial and otherwise. And yet, at the same time, if our institutions aspire to continued relevance and excellence—if the arts are to continue moving, inspiring, challenging, provoking—then we all have to change.

All of us.

So this is why we are here: To engage. To explore. To embrace a more inclusive way of overseeing our institutions.

Ultimately, our commitment must be crystal clear: The arts cannot be the exclusive purview and playground of the privileged. They must be a forum in which inequality is neutralized, democracy is realized, and diversity is valued.

ON THE ART OF CHANGE

Skoll World Forum
Oxford, United Kingdom
April 17, 2015

For as long as I can remember, the arts have imbued energy and meaning into my life.

As a small child in a little Southeast Texas town, I pored over the glossy pages of art magazines that my grandmother, a domestic, brought me from the homes of the wealthy families for whom she worked. Page after page, hour after hour, my mind visited worlds from which I otherwise would have been excluded. In many ways, because of the arts, my economic situation never limited my expectations for myself. The arts broadened my horizons—my very sense of the possible.

As a student at The University of Texas at Austin, I first saw the Dance Theatre of Harlem, and everything clicked. My life was changed forever.

As a young professional in New York City in the 1980s, I fell in love with the city's museums and galleries and treasured institutions, the likes of which I had never experienced before. I found a passion for the performing arts—for Alvin Ailey and others—and for the theater, documentary film, and the writers of Harlem, especially Langston Hughes and James Baldwin.

It was Baldwin—a Ford Foundation grantee—who wrote, "The artist cannot and must not take anything for granted, but must drive to the heart of every answer and expose the question the answer hides." To me this rang true because I was insatiably curious about the world, and in art I found meaning. This was at a time, by the way, when I fell in love with an art dealer—and was introduced to a new world of artists, collectors, curators, and critics.

As a result of all this, I am a fervent believer in the transformational, uplifting power of artistic expression. In fact, I am a product of it.

I ardently believe I would not be standing before you today as the president of the Ford Foundation if not for my exposure to the arts. And, in turn, throughout my two-decade career in philanthropy, I have advocated for creative visionaries. I have sought new ways to support them, and to amplify voices of those artists around the globe who are not being heard.

OUR MENTALITY OF INSTRUMENTALITY

And yet, given the importance of art and culture in my life, and in society, I have noticed a troubling trend during the last few years.

We all know how repressive regimes stifle creativity and persecute artists who rouse public sentiment for the sake of public good. But even where artists do enjoy freedom of expression, artists and art institutions are forced to justify their contributions in economic terms alone. Their relevance—their very existence—is often defended with studies and statistics.

All of this reflects a larger trend, of course: Our culture has bought into the idea that if something cannot be measured, then it somehow does not matter.

No doubt, it is not easy to quantify the so-called impact of a musician, dancer, painter, or filmmaker—let alone a graffitist or video-game coder. In my eyes, though, this is no excuse for only supporting those things that deliver immediately quantifiable returns.

SHORT-TERMISM IS THE ENEMY OF ART

This is a problem not limited to art and artists. It reveals and reinforces a societal illness—a perversion and distortion. With increasing regularity, we prioritize short-term gain over long-term good.

This kind of short-termism has infected so many dimensions of our lives. Education. Health care. Development. Business. Government. It has disrupted the way our society makes decisions.

Take an example from our own recent experience: Helping the city of Detroit, Michigan, to navigate its unprecedented bankruptcy without losing its soul, or the Detroit Institute of Arts, whose collection was owned by the people. At the Ford Foundation, we watched as billionaires circled above the city, waiting to strip down and sell off the museum and its masterpieces. Such "asset monetization" may have made sense in the short term. In the longer term, however, it was unacceptable. These potential buyers simply were not invested in the Detroit of 2020, of 2030, of 2050—let alone in the people who live there now.

The Grand Bargain that emerged—which we were proud to support—preserved the pensions of hard-working citizens and a cultural institution that will be treasured for generations to follow. It is precisely this focus on the next decade—on the next century—that must animate our thinking and working.

ECONOMIES OF EMPATHY

The good news is we can change our pervasive shortsighted outlook. We can prioritize long-term investments in community and in culture.

And the arts? The arts are an indispensable ingredient in the recipe for progress and change.

Apart from generating economic value, the arts and culture create economies of empathy. And because of that, we have seen them play an integral part in building a wide range of social movements, from the Civil Rights Movement to the Arab Spring.

Artists challenge the status quo and give voice to those left out and left behind. Artists imagine a better world and inspire others to join in building it. They move us to hope, joy, compassion, resolve, and, ultimately, action.

THE ART OF CHANGE

Because our work at the Ford Foundation is rooted in building social-justice movements, my colleagues and I are devoting the next year to a process of rediscovery—exploring how the arts and creativity can intersect with, interact with, and inspire all of our work for social change.

As a step of this process, we have invited a number of cultural visionaries to join us as fellows—to prompt and inform our own thinking. Their work will challenge us to reimagine ways the arts can help solve social problems.

We work on complex issues, but we have seen, time and again, how the arts can play a role in stirring our passions and awakening our creativity and empathy.

This role of arts and culture is not an add-on to our other work to improve lives. Rather, it is part and parcel—it is central, really—to changing beliefs and behaviors.

WHY THE ARTS ARE AT THE HEART OF OUR MISSION

Today, our reliance on and reverence for short-term, market-based justifications reveals a profound imbalance in the way our society is organized—an inequality of the highest order.

For some of us, less access to art means our shared insights are shallower, our collective creativity is duller, and our lives are just more boring. Plain and simple.

For those among us who struggle the most, however, the stakes are significantly higher.

When people in the twenty-first century's equivalent of my childhood town—all around the world—are denied an opportunity to connect with art, their imaginations are starved of the fuel to fully fire. Their horizons are pulled in and closed off. Their dreams are curtailed and senses of possibility diminished. Their social movements are deterred and derailed.

We cannot allow this to continue. We owe ourselves better.

We still can be a society that celebrates art—that, literally, treasures creative expression. And we must continue working to translate this aspiration into action.

Twenty-some months into my presidency at the Ford Foundation, I hear friends and colleagues asking, where does the foundation stand on arts and culture today?

My answer is that, for us, they remain right where they belong—at the heart of everything we think about, invest in, and stand for.

Simply put, less art leads to more inequality. More inequality leads to less justice. And this is not something with which any of us should be comfortable.

THE DETROIT INSTITUTE OF ARTS BELONGS TO THE PEOPLE—AS DOES THE CITY OF DETROIT

Ford Foundation Board Meeting
Detroit, Michigan
June 16, 2015

In 1932, during the depths of the Great Depression, Edsel Ford sought to honor Detroit's industrial triumphs in its still-somewhat-new, public art gallery. So, he reached out to a muralist from Guanajuato, Mexico, Diego Rivera, who soon came to the Motor City with his wife, also a painter, Frida Kahlo.

Only four years before Ford established the foundation that still bears his name—endowing it with $25,000—Ford commissioned Rivera's and Kahlo's *Detroit Industry, or Man and Machine*, for the same amount, as coincidence would have it. You might even say we are sister institutions.

Rivera's and Kahlo's five massive fresco murals—comprised of twenty-seven panels—depict doctors and scientists, accountants and secretaries, farmers, and, yes, artists. And the frescos center on workers at Ford's River Rouge auto plant, which served as the inspiration for Rivera's and Kahlo's monument to human endeavor and achievement. The piece, quite simply, is an icon for the ages.

Today, the Garden Court is known as Rivera Court. Although not without controversy, *Detroit Industry* remains a potent, powerful force. It captured culture, sure. But, more than that, it changed culture. It brought honor and dignity to the hard work—the honest labor—of manufacturing a city and civilization. And this is why, when Detroit found itself in an unprecedented municipal bankruptcy, we felt it was essential that this museum and its treasures be saved—at the same time as Detroit's workers and retirees, women and men who served their city for their entire lives, receive the pensions that they had earned.

You see, the arts are an indispensable ingredient in the recipe for progress and change. The arts challenge the status quo and give voice to those left out and left behind. The arts imagine a better world and inspire others to join in building it. They move us to hope, joy, compassion, resolve, and, ultimately, action. And the DIA is a place where art, like democracy, is not just of the people, but for the people, owned by the people.

For our part, we at the Ford Foundation committed $125 million to the Grand Bargain. The DIA itself committed $100 million toward the Grand Bargain. Many other community leaders, businesses, and foundations—to say nothing of Michigan's taxpayers—shouldered more than their share of the burden as well.

This is what we celebrate here, this evening.

This great cultural institution represents the potential of Detroit: The potential for its *industry* and ingenuity to take us forward. For its people to flourish, and its culture to thrive. For the Motor City to be the engine of equality.

Indeed, now the Detroit Institute of Arts belongs to the city anew—and to the people. And so does the future of Detroit.

OUR NATION'S MOST PRECIOUS HERITAGE

Address to the President's Committee on Arts and Humanities
Washington, DC
September 10, 2015

Thank you for that most generous introduction—and thank you, all, for the warm welcome. I'm honored—humbled, frankly—to join such a group of extraordinary visionaries and luminaries: Singular players in the symphony of American history.

I see scholars and poets, professors and authors, individuals whose inspired writing graces my conference table, my coffee table, and my bedside table. I see composers and musicians, performers and presenters, whose creative genius provides the setting, the staging, the soundtrack of our lives. I see actors and activists, who inform and transform the way I see the world, and who inspire me every day.

For as long as I can remember, the arts and humanities have infused energy and meaning into my own life—just as they do in our collective life, as a nation.

As a child in small-town Texas, I pored over the glossy pages of art magazines and books that my grandmother, a maid for a wealthy Houston family, brought me from their home. The things they discarded became my treasures. Page after page, hour after hour, my mind visited worlds from which I otherwise would have been excluded.

In many ways, because of the arts, my economic situation never limited my expectations for myself. The arts broadened my horizons—my very sense of the possible.

As a student at The University of Texas, I first read the writers of the Harlem Renaissance, and I was transported to this magical place—to Harlem—through the provocative prose of Langston Hughes, Zora Neale Hurston, and James Baldwin.

And when I moved to New York in the 1980s, I fell in love with the city's museums and galleries and its jewels of culture—the likes of which I had never experienced before.

I found a passion for the performing arts—for Alvin Ailey and others— and for Joseph Papp's Public Theater and documentary film.

This was also when I fell in love with an art dealer—and was introduced to an entirely new world of collectors and curators and critics.

My point is: I am a fervent believer in the transformational, uplifting power of artistic expression. If not for my exposure to the arts and humanities, I would not be standing here. I am enormously grateful tonight because my story has been made possible because of your stories, and the stories of artists and humanists who came before you.

I sometimes despair that our culture has bought into the notion that if something cannot be measured, then it somehow does not matter. But your work is all the proof I need to dispel this insidious idea.

Certainly, NEA data tells us that the arts contribute $700 billion to the US economy—some 4 percent of our GDP. But the larger impact of your work is unquantifiable. Statistics cannot begin to tell the story of what you have done—and continue to do—and how much it matters to our democracy and our humanity.

From the basement of a community center to the Edible Schoolyard, you give us food for thought, and teach us what it means to find sustenance—mind, body, and soul.

You help us to, and I quote, "unearth the lives of thousands of [the] little known and … completely unknown," and work to preserve the places and spaces where their histories happened.

You humanize the marginalized, and restore dignity to us all, whether by sharing the story of a woman seeking justice in the cotton mill where she works or documenting the actual stories of Mexican women working in canneries in Southern California.

You take these stories *From the Shadows*, and carve for them places in our hearts.

You break barriers—at schools, on stages, and on screen. You challenge the status quo and inspire our *Righteous Discontent*.

You blaze trails for the next Puerto Rican to study at the Actor's Studio; for the next young Black man to transfix us from the stage of the Metropolitan Opera; and for the next generation to raise its voice with authentic confidence.

Indeed, you support students and other artists and scholars, and in more ways than one you provide *Medicine for the Soul*.

Your foundation carries on the legacy of an unconventional American heiress, a woman who had a prescient interest in the art and culture of the Muslim world, who moved comfortably from Newport to Newark. Today, in her honor you provide millions annually for artists to do the unconventional.

Through your advocacy and space for artists, you provide and promote opportunities for artists to present their talents, and for communities to benefit.

You explore the complexities of our global reality, and effortlessly transport us to *The Streets of Laredo* and *The Dark Tower* and *Timber Creek*.

You put *Plato in the Googleplex*, and creativity, philosophy, and humanity back at the center of our modern, technology-crazed lives.

You declare, "*I Will Not Make Any More Boring Art*," while continuing to bore to the heart of what is most important.

You obscure—with bright colors or cloth or video or voice—in order to reveal, to call our attention to the things we would rather ignore.

You pioneer new thinking and ideas, like handseeing—to help us grasp the essential ways that we communicate and interact with one another.

You affirm the *Politics of Quiet*, and the importance of being heard.

You remind us that what some may call the *Undesirable Elements* in our societies, are beautiful, and interesting, and valuable.

You are not only *Interpreters of Maladies*, but interrogators of them.

You are investigators of culture and culpability, the found and forgotten, the domestic, and, yes, Stephen King, even the demonic.

With thoughtful, honest prose, you've taught us that *This Boy's Life* can teach us about this boy's life. And that your story is our story.

You invite us in to vast continents and neglected corners of human experience, which heretofore have been—and in many ways still are—the victims of staggering, systemic exclusion from our mainstream public discourse: The Black experience, the Latino experience, the immigrant experience, the female experience.

Your work is a reminder not that, and apologies to Sally, "you *like* me." But that you *are* like me. That we each are like one another. That we share something, whether we're from East Texas or Eatonville, Florida; Chinatown or Cooperstown; Denver or Detroit.

And it's this connection among all people—those essential things that we share—that make, for me, the alarming disparities we face as a nation all the more personal.

You see, I am convinced that inequality, in all of its forms, is among the greatest threats of our time.

While we often talk about widening economic inequality, there is also a kind of inequality that is harmful to our democratic ethos: The idea that market thinking must be elevated above all other forms of thinking and that one's value only matters in relation to capital. And that the arts and humanities must be justified in market terms alone.

But you know better than anyone else that the arts and humanities create markets of empathy, which is why Earl Shorris called the work of the Clemente Course in the Humanities "in itself a redistribution of wealth"—a wealth of human experience and knowledge and insight and understanding.

It's why, at the Ford Foundation, when we talk about supporting visionaries on the front lines of social change, we include artists and humanists who push us to think radically and deal with inconvenient reality.

Throughout our history, we have seen artists, humanists, and cultural leaders, and their ideas, play an integral part in building a wide range of social movements, from the Civil Rights Movement to the Arab Spring. I was at the new Whitney Museum and saw a quote that reminded me of this.

The printmaker Mabel Dwight once said of the Federal Art Project, the soul of the New Deal: "Art has turned militant. It forms unions, carries banners, sits down uninvited, and gets underfoot. Social justice is its battle cry." Indeed.

And each of you medal recipients has contributed in some way to the larger American project of social justice.

In 1965, upon signing the act that created the NEA and NEH, President Johnson remarked: "Art is a nation's most precious heritage. For it is in our works of art that we reveal to ourselves, and to others, the inner vision which guides us as a Nation. And where there is no vision, the people perish."

This is why the work you do is so important. You demand that America fulfill its promise. You hold up the mirror to our society and you challenge us as a nation to be, as Langston Hughes said: "The land that never has been yet—And yet must be—the land where *every* man is free."

When young people today in small towns in Texas—or on the Southside of Chicago or Ferguson, Missouri—are denied an opportunity to connect with art in schools, their imaginations are starved of the fuel to fully fire. Their horizons are pulled in and closed off; their dreams curtailed; their sense of the possible is diminished.

We owe ourselves better. And we have it within ourselves as a nation to be better.

Let's be what we "*never have been yet—And yet must be.*"

Let's be an America that protects and promotes the arts—even when schools and cities (to say nothing of the House and Senate) are willing to sacrifice them in the name of belt-tightening.

Let's be an America that preserves affordable housing for artists—even when the neighborhoods they've revitalized start to price them out.

Let's be an America with cultural institutions whose boards, staff, and programming reflect the diversity of our country.

Let's be an America in which everyone—the young and the young-at-heart—has access to the art that glorifies and challenges, that instigates and infuriates, that heals and renews, and that moves our hearts and minds.

So thank you for all the work you do: Pushing our country's consciousness, pushing humanity forward, and advancing hope. Hope for the future of this country—hope for the future of *all* American dreams.

YES JUSTICE, YES PEACE: THE ROLE OF ART IN CONFRONTING INEQUALITY

Frances Tarlton "Sissy" Farenthold Endowed Lecture
Rothko Chapel
Houston, Texas
October 3, 2016

Thank you for the extraordinary honor of joining you in the name of the incomparable, legendary Sissy Farenthold, who just turned ninety years old yesterday. Sissy: You have served as an inspiration to me and countless others—a Lone Star North Star, guiding our higher angels toward progress, no matter the barriers in the way; from your time in the Texas House of Representatives, when you fought for economic opportunity and civil rights, to your fights for human rights around the world, be it as part of the Helsinki Watch Committee or the Institute for Policy Studies or the Nairobi Peace Tent.

I think it's safe to say that we probably would not see a brave, bold woman running toward the White House if you had not blazed the trail first. And so, on behalf of countless friends and fans, thank you.

It's also wonderful to be with you all, this evening, in the special and unique Rothko Chapel. This is a sacred place—where so many spiritual leaders and Nobel Laureates have traveled, where thousands have prayed. As many of you know, this hall is the crown jewel of the de Menil family's philanthropy, affixed right at the intersection of arts and social justice. And it's *this* relationship—the interplay between art and justice, the extraordinary symbiosis that this chapel embodies—that I would like to discuss with you this evening.

Dominique de Menil once described how some people feel as they take in this chapel—as it charms, and challenges, and changes them. She said, and I'm quoting: "They feel plunged into the night. Indeed it is the night—but not quite. Even in the dim light, purplish color slowly emerges from the darkness … it is predawn."

This description feels so apt for this place, but also so appropriate for the moment in which we find ourselves.

Right now, our country and our world can feel plunged into night, into many kinds of darkness. We feel that darkness when we see videos of police violence against African Americans, or when we hear that police officers have been killed while defending peaceful protesters in Dallas. We see that darkness around the world, when immigrants and refugees are vilified, and when entire religious groups are denigrated because of terrorism perpetrated by an extreme, radicalized, fanatical minority. We see the darkness of racism and sexism continuing to metastasize throughout our politics. We see the darkness of fear and hate wielded as a weapon to divide us.

Of course, there is also our own ignorance—which keeps us in the dark and prevents us from confronting uncomfortable truths about privilege and injustice and inequality in our daily lives.

Even in Houston, we see some of this darkness. Yes, this city is one of our nation's most diverse but also one of the most segregated. Yes, this city is one of the nation's fastest growing but we also see rampant economic disparities.

So, the question we must ask is, how do we look at the things that might cause us despair *and* see reasons for hope? How do we take the world as it is *and* imagine what it could be? In other words, how do we stare into the darkness *and* see the dawn?

In my own life, one of the most powerful ways to see that light—and to live by it—has been through the arts.

When I was a child growing up not far from here, in Liberty County, my grandmother worked as a domestic in the homes of wealthy families in River Oaks—not far from where the de Menil family lived. And sometimes she would bring me back art magazines from the homes where she worked. I pored over the glossy pages of those magazines. Page after page, hour after hour, my mind visited worlds from which I otherwise would have been excluded.

In many ways, because of the arts, my economic situation never limited my expectations for myself. The arts broadened my horizons and my very sense of the possible. So I am a fervent believer in the transformational, uplifting power of artistic expression. And I think Sissy herself put it best more than thirty years ago. She said, "Imagination invites one to envision possibilities other than the status quo. We have had the expansion of 'respectable thought' to include imagination and vision. Actually, they offer world peace in the only place it can begin: The heart, the mind, and the dream."

In other words, the only place that *peace*—and *justice*—can begin is in our hearts, and in our minds.

And so it is no coincidence that Dr. Martin Luther King's most famous speech about civil rights begins with a *dream.* It is no coincidence that artists and activists both envision and enact possibilities other than the status quo. And it is no coincidence that, at the Ford Foundation, when we talk about supporting these visionaries on the front lines of social change, we include artists who push us to think radically and deal with our uncomfortable reality—who interrogate the world as it is and imagine how it could be.

And throughout our history, we have seen artists, cultural leaders, and their ideas *together* play an integral part in building a wide range of social movements, from the Civil Rights Movement to the Arab Spring.

Now, the reasons for this are many—but among them is something simple and profound: Art not only creates feelings of *possibility*; it also engenders feelings of *empathy*.

Mrs. de Menil once wrote, "Through art … God constantly clears a path to our hearts." Rothko himself put it differently. He said, "The people who weep before my pictures are having the same religious experience I had when I painted them." He also added, if you "are moved only by their color relationships, then you miss the point."

The point of Rothko's work is not color relationships—but *human relationships*, the relationship between the artist and the observer, between people who share an experience of a particular painting or photograph or performance, and who leave with a shared and expanded understanding of the world. And in this way, the point of all of our work—in art and in social justice—is creating these human relationships. It's opening up our imaginations so that we can see ourselves in the place of others, understand their experience, and, hopefully, make it better.

Of course, we must also *work* for adequate representation. We must model the equality we wish to see in our world, and elevate voices and visions different from our own.

When the de Menils opened up their revolutionary exhibit in the DeLuxe Theater forty-five years ago—one of the first racially integrated, contemporary art exhibits in the country—they opened up perspectives of so many here in Texas. And, in turn, they did for Texas what art can do for the world. They took their privilege and turned it into public good—and now we can enjoy their collection and enlarge our consciousness.

When Dominique put together her seminal volumes, *The Image of the Black in Western Art*, she said, "They are for all those who need to know about the past in order to keep fighting for the present and the future."

And so we keep fighting.

When Sissy Farenthold helped women in the Peace Tent in Nairobi express their joy through music and dance and art, she helped us recognize our interconnectedness and shared humanity. And when she told gay rights activists here in Houston, "No one is free unless we are all free," she expressed the kind of radical empathy required to bring people and movements together.

These two incredible women, each in her own way, have held up the mirror to our society—and challenged us to imagine a better world, even when others might have turned away.

I'm sure some of you know this story.

In 1969, not long after Dr. Martin Luther King Jr. was assassinated, the de Menils wanted to donate a sculpture, Newman's *Broken Obelisk*, to the city of Houston, in honor of Dr. King.

At the time, the city refused.

Not long after, the sculpture came here, to the Rothko chapel.

While it might not be physically outside tonight, it's clear and present to all of us. Because, yes, we might see *Broken Obelisk*, and think of it as broken. But when I see it, I can't help but imagine it as incomplete. Because there is so much more work to be done.

So whether it's Dr. King or Mrs. de Menil or Sissy Farenthold or any of the other visionaries and artists fighting for social justice throughout the world, we know—by reason and intuition alike—that art has a role in advancing justice.

As Dr. King himself once said, "Darkness cannot drive out darkness; only light can do that. Hate cannot drive out hate; only love can do that."

And it's incumbent upon us to remember—especially in these times—that division and bigotry and racism and blame and ignorance *cannot make any nation great*. Only empathy can do that.

Without art, there is no empathy. Without empathy, there is no justice.

But with all of us, working together, we can make our vision into reality. We can make those human connections and achieve justice once and for all. And we can march proudly out of the darkness and into the dawn we have imagined and brought into being and brightened for one another.

THE ART OF DEMOCRACY: CREATIVE EXPRESSION AND AMERICAN GREATNESS

Nancy Hanks Lecture on Arts and Public Policy
The Kennedy Center
Washington, DC
March 20, 2017

Good evening, everyone. Thank you, Thelma Golden, for your gracious introduction—and, more importantly, for your groundbreaking, visionary leadership at the Studio Museum in Harlem. And thank you all for this extraordinary honor: The privilege of delivering this thirtieth annual lecture in tribute to the incomparable Nancy Hanks.

Unfortunately, I never met Nancy in life. I was a senior at The University of Texas the year of her death. But it was around that time when I was exposed to her remarkable legacy—when I first experienced the Dance Theatre of Harlem; when the company stopped in Austin on a national tour, a tour funded by the National Endowment for the Arts.

The beauty of their performance astonished me. To see people who looked like me, dancing and expressing themselves in a way that was so dynamic, kinetic, and new—that night moved me deeply.

Once I picked my jaw off the floor, I became a lifelong lover of dance, from Alvin Ailey to the New York City Ballet, where I'm honored to serve as vice chairman of the board. And this performance was just one of the many times in my life when an experience of the arts broadened my perspective and expanded my world.

When I was growing up in rural Texas—in the era before Nancy—our democracy had yet to make a *public* commitment to the arts. There were no state art councils. No broad commitments to funding the arts in rural communities. So I was exposed to art as a matter of circumstance—a happy accident.

As a little boy, I lived with my mother and sister in a little shotgun house—in an African-American community in rural Liberty County, Texas. My grandmother worked as a maid in the home of a wealthy Houston family. And every month, she would bring me old art magazines and programs from arts events the family attended.

I remember, vividly, feeling transfixed by the magic I saw on those pages—by images of worlds to which I had no other exposure. I remember flipping through those magazines and programs, and falling in love, swiftly and deeply. Those pages unlocked my capacity to imagine a world beyond my own—and to imagine my place in it.

Simply put, the arts changed my life. They imbued me with the power to imagine, the power to dream, and the power to know I could express myself with dignity and beauty and grace.

But here's the thing: I was lucky.

I was lucky to have the right grandmother. Lucky that she worked as a maid in the right house. Lucky that house was inhabited by the right wealthy family who subscribed to the right magazines and had diverse interests in the arts. Lucky that family showed their love by giving me their discarded magazines and programs.

When I think about it now, the chances of my exposure to the arts were so improbable that I really should not be here with you tonight. And I imagine each of *you* can name a time when the arts changed *your* life or *your* perspective—a moment when the arts moved you to empathy or to action; a moment when art made it possible for you to be the person you are today. And I encourage you to reflect on those moments tonight and in the days ahead.

You see, all of us here tonight, we are all the lucky ones. Because there are children across the country growing up in circumstances not unlike those of my childhood—children who, day after day, experience in their lives the most terrible manifestations of inequality.

For them, exposure to the arts, to imagination and ambition, remains a matter of chance or circumstance. But it shouldn't be. It can't be. Not in a democracy like ours.

Everyone deserves to experience the arts. No child should need a permission slip to dream.

Art is not a privilege. Art is the soul of our civilization; the beating heart of our humanity; a miracle to which we all should bear witness, over and over again, in every home—from the most modest and humble to the grandest and well-fashioned.

And tonight—in this place, our national cathedral to the arts, and in this moment, these perilous and challenging times in our nation's history—I would argue that we need the arts and humanities more than ever before.

A POVERTY OF IMAGINATION

My friend, Judge Albie Sachs—the great South African freedom fighter and one of Nelson Mandela's first appointees to the country's Constitutional Court—was asked the question, and I'm paraphrasing: *Is it right for the government to fund art when there is still so much hunger and homelessness?*

His answer was: "It's not only right, but necessary."

Albie's contention was simple: Of course, the poor should be fed and clothed and housed; we all have these essential needs.

But all people also yearn for beauty, also long for grace, also have hearts as well as stomachs that need to be fed and filled. And people inevitably create beauty and grace when they lift their voices in song, move their bodies to music, shape color and form on canvas or in sculpture, or use language to tell stories in ways that delight and surprise.

The notion that low-income and working-class people, or people with backgrounds different from our own, do not derive meaning from the arts or do not value free and full expression—this notion is equal parts insulting and ignorant.

In fact, the arts and humanities are necessary to address a kind of poverty that goes beyond money—a hunger that lives not in our bodies but in our souls, a uniquely human hunger for dignity and for transcendence.

The arts lift us toward this dignity, and open us to this transcendence.

Now, this grand monument—the Kennedy Center—is a temple to this idea. It's one such place where dreams are born and beauty made—where all Americans are welcomed. Tonight, as we gather here, I am reminded of President Kennedy, who said: "This country cannot afford to be materially rich and spiritually poor."

Today we may well be the wealthiest nation in the world—but I believe there *is* a spiritual poverty that plagues America.

It's a poverty of imagination that corrodes our capacity for generosity and empathy. It's a poverty of imagination that diminishes our discourse, curtails curiosity, and makes our interactions petty and small. A poverty of imagination that breeds distrust for institutions and, increasingly, for information. A poverty of imagination that breeds distrust of other people who do not look or think like us. A poverty of imagination that shrinks our sense of self and our sense of a lofty and inspiring common purpose, luring us to the extremes rather than leading us toward the extraordinary.

And I believe this poverty—of heart and mind, of spirit and soul, of civic imagination—has brought us to our current moment of crisis.

THE CHALLENGE OF OUR MOMENT

Across this country, we see inequality of every kind and category.

We see it in the growing income of the very wealthy versus the static income of the rest. We see it in who holds power in our government, and who does not. We see it in who our culture respects, and who it diminishes or renders invisible. We see it in the imbalances of our criminal justice system, and in whose lives matter. We see it in the rise of hate across the country, and in who we choose to vilify.

Ultimately, we see it in our unpreparedness to *compromise* (instead of polarize), our unwillingness to *empathize* (instead of ostracize), and in our unreadiness to *humanize* (instead of demonize).

All of this reflects a poverty of imagination—a poverty of imagination that has metastasized into a paucity of hope.

I've said many times, in many parts of the world, that the greatest threat to democracy—that one of the most dangerous consequences of growing inequality—is hopelessness. Democracy cannot breathe without hope.

Hopelessness breeds discouragement and despair, disillusionment with our government and other institutions that bring order and meaning to our lives, and desperate actions that threaten our collective self-interest. Hopelessness hardens our hearts, and makes it harder to hear difficult truths. When hopeless, we can't see beyond our own struggles, or imagine that there may be light at the end of the tunnel.

Too many people around this country feel hopeless—many millions of us. And yet, at a moment when art could be the light—when art's potential could bring us hope—we who support the arts find ourselves with our backs against the wall.

Those who discredit art's value and power surround us, parroting the canards and memes we have heard for decades. They claim the arts are for the elite. They claim the arts are too expensive so government shouldn't fund them. They tell us that art has no place in an economy in need of jobs, in a nation that is struggling to make itself great.

To be abundantly clear: They are wrong.

ONE COMMON ARGUMENT AND ITS LIMITS

Some who currently target the National Endowment for the Arts and the National Endowment for the Humanities and the Corporation for Public Broadcasting see themselves as cutting waste. But we know, as Nancy Hanks herself knew in 1968, that compared to all our other national crises—be they poverty or inequality, civil rights or criminal justice reform—the expense is small.

To use her phrase, "The requirements for the arts are minuscule." The resources of the NEA, NEH, and CPB combined amount to *less than* one tenth of 1 percent of the federal budget.

Needless to say here, the benefits of the arts far outweigh their funding. These dollars achieve tremendous bang for the buck. And for every measure that concerns the opponents of the arts, we have the numbers to prove the value of our investment—an arts-multiplier effect, if you will.

Don't take my word for it. Listen to the United States Bureau of Economic Analysis. If the issue is jobs, the arts and culture sector employed 4.8 million people in 2014. If the issue is trade, our arts and culture sector produces a trade surplus. And if the issue is the economy, just remember that the arts contributed more than $730 billion to our economy in a single year.

And yet, even as I say it, it pains me to make this argument. It pains me to reduce the importance of the arts and humanities to their instrumentality—to express their enormity in mere economic terms.

Now, I'm not naive. I know that some people need to hear this before they cast their vote—or at least to defend their vote. But this argument is not enough. These numbers are not why we support the arts. They can't be.

Because while we know these numbers matter, we also know that conventional metrics will always fall short.

To me, numbers will never explain what happens the moment the curtain rises or the lights go up. They don't measure the quickening of our hearts in time with the music, the widening of our eyes, or the suspension of our disbelief. They don't capture the changes of heart, the new questions sparked, the sense of possibility that is opened. They don't capture the impact on a life trajectory that the arts can have. Like their impact on that small boy in rural Texas in the 1960s.

There is too much emotional value that cannot be measured. Beyond employment, there is enjoyment. A trade surplus does not capture the overflowing surplus of inspiration or express the importance of cultural and aesthetic exchange. And the GDP is not a measure of what makes America great.

THE NECESSITY OF GOVERNMENT INVESTMENT

Now, these days, we also hear another argument with increasing frequency—and it's an argument that I hear often as a foundation president.

Some say, "Sure, Darren, the arts are important, but why does the government need to support them?"

Others ask questions like this: "There are a lot of rich people in the country, can't the arts just live off of private philanthropy?" Or, when I'm talking with millennials, they ask, "Doesn't Kickstarter contribute more to the arts than the NEA?"

Well, here are the facts: For the past thirty years, American charitable giving to the arts has rarely risen past a meager 5 percent. Which means the arts already live on a shoe-string budget. They can't afford another pay cut.

As for the suggestion that we replace the NEA with Kickstarter, that's like saying we don't need the National Institutes of Health or publicly funded medical research because the Internet has given us WebMD.com.

Neither philanthropy nor Kickstarter is sufficient to support the arts in America—and we shouldn't want them to be. Because while private donors support elite and mostly urban institutions—and while crowdfunding favors those projects that can be marketed online—government investment in the arts has a much broader reach, a deeper and more profound impact.

This is an essential component of our democracy.

It is "we, the people" who make our nation great. It is "we, the people," not some faceless government, who choose to invest in ourselves and our culture. It is "we, the people" who believe in supporting the small rural museums, and local theater groups, and mom-and-pop music festivals that bring people together across this country.

So, if we see ourselves as great, we must invest in that which makes us great, things that the GDP has never been able to measure: Investments that make "we, the people" richer, better, more complete human beings.

We must invest in our ambition, in our aspiration, in that American spirit of ingenuity and sense of *imagination* that has always propelled this great nation forward. This is *no time* for a poverty of imagination in our country.

Right now, this is the argument we should be making. This is the argument for our times. As we watch the spreading disease of cynicism, the widening divides, and coarsening of our discourse, the arts may be the very thing to save us from hopelessness and selfishness, and the ugliness they permit and promote.

AN ARGUMENT FOR OUR CURRENT MOMENT

In this hall, it is too tempting to quote President Kennedy—so please indulge me—but it was Kennedy who so eloquently wrote: "There is a connection, hard to explain logically but easy to feel, between achievement in public life and progress in the arts."

He wrote, beautifully, "The age of Pericles was also the age of Phidias. The age of Lorenzo de Medici ... also the age of Leonardo da Vinci." And "the age of Elizabeth also the age of Shakespeare."

This insight has never been more true. If you are here tonight, I imagine you feel that connection as strongly as I do. For the age of Dr. Martin Luther King Jr. was also the age of James Baldwin. The age of Gloria Steinem, the age of Judy Chicago. What would the gay rights movement be without Larry Kramer or Keith Haring or Tony Kushner? The fight for immigrants without Lin-Manuel Miranda's *Hamilton* or Black Lives Matter without Ta-Nehisi Coates's *Between the World and Me*?

My point is: Without art, there is no empathy. Without empathy, there is no justice.

The arts have the power to lead us forward, to heal us, to bring us together and help us bridge real divides. The arts are the key to building and rebuilding bridges in our society—between cities and rural counties; between the poor and the prosperous; between the past, the present, and the possible.

And in this way, investment in the arts is an investment in *moral* imagination, in our capacity for empathy—an investment in the kind of greatness that comes with a deeper, richer understanding of one another and ourselves.

ON AMERICAN GREATNESS

Yes, there has been a lot of debate during this last year about what makes America great. Some believe it is the size of our economy or the might of our military. Some believe it lives in the power of Congress or the prose of the Constitution.

I believe what makes us great is the size of our hearts. It is our capacity for generosity and the grandness of our imagination.

And if this is true, then the connection between American art and American greatness is easy to see *and* easy to feel. It is easy to nurture and spread and grow.

So, let us talk about what makes America great.

Our greatness manifests in an enduring, storied, and honorable vision that welcomes those who come to America seeking refuge from hatred, persecution, and injustice.

Our greatness stretches to every state in the union, to local communities far and wide.

Our greatness fills the air, every summer, at the Magic City Smooth Jazz Festival in beautiful Birmingham, Alabama. It fills the streets with warmth—and performances, and art installations—as part of FREEZE in Anchorage, Alaska.

Our greatness is seen on the faces of Navajo and Hopi students who fill the Grand Canyon with their original compositions. It helps students in Puerto Rico to dream of college—to build "A Bridge to the University and the World."

Our greatness is giving ballet dancers in Des Moines, Iowa, a leg up—and lifting the voices of poets like Hope Wabuke, whose family fled Ugandan genocide to find safety and opportunity in America.

Our greatness connects people from different walks of life. It brings the Harlem Quartet to Maize, Kansas. It helps a professor from Utah State University translate *New Voices from Vietnam.*

Let me tell you about American greatness. It is everyone and every program I've just told you about. And all of that astonishing and enabling work is made possible because of support from the NEA and the NEH.

In my home state of Texas, greatness is seen on a stage in a barn in the historic town of Round Top, where thousands of Texans converge every spring to bear witness to extraordinary music and poetry.

Greatness resides in the papers of George Washington and movements of Martha Graham. It is the Hudson River School and the Harlem Renaissance. It is the poetry of Walt Whitman and Maya Angelou. Yes, we contain multitudes. Yes, we still rise.

It's the work performed by Anna Deavere Smith tonight, in *Notes from the Field*—the work of transforming ourselves and inhabiting the lives of others.

It's the reminder of Langston Hughes in his iconic "Let America Be America Again":

> *I am the poor white, fooled and pushed apart,*
> *I am the Negro bearing slavery's scars.*
> *I am the red man driven from the land,*
> *I am the immigrant clutching the hope I seek—*
> *And finding only the same old stupid plan*
> *Of dog eat dog, of mighty crush the weak.*

Because when we do the work of the arts, when we hold the mirror up to ourselves and our society, we not only experience our shared humanity, we arrive at our shared obligation to humanity: Our connection with and obligation to all people who suffer and struggle and seek to be heard.

KEEPING AMERICA GREAT

This greatness—of our culture and our character—is worth fighting for. And nobody—*nobody*—knew American greatness better than Nancy Hanks.

Forty-some years ago, there was a congresswoman who Nancy Hanks needed to convince about the power of the NEA. Nancy charmed and pushed and cajoled—as she famously did—but the congresswoman said: "Nancy, no one is sending me any letters."

As the story goes, Nancy said, "Letters? You want letters?" And soon there were flyers on the seats of concert halls and theaters across the country. The letters to the congresswoman's office started pouring in—by the mail bag, by the thousands.

The letters didn't materialize just because of Nancy. These letters were written by people—people who sat in theaters like this one, people who read those fliers, and people who decided to take action.

At the end of the day, it will always be the people who love the arts who will spread the love of the arts. It will always be the people who love the humanities who make the strongest case for our shared humanity.

And it will be us, *all of us*, who will be the best advocates for the work that changes our lives, and the artistic greatness that makes us greater still.

So, friends: Let us resolve that each of us will do our best to be like Nancy Hanks.

Let us resolve to make our voices heard. To bridge the seats in the theaters to those seats in Congress. And to explain the value on the walls of museums to those in the halls of power.

Let us resolve to take this Arts Advocacy Day as our next opportunity, and after that, to make every day an opportunity to advocate for the arts.

This work has never been more important. But, together, we will rise to meet this defining challenge of our time.

CELEBRATING DEMOCRACY'S ART

Address to the Foundation for Art and Preservation in Embassies
The United States Department of State
Washington, DC
April 16, 2018

Thank you for this extraordinary and humbling honor and for including me in this special tribute to the lives and legacies of Lee and Walter Annenberg.

We are gathered tonight in the Benjamin Franklin State Dining Room—named for the father of the foreign service—itself a monument to the power of diplomacy.

From Alexis de Tocqueville on, countless observers and historians have regarded Franklin as "the first American." But if Franklin was the first, then surely Lee and Walter Annenberg were among the most quintessential.

As collectors and connoisseurs of art, they understood that art has a power to move and persuade—to stir empathy and action in ways that talking points and trade deals sometimes cannot. As an ambassador and a diplomat, they understood the value of cultural exchange—that sharing our ideas and our art, our language, and our culture heightens empathy and understanding. And above all, Lee and Walter were patriots who believed in the power of culture to bring people together.

They built bridges. They celebrated the rich and diverse fabric of our nation. And they worked their entire lives to foster mutual understanding among cultures, countries, and continents.

These are the same values that FAPE embodies, and represents, and advances. They underlie FAPE's mission of spreading American art around the world, filling our embassies with masterpieces that represent our people, expressing and extending the American idea.

And it's this vision that Lee and Wendy Luers, and so many others, helped to imbue and energize and enshrine within this foundation. Today, the torch has been passed, and Jo Carole Lauder and Eden Rafshoon carry on this legacy. And together with Jennifer Duncan and Caitlin O'Connor, they have reinvigorated this institution for our current moment.

All of us are gathered tonight because we share in this vision. Like Lee and Walter, we believe in the importance of forging strong relationships between people and nations, of supporting civic institutions that bring people together, and of sharing and lifting up art that breeds empathy and understanding.

That notion—that art can allow us to make sense of the world we live in, and imagine a better one—is in fact quite personal to me, too.

When I was a little boy, I lived with my mother and sister in a small shotgun house—in an African-American community in rural Liberty County, Texas. My grandmother worked as a maid in the home of a wealthy Houston family. And every month, she would bring old art magazines and programs from events the family attended.

I remember, vividly, feeling transfixed by the magic I saw on those pages—by images of worlds to which I had no other exposure. Those pages unlocked my capacity to imagine a world beyond my own—and to imagine my place in it. I can honestly say I would not be here now if not for my experience with the arts.

Without the arts, there is no way I could picture myself going to college or law school, or leaving home or even the state of Texas, let alone accepting this honor in America's greatest temple of diplomacy.

And I know that a story like mine couldn't happen anywhere else except the United States. Because of this, I have always been passionate about working with others who share my passion for the arts: People like all of you. And the artists we get to work with, the work they produce, exemplifies the best of America—the best of FAPE and its contribution to the world.

There's the iconic Carrie Mae Weems, whose extraordinary photographs grace the walls of the United States' mission to the United Nations. So much of her work considers how people like me might recognize themselves and understand our place in the world—be it outside the Philadelphia Museum or the Louvre in Paris or the Pyramid of Rome. She reminds us that our place in the world is shifting—and that the arts can engage with the ways nations interact, too.

And then there's the great Ellsworth Kelly, and his phenomenal contributions to the work of this organization. His *Beijing Panels*, commissioned by FAPE for our embassy there, greet thousands of Chinese citizens every day. Those two sculptures—identical in shape and reflecting the colors of the American and Chinese flags—emphasize similarity while acknowledging difference. It's a sentiment that goes beyond language, conveyed through color and shape—a principle at the heart of diplomacy.

Beyond the relationship between any two countries, these artists and their work also can capture our deeper connection to one another. Think of the people who come to the American embassy in Kingston, Jamaica, and are met with Dorothea Rockburne's *Folded Sky*. The forty-one-foot mural, commissioned by FAPE to honor Colin Powell, depicts the night sky in Harlem as one of our great diplomats who was born from Jamaican immigrants. The art connects us to Jamaica—not just through one distinguished

American, but, in the artist's words, through "the same night sky we all share as humans of a collective earthly experience."

That is the power of art: To remind us of what we share, to connect us through beauty and free expression, and to inspire us to believe in a more peaceful, more harmonious world.

These three artists remind us how art can benefit us all. How the arts can reveal our place in the world. How they can communicate the connection between countries. And how art can bring us together and remind us of our common humanity.

This is why, at a time when the arts are beleaguered and besieged, at a moment when art's value—and the value of soft power—is openly questioned, we must defend it at all costs. We know the value of a piece of art goes well beyond its price at Christie's or its standing among critics.

Our passion for American art is a passion for America. Our unwavering love for spreading the arts comes from an unwavering love for our country—which is why defending and supporting the arts is our patriotic duty.

Lee and Walter saw the collection and promotion of art not just as pastime, but as patriotism—as a mission to bring art to more people in more places. It's why when discussing a plan to teach the American public more about art, Walter said: "I still believe in that idea of making all of the world available to all peoples."

That is what they spent their lives doing. And that is the core of FAPE's mission—bringing art across the globe, and in doing so, unlocking our ability to connect with people near and far.

This mission is why I am so proud to count myself among you today, with Benjamin Franklin looking on. Thank you for this great honor, and for the privilege of serving this noble organization.

I am grateful for your company, for your leadership, and for your continued support of our democracy's art—and the art of our democracy.

MUSEUMS NEED TO STEP INTO THE FUTURE

The New York Times
July 26, 2019

America's museums are more than repositories of ancient Greek statues and Renaissance paintings. They are guardians of a fading social and demographic order.

On Thursday, Warren Kanders resigned from the board of the Whitney Museum of Art, after protests over his company's sale of tear gas grenades that were reportedly used on asylum seekers. His case reveals the extent to which museums have become contested spaces in a rapidly changing country.

On one side of the crossfire are trustees who benefit from a distorted economic system that protects and promotes inequality. Wealthy donors and collectors decide what is valued. They expect appreciation, not scrutiny, for giving generously as government support for the arts wanes. And they are offended by the accusation that they use museums to launder, or "artwash," their reputations and increase the value of their personal collections.

On the other side are people whom the system excludes and exploits. An increasingly diverse viewing public, and growing protest movements, are calling for installations and institutions that represent a broader cross-section of America. They demand museums serve more than the interests of the elite.

Museums find themselves in the same struggle tearing society apart—a struggle fueled by worsening inequality of every kind.

Consider how this is playing out in New York City. The Metropolitan Museum of Art announced it would no longer accept gifts from the Sackler family, owners of the opioid maker Purdue Pharma. Before Mr. Kanders resigned, eight artists in the Whitney's 2019 Biennial withdrew in protest. (They have since rejoined the show.) Employees of the Guggenheim and New Museum, whose wages have largely stagnated as those of top museum executives rise faster than inflation, have recently unionized, inspiring other such efforts.

I believe that museums have the responsibility to hold a mirror up to society. As the country becomes younger and more diverse, and as its immigrant population grows, museums must shift. This is not about "political correctness"; it's about how these institutions can achieve excellence, now and in the future.

At stake is not just the work or prestige of a particular institution, but the underpinnings of democracy: How do "we the people" tell our story— who is included, and who is locked out? And how do museums resist reinforcing biases, hierarchies, and inequalities?

To start, museums should prioritize hiring curators from academic programs that invest in diversity. Donors need to support artists and academics of every background; the people entrusted with analyzing and exhibiting the American story ought to reflect the future, or risk not being a part of it.

Fortunately, there are signs of progress. A 2018 Mellon Foundation survey found that educational and curatorial departments have grown more racially diverse since 2014. More than a quarter of museum education positions are now held by people of color. A number of prominent museums, from the Getty to the Museum of Modern Art, have announced the appointment of curators of color recently.

One of the most successful traveling exhibitions of the past year, "Soul of a Nation: Art in the Age of Black Power," generated critical acclaim and enormous attendance, demonstrating the hunger for such programming. The fall cultural calendar in major museums promises to be among the most diverse ever, with solo exhibitions devoted to artists including Teresita Fernández, Julie Mehretu, Wangechi Mutu, and Mark Bradford.

Many organizations that support art institutions are demanding more. New York City, for instance, now requires diversity reporting from the cultural institutions it subsidizes. Beyond the numbers, the fact that the city will hold institutions accountable is starting to shift the focus away from merely seeking donations.

Major arts foundations—from Annenberg to Walton—are emphasizing diversity and inclusion in their grantmaking. By doing so, they are offering funds that are not contingent on naming rights for new buildings, but rather to build more diverse staffs and invest in a broader range of stories, of which there are still too few examples.

And yet, everything that moves an institution forward, or holds it back, can be traced to its board. So, boards need to include members from more diverse perspectives and backgrounds. After all, no institution in a democracy that aspires to reflect society, or serve the public, can do so without representing the communities that constitute it.

To engage diverse leaders, museums should redefine the terms of trusteeship. At a time when institutions face greater pressure than ever to raise resources, their boards have veered too far toward only appointing trustees with wealth. But we know there are other valuable forms of capital not easily measured in dollars and cents. And so boards need to stop seeing diversity as subtracting from their annual revenue, but rather as adding strength. Diversity helps them attract new visitors, artists, communities, and constituencies.

In other words, museum boards must move from tokenism to transformation—the kind of transformation that only meaningful inclusion can bring.

Transformation will take hold only if it happens at every level of the museum. That's why boards have a responsibility to support and hire a diverse staff and to compensate them responsibly. Only then will the public begin to see themselves and others robustly reflected and represented.

Static, monolithic history must be supplanted with histories, plural—even as museums continue to safeguard the past in the objects they conserve and display. Directors and their staffs can enact bold, forward-looking visions only when their boards support them in seeing museums as spaces to challenge, take creative risks, and not simply conserve.

Museums have the chance to redefine excellence and relevance. They should be civic spaces where we can gather and do the exhilarating work of building community. For that to happen, institutions should look beyond the gilded frames of this new Gilded Age, and better reflect the public they serve.

THROUGH ART, HOPE—AND THROUGH HOPE, JUSTICE

Address to the Bennington College Class of 2021
Bennington, Vermont
May 28, 2021

To my dear friend, President Laura Walker: Thank you for hosting me. Friends, family, beloved community joining us on the livestream: Welcome. Most importantly, to the Class of 2021: Congratulations.

I'm honored to be here. And I want to share a word about why I'm here, and why it means so much to me.

This is my first time visiting Bennington. I'm reveling in the majesty of the mountains and the meadows you've called home for most of the past four (or more) years. But the truth is, I loved Bennington long before today. In fact—and I'm dating myself here—I've loved it as long as most of you have been alive.

I love Bennington because, for twenty-six years, I loved a man named David.

David arrived at Bennington in 1980. He entered the MFA program with a love of the arts—and he left, in 1983, with a calling. This community embraced him, pushed him, affirmed him—as a queer man, as a thinker, as an artist. In other words, Bennington changed David's life. And David changed mine.

David introduced me to painters, performers, and warriors for justice, many of them Bennington grads. He filled my life with light and laughter—the kind that many of you have shared in your days together. So, I owe something real and meaningful and enduring to the Bennington community. I am so grateful for the invitation to be with you today, celebrating you and your achievement.

I also should say, for me, today is bittersweet. When I first received the Bennington commencement invitation, I pictured David by my side: Strolling across Commons Lawn. Admiring your brilliance at VAPA. Applauding you as you receive your diplomas. He would have relished it all.

But two years ago in January, David passed away suddenly. I mention this not to bring anyone down, but because I imagine I am not the only one feeling both gratitude and grief today. I imagine many of you are celebrating your accomplishments, while also struggling with the fact that this is not the commencement you envisioned or the senior year you expected. And that's okay.

We all have faced losses in our lives, and especially in the last year—losses big and small. There were the plans we made, and the plans we changed.

You might have pictured a cheering crowd or an extended family hugging you close. A senior year on campus—and all the memories that go along with it. Hours in the library. Days in the studio. A final performance. You might have imagined someone in the audience, or by your side, who is not here today.

And so, graduates: I see you—both your joy and your sadness—the gift of this moment and its grief. And we honor both.

And there's one more feeling on which I'm reflecting today: Hope. You see, I have come to believe the single greatest threat to our democracy is hopelessness.

That's because hopelessness hardens our hearts and limits our capacity for empathy, for generosity, for justice. When we feel hopeless, it's hard to imagine what comes next: That there may be light at the end of the tunnel, or possibility ahead. Hopelessness makes it easy to hold back, even when the world invites you in. We see forms of hopelessness all around the world.

Hopelessness (and selfishness) can lead nations to hoard their vaccine supply, leaving millions across the globe vulnerable and dying. Some justify it, saying, "We must prepare for the next wave."

Hopelessness leaves world leaders resigned in the face of climate crisis, even as fires, floods, and droughts abound. And they rationalize it, lamenting, "What could we do to stop it anyway?"

Hopelessness might convince people to ignore racist police violence and voter suppression—to succumb or even numb ourselves to its inevitability, especially when these policies threaten people who may (or may not) look like us.

And yet, despite all our losses and challenges, I have hope. Looking into your faces, I see hope. And we all have such high hopes for you.

So, Class of 2021, for this very last in-person lecture, let's reflect on how to find hope in a time when there's too much hopelessness.

For me, the first place I look for hope is in the arts.

As a little boy, I lived with my mother and sister in a shotgun house—in rural Liberty County, Texas. My grandmother worked as a maid for wealthy Houston families. And every now and then, I would go along with her and help clean or work in the yard.

One family for whom my grandmother worked was a major arts patron in Houston. And when I was over, I noticed stacks of programs and magazines from the Alley Theater and the Houston Museum of Fine

Arts—materials they planned to throw away. And so, quietly, I would wrap a few in a brown paper bag and take them home with me.

I remember, vividly, feeling transfixed by the magic of those pages. Flipping through those magazines and programs unlocked my capacity to imagine a world beyond my own—and to imagine my place in it. I know I'm not alone.

How many times have you stood before a painting and felt yourself moved in its presence? How many times have you read a classmate's poetry or prose, and found yourself entranced? How many times has a song brought you to tears? A play coaxed you to laughter? A film nestled into your heart, your lungs, your gut?

How many times have the arts—in their creation or experience— moved you, opened you, asked you to see the world more clearly, and imagine what could be?

That's why the arts—and artists like so many of you—are so important. And why a life in the arts, and informed by the arts, is not a frivolous luxury or selfish pursuit—but a *necessity*. The arts allow us to dream of—and empower us to create—futures that do not yet exist.

They cultivate within us the empathy, the understanding of human experience—our shared dignity and potential—that is the seed of hope.

Now, if one place we can find hope is in the arts, then another is in movements for justice.

Across the world, we've witnessed the largest civil rights movement in history—a movement that stands against violence and repression to say, "Black Lives Matter." We've seen millions of girls and women and nonbinary people share stories of survival, and many millions more respond with #MeToo and #NiUnaMenos.

We are living through a renaissance of solidarity led by Black women and girls; by Indigenous people around the globe; by survivors speaking up for disability justice; by trans people pushing for food and water security; by all of us, aware that our lives intersect in countless ways.

These movements are hope in action. I know many of you have raised your voices in pain and protest over the past year. And I am sure you have seen, in your intersectional work and interdisciplinary studies, the way art illuminates and elevates and emboldens our calls for justice—and vice versa.

For me, this relationship is essential.

Both art and justice require collaboration and creativity. They ask us to reexamine our assumptions and familiar narratives. They challenge us to acknowledge who is centered—and who is forced to the margins. Art and justice need our discipline, patience, and daily practice. They both demand honesty with ourselves, openness to others, and hope for what can be.

So, the pursuits of art and justice are intertwined. Both require intention and energy and hard work. They may not be perfect synonyms or substitutes. But they exist in mutuality—we need *both* in order to thrive—and to heal.

I see that mutuality in Amy Sherald's beautiful, regal portrait of Breonna Taylor, who was killed by Louisville police officers in her own home. Sherald casts Ms. Taylor in a flowing teal gown with a hand on her hip—brave, bold, loving, loved.

So, rather than see this painting sold off to a private donor, the Ford Foundation and the Hearthland Foundation donated it to both the Speed Museum in Louisville and the National Museum of African American History and Culture.

We believe in the power of Amy Sherald's art not because we want Breonna Taylor to be seen as an icon or a symbol but because we want the world to understand the humanity that has been stolen by her murder.

We believe in this painting because it has the power to heal. It holds the potential to comfort a grieving and enraged city—and a grieving nation grappling with its history of racism. And while art cannot replace accountability, it can encourage it. It can enrich it. It can drive us closer to the reckoning our communities so deeply need and deserve.

After all, that is why we find hope in justice, and art, and all the spaces in between—not because we pursue them in isolation or preserve them for the few; but because we share them with everyone.

So, Class of 2021: No matter what you do, no matter the art or justice you choose to pursue—I ask you to hope.

I ask, knowing hope is always difficult—that, at moments like these, it is radical. Because when the future feels unknown, unsure, uncertain—it's easy to languish.

But I want to be clear: There is a difference between being uncertain and being unprepared. We are all uncertain. No one knows what the future holds or what will be different about the world a year from now or a decade from now.

But know that you are *prepared*. If your future is a blank canvas, Bennington has prepared you to fill it—and see the world in its fullest form.

Bennington taught you, as it taught my David, to relish in your craft. To be relentless and unwavering in your commitment to both art and justice. To be resilient as the world shifts under our feet. To find hope and spread it to others.

Graduates, in the words of the abolitionist activist and organizer, Mariame Kaba, "Hope is a discipline."

It is a choice—yours to make and always in reach. I see it at your fingertips, in your eyes, on your horizons. In our life together, I was so lucky that David shared his hope—the hope he garnered in this place, from this community—with me. He left me enough to last a lifetime.

I urge you to choose hope as he did, to cherish it as we did, to practice this discipline—however you can.

THE URGENCY OF ART: ART AND JUSTICE DURING A TIME OF CRISIS

Rothschild Foundation Lecture
The Royal Academy of Arts
London, England
November 7, 2023

Good evening, everyone. Thank you for the generous introduction and warm welcome. To the incomparable Axel Rüger: Thank you for your visionary leadership of this extraordinary institution. And to my friend Hannah Rothschild: Thank you for your gifts of your beautiful prose and poetry, your trailblazing philanthropy, and your abiding commitment to the Royal Academy—and for facilitating my visit from across the pond.

I'm honored by the opportunity to add my voice to the conversation. And I feel deeply privileged to do so here, in this temple of the arts, created and led by artists: A singular institution in the firmament of our cultural landscape—across the UK and around the world.

I must start by acknowledging: We meet during a moment of roiling crisis. Hamas' October 7 terrorist attack has sparked the tinderbox of war in the Middle East. We grieve for the hostages—and many lives—taken in Israel and Gaza during the days since. Vladimir Putin's wanton, unlawful invasion of Ukraine endangers a proud people and culture—and imperils our rules-based global order.

Conflicts between authoritarian ideology and democratic values rage in other theaters, near and far—including in my own nation, the United States. Our shared sense of a common good has frayed, torn apart by resentment and grievance, mendacity and impunity—a nihilism that poisons our discourse. We suffer from cancers on our democracy and market system, from a changing climate that is pushing our life-sustaining ecosystems to the brink. One could be forgiven for feeling dejected and depleted by it all.

And yet.

Every time I visit London, every time I walk off Piccadilly into the grand courtyard here, I find myself replenished. I find myself overwhelmed with awe and wonder. I remember that it is through art—it is because of artists—that we rediscover inspiration and renewal and hope.

It is through art that we find ourselves; that we find one another and our shared humanity; that we find our ways through, and over, and forward.

On my many pilgrimages to the RA, I have been moved by the works of Academicians like Sir Anish Kapoor and Sir Grayson Perry. My Ford Foundation colleagues and I are proud to support the RA's forthcoming *Entangled Pasts*, as Axel mentioned—an extension of our partnership on other exhibitions, including this year's *Souls Grown Deep Like the Rivers*, which showcases Black artists from across the American South.

You see, as a child of the American South, I first came to know the power and promise of the arts—which is not to say that the arts were always close at hand.

As a young boy, I lived in Ames, Texas—a small, poor, rural town—in a shotgun house, the son of a single mother. My generation was the first to attend integrated schools, but we had no arts education or museums to visit. Instead, I was exposed to the arts by happenstance.

My grandmother worked as a maid in the home of a wealthy Houston family. And every month, she would bring me a paper bag of old art magazines and event programs that they had discarded.

I remember those pages would mesmerize me—intoxicate me. I remember flipping through them, my eyes and mind and sense of the possible widened. They unlocked my capacity to imagine a world beyond my own—and to imagine my place in it.

The arts continued to work their magic on me when I attended college at The University of Texas—when I was fortunate enough to attend a performance of the Dance Theatre of Harlem, which had visited Austin. Seeing people who looked like me—dynamic and expressive and joyful in a medium that had long felt out of reach—instilled a profound sense of belonging that I have carried with me since.

I know I'm not alone. Every one of us can think of a moment when the arts shifted our perspective, awakened our empathy, or inspired us to act because art is the beating heart and the soul of our lives—individually and collectively. And we need art now more than ever before—to reveal truth, to share beauty, to confront injustice. To mobilize us as advocates and move us to build a more just world.

Now, I want to be clear: As a lover of the arts, I believe in their intrinsic value.

When South Africa was first rebuilding from apartheid, a journalist asked a pointed question of Judge Albie Sachs, who President Nelson Mandela appointed to the Constitutional Court. He pressed if it was right for South Africa's new government to fund the arts when many in the country were facing hunger and homelessness. Albie responded, as you might imagine he would: "It's not only right, but necessary."

He understood that every person has a heart that must be fed and filled, not just a stomach—that beauty and grace are not luxuries for the few but the birthright of all. He understood that the arts make us whole. They bring us together in community. They tell the story of our tragedy, our trauma, and our transcendence. They lead us from truth to reconciliation.

Sometimes, we can grow defensive about this—and understandably so, in this age of restraint and retreat. We cite the collective economic boost that galleries, shows, and festivals generate.

No doubt, the arts do contribute to GDP. But I believe that when we allow a mentality of instrumentality to reduce their contribution to a monetary value, we see a symptom of a deeper sickness in our society that compels us to define everything about everything in relation to capital—that has raised market-oriented thinking above all other kinds and categories of human understanding.

Think about it: In medicine, we talk about cost curves and insurance schemes—with relatively scant attention to the *care* in health care.

We champion the STEM disciplines in our schools at the same time as we cut arts programs because we accept the zero-sum thinking, the false choice, that preparing students to join the workforce is somehow at odds with preparing them to be human beings. This intellectual inequality—thinking economically rather than holistically—this perpetuates economic inequality and social inequality and political inequality.

And let me suggest something else provocative: We are similarly misguided when we suggest that the arts are only a means to an end; when we suggest that the arts are exclusively a tool for advancing social change (though that is certainly part of their power); when we suggest that the arts are somehow unworthy of funding if we can't measure their direct impact on social or environmental causes in three or five or seven years.

The reasons to celebrate and affirm the arts are as multifaceted as artists and their work. They bring us whimsy and surprise, delight and disgust, the full spectrum of what it is to feel and to be alive.

So, as I see things, it is not true that the arts exist only for justice. But where justice lives and thrives, it flourishes because of the arts. This is because the arts underpin our understanding of our shared humanity and dignity.

In other words: Without art, there is no empathy. Without empathy, there can be no justice.

These days, as we know, there is already too little of each. Our empathy deficit drives analog and digital threats alike. It's at the root of the algorithmic inequality perpetuated by AI and other emerging technologies, developed by engineers and promoted by investors without regard for the common good. And it's beneath the rise, once again, of the many *isms*: The hateful rhetoric and horrific policies that endanger the most historically marginalized.

There is little doubt why crackdowns on creativity and free expression are the hallmarks of authoritarian regimes—of tyrants who fear the arts as a powerful expression of protest. There is little doubt why those championing policies that dehumanize everyone who looks or loves differently than they do are so often the ones trying to ban the images, songs, and stories that celebrate diversity. They are threatened by the singular ability of the arts to heal, to gather, to bridge—to kindle sorrow, joy, compassion, resolve, and an irreversible empathy, such that we can no longer accept inequality nor turn away from injustice.

I have seen this firsthand through the brilliant work of my friend, the legendary arts patron and philanthropist Agnes Gund. Agnes—Aggie, to her friends—was profoundly moved by watching Ava DuVernay's documentary *13th*, about the Thirteenth Amendment to the US Constitution, which freed enslaved people, families, and communities, but still allowed for the incarcerated to serve as forced, unpaid labor—up to this very day.

As a filmmaker, Ava paired a meticulous exploration of the facts with powerful visual and audio media, illuminating the connection between slavery and mass incarceration in the United States. As a viewer, Aggie was open-minded and empathetic—perhaps by nature, but also by virtue of years of exposure to the world's greatest works. She had practiced and cultivated a skill in looking from the perspective of others.

And so, when Aggie watched Ava's film, it grabbed hold of her, as great art so often does—and it refused to let go. It spurred her to direct her philanthropy toward justice.

In 2017, Aggie sold a literal masterpiece—Roy Lichtenstein's *Masterpiece*—and used some of the proceeds to establish the Art for Justice Fund. During the years since, it has directed more than $100 million toward criminal justice reform in the United States.

One of the exhibitions that Art for Justice supported, *Marking Time*, showcased the work and experiences of incarcerated artists, bringing their stories out from behind bars and into galleries at the Museum of Modern Art. Another initiative supported a first-of-its-kind Center for Art and Advocacy, which, among other efforts, provides fellowships, residencies, and a network of support for formerly incarcerated artists.

Art has been both the catalyst and the engine for this change. And I am always struck by the ways in which art and justice are inseparable within Aggie's journey—and the journeys of so many others.

Indeed, the line from art to justice is clear. It charts a course through empathy, conferring dignity upon both subject and audience.

The truth is, through the centuries, we all have denied far too many the dignity and empathy they deserve. We have coalesced around an art-historical cannon that idealized certain standards of beauty, while also elevating stereotypical portrayals of people of color, Indigenous people, and other minorities—or erasing them from the record altogether. We have kept those canvases on our gallery walls, while keeping talented artists of color outside our gates, which were in turn kept by predominantly white guardians.

When it comes to what we value as art—who makes it, where it is seen, and how it is shared with the world—we have at times been part of the problem. And I use "we" intentionally.

When I first joined the Ford Foundation, our own art collection failed to capture the richness of human experience and perspective. We owned more than four hundred works, virtually all by white European and American men—and only one woman, Sheila Hicks.

We weren't alone. A 2019 study of major US arts museums suggested that 85 percent of all featured artists were white, and 87 percent were men. One should not be surprised, then, that the subjects of those works also fail to reflect the fullness of the human experience. One shouldn't be surprised that our collections include more portraits of conquerors than portrayals of the dispossessed and disenfranchised—that pastorals and still lifes examine landscapes and objects with a more unflinching perspective than their creators cast on some of the more painful facets of our history. Nor that some of the more complicated, contradictory truths of our existence have been covered up—literally—in our artistic renderings of the past.

One nineteenth-century portrait of a Louisiana family recently became Exhibit A of the art world's ongoing negotiation with historical truths.

For decades, viewers thought it depicted the Frey family's three white children at ease in the idyllic countryside. Then, collectors noticed something: A fourth figure, hidden at the right edge of the frame—painted over as part of the landscape. And then, restoration revealed something wholly unexpected: This fourth figure was a Black child, somewhat older than the Freys, leaning against a tree—slightly removed but still part of the scene.

Historians identified this young man as Bélizaire, an enslaved young person who likely was charged with the care of the young Freys. The painting does not portray him as part of the family, but neither does it degrade him. He is depicted with the same care as the other subjects and with a great deal of interiority, at ease in a powerful pose, gazing into the middle distance.

Such depictions of enslaved people are and were rare. We still do not know why the Freys chose to include Bélizaire in this portrait. But now we do know his name and part of his story. We know that he existed, in life and in memory. And we know that, some years later, someone decided it would be better if he didn't.

Art conservators have surmised that Bélizaire was painted over sometime around the turn of the last century. He was simply erased. It was a metaphor for Jim Crow and segregation across the American South—an expression of the white supremacy that plagues the United States still.

Another illustration: Even when they are not painted over, subjects of color have historically been overlooked and under-studied. No example is more famous than Édouard Manet's *Olympia*, which shook the art world with its depiction of this titular woman, staring directly at the viewer.

Critics have spilled endless ink, first debating the painting's propriety, then memorializing it as a foundational work of modernism. Yet, for more than a century, they were all but silent on its other subject: The Black woman offering Olympia a bouquet of flowers.

In the work's original description, she has no name. Today, thanks to curator Denise Murrell, we know that she was called Laure. We know that Laure modeled for *Olympia*—and for other works and artists—neither degraded nor exoticized but shown as she was. We know that the figure she represented in those early modernist works became a point of reference for Bazille, Matisse, and more. And we know that she is—and always has been—worthy of attention not just from the artists who painted her but from us as well.

My hope is that these instances of rediscovery and reexamination are indicative of a change in our work and our world—indicative that we can finally embrace the opportunity, through art, to confer dignity equally; to confront the sins of our past that have diminished it; and to celebrate the fullness of the human experience in ways that expand it.

Today, the painting of *Bélizaire and the Frey Children* hangs in New York's Metropolitan Museum of Art, accompanied by an explanation of the work's complicated and revealing history—a model for others to emulate. And while *Olympia* remains in the Musée d'Orsay, students of art history around the world now regard Laure with greater appreciation.

In turn, we all might take a lesson—and conduct the same excavation of our own biases: To uncover the uncomfortable truths hiding beneath the surface of both canvases and institutions, sometimes hiding in plain view; to bring our work and our world closer to justice.

At the Ford Foundation, we reckoned with the fact that our storied art collection no longer reflected our mission and values. So we sold every single piece. And with the proceeds, we have built a new collection that showcases the work of artists of color, women, queer creators, and more.

I'm often asked how an institution of the Ford Foundation's scale and complexity decides what to fund, amidst so many competing priorities. These can be hard choices, but we filter each through an enduring commitment: We support what I call the three Is—individuals, their ideas, and their institutions—in order to address the causes of inequality. We prioritize systemic solutions. We center the voices and perspectives of the people closest to the problems—in shaping our strategies and in hiring the talent to execute them.

In the arts, our principles and people have led us to invest in lesser-known artists, whose voices and perspectives are less often, less fully heard. And more broadly, our values have led us to funding transformative work: Toward programs like the Dance Theatre of Harlem, whose dancers captivated me so long ago; toward exhibitions for artists like Kehinde Wiley, whose portraits of young Black people slain in an epidemic of racist brutality recasts them in the classical poses of martyrs.

Each morning that I walk into the Ford Foundation offices, I am greeted by Wiley's portrait of Wanda Crichlow, a twenty-first-century New Yorker painted in the dress and pose of a Dutch aristocrat.

She affirms, for all of us: We believe in the inherent dignity of all people. And now, our art must affirm it, too.

I have been heartened to see institutions around the world, including the RA, undergo similar reckonings with their own history and collection—not only because this is our responsibility, but also because it is how we ensure our relevance for a new generation.

We should be encouraged by undertakings like the Decolonial Research Project, which lays bare the ways in which past Royal Academicians have engaged in or benefited from the ownership of enslaved people.

We should be proud to experience the invisible made seen, through research on Fanny Eaton, a Jamaican woman whose uncredited likeness appears in the works of many Academicians, and who is finally getting her due, and through belated public recognition of Black artists' models—like Laure—in exhibits like *Posing Modernity*, curated at the Met by the legendary Denise Murrell.

We should be inspired by the breadth of excellence reflected among creators in our global art community: By Jeffrey Gibson's multimedia representations of indigeneity at the Venice Biennale; by the São Paulo Museum of Art's exploration of *Afro-Atlantic Histories*.

We should be gratified to see diasporic artists in the UK, like filmmaker Sir John Akomfrah and photographer, printmaker, and educator Sonia Boyce, both Royal Academicians, recognized for their vital contributions to a bold new cannon.

We should be galvanized by efforts to bring that art—including these—to new audiences through projects like Alice Walton's Art Bridges, which leverages the vast, undisplayed collections of great museums to bring pieces out of storage and into smaller, rural venues so that everyone has access to art.

I reflect often on Dr. Martin Luther King Jr.'s admonition: "Philanthropy is commendable, but it must not cause the philanthropist to overlook the circumstances of economic injustice which make philanthropy necessary."

At the Ford Foundation, Dr. King's challenge pushes us, each day, to address the causes, not just the consequences, of inequality.

And to paraphrase Dr. King, I would submit to you tonight that art, too, is commendable. But we must not overlook the circumstances that make protecting and celebrating creative expression—and protecting artists themselves—necessary, as well.

What does this look like?

For curators, it looks like embracing the opportunity and obligation to find excellence across a broader array of communities.

For museums, in turn, it looks like cultivating curators and recruiting trustees from a wider variety of backgrounds—changing the guard among the gatekeepers that interpret, assess, translate, and transmit art to increasingly diverse audiences.

For supporters of the arts, from individual patrons to major funders, it looks like rising up to support this noble mission—empowering artists and institutions with the unrestricted resources to invest in capital and human-capital needs, not just naming opportunities and building projects.

And to a new generation of donors and advocates, it looks like continuing to speak truth to power, to hold our old feet (even mine) to new fires, to keep pressing, to keep pushing. We can always find smarter, better ways—insights and innovations—with which to harness and direct our efforts to include those who have been excluded, whether through impact investing, or mission-related investing, or instruments like social bonds.

Ultimately, it remains incumbent upon all of us—using all of our voices in harmony—to affirm the countless ways in which the arts are central to our broader missions: To confer dignity and inspire empathy; to reflect our shared humanity and remind us of our shared obligation to humanity; to bring us together on special evenings like this—and to inspire our work each day after.

PART V

DEMOCRATIC CAPITALISM: ECONOMIC OPPORTUNITY AND SHARED PROSPERITY

If we are to keep the American dream alive, our democratic values flourishing, and our market system strong, then we must redesign and rebuild the engine that drives them....

Our economy is unbalanced because conscious choices, in the aggregate, amount to a conscienceless capitalism. These choices erode democracy and foment distrust. We, the people, can make different choices. And we, the wealthy and privileged, should lean into our discomfort.

This is the most pressing work of our time, and it will be difficult. Our present is deeply rooted in historical inequalities that must methodically be rectified. But difficulty is not an excuse to allow American capitalism to grow more distorted, corrupt, and unjust. It does not relieve us of our duty to strengthen and improve a system that, if rebalanced, could once again make America a beacon for upward mobility.

Without hope, American dreams deferred or denied will continue, as the poet Langston Hughes wrote, to explode. With hope, and through it, we can reimagine the dream and invite many millions more to share in its promise.

The New York Times
June 25, 2020

WHERE MARKETS LEAD, JUSTICE MUST FOLLOW

Address to the Presidio Graduate School Class of 2015
San Anselmo, California
May 30, 2015

To the deans, the faculty and staff, the family and friends of the graduates, and, of course, the Class of 2015: Congratulations!

Before we get too far along here, I need to be honest with you. This is not a typical commencement address. Far from it. Just look around.

At organizations large and small, at established corporations and exciting startups, at consulting firms and civil-society organizations, you already have blazed the trail toward a more sustainable world.

Now, not to make this about me, but for yours truly, this presents something of a challenge. You see, this podium is definitely not a platform for some wise old man to offer advice to the young and energetic leaders of tomorrow.

First of all, I'm not that old. But second, you are leaders today.

Usually, when I'm asked to talk about sustainable businesses, I tell people what they are. But you already know that. I usually explain why sustainability is important. But you already know that, too. And I usually share some perspective on how organizations and institutions can make more sustainable choices. But as seasoned practitioners, on the front lines of business-sustainability challenges, you know this work better than I do.

So in light of all this, I hope you'll forgive me for eschewing the formula of tradition and, instead, engaging in a conversation about the bridge between where we are and where we need to be, because while the work never stops being rewarding, it never starts getting easier. And, more than that, we're dealing with a complex, shifting set of issues—all emerging from, and evolving in dialogue with, an underlying crisis of inequality.

For my part, I believe that inequality—in all of its forms—is the greatest threat that our society faces. We see it in our economy, in our culture, in our politics and participation. And the level at which we see it is wholly unjust, to say nothing of unsustainable.

Last fall, at the Ford Foundation, we began a conversation about exactly these issues. We spoke with experts from around the world. And we asked the question: How can we make capitalism work *for good*?

In other words, we asked, where markets lead, can justice follow? And the answer, simply put, is three words: It can, if.

It can, if our businesses strive to optimize all kinds of value—social, environmental, cultural—not just to maximize shareholder value. It can, if we invest based not only on short-term gain, but also on long-term good. It can, if we learn to resist the impulse to define every element of our lives in relation to capital, if we stop elevating market-oriented thinking above all other kinds and categories of human understanding. It can, if we think about markets and human dignity not as competing priorities, but as complementary ones.

Take a not-so-old example from when I was standing in your shoes and not far removed from sitting in your seats. Between my stints in global finance and global philanthropy, I worked with a community development corporation in Harlem. In those days, many of the so-called advocates and experts—people I respected and admired—would speculate about the concerns of the community without ever so much as visiting with local residents. These outsiders had all the best intentions.

And yet, they tried to impose social change on the neighborhood, without regard to the people in the neighborhood. This was the textbook example of what my friend the eminent scholar William Easterly calls "the tyranny of experts." And the tragic irony, of course, is that if these experts had listened, not lectured, they might have learned that the biggest issue on people's minds was not the lack of some complicated, rights-based "theory of change." It was the lack of a supermarket.

You see, the last supermarket had left the neighborhood some four decades earlier. And people in the community believed that they—citizens of the symbolic capital of the world's wealthiest nation—had a right to basic services like groceries. Not the craziest idea in the world.

Well, during the late 1990s, our community development corporation helped attract a full-service Pathmark store to Harlem. And when we did, we broke the bottleneck—in a way that no technocratic development plan ever could have.

By bringing in one business, we created an environment in which others soon followed. As businesses went in, people wanted to stay or move in, too. And thus, we set in motion a virtuous cycle—a new Harlem renaissance for the twenty-first century.

What did I learn from this experience? Something that's, in a word, disruptive. (As they say, when in San Francisco ...)

Too often—and this is the case everywhere—we retreat into our separate ideological corners.

On one side are those who are exclusively rights oriented. They believe that ordinary people deserve certain benefits and protections—to make the system equal and fair—and that businesses should adapt accordingly.

On the other side are thinkers and advocates who believe that the only way to achieve inclusive, fair development is through market-based approaches that allow the invisible hand to sort everything out. In their view, economic growth is the solution to every problem.

But the truth is, after decades of experimentation, we know that each of these two arguments has merit. Each camp has the data and metrics to affirm the rightness—and righteousness—of their cause.

And so, today, more than ever before, it is incumbent upon each of us to find ways to draw on the new ideas and best practices of both community-oriented and market-based approaches—not either one or the other.

Because it hurts us to privilege one over the other. It's a form of intellectual inequality, which perpetuates actual inequality.

Put slightly differently, if capitalism can be a force for good, why not harness it? And if doing good can help businesses do well, why not encourage it?

We need to create a new paradigm that embraces each—simultaneously. We need to build bridges of understanding. After all, more often than not, we share the same objectives.

I saw this same dynamic play out again, more recently, in one of the great turnaround stories of our time, in Detroit, Michigan. The Motor City. The Arsenal of Democracy. The D.

I'm sure you all know something about Detroit and its unprecedented bankruptcy. Well, my colleagues and I were proud to join a collaborative effort that helped the city navigate this crisis—while balancing the demands of the market with the dignity of the community.

As you'll recall, there were a number of differing, sometimes opposing, positions on what to do in Detroit. To oversimplify: On one end of the spectrum, we saw billionaires waiting to strip down the Detroit Institute of Arts—the second-largest city-owned museum in the United States—and then sell off its masterpieces. They saw the bankruptcy as a liabilities-and-assets issue. The city had too many liabilities, and they were looking to sell off assets.

On the other end of the spectrum, plenty of people ignored the economic realities entirely. They believed, and rightly so, that citizens who had spent their lives working for the city should receive the pensions that they had earned. Never mind the endless red ink and bottomless unfunded deficits and debt.

So the question for Detroit—and all of us—was twofold: How do we save the city? And, more than that, how do we make sure that Detroit remains a city worth saving?

Well, the answer—much like in Harlem—was to jettison blind allegiance to only one way of thinking or another and, instead, to come together. To forge a grand bargain—in which everyone gave more than they wanted, but got what they needed. Like the Rolling Stones said.

This was, in short, "it can, if" thinking.

We can save Detroit, if we think about this not in one way, but in all ways, and with everyone in mind. We can save Detroit, if we come together. We can save Detroit, if we build—and become—bridges.

Visiting San Francisco, I'm struck—as I always am—by the majesty of the Golden Gate Bridge. And this beautiful bridge is the perfect emblem not just for Presidio but for everything I'm talking about. So, let me close by getting at this from a slightly different angle.

As many of you know, this year marks the fiftieth anniversary of the Civil Rights Movement's Bloody Sunday. Back in March, I was privileged to attend the deeply moving celebration and to spend time with one of my personal heroes, Congressman John Lewis, who marched in the vanguard of justice on the Edmund Pettus Bridge in 1965.

Fifty years ago, he was just a twenty-five-year-old kid, younger than all of you, I imagine. But John yearned for a better world. He was willing to put his life on the line for it. And he didn't just cross a bridge; he built one.

He—and a generation of heroes marching in unison—bridged the divide between an America that failed to fulfill its promise, and an America in which a Black, gay kid from a working-class, rural, Texas town could become the president of one of philanthropy's flagship institutions. His life's work made mine possible.

Colleagues and friends: As I said before, you, too, are crossing—and building—a bridge between the country we are and the country we ought to be. A bridge between the economic concerns that too often dominate our stale public discourse—and the social, cultural, and environmental concerns that comprise a new constellation of business imperatives in the twenty-first century. A bridge between the status quo and a new paradigm.

And bridges are what we need—now more than ever.

As Dr. Martin Luther King Jr. admonished, "One of the great tragedies of life is that men seldom bridge"—bridge—"the gulf between practice and profession, between doing and saying."

So our challenge is how do we transcend these gulfs? How do we take your promising successes and turn them into best practices? How do we take what you have practiced here as students and bring it to the practices of your employers?

No matter what company you work for—or what calling you answer— you will have the opportunity, and the obligation, to be the bridge. And this will be ongoing. Because just like on the Golden Gate Bridge, the work never stops.

Ultimately, I have more faith than ever that our future is a sustainable one. Or maybe I should say, it can be, if.

And I'll give you forty reasons why: You.

Our future can be more sustainable if you build markets—literally and figuratively—and make sure they work for everyone.

It can be, if you make the small compromises that usher in big change. It can be, if you negotiate your own grand bargains, and build your own grand bridges. It can be, if—together—we commit ourselves to ensuring that social justice and economic growth are not mutually exclusive but mutually reinforcing and mutually beneficial.

Class of 2015: Today, you walk across a stage. Forever, you march in the vanguard of a powerful movement.

INTERNSHIPS ARE NOT
A PRIVILEGE

The New York Times
July 15, 2016

Talent is equally distributed, but opportunity is not. And while many Americans believe fervently and faithfully in expanding opportunity, America's internship-industrial complex does just the opposite.

As the summer internship season gets into full swing, consider how a plum internship may alter a young person's career trajectory. While some students take a summer job in food service to pay the bills, others can afford to accept unpaid jobs at high-profile organizations, setting them on a more lucrative path.

I remember my own paid internships with fondness and gratitude, especially my formative experience working for the Texas legislature. As a low-income kid from a small town who entered college without an extended network, my internships equipped me with the skills, confidence, and relationships to channel my potential into a rewarding career.

And whether it's an internship, college admission, or any of the many other factors that determine a successful life, leaders who say they want to address inequality actually—and often unconsciously—reinforce the dynamics that create inequality in their own lives.

Even when financial considerations are no object, networking—the role of parents and others in helping young people score internships—disadvantages students from places that are underrepresented in positions of leadership.

We often hear that success is all about the people you know—as if it's just a matter of equal-opportunity relationship building. We rarely talk about *how* one knows them or about the privilege that has become a prerequisite to knowing the right people. I sometimes get calls and emails from friends seeking help in landing internships for their children. I understand what they're doing; this is part of being a parent. Still, it's a reminder that America's current internship system, in which contacts and money matter more than talent, contributes to an economy in which access and opportunity go to the people who already have the most of both.

The stakes of America's broken internship system are high. As report after report reminds us, this generation of students faces significantly worse job prospects than its predecessors. Without the short-term opportunities to help them learn, grow, connect with mentors, and begin climbing the earnings curve, many promising young people with limited means are denied the chance to rise as high as their talent will take them.

The result is not limited to the labor market. The broader implication is privilege multiplied by privilege, a compounding effect prejudiced against students who come from working-class or lower-income circumstances. By shutting out these students from entry-level experiences in certain fields, entire sectors engineer long-term deficits of much-needed talent and perspective. In other words, we're all paying the price for unpaid internships.

Fortunately, there is another option. Many organizations are beginning to pay interns. This is important because employers should not only compensate students for their time and contributions but also eliminate barriers that prevent low-income and underrepresented students from pursuing these opportunities.

While some nonprofits may be unable to pay their interns—even though they depend on their contributions of energy and know-how—the government can help turn unpaid positions into paid opportunities for those at risk of getting left behind.

A few years ago, researchers at the Economic Policy Institute and Demos proposed using existing student aid programs—including Federal Work-Study and the Free Application for Federal Student Aid—to facilitate internship grants for low-income students. Their proposed Student Opportunity Program would provide funding equal to $3,500 for three-month grants and $7,000 for six-month grants to students who couldn't afford to work without compensation.

At the same time, while compensating interns is necessary, it is not sufficient.

At the Ford Foundation, we take seriously the responsibility to ensure our paid internships help dismantle privilege. In addition to screening for strong academic performance and an interest in social-justice issues, our managers require that interns be recipients of needs-based financial aid. In this way, we offer sought-after positions to young people who otherwise might not have the chance to pursue them.

The right internship can put a young person onto a trajectory for success. This is precisely why those of us who oversee internship programs ought to make sure they provide a hand up to all people of promise, not merely a handout that, best intentions aside, accelerates a cycle of privilege and reward.

For countless Americans, me among them, internships have provided a foothold on the path to the American dream. Simply by making them more accessible to all, we can narrow the inequality gap while widening the circle of opportunity, long after the summer ends.

BUILDING INCLUSIVE ECONOMIES IN AN ERA OF INEQUALITY

Address to the Organization for Economic Cooperation and Development Summit on Inclusion, Innovation, and Resilience
Paris, France
November 22, 2016

We gather here at a time of uncertainty and upheaval. Political systems and institutions around the world are in flux, as movements claiming populism and predicated on fear gain traction in the United States and here in Europe. From Brexit to the election of Donald Trump to the rise of the National Front here in France, the world is in the midst of massive political change.

The cause of this disruption and, consequently, one of its effects is a corrosive and compounding inequality.

Not just economic inequality, of course. I mean inequality in all its forms. Inequality based on gender, race, and religion. Inequality of opportunity and education. Political, social, and cultural inequality. And even the rather unequal experience of globalization.

Some of the implications of inequality in our society are harder to measure, but easy to feel. Whether it's the lack of trust in our institutions or the anger and anxiety of so many who feel forgotten by the global economy or global elites.

I realize that many of these frustrations and fears can be tied back to one's economic experience. But all of these effects of inequality, all of these disadvantages, are compounding on each other, creating the conditions for inequality to persist.

That inequality can replicate itself makes it a particularly difficult problem. And I think inequality is the greatest threat to our society, in part because not only can it lead to violence and extremism at its worst, but by limiting opportunity and mobility, ultimately it generates hopelessness.

And that hopelessness makes it harder to believe that change is possible.

I choose to be hopeful. I choose to believe that change for the better is possible. But I also believe that change will require all of us to step up in a substantial way.

That's why I am here in Paris to join the mayor of Paris, Anne Hidalgo, in signing a call for global action for inclusive, innovative, and resilient cities. Because in cities around the world, we see how some people benefit more from urbanization than others, whether that's because of housing or transit or the existing infrastructure.

We also know how, in the course of their development, cities can be designed and planned in ways that promote inclusion or in other, more insidious ways that further and deepen inequality.

And this is true not just of our cities, but of all our larger systems and structures. Inequality happens because of how these are built—and that means we can thoughtfully, purposefully, deliberately build toward inclusion too.

But that won't be easy, and we need to be mindful of addressing the interlinking root causes—and not just the manifestations—of inequality.

As we think about cities, and celebrate the work of mayors on the front lines, we can also widen our focus. Because while it's true that two-thirds of the world's population will live in cities by 2050, we also know that the divide between urban and rural people has never been greater. We need to think about the ways we can link urban and rural communities, and think through how we engage with those people who live outside metropolitan areas.

Too often, we come to dialogues like this one with preconceived notions or an inherent sense of how the world works.

Too often, we surround ourselves in self-reinforcing bubbles that support our side of the argument and leave little room to consider those who disagree with us.

And too often these factors feed one another, further isolating us from the real problems—and the real pain—felt by people we do not see or cannot hear.

This is how pervasive inequality is. It affects even our most well-intentioned approaches and makes them less inclusive.

So as we continue to address the major challenges of this moment—be it inequality, climate change, or the refugee crisis—we need to get out of our comfort zones, listen to communities, and develop unlikely, unconventional partnerships. We need to tap into relationships and resources that we don't normally consider.

And in that spirit, I believe one of our most important opportunities to disrupt inequality is building an inclusive economy—a market that works better for more people.

To improve market outcomes, it will not be enough to rely solely on governments or philanthropy. We will need to meaningfully engage with the private sector, and find opportunities for increased partnership.

Already, there are so many places from which we can draw inspiration. In the United States, we've seen what happens when business, policy, and civil society come together to create innovative solutions. Meanwhile, in

Northern Europe, we've seen what's possible when we use a social-partners approach, and bring together industry and labor and government to negotiate major changes. And when we think about work being done across our global supply chains, we can't ignore the impact of an economy that doesn't just react to inequality and redistribute resources, but instead is built to improve outcomes and invest in people at every level.

Of course there is still more work to do. As technology becomes more important and our financial systems become more opaque, it will be up to us to push for competition policy, tax reform, and more transparency.

For our part, over the last few years, my colleagues and I at the Ford Foundation have been seeking out unusual allies and forming unprecedented alliances. And our work with the OECD to understand and address inequality is a testament to what is possible when we get out of our comfort zones and form these new relationships.

At the same time, we've seen a growing movement for inclusive capitalism and partnered with organizations that work at the intersection. For example, we've been involved with groups like JUST Capital and the B Team, which attempt to use the market as an engine of social change.

Additionally, we see the burgeoning field of impact investing as yet another way we can direct our resources toward justice. Since financial capital is the lifeblood of the global economy, we can wield capital in a way that benefits more people.

When capital is put to positive use, companies, governments, investors, and others will be able to drive scalable, sustainable impact that will create a more inclusive society. For instance, we can invest in the housing, transportation, and infrastructure solutions that will give more people access to cities and jobs and markets. And we can build these kinds of inclusive systems in other parts of our society and create a virtuous cycle.

We cannot deny that big business has a role in helping us solve our biggest problems. Whether we think about climate change or inequality—any of these massive problems—we must also remember that businesses have the ability to invest and innovate at scale.

And, given the political climate, it will increasingly be up to corporations to speak out and speak up—with their voices, their dollars, and their business—to defend civil society and the values we all hold dear.

Now, I will admit, we do not yet have a full playbook. We are still learning what kinds of policies and partnerships work, and how best to change outcomes.

But ultimately, I believe that inclusion—be it in our economies, our cities, or our communities—is not something we can just idealize or demand. It's something we must model.

We have to open ourselves up to more inclusive partnerships that bring together organizations from every sector, experts from every field, and voices from every community in which we work. In wealthier nations, we have to create the conditions that allow developing countries to do their part.

We have to adapt to new and changing conditions, such as our current refugee crises, and find ways to extend and expand our established ideas—like social protection—into previously uncharted territories. And it will take all of us working together to make this vision a reality.

While uncertainty in many countries threatens our pursuit of equity, it is imperative that during such tenuous times we recognize our shared responsibility, and double down on partnerships that build faith and demonstrate progress.

It was in similarly turbulent times that Dr. Martin Luther King Jr. looked out on the United States and the world and saw, as he put it, "a burning house."

And in response, he said, "we're just going to have to become the firemen."

We must all prepare to become firefighters for inclusion, firefighters for equality, and firefighters for justice.

Indeed, despite these uncertain times, I am certain—optimistic—that we can build an economy and a society that is more inclusive, more innovative, and more resilient.

ON THE FUTURE OF WORK(ERS)

October 1, 2018

At the beginning of this year, I shared my concern about the grave threat inequality poses to democratic values and institutions. Indeed, when individuals no longer feel they have equal access to opportunities or the power to control their own future, hopelessness begins to set in. This hopelessness breeds discouragement and despair, disillusionment with government, and disconnection from the institutions that bring order and meaning to our lives.

Worst of all, hopelessness can undercut individual potential and collective possibility. And nowhere does it loom larger than in the so-called fourth industrial revolution, which threatens to rob many people of their livelihoods, their dignity, their security, and their ambitions.

But we do not need to be driven by hopelessness or fear. Yes, there are daunting challenges on the horizon: Unprecedented technological change—including automation, artificial intelligence, and algorithmic decision-making—will impact workers around the world and transform labor markets with a speed we can scarcely imagine now. We know that different places and demographic groups will not all be affected in the same ways.

Technology is not the only factor, but the seemingly uncontrollable quality of it leaves us in a quandary with myriad questions.

ADDRESSING URGENT QUESTIONS

The questions on the so-called future of work are clear: How will technology affect jobs and the labor market? Which kinds of jobs will be replaced, what new jobs will be created, what is the quality of those jobs, and how will the relationship between employees and employers change? Which of these changes are around the corner, and which are years away? And how will we ensure that those who have been historically excluded—whether by race, gender, geography, or immigration status—are not further marginalized by these labor market shifts?

Too often, discussions about the future of work center on technology rather than on the people who will be affected by it. And they rarely acknowledge how the concentration of political and economic power shapes the way technology is developed and deployed. Instead, the entire discourse is led by champions of technology—management consultants, engineers, venture capitalists, and scientists—and tinged with inevitability, rather than being the product of thoughtful human decision-making, the consequences of which will affect countless lives.

These conversations are happening in the United States and across the globe, at truck stops and in breakrooms, in the headlines of publications, corporate boardrooms, and the hallways of political power, as so many of us try to understand our place in this future. But while lessons from history can serve as a guide, we remain unprepared to answer many of these questions, or to enter the uncharted territory ushered in by this era.

INEQUALITY AND THE FUTURE OF WORK

For us at the Ford Foundation, the question of work could not be more vital or more tied to our larger fight against inequality. Addressing this issue is central to our mission, and essential to the stability and success of our democracy as well.

And so, while more and more workers, families, and policymakers around the world are concerned about the future of work and workers, we at Ford remain focused on the underlying forces that are driving greater economic inequality. In the United States, for example, with stark and growing inequality, the very *idea* of the American dream is based on the opportunity to work and find a ramp onto the mobility escalator—to secure and steer your own life and the lives of your loved ones, to strive for more and hopefully succeed. And that dream is gravely threatened.

At the same time, it is clear that technology is not the only force or factor threatening the dignity and quality of work, or the security of workers. The US is an extreme case in point. Even during a time of tremendous corporate profits and unprecedented stock market success, we see the stubborn persistence of decades of wage stagnation. Furthermore, a number of factors make workers today more vulnerable and insecure: The continued weakening of workers' collective bargaining power, lack of access to paid leave, the ever-widening racial and gender wealth gap, the dilution of corporate responsibility to workers increasingly distanced from the bosses they benefit, the belief in shareholder primacy above all, and the decline of public investments in public goods and services (infrastructure, public education, etc.).

Meanwhile, campaign finance laws expand the influence and voice of corporations and the wealthy, while labor is more productive and therefore more profitable than ever—in part because of technology—but workers don't feel they are getting their fair share of the rewards. Unsurprisingly, there is a growing feeling that the economic system is rigged. All these things have eroded the place and power of working people in American society, and contributed to a belief that shared prosperity is an increasingly remote possibility.

FOCUSING ON WORKERS

At the Ford Foundation, we believe the people closest to a problem should be at the center of the solution. In this case, that means workers should have a seat at the table where the discussions and decisions are happening. Too often, employees are effectively disenfranchised in the decisions that affect their lives and disconnected from the executive suites where their livelihoods are determined. That is why we are supporting those helping to shape the future of work—and more to the point, the future of *workers*.

Despite today's focus on technology, the debate about the future of work originated with workers. The original policy discussion was initiated by labor organizers in the 1980s when concerns about technology's impact on unions and the labor market first emerged. In 1983, the AFL-CIO's Committee on the Evolution of Work even produced a report entitled, presciently, *The Future of Work*. Yet today, workers' voices seem to be the most neglected and forgotten, their power the most under siege. And so first and foremost, we need to ensure that workers remain the focus of all future of work efforts.

We will continue to invest in essential institutions and individuals that are advocating for workers today, and creating policies and systems to ensure workers have power in the workplace and the global economy tomorrow—organizations that include the National Domestic Workers Alliance, Jobs With Justice, the National Employment Law Project, and many others. As much if not more than artificial intelligence or automation, these twenty-first-century labor movements and the people they represent—the inheritors of a long tradition representing the dignity of working people—should be driving and informing the future of work.

BROADENING THE CONVERSATION

We aim to support a wider range of stakeholders who can shape the future of work, and find ways to include the worker perspective in their discussions, too. Right now, although leaders in many different sectors of the economy are discussing this issue, both globally and more locally, they rarely engage with each other. These siloed conversations raise narrow sets of issues and one-dimensional solutions like the proposed universal basic income—in effect, a way to replace the income from work on the premise that work will inevitably disappear—rather than adopting a more holistic view of what workers face.

Knowing these isolated conversations will be insufficient, we will support organizations that strive to change the prevailing narrative around the future of work, and seek to connect experts and elevate new ideas. In doing so, we aim to spark and strengthen platforms and processes that will give all stakeholders—especially workers—a voice in the public policies and business practices discussions that impact their lives. I will underline that investment practice is one very important element of that; investors can be part of moving business to the "high road" that is worker-friendly, as well as environment-friendly.

And as we support what I call the three Is—institutions, individuals, and ideas—fighting for workers, we will invest in solutions that address these concerns, from strengthening public policy to encouraging corporate practices and business models that improve families' economic security. Whether it's the innovative work of the Labor Innovation for the Twenty-First Century Fund or the analyses of the UC Berkeley Center for Labor Research and Education, we hope to build on the policy successes of the last decade and explore new protections that reflect the varied forms of employment today—from gigs to subcontracting to more traditional salaried employment—and fill in the gaps in the larger system.

Of course, we recognize that labor markets—and the issues affecting them—are global and deeply interconnected, and so we are considering how we can help craft a more equitable future of work with our partners around the world. In many parts of the Global South, precarity is the norm rather than the exception for workers, and what has been true for the vast and unregulated informal sector could threaten the promising middle-skill jobs—in manufacturing, medical diagnostics, coding, and other occupations—that emerging-market economies have created over the last generation.

Most importantly, we know that the resources of the Ford Foundation are very modest when compared to the scale of the problem, and partnership is the only way to forge lasting solutions. Indeed, to build the future we seek—full of dignity, opportunity, equality, security, and hope—we need business, labor, government, philanthropy, civil society, and academics around the world to join this effort.

THE STAKES ARE HIGH

It's not hard to imagine what might happen if we do nothing. In past industrial revolutions, vast new wealth was generated, but there was massive dislocation in the labor market. Many people lost their livelihoods. Countless families and communities were hurt and hollowed. But this time, the scale and pace of change are greater, as are people's expectations of economic mobility. The implications are beyond anything we've experienced before. We can't afford decades of dislocation, unemployment, and downward mobility, or the political and social conflict that would ensue. Societies already plagued by inequality can't bear such levels of upheaval and tumult.

Let us remember that it is "we, the people" who ultimately determine the place and the impacts of technology in our society. As we press ahead into this new era, we look forward to funding leaders and organizations who are dedicated to protecting the dignity of work and ensuring that technology improves workers' lives. Together, we can advance the cause of justice by ensuring it for workers—now and into the future.

THE VALUE OF WHAT MATTERS

Address to the IE University, Madrid, Class of 2019
Madrid, Spain
July 19, 2019

I do not need to tell you, you graduate at a moment when our planet faces two interconnected crises. Crises that affect us all.

First, there's inequality.

Income inequality continues to increase, widening the gaps between the richest and the rest of us. Right now, eight families have as much wealth as a full half of the world's population. And this does not even begin to capture the other forms of inequality that keep so many people from rising. Inequalities experienced based on gender, based on race, based on sexual orientation, based on the disabilities a person lives with. The list goes on and on.

The second crisis is climate change.

The United Nations has recently warned us that we have only twelve years to make drastic changes to the way our governments and companies and society operate. Let me say that again: *Twelve years.*

If we do nothing, or only take small steps, we will not be able to slow the effects of extreme heat, drought, and floods—and all of their consequences, from food shortages to refugee crises. And it will not surprise you that climate change has and will continue to affect the most vulnerable in our society.

Whether we're talking about rising inequality, or rising temperatures and sea levels, it's clear that our society needs to change. And that change will need to come from all sectors of our society—from governments, from nonprofits and philanthropy and civil society—but especially from our economic system.

Both of these crises have been aggravated by capitalism—irresponsible capitalism that prioritizes short-term gains over long-term value. And because of these two problems coming to a head, capitalism is at a tipping point.

Right now, businesses and their leaders can choose to continue contributing to the problem, or start building the solution. And I'm not the only one who thinks this. According to the most recent Edelman Trust Barometer, 76 percent of people say, "CEOs should take the lead on creating needed change."

Graduates, while I know that you are not CEOs yet, as rising leaders of the global business community, I believe you, too, can—and must—help advance this needed change. And today, as you prepare to write the exciting next chapter of your careers, I'd like to talk about how we can advance such change.

If we are going to change the world of business, we need to change how businesses—and business leaders—approach the world. We have to examine our current systems and reconsider how they work on behalf of all people. In particular, I believe there are three things that all twenty-first-century business leaders will need to do: First, build long-term value. Second, recognize all of our stakeholders. And third, measure our social impact.

And I want to talk about each of these for just a moment.

First, we need our business leaders to stop thinking in terms of short-term gain and start thinking about building long-term value.

This is the reason you're here at IE. With every class you took, and every lesson you learned, you have invested in the long-term value of your skills and your career. And companies need to do the same. They need to look past quarterly returns and see the bigger picture.

Could you imagine if in three months, your supervisor asked: I know you earned a degree last quarter, but how many degrees have you earned this quarter?

Of course not.

But this is how too many managers, investors, and market analysts have come to view business performance and success. And this short-term mindset doesn't merely prioritize shareholder value. It also devalues the investments we make in our future.

The future of our employees. Of our communities. Of our organizations. And of our planet.

And our businesses too. Companies that focus on long-term value outperform. In the words of a classic text, those companies are built to last—to contribute and innovate for the long haul.

So, first, we have to start valuing the impact our choices and investments have over the long-term. And to do that, we need to understand who our investments affect.

That's why, second, we need to recognize all of the stakeholders in our work—not just the shareholders.

We know that every action we take—or an organization takes—affects countless people. This is particularly true in our interconnected world and global economy.

While trust in government institutions has declined, and while some seek to close off connections and relationships—to build walls instead of bridges—many of the companies you will work in cannot afford to do that.

International corporations operate across borders and continents, defining how billions of people live and work. And the best way to recognize stakeholders, and address the problems they see, is to listen to them. To lift up their experiences of the world. Give them a seat at the table and a role in the decision-making process that affects their lives.

To that end, there is a powerful principle I learned from the disability justice movement, one that seems to be the best guidance for how we can be more inclusive of stakeholders outside a boardroom or an earnings call.

The principle is simple: "Nothing about us without us."

And for businesses, the implications are clear: No decisions about workers without consulting those workers. No policies that impact a local community without listening to the local community—whether here in Spain or anywhere else across the globe. No actions that impact our environment without considering how it affects the planet and people who share and depend on it.

And even if you are not in the most senior positions just yet, as an employee you can ask for—and even demand—the kinds of shifts in perspective we need.

And finally, we need to start looking at the bigger picture, beyond profit, and measure other kinds of value.

And this doesn't only apply to businesses. As students, you have a clear analogy for measuring different kinds of value.

In educational settings, the way we typically measure success comes down to grade points or class rankings—the marks you get on exams or other forms of evaluation. Here at IE, when you finish a class, if you did well, you might get honors, or excellence. If you didn't do as well, you might get a pass, or even a fail.

Of course, these academic assessments and achievements are important. These measurements are necessary. But there is so much more that goes into your education that does not make it onto your transcript.

There are other measures of success that will serve you in your life and career, that contribute to your overall excellence as a person: Did you grow in your understanding of the world? Did you experience the city where you lived, take in its art and culture and community? Did you contribute to that community? Did you build relationships and friendships with your classmates and faculty? Did you come to understand experiences different from your own and expand your perspective?

In the same way that we do not expect universities to do away with academic assessment altogether, we cannot expect that businesses will ever stop caring about financial performance.

And they shouldn't. That kind of information is still important. It's part of the scorecard that matters—but only a part.

We can expand the assessment of businesses to other kinds of value, and we have ways to measure it. We can ask: What contributions does this business make to the places it operates? What investments have you made for the long-term health of this community? How many workers escaped poverty or attained a middle-class income in your supply chain or among your employees? In other words, are people and the planet better off because you were around?

If we can get comfortable with those indicators of value, we will see lasting, tangible benefits for the world around us.

Class of 2019: Even though I am the president of a philanthropic foundation, what I am suggesting is not about philanthropy. It's not giving something away.

It's taking the larger, more inclusive view of the very purpose of business and its relationship to society. It's about better business strategy—and better leadership.

Most importantly, we need a strategy that transforms our economy and society. That lifts up all stakeholders and communities. That encourages responsible, sustainable, shared success. Not just today, but long into the future.

Fortunately, there are already companies around the world starting to lead this change—from Chobani to Costco, Natura and Nestlé, Patagonia and Unilever.

And beyond individual organizations, there are global movements pushing for a more inclusive capitalism. Just look to the rise of benefit corporations and impact investing, or the recent calls of chief executives for corporate purpose and long-term value.

As graduates of this extraordinary institution, you are prepared to take the progress happening right now and spread it far and wide.

You value the very kind of economic and social innovation that will be necessary if we are going to make these drastic changes before time runs out. You understand the need for humanity—not just as part of the business education, but as core business practice. And you have the global vision necessary to inspire global action and build lasting global relationships. Indeed, you've already created a diverse and connected global community right here at IE.

That's why, despite the enormous challenges we face, I remain optimistic—radically optimistic—because I know that your energy and intelligence, your creativity and drive, your purpose and passion will help push every organization you work for closer to justice.

So, I urge you to be the leaders we need. I urge you to keep building long-term value—for yourself and for others. Keep listening to all your stakeholders, and including them as you make decisions. Keep valuing what truly matters.

Thanks to you, and your leadership, I know we will be prepared to take on the challenges ahead, and build a better future.

HOW TO SAVE CAPITALISM FROM ITSELF

Fast Company
October 17, 2019

Capitalism is in crisis. The United States and our democratic values, discourse, and institutions are suffering from unprecedented levels of inequality.

Today, the three richest Americans collectively own about as much wealth as the bottom half of the population combined. Worse, extreme levels of economic inequity are only one of the many forms of inequality that plague our nation. We also face rampant discrimination based on race, gender, sexual orientation, ethnicity, religion, and ability. Looming over all of this is the threat of a global environmental catastrophe, which will make every one of these disparities more extreme through droughts, food shortages, and refugee crises.

When I was a child, I had the distinct sense that America was rooting for my success. Despite living in a small, rural town in East Texas—and despite the prejudices I faced growing up Black and gay in the South—I experienced the benefits of individuals and institutions working in concert to cheer me on. Time and again, I felt the wind at my back. But as I reflect on our system today, I find myself wondering and worrying: Do today's underprivileged children feel optimistic? How could they?

Clearly, we the people cannot wait for the next election to address the crisis of capitalism. And thankfully, we haven't been waiting, because we know what's possible when we reclaim the purpose of business and allow the benefits of capitalism to reach all corners of our country and beyond.

Today, a growing number of leaders in the business and social sectors are finding ways to make our capitalist system fairer. They recognize that if we create the context and conditions for an inclusive and just economy, the more we can use capitalism's undeniable productive power to unlock better ideas and outcomes for humankind.

Early positive signs of that recognition came in late summer, when a group of 181 CEOs from the Business Roundtable announced that they had redefined the purpose of a corporation. These CEOs committed to "lead[ing] their companies for the benefit of all stakeholders—customers, employees, suppliers, communities, and shareholders." The idea is simple: Everyone affected by the policies and practices of a firm should have a voice in shaping them.

This is the value reset that many of us have been clamoring for, a shift from late-twentieth-century capitalism run amok to a more equitable twenty-first-century capitalism.

Moving to stakeholder capitalism is not only a matter of doing the right thing, economists such as Harvard University's Oliver Hart and the University of Chicago's Luigi Zingales argue. In many cases, it's also economically more efficient—which will in turn help everyone's bottom line. It's less expensive to not pollute the environment than it is to clean up pollution. It's less costly to not sell addictive opioids than it is to provide mental and physical care for those who become addicted. By considering the perspectives of all the stakeholders involved, we can avoid cases like these where everyone involved ends up suffering.

The Business Roundtable's statement is only meaningful if its signatories follow it up with real commitments and actions. Now that these businesses have declared their values, it's time for them—and everyone else, from new business-school graduates to longtime CEOs, from advisory nonprofits to lobbies for corporate governance—to turn those values into action.

This starts by putting more and different stakeholders into positions of power. We can look to Germany, for example, where codetermination has been the law of the land since 1976: Large corporations there have to allow half of their supervisory boards of directors to be elected by workers. This rule hasn't slowed the country's economy. In fact, Germany's annualized growth in real per capita gross domestic product has been faster than ours since then. Plus, they have less income inequality and higher life expectancies. It's little wonder that here in the United States, workers have been pushing to increase the minimum wage (which a full two-thirds of Americans support raising to $15 an hour, according to the Pew Research Center) and demanding better working conditions.

American democratic capitalism once worked in a similar way. My own grandfather, with just a third-grade education, served as a porter in an oil company for nearly forty years. Because the company managed a profit-sharing plan for every employee, my grandfather was able to retire with financial security.

The most recent numbers suggest, however, that a mere 16 percent of today's Fortune 500 companies offer a traditional pension to new employees. Too many corporations are selling their workers short. While Americans are now working harder and more efficiently than ever, wage growth lags far behind that increase in productivity. Simply put, Americans are working more—and better—for less.

Together, we can—and must—reverse these trends. One of the companies highlighted in this issue, Patagonia, offers an example for how we might do so, with its exemplary family leave policy. For more than three decades, the company has provided high-quality, on-site childcare that allows parents to take lunches and breaks with their children. It offers sixteen weeks of fully paid maternity leave (and twelve weeks of fully paid leave for fathers and adoptive mothers) and nanny services for when employees need to travel, among other policies. The results are quite clear: Over the past five years, 90 percent of women at Patagonia who took maternity leave returned to work. That retention rate is something every company should strive for.

To reach goals like these, companies need to start keeping track of them. After all, the best way to ensure that promises come paired with progress is to measure and monitor. Traditionally, though, measuring something like social impact has been a challenge. Thanks to a constellation of leading institutions, however, these measurements are now far more precise.

The Sustainability Accounting Standards Board, an independent council, has worked to standardize corporate reporting of material nonfinancial data in areas such as employment, environmental sustainability, and governance. IRIS (Impact Reporting and Investment Standards), an initiative of the Global Impact Investing Network, offers a catalog of accepted performance metrics that helps guide investors who want to consider the social and environmental impact of their holdings. And the Global Impact Investing Ratings System (GIIRS) rates companies and funds based on their environmental and social impact, in a manner similar to Standard & Poor's credit-risk ratings. In short, companies can now measure social performance right alongside financial progress—and the next step is to streamline all of these different measurement systems so that we have clear, accountable, and universal metrics for assessing social value.

Of course, in a broader sense, we must replace the tyranny of quarterly financial reporting with a commitment to longer-term planning and sustainability. Larry Fink, chairman and CEO of BlackRock, the world's largest asset manager, has written passionately about this issue, having declared that the companies in which BlackRock invests must publicly delineate their "strategic framework for long-term value creation." As with the Business Roundtable, I hope that BlackRock's strong words will be met with equally strong action.

Fink's bold declaration is sound advice outside the world of finance, too. Across both the public and private sectors, we need to start thinking more about long-term value. This means, for example, thinking about the future of workers in an era of automation; after all, America needs workers to have a sustainable future so they can buy the products that these companies are making, an idea pioneered by Henry Ford, whose family established the foundation that I am privileged to lead.

In that position, it has become increasingly clear to me that solving today's challenges requires unprecedented collaboration between business and philanthropy, private and public sectors. For our part, the Ford Foundation is working to reimagine the philanthropic model—to shift our work, and our sector's work, further along the spectrum of generosity to justice. The idea is to address directly more of the root causes of injustice, rather than just addressing the symptoms of those problems with charity. The deeper we have dug into this work, the more we have discovered how interconnected business and philanthropy truly are, which is why it's so important that we work together to produce a more inclusive capitalism.

Capitalism only works if it works for everyone, which makes it our obligation to push it to be better.

The imperative of the twenty-first century is to build a new economy that recognizes the role of business and corporations in creating value in ways that better benefit society. We owe it to the next generation—to ensure that they have just as many reasons to be optimistic about their future as I did.

ARE YOU WILLING TO GIVE UP YOUR PRIVILEGE?

The New York Times
June 25, 2020

I have lived on both sides of American inequality. I began life in the bottom 1 percent but found my way to the top. And I know, all too personally, that the distance between the two never has been greater.

Last winter, at a black-tie gala—the kind of event where guests pay $100,000 for a table—I joined some of New York's wealthiest philanthropists in an opulently decorated ballroom. I had the ominous sense that we were eating lobster on the Titanic.

That evening, a billionaire who made his money in private equity delivered a soliloquy to me about America's dazzling economic growth and record low unemployment among African-Americans in particular. I reminded him that many of these jobs are low-wage and dead-end, and that the proliferation of these very jobs is one reason that inequality is growing worse. He simply looked past me, over my shoulder.

No chief executive, investor, or rich person wakes up in the morning, looks in the mirror, and says, "Today, I want to go out and create more inequality in America." And yet, all too often, that is exactly what happens.

Even before the coronavirus, before the lockdowns, and before the murder of George Floyd—during the longest sustained economic expansion in American history—income inequality in America had reached staggering levels. Social mobility, the ability for a person to climb from poverty to security as I did, had all but disappeared.

This contributes to a hopelessness and cynicism that undermines our shared ideals and institutions, pits us against one another, and drives communities further apart. That's why I am worried about our democracy, deeply and for the first time in my life.

I still believe in the American idea and in the values to which we have always aspired. Our nation's generosity of spirit made my life's journey possible. It was expressed through the public schools I attended, and government programs like Head Start and Pell grants that helped me, along with private philanthropy. Without them, I might have been ensnared in poverty or a structurally racist policing and criminal-justice system.

So I feel a profound obligation to state what has become clearer every day: If we are to keep the American dream alive, our democratic values flourishing, and our market system strong, then we must redesign and rebuild the engine that drives them.

Inequality in America was not born of the market's invisible hand. It was not some unavoidable destiny. It was created by the hands and sustained effort of people who engineered benefits for themselves to the detriment of everyone else. American inequality was decades in the making, one expensive lobbyist and policy change at a time. It will take a concerted effort to reverse all of this and to remake America in the process.

In recent weeks, I have been invited to join dozens of conversations with many well-intentioned chief executives and generous philanthropists to talk about what they should be doing during an upheaval that feels like 1918, 1932, and 1968 all at once. The irony is not lost on me: Many of those who are eagerly extending Zoom invitations are complicit in a system that desperately needs changing.

I do see progress. I see business leaders like Marc Benioff, Ursula Burns, Ray Dalio, Paul Polman, and others acknowledge that we conduct our daily work in a system built on unfair incentives. This system puts the interests of capital over labor, while it compounds privilege at the expense of opportunity.

The boardroom elite are beginning to recognize that these unfairly structured incentives have grossly distorted our economy. I see an evolving understanding that our twisted economy is an existential threat that has pushed our republic to a breaking point.

This awareness is necessary. But it is not sufficient.

The old playbook—giving back through philanthropy as a way of ameliorating the effects of inequality—cannot heal what ails our nation. It cannot address the root causes of this inequality—what the Rev. Dr. Martin Luther King Jr. called "the circumstances of economic injustice which make philanthropy necessary."

Instead, those of us with power and privilege must grapple with a more profound question: What are we willing to give up?

If we, the beneficiaries of a system that perpetuates inequality, are trying to reform this system that favors us, we will have to give up something. Here are a few of the special privileges and benefits we should be willing to surrender: The intricate web of tax policies that bolster our wealth; the entrenched system in American colleges of legacy admissions, which gives a leg up to our children; and above all, the expectation that, because of our money, we are entitled to a place at the front of the line.

I spent the first part of my career on Wall Street, and I believe that capitalism is the best means of organizing an economy. But capitalism must be reformed if we are to save our democracy.

This will require rejecting Milton Friedman's outmoded ideology: The dogma that a company must put shareholder value above all other objectives. It will require that corporations operate, in the words of the Business

Roundtable, "for the benefit of *all* stakeholders—customers, employees, suppliers, communities and shareholders."

Reforming capitalism also requires policymakers to transform a financial system that favors short-term returns, gives companies incentives to take on huge amounts of debt, and protects the special tax treatment for carried interest, a gift for private equity.

We must further ask: How can we create new policies that advance long-term, sustainable investment? How do we encourage investment in people and their skills, not just in automation and robotics? What does it mean to write a tax code that reduces inequality?

Too often, public policy does just the opposite: In 1982, a Securities and Exchange Commission rule allowed corporations to repurchase their stock. This created an environment in which companies accelerated their use of stock options and equity as forms of executive compensation, especially after the 2008 financial crisis. This has encouraged companies to increase share prices, at the expense of wages and benefits for workers, and created perverse incentives for companies to authorize buybacks. In 2018 alone, American companies spent more than $1 trillion repurchasing their own stock.

Our economy is unbalanced because *conscious* choices, in the aggregate, amount to a *conscienceless* capitalism. These choices erode democracy and foment distrust. We, the people, can make different choices. And we, the wealthy and privileged, should lean in to our discomfort.

This is the most pressing work of our time, and it will be difficult. Our present is deeply rooted in historical inequalities that must methodically be rectified.

But difficulty is not an excuse to allow American capitalism to grow more distorted, corrupt, and unjust. It does not relieve us of our duty to strengthen and improve a system that, if rebalanced, could once again make America a beacon for upward mobility.

Without hope, American dreams deferred or denied will continue, as the poet Langston Hughes wrote, to explode. With hope, and through it, we can reimagine the dream and invite many millions more to share in its promise.

IN RESPONSE
50 YEARS LATER:
THE "SUBVERSIVE
DOCTRINE" OF
MILTON FRIEDMAN

As Submitted
The New York Times
September 14, 2020

The doctrine of "social responsibility" taken seriously would extend the scope of the political mechanism to every human activity. It does not differ in philosophy from the most explicitly collectivist doctrine. It differs only by professing to believe that collectivist ends can be attained without collectivist means. That is why, in my book "Capitalism and Freedom," I have called it a "fundamentally subversive doctrine" in a free society, and have said that in such a society, "there is one and only one social responsibility of business—to use its resources and engage in activities designed to increase its profits so long as it stays within the rules of the game, which is to say, engages in open and free competition without deception or fraud."

—Milton Friedman,
"The Social Responsibility of
Business Is to Increase Its Profits"
The New York Times
September 13, 1970

In propaganda, an accusation often betrays an admission. This kind of projection was especially pronounced in Milton Friedman's pernicious attack on "social responsibility." Indeed, the most "subversive doctrine" was—and remains—Friedman's own.

Rewind the clock by a half century, and we see American society amidst the longest, most widely shared period of prosperity in history. This was the age of a rising tide and rising boats—of a vibrant, dynamic middle class on the make and on the move.

With growth came meaningful if uneven progress for civil rights, women's rights, and social justice—advances in nearly every facet of American life. And crucial to these advances was a capable, competent national government that protected the public interest, capitalized through sufficient tax revenue to fund the public infrastructure and assets that made America the envy of the world.

Then came Friedman and his ideology distilled for a broad audience in *The New York Times*: The insidious contention that businesses best serve society by solely serving their shareholders—which informed decades of destructive public policy that distorted our political economy.

Friedman's doctrine assailed business leaders like David Rockefeller of Chase Manhattan, Tom Watson of IBM, and Pete Peterson of Bell & Howell—hardly Bolsheviks—who understood the corporation to be an engine for innovation and profit but also a social actor. He absolved the firm of its responsibility to serve as a force for racial integration and inclusion. His doctrine infected our business schools, producing generations of corporate leaders dedicated to the sacred primacy of shareholder value over all other values.

In this way, Friedman's thinking became theology—the intellectual scaffolding that allowed its disciples to justify decades of greed-is-good excess and exploitation. Emboldened by his words, they promoted deregulation of markets, a brand of amoral corporation, and a conscienceless form of capitalism.

Gone were the days when someone like my semiliterate grandfather, with only a third-grade education, could work as a porter and benefit from a profit-sharing plan provided by a company that dignified his work. In their place were new conditions in which our social contract frayed, and our economy tilted wildly out of balance—fomenting the vast, unsustainable inequalities that plague America today.

I am a proud capitalist. I believe in the market's unique power to lift lives and livelihoods, especially when it's fair and inclusive. After all, Adam Smith himself admonished that the "invisible hand" could not be blind to the condition of society—that "no society can surely be flourishing and happy, of which the far greater part of the members are poor and miserable."

Ultimately, Friedman ignored that in a democratic-capitalist society, democracy must come first, or the whole enterprise collapses. "We, the people" grant businesses their license to operate—which they, in turn, must earn and renew. And for those who abuse their license, be warned: The people can take it away.

SHARED COMPANY OWNERSHIP MAY BE THE MISSING PATH TO THE AMERICAN DREAM

with Pete Stavros
Fortune
August 11, 2022

The American dream—that foundational promise of economic opportunity, social mobility, and lasting security—looms large in our life stories. While access to this promise has been granted slowly and unevenly, at its best, our nation has been a beacon of democracy and free enterprise.

Today, corporations remain too fixated on the latter at the expense of the former—but we believe democracy and free enterprise must go hand in hand. In a principled, democratic society, every worker should have the opportunity to participate fully in the economy. That means employers, large and small, must provide their workers with more paths to ownership.

We know the power of ownership firsthand. Darren's grandfather, a Black man born in the Jim Crow South, held only a third-grade education—but as a porter for a Texas oil company, he participated in a profit-sharing plan that dignified his work, sustained his family, and left him with enough stock to retire comfortably.

Pete's father operated a road grader for nearly five decades for a construction company outside of Chicago. Despite his long hours over many years, he never participated in the success of the company beyond an hourly wage. As a result, he never felt a sense of ownership or alignment, and enjoyed few options for mobility.

Today, millions of Americans feel the same way. Gone are the days when first-generation college graduates could see doors open to them that were closed to their parents. Instead, many Americans are now downwardly mobile.

Unlike previous generations, only half of American adults born in 1980 make as much as their parents did at the same age. Two in five Americans cannot afford a $400 emergency, let alone save enough for retirement. Gaps in knowledge widen the disparity: According to the Treasury Department, only one in three Americans is financially literate.

These trends—evaporating opportunities for access, growth, and prosperity—have dangerous implications not only for the economy but also for democracy. Our social contract is fraying—and we all have a vested interest in weaving it back together. Whether we work for an hourly wage, a salaried job, or own companies ourselves, one way we can do just that is by advocating for shared ownership plans.

What does this look like in action? Publicly traded pump manufacturer Ingersoll Rand introduced an incremental shared ownership plan for its sixteen thousand employees in 2020. Employees who have been with the company since 2017 have earned free equity grants equal to 100 percent of their annual income.

In return, the company has seen its turnover rates drop from 20 percent to below 3 percent—even amid the "Great Resignation." Employee engagement scores at the company skyrocketed from the 20th percentile to the 90th. The impact on corporate culture and performance should be self-evident but, to be clear, investors have also done extremely well.

Over time, staffing giant Insight Global has increased its employee ownership, and today every one of the company's 4,500 employees has a pathway to share ownership—starting with $5,000 grants with eligibility increasing as they spend more time with the company. It's had a considerable impact on their employee turnover and culture-building—with a decline in the employee turnover rate by more than 60 percent since 2017.

Likewise, material sciences company Hyperion Materials & Technologies granted all 2,000 of its employees ownership in 2019 alongside a robust internal employee engagement effort. They've seen profit margins increase by 57 percent along with a 72 percent increase in their employee engagement scores measured by Gallup.

These results—engaged, well-compensated workers, doing fair, dignified work at healthy companies able to support them—can be replicated across our economy. Broad-based employee ownership can help get us there.

This is a crucial opportunity for everyone to participate in meaningful wealth creation. To that end, we are proud to collaborate as partners on a new nonprofit called Ownership Works, which pushes for broader profit-sharing and a sustainable, inclusive economy.

This consortium of more than sixty (and growing) investors, pension funds, labor advocates, foundations, financial institutions, and professional services organizations controls or influences trillions of dollars of capital and millions of jobs. It can have a profound social impact.

By 2030, we aim to create hundreds of thousands of new employee-owners and generate over $20 billion in wealth for working families. We see potential to meaningfully exceed these figures.

We can—and must—do more. Like all symbiotic relationships, free enterprise and democracy need each other to thrive.

We urge all stakeholders to join us in the fight for an inclusive, democratic, and free enterprise—where all of us can find dignity and ownership in our labor. Only then can we fully restore our social contract—and rebuild an American dream that endures.

AI IS CHANGING EVERYTHING—AND WE NEED NEW GUARDRAILS

with Hemant Taneja
The Washington Post
March 28, 2023

The artificial intelligence revolution has arrived. One of us is a venture capitalist, the other a philanthropist, and we see leaders in every field placing bets, by the billions, on what comes next.

That makes this a perilous moment. Machine learning is poised to radically reshape the future of everything for good and for ill, much as the Internet did a generation ago.

And yet, the transformation underway likely will make the Internet look like a warm-up act.

AI has the capacity to scale and spread all our human failings—disregarding civil liberties and perpetuating the racism, caste, and inequality endemic to our society.

Machine learning mimics human learning, synthesizing data points and experiences to formulate conclusions. Along the way, these algorithms replicate human error and bias, often in ways not discernible until the consequences are before us: Intolerable cruelty, unjust arrests, and the loss of critical care for millions of Black people, to name a few.

AI trains on our own flawed human data sets—unrestrained by a moral compass, social pressure, or legal restrictions. Almost by definition, it ignores fundamental guardrails.

This is a profound test for everyone: The private sector, the public sector, and civil society.

Businesses that research and develop AI are sharing a powerful tool with a public that might not be ready to absorb or wield it responsibly. Governments are poorly equipped to regulate this technology in a way that safeguards the people who use it or those who might be dislocated by it. And neither group feels much urgency to understand or work with the other.

All of this has our alarm bells ringing.

The time has come for new rules and tools that provide greater transparency on both the data sets used to train AI systems and the values built into their decision-making calculus. We are also calling for more action to address the economic dislocation that will follow the rapid redefinition of work.

Software developers should commit to continuous monitoring through "algorithmic canaries"—models designed to spot malign content like fake news—and external, independent audits of their algorithms. We are heartened by OpenAI CEO Sam Altman's recent commitment to open the company's research to independent auditing—as well as his challenge to the industry to avoid a reckless race to release models as fast as possible without regard to safety processes.

Policymakers and regulators must catch up on protections for privacy, safety, and competition. More than half of American workers with AI-related PhDs work for a handful of big-name companies. So, our elected representatives should initiate a whole-of-government effort—across Congress, the Departments of Commerce and Labor, the FCC, and the SEC—to build a regulatory framework to match. This would require widely shared technical literacy and expertise—one reason that the Ford Foundation and others are supporting efforts to place technologists across offices on Capitol Hill, one element of the gathering movement for public-interest technology.

In addition to government oversight, the venture capital and start-up community must evolve—and quickly. Investors cannot count on others to allay unintended consequences. We must pursue intended consequences from the start, which means in-depth investigations, scenario planning, and boundary setting before investment. We must set responsible innovation guidelines, which will standardize how we unlock the possibilities and avoid the pitfalls of this transformational technology.

No one wants capitalism to destroy itself—which is why the private sector must broaden its definition of value to include the interests of all stakeholders, not just shareholders. By retethering wages to rising productivity, firms can ensure the dollars pouring into new technologies flow beyond the wealthy investor and founder class. They can revive models of equitable wealth creation, from employee ownership to profit sharing—beginning to reduce the concentration of wealth creation among a very small subset of our workforce.

We know that technology will uproot and upend. Manufacturing communities across the country, decimated by offshoring and automation, offer a stark reminder of the stakes. Every company that endeavors to use AI ought to build retraining capabilities for its people, especially given the massive labor shortages that businesses face in complex roles that need highly skilled workers.

Finally, business leaders must stop assuming that they can reap the profits of disruption and then repent through philanthropy. All too often, corporate leaders use the language of philanthropy; corporate social responsibility (CSR); and environment, social, and governance (ESG) to mitigate harm on the back end rather than designing with intentionality from the start.

Artificial intelligence isn't just another technological breakthrough. If we are to survive this test, everyone must do business differently than in the past.

PART VI

THE COVID-19 CRISIS: EXTRAORDINARY TIMES, EXTRAORDINARY MEASURES

We are experiencing the unprecedented. The world we knew before COVID-19 has been permanently upended. Our lives—our histories—are forever split in two: Before coronavirus and after… During the Great Depression, President Franklin Delano Roosevelt affirmed the need for relief, recovery, and reform—in that order. Today, we must follow these same steps—beyond reform to a broader, deeper reimagination of our society… We live in a culture that makes these things hard—but what makes doing them worthwhile and meaningful is the hope that doing them now will create a better tomorrow. And that hope is the oxygen that allows our movements and institutions and democracy to breathe free. Ultimately, we need hope—a hope born not from idealism or naivete, but from a stubborn, determined recognition of what we owe each other; that the actions we take today and every day will bring us closer to the future we seek. We need hope that united—on the other side—we will realize justice for all.

Extraordinary Times, Extraordinary Measures
June 11, 2020

A NOTE FROM HOME

March 20, 2020

Dear colleagues and friends:

During these strangest of days, one cannot help but feel disoriented.

Our circumstances—and the way we make sense of them—are evolving so rapidly that, even as I draft these lines, I cannot know which will hold true tomorrow or the day after, much less during the weeks and months ahead.

The strangeness takes many different forms. As I work from home—practicing the social distancing that the experts counsel—the speed of news, closures, and conference calls is juxtaposed with an unsettling quiet. No one is bustling around my home office the way they would the Ford Foundation corridors.

How can things be moving so fast and also so slowly?

And yet, I recognize that my lockdown in a Manhattan apartment, while hard for me to process, is certainly no hardship. Those of us who benefit from such privilege would be well served to remember this during the days and months ahead. Far too many are facing real hardships: Frontline health-care professionals, as well as retail, hotel, and restaurant workers, and others for whom survival depends on hourly and tipped wages.

No matter where we find ourselves, though, we share the anxiety that comes with staring straight into the unknown—even if we've already been living with some elements of this altered reality. In many ways, the COVID-19 crisis is an extreme extension of trends and feelings of uncertainty that have defined the past few years: The *unprecedented* has become the *ordinary*, in nearly every facet of life.

Despite all of this, or perhaps because of it, I have been reflecting on the timeless words of Dr. Martin Luther King Jr.: "We are caught in an inescapable network of mutuality, tied in a single garment of destiny. Whatever affects one directly, affects all indirectly."

As the pandemic and its consequences threaten lives and livelihoods, we see—yet again—just how inextricably our fates and fortunes are intertwined. We see how each of us is directly, and indirectly, responsible for those around us.

And even as this interdependence reveals certain vulnerabilities—this virus knows no borders—we must take heart. For, in these moments, our "inescapable network of mutuality" also serves a common good. It serves as a kind of social immune system.

With a crisis of this scale—given the volatility and velocity—we all wonder, what can I do? What can *we* do? And apart from washing our hands, avoiding crowds, working from home if we can, and supporting those who cannot—we must ask: *What can philanthropy do right now?*

If the specifics are still hard to grasp, the principles are clear. Now is the time for leadership and action—for common cause and common effort.

Already, many in our sector are joining together and delivering. Our colleagues at the Gates Foundation and the Rockefeller Foundation, for example, have long engaged in a worldwide effort to improve public-health systems. They—along with Bloomberg Philanthropies, the Chan Zuckerberg Initiative, the Wellcome Trust, and others—are now undertaking bold and ambitious initiatives in response to this pandemic.

In real time, philanthropy is mobilizing across the United States, with foundations and funders establishing more than twenty-five emergency response funds in a matter of days—including our friends and colleagues in Detroit, Chicago, San Francisco, and Seattle. I'm pleased that the Ford Foundation is part of a group of New York City–based foundations and businesses that have raised $75 million and counting for the COVID-19 Response & Impact Fund.

Meanwhile, the United Nations Foundation, the World Health Organization, and numerous international foundations have launched the Solidarity Response Fund to address COVID-19's spread in the Global South.

In all of these ways and more, philanthropy is stepping up and stepping in. And these examples represent but a small slice of the total philanthropy nationally being marshaled at the regional and local levels.

Meanwhile, as funders play a modest short-term role in ameliorating this crisis, our grantees are providing the pathways to long-term solutions with powerful policy ideas and innovation. Organizations like the National Domestic Workers Alliance, National Employment Law Project, Family Values @ Work consortium, and others are championing bold ideas—once considered marginal—like paid sick leave, increases to the minimum wage, and even cash transfers to low-income households. All of these policies are now under serious consideration by policymakers in Washington and state capitols as leaders look to help communities that will be disproportionately impacted by this crisis.

As funders, we must continue to provide support—general operating support—to fortify their organizations so they are prepared to work with the private sector and government over the long term.

Speaking of government, the current crisis has brought in sharp relief and made crystal clear the compounding, pernicious effects of the decades-long assault on competent, productive government: We are relearning, once again, that a sclerotic and eroded public sector is not a point of political pride but a matter of life and death for thousands. Now, more than ever, we see the necessity of a robust, capable, and coordinated federal government *and* thoughtful, inclusive, and trustworthy leadership.

No doubt, these are frightening times. And yet, from history, we can draw hope.

In the depths of the Great Depression, President Franklin Delano Roosevelt famously exhorted that "the only thing we have to fear is fear itself."

Today, of course, we do have much more to fear: The unknown. The COVID-19 virus already has taken thousands of lives around the globe and likely will take more. The markets are in freefall and economies are in turmoil, locally and globally. But even as the workings of the world slow down, we cannot be paralyzed. We cannot abide the anxiety or fear that keeps us from moving forward, and doing what must be done.

So, while the employees of most foundations today are working from home, we will not be sitting on the sidelines. None of us can. We need the same boldness and truth-telling and endurance for which President Roosevelt called, all those years ago.

We need caution and courage and calm.

And for all that remains uncertain—about the extent of this crisis and the ways that things may change—there is plenty we do know:

We know that facts matter—and that there is a difference between educating the public and stoking anxiety with hearsay and speculation. We must not succumb to fear and falsehood (especially online), and instead find ways to cope with our anxiety and console others. Above all, we must keep our heads and our cool.

We know that the devastating impacts of this crisis will be measured in cases and deaths, as well as the economic ripple effects for workers and their families. As with so many crises, inequality in the United States and around the world accelerates and intensifies these effects for untold millions.

To paraphrase the old line, when the privileged sneeze, the poor get pneumonia.

We know our systems—our health systems, and our economic and political systems—will need to be rebuilt and repaired in order to address all manner of inequalities, and in order to handle continued disruption and dislocation.

We know that as this pandemic continues to evolve, we will need to bend without breaking—to be nimble, and agile, and flexible as the times require.

We know we must not act as though we are headed "back" to some kind of "normal"—because we also know this will not be the last crisis. We ought to learn from this moment and prepare for the next.

And we cannot say it enough: We will get through this, even if it is difficult to remember at every moment of every day. We know we will.

We will get through this. And *we* will be the reason.

After all, our "inescapable network of mutuality" is more than a web that ties us together. It's the way we serve and give to and honor and love one another—especially in times of trial. If our destinies are bound together, let us wrap ourselves in this garment of care, and let it shield us from the storm.

Wishing you renewed *mutuality* and good health,

Darren

WHY FOUNDATIONS LIKE MINE NEED TO GIVE MORE TO STAVE OFF THE COLLAPSE OF VITAL NONPROFITS

The Chronicle of Philanthropy
June 8, 2020

During the coronavirus pandemic, government leaders and the news media have focused their attention on the economic struggles facing business. But America's nonprofits are in the gravest danger. Organizations that help feed the hungry, fight for social justice, tend to the sick, and enrich our lives through arts and education will be irreparably harmed without urgent action from government, business, and philanthropy.

An astonishing 75 percent of nonprofits surveyed by the Nonprofit Finance Fund do not have six months of cash reserves. In the wake of canceled fundraising events, postponed programs, and lost revenue, nonprofit leaders are taking drastic action to cut costs to save their organizations.

Furloughs, layoffs, and terminations are hitting nonprofits hard. One executive director called me recently in tears to share the news that she and her board had decided to close their doors. Many more are on the brink of doing the same.

If we fail to act, the economic toll will be devastating. Nonprofits employ more than 10 percent of the private workforce in the United States, some 12.3 million people at last count, according to the 2019 Nonprofit Employment Report from Johns Hopkins University.

In addition to economic harm, the loss of nonprofits would deprive all Americans of a platform we depend on to build a more vibrant and just nation. Throughout American history, social progress has been made possible by civil society—by people joining together to fight for the abolition of slavery, women's suffrage, and civil rights. As the United States faces the most profound racial-justice crisis since the Civil Rights Movement of the 1960s, the loss of these institutions would result in a retrenchment of our public life and a profound weakening of our democratic republic.

How, then, do we meet this challenge? During the Great Depression, President Franklin Delano Roosevelt affirmed the need for relief, recovery, and reform, in that order.

Governments need to take urgent action. More than four hundred nonprofits joined with the National Council of Nonprofits to write a letter outlining policies that governments need to enact to help save nonprofits, such as expanding grants and loans that keep staff employed and doors open.

Businesses, too, must deploy the myriad resources at their disposal, from charitable giving to consultation and technology. Corporate foundations give away billions each year in cash, products, and services. But we need companies to make new commitments that go above and beyond. Last year, 181 CEOs—members of the Business Roundtable—called for a broader, purpose-minded definition of the corporation. If each of their companies contributed another $5.5 million—a pittance compared with their profit pools—we could raise $1 billion for nonprofit relief and recovery.

Already, philanthropy has stepped up. In New York, a consortium of foundations and donors created a response fund that has raised more than $105 million in emergency support for human services and arts nonprofits. In Chicago, Seattle, Atlanta, and many other communities, similar emergency-response funds have been organized.

We must do more. Foundations like mine have often provided the financial oxygen and lifeline for nonprofits. Our ordinary practice is to annually pay out in the range of 5 percent of the value of our endowments, the legal minimum.

But this is no ordinary time. We cannot do the minimum when faced with the overwhelming threat to the survival of nonprofits and, by extension, our democracy. Foundations must use the full arsenal of tools and assets at our disposal, including our flexibility, ingenuity, and longevity. Imagine if each of our institutions distributed three or four extra pennies on the dollar. The impact would be significant.

Established by visionary industrialists—and endowed with vast resources and noble missions—America's first foundations afforded broad powers to future generations to rise to the problems of future eras. Today, our generation of foundation trustees and leaders must take extraordinary steps to carry out these missions in the face of an existential threat to our democracy.

Much like the proverbial stool, our society rests on three legs: Government, free enterprise, and civil society. To date, our collective actions toward relief and recovery have focused mostly on the first two, but insufficiently on the third.

Long before this crisis, the nineteenth-century observer Alexis de Tocqueville remarked on the splendor of American "associations," groups of people who joined together in common cause for a common good.

These "associations," small and large, have served as the heartbeat of democracy.

In the 185 years since de Tocqueville's words, American civil society has ushered in immeasurable national and global progress. But what we choose to do together and for one another is what makes us unique among nations. During the challenging days ahead, we need to once again meet the moment with common purpose and unified action to save America's vital nonprofits.

EXTRAORDINARY TIMES, EXTRAORDINARY MEASURES

June 11, 2020

We are experiencing the unprecedented. The world we knew before COVID-19 has been permanently upended. Our lives—our histories—are forever split in two: Before coronavirus and after.

Beyond overflowing hospitals and understocked grocery stores, our economies have fallen off a cliff. Today, a full quarter of American workers—more than forty million people—have filed for unemployment. Fewer than half of Black adults have a job. In a mere two months, Americans have lost twice the number of jobs as in the Great Recession.

And, during these last few weeks, one pandemic has collided with another, as tens of thousands of protesters take to the streets to demand justice for George Floyd's murder, for all the violence against Black people that has gone unfilmed, and for a history of white supremacy and racial terror that remains unreconciled.

But in this moment when we, the people, are demanding more action and in need of more support, the organizations on the front lines—championing essential workers, fighting for the rights of Black and other marginalized communities, and building the systems that will be central to an equitable recovery—face their own crisis. Indeed, the economic realities brought on by COVID-19 threaten the very survival of the people, organizations, and movements behind this crucial work.

CIVIL SOCIETY: NEEDED AND IN NEED

At another unprecedented moment, in the early days of our republic, the nineteenth-century French historian and political scientist Alexis de Tocqueville traveled across America and was taken by its "public spirit" of cooperation. He remarked on these American "associations": People who joined together in common cause for a common good, identifying an emerging civil society. This "autonomous area of liberty incorporating an organizational culture that builds both political and economic democracy"—America's unique third sector—has, in the 185 years since his writing, ushered in immeasurable national and global progress.

This third sector encompasses remarkable breadth, the wide array of organizations, institutions, and movements that educate, congregate, support, organize, and inspire—the organizations that stitch our nation together. Civil society is concert halls and civil rights advocacy, scholarship and prayer, food banks and fine arts programs, after-school programs and end-of-life care, local charity and global aid. And, of course, it includes the hundreds of organizations we support—like Color of Change, the Equal Justice Initiative, Black Youth Project 100, and the National Employment Law Project—whose work remains indispensable.

These small and not-so-small "associations" have served as the beating heart of our democracy. And they are in jeopardy, as I argued in *The Chronicle of Philanthropy* this week.

Because of COVID-19, the nonprofit sector faces overwhelming need paired with existential threat. According to the Nonprofit Finance Fund, three out of every four nonprofits do not have six months of cash in reserve. Many have less. Already, furloughs and layoffs are hitting nonprofits—hard.

Postponed fundraisers, canceled seasons, fewer grants from foundations anticipating decreased endowments, reduced corporate sponsorships and government contracts due to internal budget cuts—all of this puts the world's vital nonprofits at risk.

If we do nothing, the economic toll, alone, will be devastating.

According to the 2019 Nonprofit Employment Report from the Johns Hopkins Center for Civil Society Studies, nonprofits employ more than 10 percent of America's private workforce—some 12.3 million people at last count. These nonprofits, based on research from the Urban Institute, contribute an estimated $985 billion to the economy.

Of course, losing nonprofits would hurt more than our economy. Especially at this moment when we cannot physically be with each other, civil society—the spirit and sinew of our collective civic life—is vital.

And so, we cannot simply do more of the same. Extraordinary times call for extraordinary measures. Our challenge is not to save any particular organization; it is to save the soul of our democracy itself.

A ONCE-IN-A-CENTURY RESPONSE

During the Great Depression, President Franklin Delano Roosevelt affirmed the need for relief, recovery, and reform—in that order. Today, we must follow these same steps—beyond reform to a broader, deeper reimagination of our society.

Philanthropy has already stepped in to provide timely relief to the nonprofit sector. In New York, a consortium of foundations and funders, including the Ford Foundation, created the NYC COVID-19 Response & Impact Fund, which has raised more than $100 million to date. Hundreds of philanthropic institutions, nationally and globally, have also committed to more flexible funding to help their grantees navigate the unanticipated consequences of the pandemic.

Now, we must focus on recovery, so we can lay groundwork to reimagine what is to come.

Government ought to implement additional public policies that support civil society—including grants and loans that keep staff employed and doors open. More than two hundred nonprofits joined with the National Council of Nonprofits to author a letter outlining such policies.

Businesses, too, must deploy all of the resources at their disposal, from charitable giving to consultation and technology. Companies also need to protect their workers—especially low-wage workers and workers of color—to take pressure off the nonprofit safety net.

And nonprofits, themselves, will need courageous, creative leaders willing to face what lies ahead and reinvent their operating models and budgets to stay viable and thrive in a post-coronavirus world.

The Ford Foundation recognizes that this once-in-a-century crisis—and the overwhelming need to emerge from it with a more just and equitable society—requires a once-in-a-century response.

As foundations, our standard practice is to spend the 5 percent of our endowments each year as required by law to support the financial viability of the institution into the future. We will not spend down our assets but, as I've written previously, we cannot limit ourselves to this 5 percent. We must explore and expand new ways to deploy all of our assets—including the other 95 percent—in the fight for justice.

Given these intersecting, cascading crises, Ford's trustees and I have concluded that we cannot and will not merely pay out what we would in a normal year. We cannot and will not allow this economic crisis to decrease our grantmaking next year or going forward. We cannot do the minimum when faced with maximum threat.

If we fail to act, civil society will suffer irreparable damage—and so will the health and vitality of our most vulnerable communities, and the future of our democracy.

And so, today we're announcing that, for the first time in Ford's history, the board of trustees has authorized up to $1 billion—financed through the sale of bonds—to help stabilize and strengthen the nonprofit sector. This is only possible because of the board's unwavering, unstinting support, energy, and commitment, which serves as a source of inspiration to all of us at Ford that this is possible, and for that I want to express my deepest gratitude.

With this new source of funding, the foundation will make strategic investments in the individuals and organizations that are not just fighting against inequality and injustice but preparing to lead us through a post-coronavirus recovery.

A CALL TO UNLEASH EVERY RESOURCE

Historically, foundations have issued debt for building acquisition and construction projects—as we recently did to renovate our New York headquarters. Never has debt been used as a tool for expanding philanthropic grantmaking.

This changes now.

A number of US foundations—including the Doris Duke Charitable Foundation, W.K. Kellogg Foundation, John D. and Catherine T. MacArthur Foundation, and Andrew W. Mellon Foundation—have joined us and, collectively, our joint commitment to additional grantmaking will add more than $1.7 billion to the nonprofit sector. I'm enormously grateful to the presidents of those foundations who have my admiration and affection: Elizabeth Alexander, Ed Henry, John Palfrey, and La June Montgomery Tabron, who have dedicated countless hours to our collective action. They are the very best examples of foundation leaders with bold and ambitious visions for their organizations.

If more foundations take this brave step, our sector could generate untold billions of dollars to rescue nonprofits. We could ensure that civil society emerges from this pandemic and economic collapse more resilient and effective than ever.

Philanthropy has a special responsibility. Given our resources, we can support programs and initiatives that others might consider a financial burden. We can, will, and must invest in organizations that attack the roots of systemic inequality this virus has laid bare. And as we fund these vital recovery efforts, we must reimagine our systems—reimagine our democracy, our economy, our culture for the better.

In another tumultuous and violent year, 1968, Dr. Martin Luther King Jr. shared his concern with friend Harry Belafonte that, despite the progress they had seen, America and its systems were still "a burning house."

When asked what to do about it, Dr. King said, "I guess we're just going to have to become firemen."

I return to this exchange often. It clarifies that, despite the scale and complexity of the problems we face, we still share a universal imperative—to become firefighters for justice. To do, whatever it is we do, for justice.

At this moment, it is not enough to douse the "burning house" in front of us. It is not sufficient to lend a hose and then move on. We must, further, think, and act, like firefighters. We must make it our mission to save lives—to rush in where others turn away, take brave and extraordinary action, and attend to the emergency at hand.

We must stop the forces of destruction at their source with every tool and resource we have at our disposal. We must assess the damage caused by these inequalities and set the conditions in which we can build something new.

The lifting will be heavy. It will require humility and selflessness, listening and elevating the lived experience over ego and abstract expertise, and the moral courage to stand up for the rights and dignity of every human life. It will demand that the privileged among us not only give something back, but also give something up.

We live in a culture that makes these things hard—but what makes doing them worthwhile and meaningful is the hope that doing them now will create a better tomorrow. And that hope is the oxygen that allows our movements and institutions and democracy to breathe free.

Ultimately, we need hope—a hope born not from idealism or naivete, but from a stubborn, determined recognition of what we owe each other; that the actions we take today and every day will bring us closer to the future we seek. We need hope that united—on the other side—we will realize justice for all.

TO END THE PANDEMIC, EVERY BUSINESS LEADER MUST PUT WORKER HEALTH AND EQUITY FIRST

Fortune
February 23, 2021

COVID-19 has upended every part of society. But now that we are a year into the pandemic, we have come to better understand how it spreads, and the remarkable risk and sacrifice so many employees are taking to keep our shelves stocked, our health-care institutions staffed, our children educated, and our communities moving.

It's noteworthy that among President Biden's first actions to take hold of the pandemic was an executive order calling on the Occupational Safety and Health Administration (OSHA) to revise existing safety guidelines, ramp up enforcement, and use its resources to protect America's most vulnerable and hardest-hit workers. With that directive, the new president made clear what we all know to be true: America's workers are on the front lines of this pandemic, and they must have the protection and support they deserve from their employers.

We have witnessed how workplace transmission is contributing to the country's mounting case count. Inequality has also exacerbated the spread of the virus. President Biden's order points to the social, racial, health, and economic inequities that frontline workers are experiencing today, and this is a clear signal that every business must not only root out inequality by reshaping leadership strategies—businesses must also have clear frameworks for understanding and addressing how certain groups are disproportionately impacted.

So, facing these multiple crises—a pandemic, a needed economic recovery, a reckoning with racial inequality—what is the role of employers, and how do leaders need to change? In our view, businesses must focus on their people, placing their voices, their health (both physical and mental), their safety, and equity at the top of business priorities. Thinking about employees shouldn't be a function of human resources—it's a competitive differentiator, and it's needed now more than ever.

Cisco, for example, has been guided by its social-justice principles to examine and, where possible, strengthen employee health benefits through a racial equity lens. Employee-focused initiatives in mental health, workplace safety and privacy, and childcare all sit at the same level as business strategy to ensure that issues of inequity can be elevated to leadership.

By advocating for internal safety measures, effective policy, and racial equity, companies can put purpose-driven leadership into practice to protect their workers and fuel an inclusive recovery. For many businesses, this will mean changing the way they view their people strategies—applying the same rigor, creativity, and care they used to pivot and keep their business strong during this crisis. For every business, this will mean listening to and protecting those most at risk. As we continue to distribute vaccines, a process that will still take time, business leaders can use their ingenuity, energy, and resources to place the well-being of workers at the forefront.

Black and Latino workers account for 36 percent of employees in frontline jobs, with many lacking access to the paid sick days and quality health insurance needed to care for themselves and their families. Black frontline workers are also more likely to report experiencing retaliation by managers for raising concerns about the coronavirus. With Black Americans losing their lives to the pandemic at more than twice the rate of white people, businesses must double down on commitments they renewed in the wake of last summer's racial reckoning and widespread protests by making worker safety a key part of their social-justice efforts.

First, businesses can reduce spread by offering paid sick days to all workers, whether they are full time, part time, or contractors. Over a quarter of people know someone who has gone to work sick during the pandemic because of financial stresses, thereby risking the health of customers and staff. Now, companies can make clear that economic security and public health are not options workers have to choose between, but two sides of the same coin.

Second, we must provide essential protections for workers, including supplying and mandating personal protective equipment, enforcing social distancing protocols and the use of face coverings, immediately notifying employees of exposure or infections, and implementing workplace contact tracing.

Next, while many companies have already embraced these measures, it's crucial to ensure they are consistently implemented and that organizations can rapidly course-correct when something goes wrong. To do that, companies must give their employees a voice in designing and managing workplace health and safety. Workers know the problems best and often have a unique, early window into where efforts may be falling short.

This pandemic has made clear that taking deliberate steps can be the difference between being part of the problem or part of the solution. Our country relies on working people to keep the economy functioning, and communities safe. So, when we look back on this pandemic, history will ask how business leaders rethought their approach to employees and protected them. The choice is clear, and there's no time to waste. Together, we can build an inclusive future that ensures all workers are safe, healthy, and thriving. With everything connected, and everything at stake, we must build that future today.

REBUILDING OUR POST-COVID WORLD TOGETHER

March 24, 2021

One year ago, the world changed. To paraphrase Ernest Hemingway, it happened slowly, and then all at once.

Weeks of uncertainty became a season of suffering, and then the deadliest year in the history of the United States, as well as Brazil, India, and now Mexico. Around the world, COVID-19 has taken more than 2.7 million lives and counting. It has upended the hopes and dreams of untold millions more.

I have long resisted the simple binary—rejecting, as best I can, the false choices and zero-sum calculations; the unnuanced punditry on an increasingly complex world. And yet, as we mark the one-year anniversary of life with coronavirus, the beginning of a new era is in sight.

The last year constitutes a watershed. On one side, history's tributaries run in one direction; on the other, toward something new. Years from now, we will refer to these periods as the B.C. and P.C. eras: Before coronavirus, and post.

THE BEFORE AND THE AFTER

Before COVID-19, we knew we lived in an interconnected, multipolar world, even as globalization was on the retreat and global cooperation on the decline. Now it's clear that we are not just interconnected but also deeply interdependent.

Before coronavirus, many took for granted that democratic values and institutions, especially in the US, were strong and, in Lincoln's words, would "long endure." Now it's clear, they are vulnerable to autocracy in ways many Americans never honestly acknowledged.

Global inequality had pushed us to a precipice well before 2020. But through this pandemic, we've seen the wealthiest get wealthier, while essential workers, women, and communities of color suffer the virus's worst devastation, Indigenous people, especially those in Latin America, are threatened by extinction, and entire societies become more vulnerable.

And the reckoning underway transcends the virus, too.

We knew—well before the murders of George Floyd, Breonna Taylor, Ahmaud Arbery, and the recent surge of anti-Asian hate—about pervasive police violence and that racial inequality was, and is, as central to the American experience as the democratic values it belies. We knew, fundamentally, that the dehumanizing ideology that justified slavery and colonialism, apartheid and Jim Crow, was not, somehow, a relic of the past, but a reality, clear and present. And now we're seeing a renewed, global, intersectional movement committed to fighting racism, white supremacy, sexism, and more.

And so, even as we look forward to the day we return to offices, schools, and other places, we cannot—we must not—return to our old ways of working, learning, and connecting. Too much has been permanently disrupted, too many long-held beliefs disproved. We cannot permit ourselves to resume what was; we must reimagine what can be.

WHAT CAN WE BUILD TOGETHER

If 2020 was, in many ways, unprecedented, what defines the P.C. era is still undetermined.

Now that COVID-19 has stripped away old expectations and assumptions, what actions can we take—collectively, collaboratively, concurrently—to secure and advance progress?

If coronavirus revealed the starkness of inequality around the world, how can we respond with proportionate force?

If the pandemic revealed our global web of mutuality, how can we better support leaders on the ground, connect across countries and continents, and rebuild multilaterally?

I do not pretend to have the answers, but I know where we might start.

For one, in light of our global interdependence, the cult of individualism that has dominated America's economy and politics since the 1970s has become outmoded and outmatched. If the pandemic called for collective action on an international scale, it is hardly the only such crisis our species and our planet face—from climate change to gun violence. Time is running out, and only collective action, at scale, has any chance of mitigating what might come next.

Indeed, the cult of the individual not only prevents collective action; it perpetuates inequality. Look no further than the billionaires profiting off global catastrophe, and it becomes clear our conscienceless breed of capitalism is in need of conscientious reinvention. Adam Smith would be appalled by Ayn Rand, Milton Friedman, and all their disciples, and by the individual hands visibly, violently tearing at society's seams.

We must move away from a culture of individualism toward the restoration of a common good. We must shed our obsession with the idea of rapid growth at all costs and establish, instead, a clear, shared understanding of inclusive, sustainable growth—in which the goal is both equal opportunity and equitable outcomes. And we must push ourselves not merely to answer the call for justice, but to reckon with a history of injustice.

We can build on the successes of collective action—from global climate activists and racial justice organizers to the record number of voters in the US and the women who recently took to the streets in Mexico and the United Kingdom demanding safety from male violence.

And we must include equity in our execution of every policy and cultivation of every movement—whether that's vaccine distribution across the Global South or supporting the people, from women to Indigenous and Afro-descendant communities, behind gathering movements around the world.

A NEW PROGRESSIVE ERA

At the height of America's Progressive Era, the pioneering journalist Walter Lippmann observed that democracy is "a way of life, a use of freedom, an embrace of opportunity." Democracy is "a weapon in the hands of those who have the courage and skill to wield it."

As we work to shape the P.C. world, Lippmann's words might inform a new, more inclusive, more global Progressive Era. After all, the P.C. era is more than the absence of violence or presence of a vaccine. It is "a way of life," a way of being and understanding, "a use of freedom" for a common good.

This new era is "an embrace of opportunity"—mindful of the world's fragility and energized by the possibility that if everything can change *forever*, then the power to change everything *for good* rests in the hands of the just and the righteous, on the front lines of necessary, overdue change.

It will require courage, a willingness to be honest with ourselves and confront the realities the pandemic has laid bare, and a sustained commitment not to restore the world we once knew, but instead to imagine what we want to be different—and to work together to define a new age of solidarity, connection, and equality.

We must meet the challenge, the charge, and this unique chance to push justice forward. This is the work of the P.C. era. We must at once offer *relief* to the communities still suffering—and help bring *recovery* to institutions on the front lines that need our support. We must *reform* systems and structures, while we *reimagine* what's possible with our partners around the world, heeding their best ideas.

Relief, recovery, reform, reimagination—this remains the path to better days.

AN EQUITABLE VACCINE ROLLOUT MUST PRIORITIZE THE MOST VULNERABLE

The Washington Post
April 6, 2021

Many Americans are breathing a sigh of relief. Across the United States, the vaccine rollout is gaining speed. By May 1, every US adult will be eligible for inoculation.

But eligibility is far from equity—and, around the world, the pandemic is far from over. Already, vast disparities are emerging in vaccine access—both *within* countries and *between* them—especially for Afro-descendant and Indigenous communities.

Within countries, the gaps are stark. In the United States, for example, white people remained nearly two times more likely to be vaccinated than their neighbors of color at the end of March. In Brazil, Indigenous populations are *ten times* more likely to die of COVID-19 than the general population, even as wealthy Brazilians travel abroad to secure shots. And in

India, many members of poor Muslim and Dalit communities are denied access to the limited vaccine supply that is available.

These blatant inequities also are apparent in the disparities *between* countries. Wealthy nations such as Canada and the United Kingdom have preordered enough supply to vaccinate their entire populations six and four times over, respectively. In fact, the world's richest countries controlled more than 80 percent of the world's COVID-19 vaccines as of last week. Meanwhile, low-income countries can access only one tenth of 1 percent.

All told, nearly six hundred million doses have been administered thus far—which is good, but not good enough. With only 4 percent of the world's 7.8 billion people vaccinated, we still have a long way to go.

The reasons for the gap are clear: Rich nations are hoarding the vaccines. Whether it's the European Union blockading international vaccine exports entirely, or the United States stockpiling thirty million AstraZeneca doses, a wave of vaccine nationalism is depriving the world of much-needed supply.

Vaccine nationalism is not without consequences. It delays our global recovery even further. Indeed, until we are all vaccinated, we are all vulnerable.

And many people—especially those working on the front lines of the fight for equity around the globe, including many NGO partners of the Ford Foundation—are needlessly dying. At last count, at least a dozen of our courageous grantee colleagues have succumbed to the virus. This is a heartbreaking loss of life and an incalculable loss of leadership.

In other words, our vaccination regimen has become the latest harrowing outcome, and potential accelerator, of vast, underlying global inequalities.

To address these disparities, three immediate steps come to mind.

First, the United States could dip into its vast reserves and vaccinate the world—mobilizing the resources of the US military and other agencies to manufacture, ship, and distribute doses around the world, perhaps in the style of former president George W. Bush's Emergency Plan for AIDS Relief. To paraphrase Dr. Martin Luther King Jr., vaccine inequality anywhere is a threat to global health everywhere.

At the same time, the European Union, United Kingdom, and United States could waive patent protections and allow more countries to manufacture and distribute vaccines themselves. Officials from India and South Africa already have drafted a World Trade Organization proposal temporarily lifting patent protections on COVID-19 vaccines—and fifty-seven member states have joined them as cosponsors. A temporary patent moratorium would reset and realign the tattered relationship between democratic values and capitalism.

Finally, we must strengthen multilateral initiatives and create more robust, resilient health systems, for this pandemic and the next. Here, concerned philanthropists can follow the lead of pioneers such as Bill and Melinda Gates. Their foundation's support and advocacy for Covax—a vaccination partnership among nonprofits, governments, and the World Health Organization—has pushed global institutions away from vaccine nationalism and toward vaccine equity. Covax already has played a crucial role in allocating a projected two billion doses to low-income countries.

We must center the people and communities that continue to suffer the highest death tolls around the world. An equitable vaccine rollout must prioritize and protect the most vulnerable in our societies—from the Dalit community in India to Indigenous populations in Brazil to essential farm workers and grocery store clerks throughout the United States.

Vaccine inequality is not only a crisis to solve, but an opportunity for individuals, institutions, and industries to build back our health systems, economies, and democracies better than before.

HOW TO END GLOBAL VACCINE INEQUALITY

with Charlize Theron
TIME
October 6, 2021

This month, for the first time in two years, the G20 will meet in Rome to discuss a global, multilateral agenda. The stakes could not be higher.

Certainly, member states are feeling the COVID-19 pandemic's ongoing consequences. But, sadly, the 175 countries not at the table—most in the Global South—still face the gravest suffering and highest rates of death.

Nowhere is the disparity more apparent than in vaccine access. In places like Los Angeles and New York City, where we respectively live and were vaccinated, large distribution sites like the LA Forum and the Javits Center have helped the two cities administer a total of twenty-three million doses, collectively.

Meanwhile, we've heard from partners and colleagues across the globe about the barriers to getting vaccinated in less wealthy parts of the world—from months of waiting to lack of Internet access to clinics running out of doses. These barriers add up fast, while the number of vaccinated people rises too slowly. To date, all of South Africa, Charlize's home country, has administered just seventeen million doses. Indeed, while seventeen of the G20's member states already have vaccinated at least two-thirds of their populations, the vaccination rate across the continent of Africa is below 5 percent.

Many countries across the Global South suffer a damning lack of vaccine doses—and even for those who do have access, uncertainty and vaccine hesitancy in vulnerable communities have been growing, due to either a lack of information, an excess of misinformation, or both. Without strong, robust, civil-society organizations working on the ground to combat misinformation and support meaningful access for those in need, progress toward a more equitable recovery will be impossible.

As global leaders, the members of the G20 have an urgent responsibility: To end the immediate crisis of vaccine inequity today and build long-term infrastructure that safeguards the world from future pandemics. First and foremost, this means supplying billions of doses to less wealthy parts of the world. President Joe Biden's recent commitment to double US vaccine donations is a welcome step—but even the 1.1 billion doses he vows to contribute will not be enough to reach global herd immunity. Ending this global health crisis requires a more robust and holistic sharing of resources.

For instance, our current intellectual-property regime prioritizes pharmaceutical profit over public health outcomes. We recognize the power of intellectual-property protections to drive research, development, and innovation. But in the context of a pandemic like this one, those protections have deadly consequences by kneecapping the ability of resource-poor countries to manufacture life-saving vaccines. G20 members must join the more than one hundred national governments and hundreds of civil-society organizations that have signed on to support a temporary waiver of the Agreement on Trade-Related Aspects of Intellectual Property Rights (TRIPS). With this waiver in place, government leaders around the world can finally build a vaccine infrastructure that empowers countries to quickly produce and distribute vaccines, in a way that's rooted in collaboration, not competition.

Crucially, we also need to ensure we translate doses manufactured into shots in the arms of those in need. That necessitates a reimagined and strengthened health infrastructure that commits to bolstering civil society, community health workers, and community-based organizations.

Civil-society organizations have played an essential role in pandemic response—as watchdogs holding governments accountable, and as trusted partners and messengers serving vulnerable communities. From Dallas, Texas, to Durban, South Africa, communities that have experienced a history of exploitation, neglect, and marginalization harbor an understandable distrust of the state. Understanding this fact is crucial, because in many places, like rural South Africa, distrust and hesitancy of the vaccines continues to rise, creating new barriers to recovery even as more doses become available.

Especially in regions marked by internal conflict, political tension, language barriers, and social unrest, even the most well-intended distribution policies will fail without strong civil-society engagement and community-led action from organizations with a well-established foundation of trust and support. We have seen time and again, in our work with frontline organizations like the Small Projects Foundation, that the messenger matters. Without robust civil-society organizations—including local newsrooms, community centers, and trusted health-care providers—to disrupt dangerous COVID-19 conspiracies, vulnerable groups like women and immigrants are most likely to lack the information needed to make healthy choices. To create pipelines for a faster, more equitable response, the G20 must meaningfully invest in the work of such organizations.

Five years ago, we both joined thousands of activists in Durban to discuss another virus and global public health crisis: HIV/AIDS. There, at the twenty-first International AIDS Conference, we encouraged global leaders to disrupt the racism, sexism, transphobia, and homophobia that make HIV a treatable illness for some and a death sentence for others. These types of inequities and fear drive pandemics. Since then, thanks to fearless leadership from people living with HIV and civil-society champions, we've seen ongoing advocacy lead to an increased focus and shift of resources to vulnerable populations like youth, and tangible policy changes like the government approval and formal rollout of the life-saving HIV preventative regimen PrEP in Kenya and increased HIV/AIDS treatment and prevention funding throughout the region.

Today, we're trying to propel similar change to fight inequity and stymie the pandemic's devastation of the Global South. At the Ford Foundation, we are proud to launch a new $16 million grantmaking initiative that will spur intellectual-property reform, fund public goods, and bolster civil-society organizations working in marginalized communities. And at the Charlize Theron Africa Outreach Project, we're working with long-standing partners to uproot harmful misinformation and vaccine hesitancy among adolescents and help remove barriers to vaccine access for young people, their families, and the under-resourced communities in which they live.

That said, no group has more influence than the G20 to redistribute vaccine supply, reinvest in medical and civil-society infrastructure, and reimagine our global systems with equity, justice, and collaboration at the heart. Together, we can build a more equal, more equally prepared world.

THE STUBBORN PERSISTENCE OF VACCINE INEQUALITY

Foreign Affairs
November 2, 2021

In the forests of Jambi Province, on the Indonesian island of Sumatra, more than half the Indigenous Orang Rimba community lacks government-issued identification cards. Until mid-August, that meant its members could not receive COVID-19 vaccines, since the government required anyone seeking a dose to have a state-issued ID number. Even now that the rule has been changed, many Orang Rimba have not had a chance to get a shot, because like most Indigenous people in Indonesia, they live in a remote area, hours away from the nearest vaccination site.

Such barriers have impeded vaccine access for Indigenous communities across Indonesia. According to Rukka Sombolinggi, the secretary general of the Indigenous Peoples Alliance of the Archipelago, just twenty thousand of Indonesia's twenty million Indigenous people—or 0.1 percent—had received their first dose of a COVID-19 vaccine as of August 4.

By contrast, more than one-third of Indonesia's general population has received at least one dose, and the government is distributing nearly 1.5 million doses each day. This tremendous progress has been mirrored in many other developing countries that initially struggled to source vaccines from wealthier nations. Yet the progress has obscured a disturbing global trend: Marginalized groups, including Indigenous people, people of African descent, and people with disabilities, have been last in line to get inoculated everywhere in the world.

Simply increasing the global supply of doses cannot ensure equal access to vaccines, either between or within countries. Governments and international organizations must therefore work together with donors, civil-society groups, and local leaders to ensure that vaccines make their way to marginalized communities. Otherwise, millions of vulnerable people will remain unvaccinated—and the whole world will remain at risk.

INTERNAL INEQUITIES

Calls to address vaccine inequity have abounded since the first COVID-19 vaccines hit the market late last year, and the world has a long way to go to ensure equitable global vaccine production, pricing, and distribution. Gaps between rich and poor countries have been slow to close. Yet thanks in part to the tireless advocacy of philanthropists and civil-society leaders, vaccines are starting to reach developing countries in meaningful quantities. There is now hope where there was none before.

But getting doses to low- and middle-income countries is only half the battle. After months of waiting in line behind rich countries to secure vaccine supplies, many developing countries are now struggling to address internal vaccine inequities—in particular, between affluent urban populations and rural, often marginalized ones. The disparities stem from a series of cascading inequalities that have only intensified over the course of the pandemic.

Misinformation has spread like wildfire over social media, discouraging many marginalized populations from seeking vaccines. Unemployment and economic hardship have widened the gaps between rich and poor. And already struggling civil-society organizations, so often the main bridge between government services and marginalized communities, are stretched thinner than ever.

Consider Colombia, where armed groups and criminal networks have flourished during the pandemic, threatening the local leaders and organizations that are vital to public health outreach. Especially in areas where the state has a minimal presence, such as those that are home to Indigenous and Afro-descendant communities, armed groups have seriously disrupted vaccine distribution by impeding the access of public health officials and restricting the flow of necessary supplies. Making matters worse, the crisis in neighboring Venezuela has pushed the number of Venezuelan migrants in Colombia up to nearly 1.8 million, putting additional pressure on the already fragile health system and complicating vaccine distribution plans.

As of October, approximately 40 percent of Colombia's population was fully vaccinated, and more than half the residents of major cities—63 percent in the capital of Bogotá—had received at least one dose. But in areas of the country that are home to predominantly Afro-descendant and Indigenous communities, those percentages are cut nearly in half. In the heavily Afro-Colombian northwestern territory of Chocó, for instance, only about 26 percent of the population is fully vaccinated.

To address these inequalities and to speed the pace of global recovery, the world needs an equitable distribution plan, one that coordinates the efforts of governments, international organizations, donors, and local communities to deploy urgently needed resources and infrastructure. One country that has made significant progress on equitable distribution and that might serve as a model is South Africa, which was slow to roll out vaccines (thanks in part to hoarding by rich countries) but is now doing so faster than most low- and middle-income countries. South Africa's public health officials and civil-society organizations have found a variety of creative solutions to reach the country's remotest populations, including setting up health-care hubs and vaccine pop-up sites in rural areas to meet people where they are. The government has even dispatched a "vaccine train" stocked with hundreds of thousands of doses to villages across the country.

GLOBAL ASSISTANCE, LOCAL SOLUTIONS

Of course, not every country can or should field a vaccine train—especially those without adequate rail lines—but the international community should help all countries overcome disparities in vaccine access. The most effective solutions are usually ones that are tailored to local conditions. That said, three overarching principles apply to every successful vaccine-distribution model—and to the infrastructure that supports it.

First, efforts should be locally driven and community oriented. Time and again, top-down solutions have failed to meaningfully alter human behavior or bring about lasting change. Donors and international civil-society organizations should therefore leverage partnerships with groups that already have deep roots in marginalized communities and empower local leaders to create solutions based on their lived experience.

For example, the Kenyan nonprofit Shining Hope for Communities, which has a long track record of working in informal settlements (including with grants from the Ford Foundation, where I serve as president), has helped curb rampant misinformation about COVID-19 by disseminating public health information through trusted local leaders. Building on their established relationships with local communities, these leaders are disrupting social media conspiracies and educating their neighbors about the importance of vaccines.

Second, improving vaccine equity requires removing barriers between people and shots. Here, civil-society organizations and other watchdog groups have a vital role to play in monitoring local, national, and international officials—and calling out disparities and discrimination. By fully funding these groups, international donors can help them reduce barriers—such as registration requirements—to vaccinating marginalized communities. The Indigenous Peoples Alliance of the Archipelago and the Indonesian Women with Disability Association, both partners of the Ford Foundation, are doing exactly that. In late July, they collaborated with over two hundred Indonesian civil-society groups to advocate for the rights of Indigenous Indonesians and Indonesians with disabilities. It was in response to their public pressure campaign that the government began to offer alternatives to the identity-card requirement, which had previously barred so many marginalized communities from seeking vaccination.

Finally, and perhaps most important, international institutions such as the United Nations and the G20 must support local efforts. These institutions have the power to identify new solutions, scale-up proven ones, and support the governments of low- and middle-income countries as they create equitable rollout plans. International institutions must use every tool at their disposal to speed this process along, freeing up governments across the developing world of the need to fight for doses so that they can focus their resources and energy on tackling distribution. By applying local knowledge and solutions on a global scale, international organizations can act as partners to civil-society groups and nonprofits, ushering in a more cohesive era of vaccine diplomacy and collective action.

Taken together, these steps will transform the way the world distributes lifesaving public goods, replacing the prevailing top-down model with grassroots ones. Ultimately, the only way to prevent another global pandemic the magnitude of COVID-19 is to strengthen the public health infrastructure across the developing world, especially in communities that have long been neglected, exploited, and oppressed. Inequality must be tackled head-on—not only because morality demands it but because public health and safety do as well.

PART VII

FROM AN AMERICAN CENTURY TO INCLUSIVE GLOBAL ENGAGEMENT

We're engaged in a generational contest between authoritarian ideology and democratic values in countries the world over, including our own, but we're responding with the cutting-edge thinking of the 1940s.

The consequences of climate change, the next pandemic, or next recession will not be relegated to one country or another, but experienced first and worst by the poor and vulnerable in every country, jeopardizing everyone's security in turn....

We must recognize that growth is good, but not good enough. We need metrics beyond GDP to measure and manage toward what matters most: The human rights and human dignity of people in every country....

We must think bigger and bolder, but also for the longer term. We know that investment in equitable development today is far more cost effective than dealing with the consequences of our failure to invest during the decades ahead.

Most important, we must ensure that the people affected by twenty-first-century crises—and the development community's responses to them—have a voice in shaping policies and pro-grams that serve them.

The global community can start immediately by releasing more resources, currently tied up in development organizations, and by listening to and learning from inspiring leaders across the Global South. Ultimately, though, we can and must reorganize our efforts around the needs of people and communities, not just nation states, so governments, civil society, and private sector entities all work in common purpose toward a global common good.

The New York Times
September 19, 2022

DEMOCRACY HAS NO FINISH LINE

Address to Ford Foundation Trustees Symposium
Johannesburg, South Africa
February 11, 2014

Thank you for joining us on this wonderful day of celebration, conversation, and reflection about our shared past and exciting future.

As we mark six decades of Ford Foundation support for South Africa, and two decades working here on the ground in Johannesburg, I am delighted to reaffirm our commitment to the courageous people of this country and to the principles of human dignity and social justice for which you have struggled and sacrificed.

We are proud to stand with you, and behind you. And we are in awe of what you have achieved in pursuing a vision that the South African people put forward a generation ago: To heal, to improve, to build, and to fulfill the promise of a true democracy.

As we begin, I'd like to spend a few minutes talking with you about democracy—about the challenge that, in my view, threatens so many democracies around the world today and about the extraordinary asset you have in South Africa's proud history of citizen-led action.

South Africa's democracy is only twenty years young. And yet no nation can claim a more democratic form of government than South Africa.

The promise of participatory democracy here remains potent and palpable and profound. And your democratic example is about far more than ballots; it is about securing human dignity and justice.

When I reflect on South Africa's courageous pursuit of democracy, I feel both reverence and resolve: Reverence for the manner in which you sought and secured reconciliation among yourselves; resolve that, by dint of your example, we Americans might find the courage to address the racial injustice that lingers in our own society.

For me, this is a deeply personal point, because I am not just an American. I am an African American.

In my very DNA, I carry the heritage and the history of two continents: A history that binds me—and millions of others across the Americas and across the diaspora—to your story almost as much as it binds us to our own. And it is because of this connection between our story and yours that the example of transitional justice that you have given the world is so compelling.

If my country had been able to accomplish in twenty years what you've accomplished, goodness, what a different world it would be.

Of course, no two nations travel the same path. Our histories are intertwined, but they are not identical. And yet I do believe there is one thing that unites us: The imperative to never give up on democracy; to never grow weary of the demands it places on us as citizens and as leaders.

Because in democracies, we—all of us—are involved in a perpetual pursuit of more perfect. And, as it turns out, perfection takes time.

It's been only twenty years since the people of South Africa wrote one of the most democratic constitutions in the world. Well, in 1807, twenty years after the United States wrote its constitution, a former vice president was charged with treason for plotting to form his own country, in Louisiana.

This was after he shot and killed another member of the president's cabinet in a duel.

This was a full fifty years before Americans waged civil war in a contest over the meaning of our founding creed, that all are created equal.

My point is: From ancient Greece to modern South Africa, democracy has not always been at work for progress. Most often it's just a work in progress.

This is why our conversation today is so important: Because we each have a long road ahead—a long walk to freedom, to borrow a phrase. And there are many challenges along that road.

When I survey the state of today's world, and consider the challenges we face, there is one that stands out: The challenge of inequality.

It is universal and it is pronounced. And while it is widening everywhere, it is also widening right here in South Africa, as you well know.

In that fact lies a significant paradox: Since apartheid's abolition, the percentage of South Africans living in extreme poverty has been cut in half. And yet, the International Monetary Fund tells us that the top 10 percent of South African earners take in half the country's income, while the bottom 20 percent of earners take in only 2.7 percent of national income.

Today, simply put, South Africa is one of the most unequal countries in the world—in spite of the fact that it's also one of the most democratic. This is the very definition of a paradox.

Years ago, Madiba would tell his fellow citizens—whom he called the real heroes of South Africa's transformation—that "the whole world is watching our progress, and willing us on."

Well, we were—and we still are—because you have been, and very much remain, on the front lines of the quest for justice.

Today, that quest for justice calls on us to overcome inequality—for inequality corrodes and undermines democratic spirit. And I know for a fact that people around the world are looking to South Africa for inspiration in this new battle: For smarter approaches to inequality not just in Durban, but in Detroit and Delhi, too.

And I believe South Africa once again has the opportunity be a leader, to blaze a new trail for the world. Indeed, you already are. You have a wealth of resources. You have an inspiring constitutional framework. And you have a vibrant and determined civil society.

Since the 1950s, the Ford Foundation has seeded and nurtured civil society around the world—including here in South Africa, where we made our first grant back in 1953. This experience has taught us, again and again, that no society can be truly civil without a healthy system of civil-society organizations.

When I look around this room, the importance and value of civil society literally comes alive. Many of you in this room played a critical role in channeling public opposition to apartheid, and in doing so created a worldwide movement for change. People in this room have been a vital voice for transparency and accountability. Some of you demanded—and helped build—more effective and more equitable approaches to HIV/AIDS. Others have led the fight against corruption. And some of you have led the way in the battle for fair and open access to education.

As a global foundation, supporting organizations in more than fifty countries, we know how important civil society is. But we know equally well the unsettling truth that, around the world, civil society is under duress, threatened by overzealous governments.

Whether in Russia, Egypt, Ukraine, or in countries across Africa, the voices of civil society are being muted. I hope that this is a trend that South Africa will help the world to break, because you recognize and honor civil society and its contributions to national well-being and human progress.

In fact, one of the questions I hope you help us answer today is: *How* can philanthropy—and the Ford Foundation—be a better resource and partner on your walk to justice?

This question, *how*, is what this gathering is all about—and I hope we can address it with openness and honesty.

We are not here simply to celebrate the last twenty years. We are here to listen to and to learn. And to renew our pledge never to give up on democracy.

The beauty of democracy is that it has no end point. There is no finish line. There is no perfect expression of our democratic aspirations. Democracy is only what we make it, or fail to make it. And more than almost any other country on earth, you have the potential to help democracy fulfill its extraordinary promise.

While you are still at the beginning of your journey, you have the momentum of your own history at your back: A history of daring and courage, of rebirth, of extraordinary citizen-led action; an unrivaled commitment to freedom, justice, and human dignity.

I can hardly wait to see what the next twenty years will bring.

A NEW GLOBAL ERA
OF URBAN DISRUPTION

Address to UNHABITAT, World Urban Forum 7
Medellín, Colombia
April 7, 2014

Thank you, Joan Clos i Matheu, for that gracious introduction—and for your leadership and your eloquence in making the case for cities that are both just and sustainable. And thank you all for lending your voices to this important conversation about how each of us can contribute to realizing our shared vision of just and sustainable cities.

I am honored to join so many accomplished thinkers and doers. In business and commerce, in job creation and community development, in industry and innovation.

Now, Dr. Clos already has clarified why you are a crucial part of the World Urban Forum: Because the private sector is absolutely essential to sustainable urban growth.

And he has left it for me, then, to explain exactly what I am doing here.

Well, what I'd like to do is stir some disagreement—to start the day by calling out some of the sensitive areas that we might as well get on the table.

In today's business parlance, this might be called "disruption." But please consider it friendly disruption.

Although I am honored to lead the world's foremost social-justice philanthropy, earlier in my career, I spent a number of years at UBS, where I learned a deep appreciation for the power of markets.

Those years prepared me for a second career in community redevelopment—and eventually led me to a third career in the foundation world, where institutions like Rockefeller and Ford have long been investors in urban innovation and inclusive growth.

But allow me to talk about disruption for a moment because this much is inevitable: At the rate that people are finding their way into urban areas, if we do nothing, disruption will come to us. It will come in the form of more human suffering, more unplanned sprawl, more economic upheaval, more environmental damage. And, frankly, I'd rather the disruption come from us.

As leaders of enterprises focused on innovation and entrepreneurship, I assume you are already disrupters. And I mean that in the best possible way.

So I am asking you to be part of a very healthy, and much-needed disruption in how we think about urban development and inclusive growth.

To find an example of what I mean, you don't need to travel far. Just walk out the door of this hall, and there it is: Medellín—a city whose leaders have completely transformed their historic reality. They've transformed one of the world's most troubled places into a beacon of inclusive development.

As many of you know, *The Wall Street Journal*, Citi Group, and the Urban Land Institute recently named Medellín "the world's most innovative city." And twenty years ago, the headlines coming out of Medellín read very differently.

What took place here was a shared effort to disrupt everything about how the city worked—by the mayor, by regional and national leaders, by the business community, and by the people of Medellín themselves. They embraced a constructive disruption—in which all the parties came to understand that their individual interests meant coming together around a shared vision and a shared process. They called it "social urbanism"—meaning that every investment made should benefit all the city's people, not just some. And this is easy to say—but very hard to do.

It means asking the people closest to a city's challenges what they need to overcome them: These are the communities whose voices are rarely heard in urban planning conversations, but who are actually the most invested in solving problems.

We ignore them at our own cost. And I mean hard financial costs, as well as opportunity costs, human costs, and the cost of lost potential of staggering proportions.

As I mentioned, years before I took the reins of the Ford Foundation, I worked with a community development corporation in Harlem. In those days, many so-called leaders and experts speculated about the needs and wants of the community without even so much as conversing with local residents on a street corner.

These big players—well-intentioned, no doubt—tried to impose social change on the community without engaging the people of the community. It was the textbook example of what my friend the eminent scholar William Easterly calls "the tyranny of experts."

The tragic irony, of course, is that if these experts had listened, not lectured, they might have learned that the biggest issue on people's minds was not the lack of a comprehensive plan for renewal. It was the lack of a supermarket.

This was something to which the community thought it had a right—but something which the private sector, based on market analysis, concluded was not sustainable. So, the people of Harlem went four decades without this basic service.

In the late 1990s—with the help of advocacy from civil-society groups with new analyses in hand—we attracted a full-service Pathmark store to Harlem. And this one store broke a development bottleneck in a way that a technocratic development plan never could. It created an environment that was inviting to other businesses and people, which set in motion a virtuous cycle—a new Harlem renaissance for the twenty-first century.

Why am I sharing this story?

Because Harlem's story is connected with the stories of cities and urban areas around the globe. And because it represents something disruptive.

Too often—and this is the case around the world—we in the business community, we in the civil-society community, we in the UN-development community, we in the human-rights community—we retreat into our own ideological corners.

We all see things from our own points of view, and we pay little heed to what others are seeing from theirs. We all are absolutely sure of our rightness.

I am here to say that it is time for us to move beyond these unnecessary divides.

Rights actors, community actors, development actors, private-sector actors—we all have a piece of the puzzle in our hands.

No piece exceeds another in importance if we are to create truly just and thriving places.

Where did we start in Harlem? Where did they start in Medellín? In Dr. Clos's Barcelona? In Detroit, today?

We start with a serious engagement of the people of the city—all of the people. This is the key to disrupting the debate over whose development model is most right. After all, once we engage the people of a place, the right answers will come.

A little more than a half century ago, a bright—sometimes brash— New Yorker with a bold idea forever changed the world's understanding of cities, planning, and urban design.

Her name was Jane Jacobs, and I sometimes find myself reflecting on the insight that animated her life's work—that cities ought to be made of, by, and for people. For citizens, in the fullest sense of the word.

Jane Jacobs is most famous, of course, for her *Death and Life of Great American Cities*. But a few years before its publication, Jacobs penned a *Fortune* magazine piece titled "Downtown Is for People."

She wrote then: "There is no logic that can be superimposed on the city. People make it; and it is them, not buildings, [that] we must fit into our plans."

Fifty years later, we must renew Jane Jacobs's mission and message for our time.

Our job—as urban thinkers and urban leaders and urban doers—is not to make people fit into our urban plans. Our job is to make urban plans that fit the needs of people—that reflect and respect their voices and values.

At the Ford Foundation, this is what our work on just and sustainable cities is all about—from Cali to Johannesburg, from Rio to Detroit. And so, let's recommit ourselves to embracing these principles—and to embracing true partnership.

Let's recommit ourselves to ensuring that people, not dogma and doctrine, are at the center of our urban solutions, and the heart of our work.

Let's recommit ourselves to ensuring that social justice and urban economic growth are not mutually exclusive, but mutually reinforcing.

If we do, and when we do, then "equity in urban development" will be more than a slogan.

When we see things through each other's eyes; when we stand in each other's shoes; when we act as constructive disrupters not just in spite of our differences, but because of them—then we can lift the lives of billions of people in the urban regions that most of us call home.

HOW CAN WE HELP YOU?

2015 CIVICUS State of Civil Society Report
July 8, 2015

During my very first days as president of the Ford Foundation, I participated in a roundtable on civil society with President of the United States Barack Obama. At that meeting, he said: "Human progress has always been propelled … by what happens in civil society—citizens coming together to insist that a better life is possible, pushing their leaders to protect the rights and dignities of all people."

I could not agree more.

Imagine what the world would be like without a strong, vibrant civil society. Imagine a South Africa still repressed under apartheid. Imagine a United States without civil rights—or voting rights—for women and African Americans. Imagine, instead all of the democratic movements mobilized, the civil-society organizations (CSOs) opened, and the lives saved, these stymied, closed, and tragically lost.

Indeed, we find civil society at the root of any real, meaningful, and lasting movement toward social justice, anywhere and everywhere on Earth. This certainly has been true throughout our history at the Ford Foundation, where we have helped to seed and support an alphabet soup of organizations: HRW (Human Rights Watch) and the ICTJ (International Center for Transitional Justice), the LRC (Legal Resources Centre) in South Africa, and the CBGA (Centre for Budget and Governance Accountability) in India. The list goes on, and includes organizations that are delivering services and achieving impact every single day, in areas as diverse and indispensable as the arts, economic opportunity, and education.

For this reason, civil society remains firmly fixed at the center of how we see, seed, and support social change. To us, nothing is more powerful than a movement of passionate and principled people, working toward a good that is greater than themselves.

From our perspective, the Ford Foundation's work has long been focused on galvanizing social movements by investing in institutions, individuals, and ideas. I think of these as our three Is.

Throughout our history we have seen and supported the full range of approaches and shapes civil society can take, whether civil society's relationships with government and the private sector are collaborative or, sometimes, contentious. From the Children's Television Workshop that brought us *Sesame Street* to Dr. Martin Luther King Jr. leading marches in the street to the deal that brought the city of Detroit back from fiscal bankruptcy to the World Social Forum out in the streets around the globe, we have always seen these three Is as the path to progress. They all are interdependent and interrelated, of course. Investments in individuals and leadership translate into stronger institutions. Stronger institutions yield stronger ideas and, ultimately, greater impact. And in each of these three cases, civil society remains the strongest medium through which movements and solutions can be brought to address the largest challenges we face.

CIVIL SOCIETY UNDER SIEGE

Yet, despite their central role—or perhaps because of it—many CSOs are beleaguered and besieged. At few moments since the movement to build CSOs began have these institutions been at greater risk, more vulnerable, and less resilient. How can this be, given the vital role of civil society? I believe there is a combination of reasons, both external and internal.

Externally, we know about the atrocities committed by authoritarian regimes, and how civil society has been repressed and restricted by those in power, and thus severely limited in their ability to operate and give voice. For years, troubling laws in Ethiopia have constrained the operation, and free association, of CSOs with foreign funding. In January 2014, we watched as the Cambodian government banned all public assembly in the face of growing dissent. Two months later, Human Rights Watch issued a report on rights violations in Venezuela, where protesters were beaten and shot. In January 2015, the founder of the Bahrain Center for Human Rights, Nabeel Rajab, was arrested for criticizing the government on Twitter. These examples are only a few among many.

The fact is that around the world, activists feel the pressure from governments, who see CSOs as adversaries rather than allies. In countries where CSOs are viewed in this way, human rights abuses are on the rise. An increasing number of legal challenges and constrictive laws impede important work. We have witnessed cases of censorship and harassment on nearly every continent. We have seen persecution, even murder, of citizens working for dignity and justice.

Of course, external pressures are not limited to authoritarian, repressive regimes. There also has been uneven, tepid support for CSOs in some democracies, despite the fact that, according to the 2015 Edelman Trust Barometer, NGOs (as it categorizes CSOs) remain the world's most trusted institutions. Given the expansion of electoral democracy around the world, the shrinking space for civil society in recent years seems as contradictory to those values as it is concerning.

Moreover, even when CSOs have the freedom to operate, they face a range of challenges from within the ecosystem of funders and fellow institutions.

One such internal pressure comes from the current attachment to— and almost a worship of—market-based solutions that ask organizations to measure progress as if they were for-profit concerns. Granted, Henry Ford II called our foundation a "creature of capitalism," but we need not be its captives.

And born from this issue is another: How we relate to one another. In 2014, CIVICUS published a powerful call to action, signed by many civil-society leaders and supporters, subtitled "Building from Below and Beyond Borders." This letter says it more potently than I ever could: "We are the poor cousins of the global jet set. We exist to challenge the status quo, but we trade in incremental change. Our actions are clearly not sufficient to address the mounting anger and demand for systemic political and economic transformation that we see in cities and communities around the world every day."

This same letter goes on to state, loud and clear, that civil society's "primary accountability cannot be to donors." And this is just one testament to a series of larger, interconnected issues.

To begin with, the entire development ecosystem has become distorted. For those CSOs that depend on big development agencies such as USAID (United States Agency for International Development) and DFID (the UK Department for International Development) to keep their doors open, they often become bound to contracts, and burdened by checklists. In the name of accountability, these groups have to show bang for the buck—and units per dollar—even if that means spending valuable time on bureaucratic busywork, rather than doing their best work. Of course, we all want to get the most value out of our investments, but when it comes to measuring that value, and holding organizations accountable for it, we need to be more thoughtful and flexible. Right now, too many organizations are bean counting, rather than problem-solving.

In short, development incentives do not reward the construction of adaptive organizations, but rather a set of donor-focused, piecemeal priorities. Sometimes, those priorities are myopic, if not downright perverse, diluting grassroots voices, artificially narrowing policy debates, or worse.

To borrow a phrase from our colleagues, we have encouraged this "trade in incremental change," at the expense of challenging the status quo. Our sector's obsession with quantifiable impact, and frequently dogmatic adherence to discrete deliverables, undercuts the expansive purpose of CSOs, miniaturizing them in their ambition.

In other words, this system is rooted in transactional short-termism—a tyranny of donors—that distorts and inhibits, rather than unleashes, the potential of civil society.

THE TYRANNY OF DONORS

Of course, we foundations are far from innocent. Not only are we unwilling to take responsibility for this ecosystem—an ecosystem we helped create and degrade—but, more often than not, we also demand control. We want credit. We want to micromanage. Often, we seem not to trust the very organizations we support.

I know I am generalizing. There are plenty of exceptions to this assessment, and certainly the Ford Foundation does not always set the best example. My point is that the larger donor culture we have collectively created speaks louder than the actions of any one funder.

Unfortunately, this culture is one in which civil-society leaders too rarely have a voice in setting their own priorities or even articulating the problem they aspire to solve. Little wonder that funders too often view themselves as patrons rather than partners.

All the while, we know that any enduring relationship, any successful partnership, requires trust. It means ceding some control, and listening to what the other side needs.

And in all candor, in some areas, there are too many CSOs pursuing the same funding. As funders, we have contributed to this phenomenon, and added to the asymmetry between the number of CSOs and the increasingly scarce available resources. The result is a marketplace where we are unable to prioritize effectively.

Simply put, we keep cutting the pie into smaller slices, and more organizations, often with overlapping interests, are left underfunded.

No doubt, for the sake of efficiency and efficacy, there are times when fewer, stronger institutions can make a more powerful impact. But from a foundation perspective, we are not yet comfortable saying to CSOs, "You should focus on a different part of the solution," or, candidly, "This space is too crowded."

In turn, we fund a group at a minimal amount because we do not want to tell the truth. Instead of doing no harm, or even being able to help, this means that we allow organizations to die undignified deaths, chasing project grants and grasping to whatever life support they can eke out.

At the same time, CSOs are not without their own vices. We certainly have seen a lack of coordination between organizations working in the same space, which results in unnecessary inefficiencies and even redundancies. Despite having the best intentions, there are times when ego and defense of territory come into play, and organizations that are meant to improve the world act like the world revolves around them.

THE GENERAL SUPPORT DROUGHT

All of this culminates in two interrelated crises for civil society: A lack of general support and an epidemic of short-termism. I became acutely aware of this when an organization that the Ford Foundation helped launch, more than four decades ago, called to advise they were at risk of shutting down. I was stunned, not only because the organization was once at the pinnacle of influence in policy circles, but also because it had some $2 million in project-based funding in the bank. And yet, for all practical purposes, the organization was broke, with substantial overhead and debt. This is not an uncommon situation. According to a recent article from the *Harvard Business Review*, global CSOs spend more on accounting than comparable for-profit companies largely because "most global NGOs today struggle to master the complexities of managing efficient, integrated operations in large part due to restrictions placed on them by funders."

For all that project-based grants can accomplish, they cannot keep the lights on. They do not provide organizations with the flexibility to meet their needs and pursue their missions. They focus on a short-term initiative, rather than long-term institutional health. And this is why, going forward, as a general principle, the Ford Foundation is committed to increasing general support.

In my experience, we too often ask what CSOs can do on our behalf, and too little about what we can do on theirs. When I was a CSO leader myself, I rarely heard foundation program officers begin a conversation with the words, "How can we help you create a stronger organization?"

And yet this is precisely the question donors should be asking.

This report should be a clarion call to change how we do our work and where we begin to think about solving these problems. And where we begin cannot be by telling you what we need you to do for us, but by asking what we can do for you.

USHERING IN A NEW ERA OF INSTITUTION BUILDING

If we believe in the work that CSOs are doing—and we should—then we must help usher in a new era of capacity-building investment, for institutions and the individuals who comprise them.

What civil society needs most, and now more than ever, are resilient, durable, fortified institutions that can take on inequality, fight poverty, advance justice, and promote dignity and democracy.

Lest I be misunderstood, I want to affirm my belief that there always will be a need for project support. Project support is indispensable and essential, although I do not think the true overhead costs of most projects are covered by the inflexible overhead formulas of donors, but that is another conversation. However, if we are being honest, and if our objective is endowing excellent institutions with excellent leadership and infrastructure, then general support ought to be our more pressing concern.

I am not always keen to make analogies for the private sector, but this is certainly a place where philanthropy can learn from it. When venture capitalists invest, they invest in leaders and ideas, and they help those leaders realize their ideas by providing them with the most flexible capital possible. In circumstances where organizations need more support, whether financial, technical, or in the form of a good, old-fashioned introduction, venture capital investors do what they can to deliver. This focus on holistically developing organizations and their leaders is what we funders should emulate going forward.

BUILDING THIS NEW ERA TOGETHER

In order to better resource civil society—and in order to be better resources for civil society—we all need to change our behaviors. Large development agencies need to rethink how they invest, and in whom they invest. Foundations and philanthropists need to rethink how we allocate resources. CSOs need to advocate for general support, and articulate why their organization deserves that general support instead of project support. And, most importantly, we need to recommit ourselves to building organizations in a different, more durable way.

We know that fulfilling a contract deliverable is not the same as delivering social change. It, by definition, is too narrow, in both intention and output. We need to broaden our approach in order to foster an ecosystem that supports broad impact. This means that everyone needs to collaborate more—donors with donors, donors with grantees, and, importantly, grantees with donors.

So much of the first wave of this behavior change falls on donors. It is easy to say we need to give more general support. But we also need to be more trusting of the ecosystem, to get our individual houses in order and then act together. We need to recognize we are not the sole investor in the organizations we fund, and remember that their budgets reflect different sources of funding, and sometimes competing sets of priorities.

More than that, we need to shift the power dynamics of our relationship with CSOs, because our traditional ways of engaging no longer work. They lack authenticity and integrity, and, in some cases, basic respect.

We need to stop treating grantees and partners as contract workers and project managers. Instead, we need to restore balance and honesty to our interactions. We need to learn from one another, communicate and iterate often, and adapt to the changing needs of both parties as they arise. As donors, we must be frank in our observations. But, crucially, we also must listen better, so our partners do not feel timid when we need them to raise their voices and advocate for themselves.

And for civil-society institutions, I hope you will put the general support question on the table, not just at the margins, but right at the center. I hope that you will feel empowered to be loyal to your principles and your mission, and to engage with your donors based on the work that you are doing, rather than the pressure you are currently feeling. At the same time, CSOs also need to take responsibility for coordinating, at times consolidating, and, as the open letter I referenced earlier put it, "insisting that the voices and actions of people are at the heart of our work." This means periodically asking the hard questions, and giving honest answers: Have we really fulfilled the need we set out to? Have we drifted from our mission? Have we collaborated as effectively as we might?

Together, we need to reset the system in which scrambling for new funding gets in the way of fighting for social change—in which development distracts from mission. This is no easy task.

At the end of the day, we all have to make some difficult choices. As ever, we stand ready to work with you, to listen to you, and to help you, not just for three to five years, but for the long haul. Typically, the problems CSOs are intended to solve are not short-term problems. These are multigenerational bets. And as we know, from our history and our present, the best bets, and human progress itself, have always been propelled by a bold, vibrant, and adaptive civil society.

OLD MONEY, NEW ORDER: AMERICAN PHILANTHROPIES AND THE DEFENSE OF LIBERAL DEMOCRACY

Foreign Affairs
October 15, 2016

The world is experiencing a realignment unlike any other since the end of World War II. Nationalism and populism are surging in the United States and Europe, at the expense of liberal internationalism and democratic values. This poses a challenge to a wide range of institutions, including philanthropies committed to international development and social justice. Such foundations played a crucial role in building the liberal international order that has come under assault in recent years, and that the United States seems less willing to defend than ever before.

During much of the last century, philanthropic foundations based in the United States exported American ideals about democracy, market economies, and civil society. That mission was made possible by ideological support from and alignment with the US government, which, in turn, imbued foundations with prestige and influence as they operated around the world. American philanthropies such as the Ford Foundation can no longer count on such support. Nor can they be sure that the goals of increased equality, the advancement of human rights, and the promotion of democracy will find backing in Washington.

As US leadership of the global order falters, American foundations must blaze a new path. The first step will be recognizing difficult truths about their history. The old order they helped forge was successful in many ways but also suffered from fundamental flaws, including the fact that it often privileged the ideas and institutions in prosperous Western countries and failed to foster equitable growth and stability in poorer countries. For all the good that American philanthropies have done, they have also helped perpetuate a system that produces far too much inequality. Their task today is to contribute to the construction of a new, improved order, one that is more just and sustainable than its predecessor.

HOW TO SPEND IT

Although it was founded in 1936, prior to World War II, the Ford Foundation as it exists today took shape mostly in the war's aftermath. The social and political upheaval that the war left in its wake and the widespread anxiety about future conflict colored every decision the foundation made from 1950 onward.

The foundation was chartered in Michigan by Henry Ford's son, Edsel, and was designed in part to protect the Ford family's estate from new federal inheritance taxes. In its early years, the foundation was a modest organization that funded projects of interest to the Ford family. But the war, along with the deaths of Edsel Ford, in 1943, and his father, in 1947, fueled the foundation's transformation into a global actor.

Their bequests to the foundation totaled nearly 90 percent of the stock of the Ford Motor Company and created an endowment that was valued officially at $417 million in 1954 but was likely much larger. (A 1955

New Yorker article put the number, based on Ford Motor Company earnings, at closer to $2.5 billion, or $23.6 billion in today's dollars.) That wealth made the foundation the largest philanthropy in the world, overtaking older institutions such as the Carnegie Corporation and the Rockefeller Foundation.

In 1948, Edsel Ford's eldest son, Henry Ford II, asked the lawyer and investment banker H. Rowan Gaither to lead a study to determine what the foundation should do. Gaither's team collected input from a wide range of figures across the American establishment, from Dwight Eisenhower to Walt Disney. Its report recommended that the organization commit itself to human welfare through, first and foremost, "the establishment of peace," a lofty goal that could be achieved only by international cooperation and global economic development. This mission aligned perfectly with Washington's push to construct a liberal order backed by US military power and composed of alliances such as NATO, multilateral organizations such as the International Monetary Fund and the UN, and trade agreements such as the General Agreement on Tariffs and Trade. In embracing this emerging order, the Ford Foundation was hardly alone among the philanthropic set: The Rockefeller family, for example, had helped secure land for the UN headquarters and facilitated the 1944 Bretton Woods Conference, which led to the creation of the IMF.

To define the foundation's role in the emerging order, Ford turned to some of the order's most influential shapers. The first person from outside the Ford family to serve as president of the foundation was Paul Hoffman, who took charge in 1950 after having overseen the execution of the Marshall Plan in postwar Europe. To Hoffman, the foundation's mission represented, in a sense, a global extension of the Marshall Plan's goals: To foster democratic institutions and free markets, ward off the spread of communism, prevent the return of fascism, and secure American influence abroad. Hoffman toured the world, identifying projects to fund in democracies that Ford and the US government deemed essential.

Hoffman's goals were to mitigate global tensions, develop understanding among peoples, strengthen international institutions such as the UN, and improve how the United States engaged in global affairs.

Other boldface names served in important positions at Ford, creating a revolving door between the foundation and the highest levels of the US government. In 1950, George Kennan, the author of the famous "Long Telegram" (and a related, seminal article titled "The Sources of Soviet Conduct," published pseudonymously in this magazine in 1947), took a leave from the State Department, during which he advised the foundation on its early programming and worked on a Ford-funded project to create, in his words, "a more up-to-date, more realistic concept of the objectives of American foreign policy: That is, what the American government ought to be trying to achieve in its foreign policies." In 1952, John McCloy, after having served as US assistant secretary of war, US high commissioner for Germany, and the first president of the World Bank, was tasked by Hoffman with investigating "the conditions of peace"—a project that led to the foundation's support of the Council on Foreign Relations (which publishes *Foreign Affairs*) and of organizations such as the Brookings Institution and the International Institute for Strategic Studies. McCloy later served as chair of the foundation's board, from 1958 to 1965.

The cozy relationship between Ford and the US government would eventually draw a fair amount of criticism, particularly when it came to the foundation's influence on American foreign policy. John Howard, a staff member who accompanied Hoffman on his world tour, remarked that in India, "there was already suspicion that the foundations were just arms of the State Department; [Indian commentators] could never make the distinction between State and the Ford Foundation." At the same time, critics in India and Latin America accused the foundation of entanglement with the CIA. It's easy to imagine how their interests might have converged during that period, given the close relationship between the foundation and the US government. Nonetheless, efforts were made to ensure that, as Francis Sutton, a foundation official, wrote, "the CIA was kept at a prudent distance."

Ford's critics in Washington were more concerned with the foundation's domestic programs than with its international ones. In the early 1950s, the US House of Representatives' Select Committee to Investigate Tax-Exempt Foundations and Comparable Organizations (known as the Cox Committee, after Representative Edward Cox, a Democrat from Georgia) sought to discover whether such foundations were using their resources for "un-American and subversive activities." In a familiar Cold War paradox, some accused Ford and other foundations of being agents of American imperialism, and others accused them of being secret Soviet sympathizers.

COLD WARRIORS

As the Cold War intensified, alignment between the US government and major US foundations became a de facto alliance against communism, which both official Washington and its philanthropic allies saw as a major threat to peace and to their joint mission. A memo from Hoffman's very first board meeting, in January 1951, makes clear that "the main danger of war stems from tension between the East, led by the Soviet Union, and the West, led by the United States." According to Howard, Hoffman's visits to places such as India and Pakistan stemmed from a "Cold War philosophy." Although Hoffman "didn't speak like a Cold War warrior," Howard later recalled, "the mere choice of the underbelly of China was in the same genre of thinking."

A foundation annual report from 1953 stated that the Ford Foundation would work "only in those nations whose political philosophy and objectives, if sustained or achieved, are incompatible with communism." Throughout the 1950s and 1960s, Ford invested millions of dollars to build state capacity in emerging democracies in Africa, Latin America, and Southeast Asia. The foundation established its first international office in New Delhi in 1952, in part due to concerns that intense poverty would imperil the newly democratic and independent India by giving communists an opening.

Fighting communism and promoting democracy through massive poverty-reduction initiatives became a mainstay of Cold War–era US philanthropy. Beginning in the late 1950s, for instance, Ford collaborated with the Rockefeller Foundation to support what became known as the Green Revolution, helping to build and fund institutions focused on agricultural research all over the world. Vastly improving agricultural output, these efforts saved hundreds of millions—perhaps billions—of lives and helped lift millions more out of destitution.

Many of Ford's activities abroad involved connecting foreign government officials with American academics and experts, who could aid postcolonial democracies in crafting plans for economic development and institutional reform. The foundation also trained foreign civil servants in fields such as business, finance, law, management, and urban planning. The Ford Foundation followed in the Rockefeller Foundation's footsteps by building academic centers abroad and creating exchange programs for policymakers and academics. By the late 1970s, Ford had invested $450 million (approximately $1.7 billon in today's dollars) in these programs.

In 1968, in coordination with the State Department, the foundation formalized these activities in the International Research and Exchanges Board, which became extraordinarily influential in places such as Hungary and Poland, and even in the Soviet Union itself. It also sought to consolidate postwar democratic gains in Western Europe. The origins of the European Union can be traced back to grants from Ford and other American foundations, which funded scholarly research on European integration in the early 1950s, the work of the French diplomat Jean Monnet (one of the founding fathers of the EU), and a series of conferences for young leaders from across the continent who wanted to forge a common European identity.

Through these kinds of projects, the foundation trained and supported a generation of civil servants, diplomats, and leaders around the world, thousands of whom went on to achieve great things—most notably the late UN Secretary-General Kofi Annan. Some, however, later served repressive, even violent regimes. These include a number of Indonesian economists at the University of California, Berkeley, who became known as "the Berkeley Mafia" when they went to work for Suharto's dictatorship. Ford also helped train the so-called Chicago Boys, a group of Chilean economists who were educated at the University of Chicago with the help of Ford grants and who later joined the authoritarian government of Augusto Pinochet. These kinds of outcomes serve as reminders that foundations such as Ford do not have complete control over the downstream impact of their grants. Inevitably, some funding will have unintended consequences and confounding results.

SHOCKS TO THE SYSTEM

Pinochet's rise was part of a larger turning point for the Ford Foundation in the late 1960s and the first half of the 1970s. In democracies across Latin America in which the foundation operated—not only Chile but also Argentina and Brazil—right-wing autocrats came to power, often with Washington's direct or tacit backing. Ford could no longer work closely with those governments and had to find new approaches to supporting democratic ideals there. It pivoted from assisting officials with national planning to supporting civil-society organizations such as think tanks, watchdog groups, grassroots organizations, and even certain religious societies. It also began to prioritize its advocacy for the rights and norms required to protect such groups, including freedom of expression and association and the rule of law. In Chile, following Pinochet's 1973 overthrow of Salvador Allende, the foundation began to support groups that protected Chilean scholars and their academic work from the dictatorship, including the Latin American Council of Social Sciences, the

Emergency Committee to Aid Latin American Scholars, and the Vicariate of Solidarity.

This new focus on civil-society organizations informed the foundation's work in authoritarian countries in other regions as well. The foundation supported a 1973 conference on legal aid at the University of Natal, in South Africa, which drew international attention to the apartheid regime's abuses. In 1975, at the urging of several staff members, the foundation's board of trustees approved a human rights program, which began with $500,000 to support reforms, individual rights, local organizations, and social movements in various countries.

Political change also led philanthropies to modify their approaches in the wealthy countries of the West. Foundations had played a significant role in building the postwar global economic architecture, including the system of international financial exchange that emerged from Bretton Woods. But in 1971, the so-called Nixon shock—which saw, among other developments, the United States abandon the gold standard—transformed the world economy. Ford adapted by establishing a program on international economic order, which supported research into new fiscal models, inflation, and national stabilization policies, and helped establish networks to connect economists and policymakers.

Ford also became increasingly known for its work on social issues in the United States, particularly civil rights and women's rights, and the creation of new disciplines at universities. Much of the research that informed President Lyndon Johnson's Great Society agenda was funded by the Ford Foundation—including Head Start, the federal program that supports early childhood education. (As a five-year-old in Ames, Texas, I attended one of the first preschools funded by Head Start.)

Whereas World War II had bred near-universal alignment between foundations and the US government on most issues, the Vietnam War had the opposite effect. By sowing public distrust of the US foreign policy establishment and reminding institutions of the danger of uncritically supporting government policies, Vietnam gave foundations ample reason to assert more independence.

MULTIPOLAR GIVING

Today, the world is once again undergoing tectonic shifts. Liberal values and the US-led global order have come under assault. If Washington continues to retreat from its traditional role as the order's principal guarantor, authoritarian regimes will grow stronger and illiberal ideas will spread. The rise of China means that foundations will have to learn to operate in a world defined by multiple spheres of influence.

This learning process has already begun. Consider, for example, the Carnegie Endowment for International Peace's establishment, in 2010, of the Carnegie-Tsinghua Center for Global Policy, in Beijing, or the Brookings Institution's investment in research centers in Beijing, Doha, and New Delhi. More foundations should follow suit by establishing partnerships outside the United States and making their programming less reliant on US-centric views of global order and economic development. Just this year, for instance, the Ford Foundation has adjusted its own programs to be more global in nature, seeking to use our footprint in ten countries outside the United States to work together toward global outcomes on global issues—issues such as imbalanced financial flows from extractive industries, violence against women and girls, and the increasingly endangered space for civil society. In order to address such problems effectively, we will have to draw on ideas and talent from all parts of the world, working toward solutions that help encourage a new kind of international cooperation in a multipolar era.

Foundations must also invest in non-US institutions and individuals who intend to stay in and serve their home countries. In 2001, Ford invested $280 million—its largest single grant ever—to create the International Fellowships Program, which funded the education of foreign scholars around the world and sought to build the capacity of universities outside the United States. By 2013, the program had paid for more than 4,300 fellows from twenty-two developing countries to earn graduate or post-graduate degrees, many of whom were educated in the Global South. When the program ended, in 2013, 82 percent of the fellows it had funded were working for social change in their home countries.

A multipolar world will also foster the proliferation of non-American philanthropy. For most of the twentieth century, international giving was dominated by the great families of US industry: The Carnegies, the Fords, the Rockefellers, and many others. During the first two decades of the twenty-first century, American philanthropic preeminence has persisted and even expanded, as foundations established by Michael Bloomberg, Bill and Melinda Gates, and George Soros have made tremendous contributions to human progress. But as other parts of the world produce greater wealth, US-based foundations will have to share the stage with foundations established by wealthy individuals such as Mukesh Ambani of India, Aliko Dangote of Nigeria, Jack Ma of China, and Carlos Slim of Mexico.

This is a hopeful development because American foundations cannot address the world's most pressing problems alone. US foundations must find ways to support the growth of philanthropy in other countries and unleash the potential of new wealth around the world.

The Ford Foundation has provided seed funding for local and regional foundations, such as TrustAfrica, and networks of philanthropies, such as the African Philanthropy Forum, the East Africa Philanthropy Network, and the China Foundation Center. By sharing ideas, best practices, and strategies for funding with these smaller, non-American groups, legacy foundations can offer the perspective they've gained through their own successes and failures. Yet at the same time, they must abandon the old habit of relying on top-down initiatives designed by technocrats in New York and Washington and listen instead to people with on-the-ground knowledge. Over the past fifteen years, Ford has moved away from the practice of staffing its offices in the developing world with Americans and has benefited from tapping deep reservoirs of local talent.

In the postwar era, American foundations—working with the US government and other countries, development agencies, the private sector, and civil society—helped build a global order that brought impressive advances in poverty reduction, the promotion of democracy, gender equality, and social progress but that also produced unsustainable inequality. Today, US foundations have a responsibility to contribute to a more just and sustainable order. Doing so will require working with a broader range of partners and including voices that were left out of the twentieth century's order-building project. The time for change is now, and there isn't a moment to lose.

SUPPORTING UKRAINE AND THE VALUES OF DEMOCRACY

March 9, 2022

For two weeks, Russian forces have ravaged the people of Ukraine, brazenly and indiscriminately attacking civilians fleeing for the safety of their families and citizens fighting for the sovereignty of their democracy.

My heart breaks for them. I grieve for the hundreds, soon to be thousands, slain—for the untold millions whose lives have been forever upended by this senseless war. I worry for our world, pushed to the brink in so many ways and places. I fear, to paraphrase the poet W. B. Yeats, that, at some point, the center cannot hold.

The fact is, President Vladimir Putin's malevolent invasion of Ukraine and subversion of its democratic government violates international law. It disregards the conscience, the calls, and the condemnation of the international community.

Moreover, Putin's actions—his assault on the Ukrainian people's liberties, freedoms, and their republic itself—are not new to history. One would be hard pressed not to notice the parallels to 1938 and 1939, when Hitler's armies marched on Czechoslovakia and Poland, sparking the last great global conflagration.

Already, Putin's campaign of terror has created a refugee crisis of epic proportions—yet another global crisis that exposes and exacerbates inequalities of all kinds, including gender-based exploitation and anti-Black/Brown racism. This cataclysm comes at a moment when the global community desperately needs to reimagine recovery and rebuild more equitably, after two full years of COVID-19 throwing us off balance all over again. And given the scale of this calamity, it, inevitably, will draw attention and resources away from other humanitarian crises and urgent intersecting issues—that pandemic of pandemics—of caste and plague and environmental catastrophe.

More broadly, beyond the borderlands between East and West, we are confronted anew with the defining conflict of our time: The generational contest between authoritarian ideology and democratic values, the world over. Ukraine may be the latest, most violently contested battleground, but it is hardly the only one.

One recent analysis from Freedom House shows that, globally, authoritarianism has been gaining and democracy losing ground for sixteen consecutive years. Another from Sweden's V-Dem Institute illustrates that 70 percent of the world's people—some 5.4 billion human beings—now live in dictatorships. Put differently, the number of people living in liberal democracies has contracted to 1989, Cold War–era levels.

In Russia, Putin has tightened his grip on power for two decades, but he and his kleptocracy are only one element of a gathering authoritarian axis comprised not only of state actors, but autocrats across and within many states. Like others, he has governed with a degree of impunity—unjustly, wantonly, without consequence.

We see it everywhere. Autocrats (and wannabe autocrats, at home and abroad) denounce and discredit both journalism and history—both journalists and historians—promoting, in their place, state-sanctioned propaganda and mythology. They disrupt and distort the free flow of information, proclaiming one totalitarian truth that belies basic facts, let alone the nuance and complexity of the past.

This new kind of authoritarian axis erodes our global institutions. It denigrates the rule of law. It undermines confidence in fair elections, self-government, and civil society. It embezzles from its own peoples—perpetuating rampant corruption.

In the case of Russia, the Ford Foundation has witnessed this up close and in person. In 2008, we closed our Moscow office, in part due to government interference and corruption. Like others, we saw then what the world sees now: Putin did not, and does not, share the West's—and the Russian people's—ambitions for a new Russia following the dissolution of the Soviet Union.

Today, as the world inches closer to the precipice, we all are asking of ourselves and each other: What can we do? And what can we do now?

For starters, I'm thinking of the old benediction: Let's do all the good we can, for all the people we can, in all the ways we can.

Everyone can give—whether to CARE, the Ukrainian Women's Fund, the Committee to Protect Journalists, the International Rescue Committee (IRC), or other essential civil-society organizations like the Urgent Action Fund stepping into the breach.

I've been energized, too, by the creativity and generosity of many private sector leaders. Businesses across industries—from food to pharmaceuticals, cosmetics to travel—are putting aside profits to offer free housing to refugees, transport medical supplies and equipment, and get food, blankets, and other essentials to Ukrainians in need.

And, of course, the arts community exhilarates and emboldens, as ever. I was moved by Yo-Yo Ma's impromptu performance in front of the Russian Embassy on Monday afternoon. "We all have to do something," he said. Indeed.

For our part, philanthropy can and should anticipate what and where ongoing needs will be—and step in preemptively to address them. At Ford, so far, we have committed $1 million to the IRC's Ukraine Emergency Response Fund. We also are contributing $1 million to the Open Society Foundations' Ukraine Democracy Fund, which will bolster the work of many civil-society organizations and demand accountability through the documentation of war crimes.

And at home in the United States, this crisis calls out for America to rise to the challenge and realize our promise, not just despite our missteps in recent years, but because of them. The world needs us to serve as a beacon for human dignity and human rights—for the tired, for the tempest-tost, for all those yearning to breathe free.

I am heartened, in this vein, by New York Governor Kathy Hochul's bold proclamation welcoming Ukrainian refugees in New York City—home of the largest Ukrainian population outside of Ukraine itself. As a nation, we must prepare to do more, better, and faster: To resettle refugees in the US at an accelerated pace; to use every one of the 125,000 slots that President Biden pledged to make available for refugee resettlement (and more if necessary); to ensure that we welcome newcomers to our shores with compassion, after they experienced the unimaginable.

Ultimately, isolationism at the expense of cooperation is a self-fulfilling prophecy. That tired, "America First" dogma ignores our interdependence, tearing at that web of mutuality in which we all are bound together.

Each of us, in our own ways, must refuel that lamp beside the golden door—not because we always, in every instance, have kept it perfectly, but because we have the strength and means and obligation to brighten its glow now.

And, at the same time, we must redouble our commitment to multilateral institutions and their work; our support to Poland, Hungary, Romania, Moldova, and other nations now literally on the front lines; to protecting and promoting civil society in nations which, themselves, are theaters in the conflict between authoritarianism and democratic values.

Like all of you, I am watching with admiration and reverence as President Zelensky and the Ukrainian people fight valiantly to defend their homes, their communities, their country, and their democratic aspirations. I am moved by their resilience, courage, and strength, but also their kindness, empathy, and grace.

Let us honor their sacrifice with our own—for them and for the values we share. As we have before, time and again, let us meet this challenge with resolve, with action, and with enduring hope for justice and for peace.

BUILDING A MORE INCLUSIVE GLOBAL ORDER

The New York Times
September 19, 2022

Our international rules-based order—the system through which the world's nations pursue global peace and development—is crashing into the limits of its founding vision. What our predecessors built some eight decades ago, after the Second World War—from the World Bank and International Monetary Fund to the United Nations—is in desperate need of repair. But it remains essential, and salvageable.

For billions of people, the stakes could not be higher. This is painfully true for the people of Ukraine, where Vladimir Putin continues his malevolent invasion of a sovereign nation and subversion of international law. It's also true across the Global South, where I believe our global development finance system has proved outdated, outmoded, and outmatched.

We must reform the architecture of our global order—the blueprint for our system of international relations and development finance.

The Group of Seven (G7), major global-development organizations, and big global foundations remain too uncomfortable, too unwilling, to expand their range of funding and planning partners, especially stakeholders from the Global South. Many of us assume that our so-called expertise is more valuable or relevant than the experience of the communities affected by today's crises.

Of course, these are precisely the individuals and organizations to whom we should be listening, because they are most proximate to the problems that we can only solve together.

According to a recent study from the United Nations Development Program, during 2020 and 2021, nine of every ten countries have actually slid backward on the Human Development Index, a first in the three-decade history of this trusted report on health, education, and standards of living. These findings set in sharp relief the staggering costs and consequences of our cascading global crises, all of which are aggravated by inequality.

During the pandemic, the global order failed to sufficiently finance vaccine distribution and access, costing countless lives and inflicting incalculable damage on the economies of poor nations. As the world transitions to recovery, the inequities are only widening, both between and within countries.

The picture is hardly better for what should be a shared effort to mitigate and adapt to the global climate emergency and to meet the United Nations Sustainable Development Goals more broadly. In 2009, for example, the world's wealthy nations pledged that, by 2020, they would contribute $100 billion every year to help poor nations prepare for the consequences of climate change. Our system has now failed to meet even that modest goal three years in a row, and counting.

This system was founded to serve a simple, powerful ideal: Peace through economic engagement. Never again would the United States and Europe allow widespread economic depression and dislocation to recreate the conditions that led to isolationism, nationalism, fascism, and global conflagration.

This vision found its consummate expression at the Bretton Woods Conference in 1944, where delegates created the World Bank and International Monetary Fund—and then in the charter of the United Nations a year later. With support from a range of institutions, including the Ford Foundation, it evolved and expanded to include a plethora of development agencies, a complex mix of government, multilateral, and civil-society organizations.

By and large, this system of international cooperation helped achieve its original objective: Preventing the horror of a third world war. It sustained peace and prosperity, at least for the West, and ushered in unprecedented (if not uncomplicated) social and economic progress around the world.

At the same time, and from the start, this order was rife with flaws. For one, it did little to impede the proxy wars of world powers, particularly the United States and Soviet Union, across Asia, Africa, the Middle East, and Latin America.

For another, it reinforced and even replicated the inequalities it ought to have dismantled, dividing the world into donors and recipients, creditors and debtors, givers and takers, winners and losers. It became a new face of imperialism and colonialism.

Today, the challenges that face this order compound on one another.

We're engaged in a generational contest between authoritarian ideology and democratic values in countries the world over, including our own, but we're responding with the cutting-edge thinking of the 1940s.

The consequences of climate change, the next pandemic, or next recession will not be relegated to one country or another, but experienced first and worst by the poor and vulnerable in every country, jeopardizing everyone's security in turn.

Global leaders should commit to three principles for reform, to repair historic wrongs and to seize new opportunities for progress.

First, we must recognize that growth is good, but not good enough. We need metrics beyond GDP to measure and manage toward what matters most: The human rights and human dignity of people in every country.

Second, we must think bigger and bolder, but also for the longer term. We know that investment in equitable development today is far more cost effective than dealing with the consequences of our failure to invest during the decades ahead.

Most important, we must ensure that the people affected by twenty-first-century crises—and the development community's responses to them—have a voice in shaping policies and programs that serve them.

The global community can start immediately by releasing more resources, currently tied up in development organizations, and by listening to and learning from inspiring leaders across the Global South.

Ultimately, though, we can and must reorganize our efforts around the needs of people and communities, not just nation states, so governments, civil society, and private sector entities all work in common purpose toward a global common good.

PART VIII

OUT OF MANY, ONE: WHY DIFFERENCE NEED NOT YIELD DIVISION

Our differences and our divisions are not the same thing. The former does not somehow inevitably lead to the latter. To the contrary, our differences are our greatest strength, not a weakness—our greatest asset, not a liability. At this moment when it is all too tempting to shut out those with whom you differ, I implore you not to build walls, but to build bridges: To transcend divides, rather than widening them; to forge new relationships, by listening with humility, and curiosity, and empathy; to find common ground, at the intersection of open minds and open hearts.

Beirut, Lebanon
June 8, 2024

THE OPPOSITE OF INEQUALITY IS JUSTICE

Address to the Hostos Community College Class of 2015
South Bronx, New York, New York
June 4, 2015

Over the years, I've been to more than a few commencement ceremonies in more than a few places. And I'm very proud that just a few subway stops away from our offices at the Ford Foundation in Midtown, there is a school that rivals almost any other—a school that stands out for both celebrating diversity and encouraging excellence.

Of course, a lot changes between 43rd Street and 149th Street, between Grand Central Station and Grand Concourse—even just between Manhattan and the Bronx. It's sometimes unbelievable to think how different worlds can exist in the same city or in the same country.

I don't need to belabor the observation that, for the United States, this is a seminal moment—a period of profound and not always equal change. Indeed, the America of your college graduation day looks, and feels, and sounds very different than the America of mine.

Consider this: A half century ago, seventeen out of every twenty Americans were of European descent. A half century from now, we'll be well on our way to the opposite. In other words, with each passing day, America looks more and more like the South Bronx. And taken together, what this means is that your perspective matters more than ever before.

Look around, and you'll see that you are waves of a rising tide. Your lived experience is shared by a growing plurality of Americans. Look around, and you'll see Raisa Valerio, the first member of her family to attend college, let alone receive a degree. The proud mother of a six-year-old son, Raisa has been accepted to John Jay College of Criminal Justice, as well as Hunter College, and is considering a career within the Department of Corrections. Raisa: Congratulations!

Look around, and you'll see Diana Eusebio. Diana started life with her family in Mexico—but came to the United States and New York as a DREAMer. She's pursuing her interest in science while advocating for herself and others like her inside and outside of school. Today she is a Lincoln Academy Student—and has earned her Regents Diploma and an Associate Degree from Hostos. Congratulations, Diana!

Indeed, I am looking around, and I see all of you. Your hard work. Your triumphs. And I stand in awe of each of you. Because I started my journey in your very seats.

You see, as a young boy, raised by a single mom, I wasn't supposed to go to college. As a young man somewhat unprepared for the world, I wasn't supposed to graduate from a top-flight law school. As a young professional, with no experience in finance, I wasn't supposed to cut it on the trading floor of a major New York bank. And when I started in philanthropy, there the skeptics and cynics were again. They told me to lower my sights. They said that because I went to public schools, not private schools, that because I had on-the-ground experience, not a PhD, that because I had never worked in the venerated halls of old, stodgy foundations, I couldn't effectively manage seasoned, polished, buttoned-up executives.

My point is: In the eyes of so many, I wasn't supposed to have the opportunities I did—and I certainly wasn't supposed to seize them.

And every time I think about how I was not supposed to be where I am, I remember how I almost was not here at all. My childhood friends were cousins—boys with talents and passions and potential no different from my own. They found themselves caught in the same cycle of despair and injustice that has trapped so many of our young Black and Brown men. By my count, five of them have spent significant time in prison.

It reminds me exactly why days like these are so special, and so important, and so precious. Because there are insidious systems at work—entrenched systems that stack the deck against people like us, that make it harder to go from aspiration to achievement. But then there are institutions at work for good—institutions like Hostos—that advance, rather than hinder, opportunity.

Graduates: Look around. Here we all are, sharing this auspicious day. And what was true for me is true for you: You have to push forward, with courage and resolve, with poise and patience, with gratitude and grace. You have to represent these institutions of good, with excellence. And you already know exactly what this takes—better than most.

Many of you are the first in your families to graduate college—blazing a trail for generations to follow. And most of you attended class while holding down a job and raising a family. You woke up early. You worked and studied, and then worked some more. You did not coast. Cruise control was not an option. You took nothing for granted. And, as a result, you remind us all that anything, that everything, is still possible.

Graduates: You embody excellence—because of where you are; because of how hard you've worked and how far you've come. Immigrant, native. Straight, gay. Wealthy in means, rich only in resolve and resilience. Daughters and sons of proud families, mothers and fathers of children who will lead better lives because of your talent and your toil. Because of your sacrifice.

And so, I ask you—I implore you—don't stop. Keep dreaming. Keep working. Keep pushing forward. But keep reaching back, too. Start a business. Join a community association. Sign a petition. Serve on the PTA. Vote. The onus is on you. To stand up. To speak out. To use the weapons that Hostos has given you to fight for social justice.

Let me close with this: As coincidence—or maybe fate—would have it, today marks the fiftieth anniversary of another seminal commencement ceremony, the 1965 Howard University commencement at which President Lyndon Johnson delivered one of his greatest speeches. In it, he said—and I'm quoting here: "We seek not just freedom, but opportunity. We seek not just legal equity, but human ability. Not just equality as a right and a theory, but equality as a fact and equality as a result."

For my part, I believe that inequality is the greatest challenge we face as a society. But the opposite of inequality is not just equality; it is justice. And justice is what we must fight for, each in our own way—but also all together at the same time. For some of you, the fight may be here in the South Bronx. For others, it may be wherever else your family calls home. But your location does not trim your responsibility. Indeed, we are bound together—by pride in our history and our desire to make better our shared future.

Graduates: Your final class assignment is one that you must carry with you always. Demonstrate your excellence every day. Climb the ladder up, and when you do, don't lift it behind you.

This is a moment you will remember and cherish forever. Earning a degree from Hostos is a great achievement. But do not let it be your greatest achievement. Because there is much work to be done. Because your work is just beginning. And I cannot wait to see what you accomplish next.

CHOOSING
E PLURIBUS UNUM

Address to the University of Vermont Class of 2019
Burlington, Vermont
May 19, 2019

Today is special for many reasons. It's a celebration of excellence—and of the promise your future holds. It's the end of one chapter—and the beginning of another.

But today is also special for an additional reason.

You came to this magical community—Burlington, Vermont—from different places; from different towns and states and countries around the world. You came to your degree by different paths, taking different courses in different majors. Even when you were on the same campus, you spent time with different people, engaged in different activities. And after today, you will go off in your different directions: To different jobs, different cities and towns, entirely different lives.

And yet, here we are. Together. And the fact that we are together—at this time, in this place—this is remarkable.

It is remarkable because this is a unique, wonderful moment in your lives. But it also is remarkable because, in this new digital world, we are too often led to believe that our differences are reasons for division, rather than unity.

Class of 2019: This is a defining characteristic of our digital era—whether it's algorithms that segment and select the information we see based on our previous clicks and likes; or media outlets incentivized to confirm our beliefs, rather than deliver facts that help educate us and make us better citizens; or political leaders who rally the extremes, rather than serve a common good.

As a result of all this, we jump to judgment—and disagreement too often turns to dehumanization. We miss opportunities to turn difficult and challenging moments into teachable ones, from which we can learn and grow. We lose touch with the shared values and shared experiences and shared aspirations that bind us together in this country and make us who we are.

My message to you today is this: It doesn't need to be this way—and it hasn't always been. And I know this to be true, from my own journey.

You see, many aspects of who I am as a person, as an American, might be labeled as "different."

I am Black. I am gay. I live in Manhattan, that tiny island moored off the East Coast and a little unmoored from reality. And I spend much of my time traveling across the country and around the world, meeting visionary, courageous, resilient people fighting poverty, inequality, and injustice. All of these things—the things that make me different—define who I am.

And there are parts of my story that equally define me, that are harder to see, which also make me different.

I was born to a single mother in a charity hospital. We lived in a shotgun shack in a small, rural community in East Texas.

I attended public schools and colleges. I was in the first class of Head Start in 1965, received Pell grants, and private scholarships.

As an African American growing up in the South, I certainly encountered bitter racism. But I also benefited from enormous generosity—from people who provided me with support and encouragement, and who believed in my potential.

You see, in spite of the differences I presented and the challenges I encountered, I always felt that my country, that America, had my back. I had good people of good will cheering me on and pushing me forward.

Indeed, my story is an American story. It's a story of what is possible, of what can happen, when "we the people," live up to our highest ideals. And when we do fulfill these ideals, the fact of our differences does not hold us back, in the very same way that the fact of our differences is not really what divides us.

Class of 2019: The differences among us and the divisions between us—these are separate things. One does not inevitably lead to the other.

We are different, yes. But our differences are our strength.

Our division, on the other hand, is a liability—a liability that has been exacerbated and exploited, I believe, because of the corrosive inequality that today is widening in American society.

More than what we look like or where we come from or how we worship, inequality is what is tearing our communities and country asunder.

Economic inequality asphyxiates the American idea—and the economic and social mobility that sustains it. It creates unprecedented wealth gaps, sorting us into circles where we only engage with people of similar means and perspectives.

Persistent racial and gender inequality cause the sins of our history to infect the present and imperil the future.

Inequality helps explain the gaps between the experience of rural Americans and urban Americans—and entrenches the polarization in our political institutions.

And inequality doesn't just cause our challenges. It also prevents us from joining together to solve our common problems.

It undermines our hope for the future and erodes our faith in one another. Because of it, we are less willing to trust one another—less willing to extend the benefit of the doubt. Too often, we rush to judgment, assuming the worst intentions of others.

Now, I'm not naive. There are people for whom hate and harm is the intention. From Charlottesville to Pittsburgh, we have witnessed the painful, pernicious impact of hate. And while there certainly are racists, anti-Semites, homophobes, and prejudice in America today, this is not the character of who we are as a nation. Most Americans believe in ideals of equality and justice for all—and in order for these ideas to be realized, we must stand up to emboldened bigotry.

And so, graduates: I ask you, I implore you, not to build walls, but to build bridges—to build relationships—because when I reflect on my own story, I know I did not get here alone.

None of us have.

It was not the simple fact of my presence, or superficial measures of diversity or inclusion, that led me to the great honor of serving as president of the Ford Foundation, or to the great honor of addressing you today. It was often people who were very different from me extending their humanity and generosity and their privilege to help me—leaving their comfort zones behind and spanning a divide.

It was people I didn't know—or came to know only later—who had faith in me, who invested in me, who sustained me on my American journey.

My story is proof of what can happen when people choose to transcend their differences and build bridges and build relationships. You, too, are proof. And, on its best days, so is this country I love.

America always has been the product of people choosing to bind themselves together. Actively choosing. We are "we the people." We are *e pluribus unum*—out of many, one.

Because of our differences, we can ascend from cooperation to collaboration to innovation. Out of our differences, there is hope. Out of difference, there can be unity. Out of difference, equality and justice.

And it's bigger than the United States. Out of many countries, we are one planet—with one future.

Which brings me back to where I started: The celebration of difference—and all of the possibility that difference unleashes.

Out of many paths—out of many graduates—you are one class. And while you have many careers and choices in front of you, I hope you keep one objective in mind: To make this a more just—a fairer world.

So, I ask you: What bridges will you build? What new relationships will you initiate? What justice will you serve? What will you make possible for someone else?

Many of the bridges you cross will not be physical structures of concrete or steel. They will be relationships you forge, through hard work and attention, respect and care, listening and love. And the best relationships are those in which you can be yourself and better yourself.

If my experience is any indication, this is especially true of relationships with graduates of this great university. My partner in life of twenty-six years, David Beitzel, was a proud member of UVM's class of 1980. He passed away suddenly in January.

David taught me so much about life, and our common humanity. We were very different. We hailed from very different places and backgrounds. But we found each other despite those differences—and enriched each other's lives because of them.

Relationships with other people—friendships and family, professional, romantic, incidental and intentional—all are essential, no matter how different we may seem to be. They strengthen our empathy, our compassion, our humanity, and widen our perspectives.

If we build bridges and bonds of connection, then when injustice affects one of us, we know—deeply, personally—that it affects all of us. When we bind ourselves to others—when we recognize that our fates are bound together—we can put the small things aside. We can make a world where stories like mine are more probable, more likely, more common. We can shrink the gaps of inequality and grow justice in its place.

It will not be easy, Class of 2019. Justice takes time. It takes work. It takes love. And it takes risk.

But I hope you find ways to build these bridges. I hope you find ways to listen and be curious—to be present and proximate. I hope you embrace difference—and reject division.

Class of 2019: I know you will answer the call—and I know the future will be much better for it. It's yours for the taking and the making, as of right now.

CONFRONTING ANTI-ASIAN VIOLENCE

March 17, 2021

Anti-Asian racism is a painful, pernicious American tradition—and yesterday's murders in Atlanta remind us that this particular strain of racism is not merely part of our history, but a clear and present crisis.

My heart breaks today for the families and communities of the eight people callously gunned down. Like our trustee Ai-jen Poo shared earlier today, we "woke up this morning just wanting to know their names." As we wait to learn—and yearn to say—their names, we already know that they lived and died in a world where Asian Americans are too often scapegoated, marginalized, and demonized, where their labor has been exploited and where their dignity has been denied. For decades, Asian Americans have been labeled a model minority, a damaging myth that diminishes the complexities of racism in the United States and downplays its role in the persistent struggles of other racial and ethnic communities, especially Black Americans.

As Americans, we must reckon with our past in order to transcend it. Our past includes Chinese exclusion and Japanese internment, xenophobia directed at South Asian and Muslim communities after September 11, 2001, and too many other instances to name. And most recently, it includes hateful, racial slurs from the highest levels of the United States government, which contributed to a significant wave of anti-Asian violence in major cities across the country.

Last night's murders are inseparable from this broader history of anti-Asian hate, and of a global epidemic of violence against women, but they also reflect and emerge from the white supremacy that devalues people of color across the United States and around the world. They're inseparable from the inequality faced by workers who labor at the margins, by immigrants othered by society rather than embraced as our fellow Americans.

As Dr. Martin Luther King Jr. once wrote, "Injustice anywhere is a threat to justice everywhere." In the same way, hate and violence directed at Asian Americans is a threat to us all.

My Ford Foundation colleagues and I stand with the Asian American and Pacific Islander community. Together with our grantee partners, we will continue the work of dismantling white supremacy and disrupting inequality in all of its forms.

BUILDING MULTIETHNIC, MULTIRACIAL, PLURALIST DEMOCRACIES

Statement upon Appointment into the Order of the British Empire
New York, New York
March 22, 2023

Thank you, Consul General Emma Wade-Smith, for your generous introduction. My sincere thanks to His Majesty King Charles III for this recognition. And my deep gratitude to the late Queen Elizabeth II, for her lifetime of leadership and service—and for extending this privilege, appointment to the Order of the British Empire, to those of us gathered here.

I feel deeply moved to join in celebrating all of you: This community of distinguished educators, steadfast advocates, and dedicated public servants.

It's been observed that the United Kingdom and United States are one people divided by a shared language.

Now, there is a healthy debate over whether Prime Minister Churchill or George Bernard Shaw or Oscar Wilde deserves credit for the insight.

But the idea reflects our shared values, our shared history, and our shared future.

Indeed, the lauded *special relationship* between our two nations endures as a beacon for democratic values and institutions the world over. At our best—in our finest hours—this special relationship represents humanity at its best: The conviction that all are created equal and endowed with inalienable human rights; the conscience that catalyzed transatlantic movements for abolition and suffrage, equality and justice; the courage to give blood, sweat, toil, and tears in battles, past and present, against tyranny and authoritarianism, all around the globe.

What began as allegiance centuries ago evolved into an unshakable alliance for centuries to come.

We are prolific partners—across culture, creativity, and commerce. In shouldering the burdens that give us purpose. In enjoying the freedoms that give our lives meaning and richness and depth.

And let us tell the truth: We also struggle with a shared legacy of colonialism, imperialism, and caste. With patriarchy and white supremacy. With the deep injustices and inequalities that have accompanied our most noble aspirations from the very beginning.

On this august occasion, we note the fullness of our inheritance not to diminish the light our two nations have brought to the world—a triumph of human achievement—but to illuminate how we got from where we were to where we are; how we get from where we are to where we must go.

Inequality has plagued us from the start. We grapple, daily, with the pernicious, insidious consequences of inequality still.

But we became more equal thanks to the sacrifices of our ancestors and elders. And we become so thanks to so many of you, on the front lines of our transatlantic fight for justice today.

I am inspired by the diversity that the sovereign has chosen to recognize—the many different people pursuing scholarship, diplomacy, and public service—advancing justice across countries and continents.

And I am gratified by our larger opportunity: To commemorate the late Queen's desire for a representative, inclusive OBE. To celebrate our nations—not despite our past, but because we acknowledge and contend with its complexity. To move closer to the promise of the democratic project—the promise of one people—closer to building multiethnic, multiracial, pluralist democracies.

In service of this shared mission, I am grateful—humbled—to accept this extraordinary honor. Thank you.

TURNING THE RISING TIDE OF ANTI-SEMITISM

September 15, 2023

Beginning tonight, millions of Jewish Americans will observe Rosh Hashanah (the Jewish New Year) and then, ten days later, Yom Kippur (the Day of Atonement). Together, these high holy days reflect a duality, even a paradox of progress: We cannot fulfill the promise of the new without first recognizing and seeking forgiveness for the pain of the old.

For Americans of every faith, this timeless tradition might inform and inspire our journeys toward a collective *tikkun olam*—repair of our world. Indeed, we cannot strive to mend without first acknowledging what is broken. And among the wrongs we must make right, one specific sin that stains the conscience of our nation is the resurgent scourge of American anti-Semitism.

Today, anti-Semitic bigotry is becoming more brazen—and dangerous.

During the last five years, the Jewish-American community has endured a record number of hate crimes, a 35 percent increase between 2021 and 2022.

This includes the horrific 2018 terrorist attack at Tree of Life Synagogue in Pittsburgh, of which American Jews are reminded every single Saturday as they walk past police officers posted at their synagogue doors—as well as the 2019 murders of Jewish people in Poway, California, Jersey City, New Jersey, and Monsey, New York. Last year, another perpetrator took four people hostage during a Sabbath service at a temple in my home state of Texas.

We hear the echoes of violence in the coded language and dog whistles of our conspiratorial and paranoid politics. We scroll through the onslaught of anti-Semitic expression up and down our social media feeds. We see it in the sinister insinuations about surnames like Soros and Rothschild. We sense its spread in the cancer of Holocaust denial, metastasizing online and off.

Anti-Semitism is among the oldest forms of hate. Its ongoing expression aggravates intergenerational trauma for a community that remains vulnerable—for a people who experience that vulnerability intensely, despite what some simplistically assume to be their full acceptance in mainstream American life.

One might even draw a parallel between the Jewish communities of the United States today and those of Germany and Austria a century ago, who thought themselves assimilated into their home countries but were condemned as the "other." Through the 1920s, hundreds of thousands of people self-identified as *German* Jews, German first. But as the next several decades unfolded, it became all too clear that the reality was the exact opposite: Their neighbors saw them only as Jews, who happened to reside in Germany.

America's history is rife with our own version of persecution and pogroms, entangling even those that our familiar stories anoint as heroes.

President Franklin D. Roosevelt, for instance, simultaneously defended the "freedom of every person to worship God in his own way" while turning away Jewish asylum seekers through the 1930s. The very ideology that they were fleeing manifested itself again in Charlottesville, where neo-Nazis brandished torches and chanted, "Jews will not replace us."

We can and must do better.

We must look to the lessons of history, which affirm—as do the Jewish high holy days this week—that there can be no reconciliation without atonement, no justice without accountability.

I feel this obligation acutely as the leader of an institution that protects and promotes democratic values, which also was founded by Henry Ford—an icon of innovation and industry and philanthropy *and* one of the twentieth century's most virulent American anti-Semites.

Further, all of us engaged in building a fairer, more just America ought to embrace our responsibility to speak out about this ancient strain of inequality—this category of caste—exactly as we call out racism, sexism, ableism, and homophobia.

To paraphrase *Pirkei Avot*, a Rabbinic text on ethics, we are not obligated to complete the work, but neither are we free to desist from it.

Making amends for the sins of our past requires a fundamental reckoning. And the first step is rejecting indifference.

Let's root out bias in our own actions and question the causes and concessions at the root of our inaction. Let's condemn acts of explicit prejudice and find the will to challenge silence as well.

Ultimately, let's regard solidarity not as a finite resource that we might somehow deplete, but rather as a muscle that we strengthen with use.

Reflecting on the last century, Elie Wiesel, a hero of mine, cautioned that "indifference is always the friend of the enemy, for it benefits the aggressor, never his victim." As we mark these high holy days, let us cast off our indifference—and forge a new beginning, with hope, worthy of the ideals we cherish.

HOLDING FAST TO OUR SHARED HUMANITY

October 22, 2023

With each passing day, my heart breaks anew.

I grieve for the victims of Hamas' terrorism and all of the suffering and trauma it has unleashed—for the more than 1,400 Jews and 5,000 Palestinians killed; for the more than 200 anguished families, anxiously awaiting word about their loved ones held hostage.

I grieve for the communities this crisis has displaced and upended, in Israel and around the world—for all those across the Jewish diaspora reckoning with the vile resurgence of anti-Semitism and the many victims of Islamophobia.

I grieve for the millions of innocent people—civilians, human beings—who yearn only for peace, but remain trapped in an escalating cycle of violence.

For me, one pressing question is: How can philanthropy make a difference?

I believe, especially in moments like these, that philanthropy must turn toward the pain and peril, not away from it. We must act with urgency and agility, in a way that catalyzes the good works of others. And at the Ford Foundation, we are proud to provide grants to both Jewish- and Palestinian-led efforts—because the long road to relief, to rebuilding, to reconciliation of any kind begins with both peoples.

As ever, we are listening and learning with empathy and compassion. We are supporting those closest, most proximate, to the people and communities in greatest need. We are giving in collaboration—in true partnership—with the public and private sectors, other foundations, and many indispensable civil-society organizations, entrusting grantees with general support and empowering them to deploy resources most effectively.

Of course, some have cautioned that I—and the institution I lead—would be well advised to stay silent and stand pat. As I've noted before, Henry Ford, our founder, was among the twentieth century's most virulent American anti-Semites. And yet, to me, our past confers a special obligation to engage, not to retreat—no matter the complications or the consequences.

Ultimately, we all must hold fast to the promise of a future in which everyone can live in equality—with human dignity and human rights, with the freedoms and responsibilities of pluralist democracy. History teaches this will not come easy, nor on its own. But together we can and must help to build a just and lasting peace, worthy of our shared humanity.

THE DEMOCRATIC VALUES THAT BIND US TOGETHER

Address to the American University of Beirut Class of 2024
Beirut, Lebanon
June 8, 2024

Today is special for many reasons. It's a celebration of your excellence and of the promise your future holds. It's the end of one chapter and the beginning of another. And as we pause on the threshold of all you will do next, it's an opportunity to reflect on the community that you have built together—and on the shared democratic values that bind our communities together across the world you are entering.

From my own life's story, I understand how—and how much—these shared values matter.

I grew up poor, born to a single mother in a charity hospital and raised in a tiny shotgun shack. I grew up gay, at a time when many people saw my identity as a psychological disorder, or a crime. I grew up Black in the segregated American South, in Louisiana and Texas, where the adults in my life were subjected to discrimination in just about every aspect of theirs.

And yet, at every step of my journey, our shared values inspired good people of good will to help me cross bridges of opportunity. Our shared values inspired public goods and public resources—Head Start, public schools and universities, Pell grants—that provided me a path forward. Our shared values inspired enormous generosity—from institutions that provided me with support and encouragement; from friends and mentors who extended my horizons and challenged me to think in new ways.

Indeed, my story is about what's possible when we live up to our highest ideals—when we embrace the conviction that from many, we are one. And Class of 2024: I know that your stories are about this, too.

I know you traveled all different paths—all different roads. You overcame different obstacles. You pursued different interests and passions and dreams. You made your way from the corner of a Zoom screen in 2020 to this campus at the crossroads of the world—to this magnificent, magical city, with its rich history and culture.

And when you arrived, what greeted you? What energized you? What intoxicated you? What, sometimes, challenged you?

More difference: People who looked or loved or worshipped differently than you. People who, perhaps, saw the world through different eyes. People who saw our problems differently. People who saw our opportunities differently.

Moment by moment, you persevered and triumphed across all different fields and disciplines—all different traditions of inquiry and exploration and engagement. And after today, you once again will go off in all different directions: To different vocations, different locations—to lead different lives.

And still, from all this difference, look around: Here you are, wearing the same robes and the same joyful smiles. Here you are, sharing the same pride in all that you've accomplished. Embracing the same responsibility— the same commitment—to make change in a world that desperately needs it.

You came here as strangers—but you leave here as lifelong classmates and friends, united by your shared journey.

Class of 2024: The fact that we are together—at this time, in this place—this is remarkable. And on this most auspicious evening, I ask you to remember this: The power of solidarity—of shared values and shared aspirations—not just despite our differences, but because of them.

Now, I don't need to tell you that division—divisiveness—is a hallmark of our era. We see it in—and in response to—the world's most intractable conflicts: In profound human suffering, in the pain and anguish across this region, a stain on our humanity. We see it in our distorted media, where the few loudest voices garner the coverage and clicks, while the conglomerates reap the rewards. We see it in the so-called leaders who rally the extremes, rather than calling us to a common good. And we see it because of inequality—inequalities of all kinds—inequalities that both aggravate our gathering crises and prevent us from joining together in common cause to address them.

As a result of all this, we—almost instinctively, reflexively—retreat into our comfortable corners, where our biases are confirmed. And we allow our differences and disagreements—we allow our diversity—to be spun into division. As the poet and activist Audre Lorde put it many years ago, difference has been—and I quote—"misnamed and misused in the service of separation and confusion."

And so, Class of 2024, my message for you today is simple: It doesn't need to be this way—and it hasn't always been. Our differences and our divisions are not the same thing. The former does not somehow inevitably lead to the latter. To the contrary, our differences are our greatest strength, not a weakness—our greatest asset, not a liability.

At this moment when it is all too tempting to shut out those with whom you differ, I implore you not to build walls, but to build bridges; to transcend divides, rather than widening them; to forge new relationships by listening with humility and curiosity and empathy; to find common ground at the intersection of open minds and open hearts.

The work ahead will not be easy. It will take comfort with discomfort. It will take risk. It will take hope—radical, audacious hope. And it will take love. But I have every confidence that you—that your generation—is up to the task ahead.

PART IX

THE PROMISE OF AMERICA

The American story we should celebrate ... is one of expanding representation—however slowly, unevenly, and imperfectly. It's the story of a small circle of white, property-owning men in Philadelphia that, generation by generation, continues to grow wider, precisely because of the patriotic struggle and sacrifice of the people who were once excluded....

I love my country. I'm grateful to and for it. And I believe, now more than ever, in the promise of 1776—in the radicalism of representation.

In their flawed genius, the founders entrusted us with the tools to fix what they were unwilling to repair. They left us the capacity to build something that had never existed: A multiracial, multiethnic, pluralist democracy that extends the blessings of representation to all.

The Washington Post
July 2, 2021

A NEW TESTAMENT
OF HOPE

Expanded Version
December 15, 2014

Nearly a half century ago, during the final days of Dr. Martin Luther King Jr.'s life, he penned what he called a "testament of hope," an epistle he could not have known would be among his last. "Whenever I am asked my opinion of the current state of the civil rights movement," Dr. King began, "I am forced to pause; it is not easy to describe a crisis so profound that it has caused the most powerful nation in the world to stagger in confusion and bewilderment."

During these last few weeks and months, as we each have attempted to make sense of Michael Brown's and Eric Garner's senseless deaths, confusion and bewilderment abound. In quiet moments and public demonstrations, we have been overwhelmed with emotion. We have staggered in disbelief, in frustration, in shame, in anger.

All too often at moments like this, we Americans have retreated into our comfortable corners—segregating not only ourselves, but our ways of understanding what Dr. King called, in that same remarkable document, "a series of separate problems" that have "merged into a social crisis of almost stupefying complexity."

Yet, confronted anew with crises as old as our country—with issues intertwined in our very constitution—we must give our own testament to hope, too.

There is hope, for example, in the fact that I can compose this essay from my desk at the Ford Foundation; that a Black, gay man—born to a brave single mother in a Louisiana charity hospital, the product of Head Start, public schools, and Pell grants—can rise to become president of a prominent global foundation.

There is hope in the knowledge that, from innumerable tests and trials of our national conscience, we can emerge—and are emerging—a more unified, more equal, more just America.

FOUNDING CONTRADICTION

This hope is anchored in an honest assessment of where we have been and how far we have come.

It bears repeating that the United States was founded on a fundamental, unresolved contradiction: Our founders pledged their sacred honor to the idea that "all men are created equal," while creating a system in which they were not.

Americans conveniently forget that among the many compromises that made possible our charters of freedom were choices to count my enslaved ancestors as three-fifths of a person; to protect, not proscribe, the bondage and sale of children; to codify society's illusory hierarchies of gender, of class, and, especially, of skin color.

While traveling across our early republic, Alexis de Tocqueville—the celebrated political observer who first imbued the idea of American exceptionalism into our national psyche—noted this dissonance. On one hand, early America was distinctive in its communitarian equality and entrepreneurial ambition. On the other, even he observed that the interrelated issues of slavery and race were more than a contradiction: They were "the most formidable of all the ills which threaten the future existence of the Union." These issues held the destructive energy to do us in.

In our time, we are fast to grab hold of the American promise and to say, "You see, we *are* special." And for good reason. My American story—among countless others—is proof.

But de Tocqueville was not *only* half right. We are the progeny of both parts of this heritage.

It should not be surprising, then, that two centuries later—on the other side of civil war and Jim Crow, in the aftermath of marches on Washington and Selma and Montgomery—we feel confused and bewildered as the legacy of our founding contradiction manifests itself once again.

GRINDING INEQUALITY AND ITS CORROSIVE EFFECTS

We know, intuitively, that our experiment with democracy—our quest "to form a more perfect union"—is a complex endeavor.

For most Americans, our nation's diversity is a source of strength and pride—*e pluribus unum*—whereas, for many other nations, it is an anathema. Nevertheless, during confounding moments, like the one in which we find ourselves now, we still can revert to old habits and patterns. And all of this is further complicated by a spectrum of inequalities—social and economic—that is much wider than racial inequality alone.

During these last few decades, American society has suffered from grinding inequality—arguably more corrosive than in any previous period.

As the economic growth of the early 1960s converged with social unrest and upheaval, Vietnam and Watergate, and then, finally, gave way to the stagflation and recession of the late 1970s and 1980s, a spirit of empathetic, inclusive optimism contracted. During the decades since the mid-1980s, most of the benefits of our booming markets have inured to the very few—never more so than in this most recent economic recovery.

As a result, Americans—and middle-class Americans, in particular—are too worried about their own plight to be magnanimous in worrying about the plight of others. Americans of every creed and color feel *less* secure. They feel *more* vulnerable, uncertain, and anxious.

In turn, as the eminent political scientist Robert Putnam has shown, we—collectively—have become less motivated to solve big problems. In this way, our "civic infrastructure" has deteriorated and our discourse has coarsened.

The problem that Frederick Douglass and W. E. B. Du Bois long ago called "the color line" has proven hard to erase, even in the best of times. And today's debilitating inequality, which eats away at our society, makes it even more difficult to engage.

OUR CRIMINAL JUSTICE SYSTEM TODAY

This is a problem with cascading consequences—and these consequences are encountered daily by some of the most courageous women and men in our national life: Our police officers.

Law enforcement is among the toughest vocations in America. When someone decides to become a police officer, they are not just choosing a career; they are answering a calling.

Police officers do not enter the profession seeking to do harm. They are making good on a noble commitment to serve and protect. As I joined with tens of thousands of marchers in Manhattan last weekend, I was struck by the powerful juxtaposition of the countless New York City police officers who helped ensure peaceable assembly in a protest against the police department itself.

At the same time, we must acknowledge that certain elements of our larger criminal justice system—no matter the best intentions of the overwhelming majority of people who comprise it—remain patently, structurally unjust. This is why many people—especially in poor communities of color—perceive the police as mechanisms of social control.

Scholar, lawyer, and advocate Michelle Alexander powerfully makes this case in her magisterial book *The New Jim Crow*. As she argues, America's unequal drug laws, mandatory-minimum prison sentences, and wholesale incarceration of Black and Brown men for nonviolent crimes have set in motion a vicious cycle. Black men have their basic rights revoked, which traps families in poverty, which contributes to increasing crime. As a result, she explains, more African Americans are part of the criminal justice system today than were enslaved on the eve of the Civil War.

To me this is intensely personal. My childhood friends were cousins—boys with talents and passions and potential no different from my own. My mother wisely moved my sister and me from a segregated small town in Louisiana to Texas in hopes of giving us a better life. My cousins, however, found themselves ensnared in the same cycle that has trapped so many young Black men. By my count, five of them have spent time in prison, including one who died by hanging himself while incarcerated.

When I was in college at The University of Texas, I knew I would be held to a different standard than my white friends when it came to recreational drug use, which was prevalent, especially among the privileged students from Houston and Dallas. At a party in my dorm, when a friend passed me a joint, I knew to decline. When he was arrested later that year for possession of marijuana, his father had it taken care of. Whatever happened was expunged from his record; today he has a wonderful life and beautiful family in a prosperous Texas suburb. As a Black kid—a young Black man without means—I knew *implicitly* that if I were ever to be brought into the criminal justice system, my hopes and dreams would be snuffed out in an instant.

My point is: The distance between promise and peril, between justice and injustice is astoundingly, terrifyingly short.

No one *wants* this—especially those who work in our justice system and law enforcement. This is not by *our* design.

But this system, remember, is rooted in that same complex web of inequality—racial, social, and economic—which predates any of us. This system is what created the context for Michael Brown's and Eric Garner's killings—for countless other stories just as heartbreaking and perplexing and infuriating. This system is the reason we find ourselves watching video of Eric Garner begging for mercy, while receiving treatment not even befitting an animal.

This is not the America we want. This is not the America we are proud of.

A NEW TESTAMENT OF HOPE

Yet, despite all of this—or, perhaps, in some strange way, because of it—I am hopeful.

To borrow a phrase from my youth, the whole world *is* watching: Up close. Aghast. Just as our parents and grandparents were a half century ago—only this time on the screens of devices in our hands, not just televisions in our living rooms.

Indeed, today's demonstrations have been heartening not only for their message, but also their makeup. People of all backgrounds, and young people in particular, are rallying together in pursuit of justice.

This can be a tipping point—a time and place where we see the bending in the "arc of the moral universe." While our history has been informed by a contradiction, it also has been defined by what James Baldwin called "the perpetual achievement of the impossible."

So, how do we escape the quagmire? How do we "achieve the impossible" again?

To start with, we need smarter investment in better policing.

We need investment in the human capacity of our police officers—in their professional development, in their training, in their ability to relate to and understand the communities they serve. We need to redirect funding to community policing, which has fallen out of favor in the age of stop-and-frisk policies, broken-widows theory, and three-strikes-you're-out theology.

What we do not need is more of the militarization we saw in Ferguson—nor more of the menacing weaponry that has been shipped from battlefields in Iraq to precincts across the United States. (And, by the way, maybe police would not have reason to be so afraid of young people with guns if guns were not so readily available virtually everywhere.) Instead, we, as a democracy, should give our police the best tools and techniques to match their best intentions and then hold them accountable.

At the same time, we need to engage with and empower communities. We need to ensure that the people affected by policy have a voice in creating it. We need to invest in our neighborhoods and cities because, while talent is everywhere, economic opportunity is not.

As I have traveled the United States—from New York to Detroit, Chicago, and St. Louis—I hear the same things. People, especially young people, want jobs. They want to do well for their families, to do right by their neighbors, and to do good in their communities. Sybrina Fulton, the mother of Trayvon Martin—another gunned-down, young, Black man—put it so well: "People are now realizing [our movement] is not just about African-American rights; it is about human rights."

And this larger movement for human rights is inseparable from the necessary work of repairing our broken politics—the heavy lifting of owning up to the biases and injustices that are deeply embedded within our system.

All of this will require political courage. We need statesmen and stateswomen to bring us together, not politicians to degrade our discourse and drive us apart. We need people of purpose to transcend the politics of division—in spite of the fact that the rhetoric of exclusion is such a successful political tactic.

MY RADICAL OPTIMISM

Ultimately, there is a larger force at work. There is something stirring us to action—demanding that we trade confusion and bewilderment for a fight for change that only hope and *radical* optimism can sustain. The memories of Michael Brown, Eric Garner, and too many others—the legacies of all those who suffered and sacrificed before us, the giants on whose shoulders we stand—deserve no less.

In that final "testament of hope," Dr. King wrote that "man has the capacity to do right as well as wrong, and his history is a path upward, not downward." "This," he said, "is why I remain an optimist."

So, too, it must be with us.

Let us continue to seek right in the face of misdirected might. Let us continue making our way upward, even—and especially—at these moments when the gravity is more than we can bear.

For my part, I have deep, abiding, and absolute faith that America will. Through fits and starts, feats and defeats, fairness *will* triumph. The irrepressible current of justice *will* carry us forward, no matter the impediments ahead.

Why do I believe we shall overcome? Because, time and again, we have.

WHAT MAKES US EXCEPTIONAL: THE ACT OF PERFECTING, NOT THE FACT OF PERFECTION

Address to the Hunter College Class of 2016
New York, New York
January 21, 2016

Today, we celebrate a wonderful occasion for you, for Hunter College, for our city, and for our country. Yes, we marvel at your accomplishments—at your resolve and resilience. Yes, we pause in awe and appreciation for your tomorrows—full of promise. But this moment also belongs to history—the histories from which you emerge and the history that you will make.

For my part, I come from a personal history not vastly different from many of yours.

As the child of a single mother—the product of Head Start and public schools—I know what it's like to enter college with family rooting me on but unable to help with the tuition.

I know what it's like to attend class while holding down more than one job; to make friends in the financial-aid office; to work through the summer because you can't take a break when on the verge of going broke.

And I know what it means to graduate from a great public institution like Hunter, one of the defining innovations in American history, colleges and universities where all young people can pursue their dreams, regardless where they begin in life.

Indeed, history is exactly what I'd like to discuss with you this afternoon—even as we look ahead to your bright and brilliant futures.

Of course, from our history, we draw more than our senses of perseverance—of grace and grit. In our history, we see the roots of many of our thorniest challenges.

We hear the echoes of history in debates over how far the right to bear arms extends or who does—and doesn't—have the right to immigrate to a nation of immigrants or the right of corporate donors to exert influence on public institutions.

Every civic argument—from the name of a professional football team in Washington, DC, to the failures, too often tragic, of our criminal-justice system to the heartbreaking fact that we still need to affirm that Black lives do matter—all of this, *all of it*, returns us to our history.

As William Faulkner put it, "The past is never dead. It's not even past."

During the last year or so, I've found myself reflecting often on the effect of history on our lives, especially in light of recent protests on college campuses from Columbia, Missouri, to New Haven, Connecticut. And I've found myself reflecting, in turn, on how this history has propped up and protected systems that perpetuate privilege and inequality.

I think about this often because, at the Ford Foundation, our work is designed to disrupt inequality in all of its forms—and because we have found that entrenched cultural narratives often lead to persistent prejudice.

You see, narratives matter.

It was a narrative about skin color and inferiority that allowed many Americans to justify centuries of slavery and discrimination.

It was a narrative about gender and ability that allowed some men to deny women the right to vote—and, for that matter, equal pay today.

It's cultural narratives of "rags to riches" and "lifting yourself up by your bootstraps" that entitle some people to ignore their own advantage—to mistake their running start for a fair start.

These narratives and others even inform the way we memorialize our history—who is included, and who is left out. What we remember, and what we choose to forget.

In America, after all, one widespread cultural narrative is that our nation is exceptional. American exceptionalism is rooted in the earliest writings of Alexis de Tocqueville.

Across this country, people are hugely invested in this idea of America—this idealized America—that papers over the many difficult pages of our history, no matter how clear and present the effects of these problematic passages remain.

This is not to say these men and women are bad people—or to deny their good intentions. But the stories that many of us believe advance a narrative that holds us back.

One recent example shows how—and how much—this all matters.

As you all know, Princeton University is one of our nation's oldest institutions of higher learning. Its renowned school of international affairs is named after Woodrow Wilson, the twenty-eighth President of the United States and, before that, the thirteenth president of Princeton.

Woodrow Wilson was a prescient visionary and remarkable leader. He signed the Federal Reserve Act. He earned the Nobel Peace Prize for efforts to create the League of Nations, an idea that became the blueprint for our United Nations.

But Wilson also was a virulent racist.

As president of Princeton, he denied admission to Black students. As president of the United States, he and his appointees demoted Black civil servants from leadership positions in government, and rolled back whatever progress remained from the reconstruction era.

Now, as a result of all this, a century later, a vigorous debate is raging about whether his name should stay on the Wilson School—about whether we still should honor this man at all.

On one side, some would remove the Wilson name, and erase any mention of him from university grounds. "It is offensive," they understandably argue.

On the other, some say keep it, maintain the status quo, and focus on the good parts of Wilson's legacy—of which there are many.

Once again, we find ourselves in a binary, polarizing debate that drives us further apart.

I will be honest. I don't think either side is right. Erasing the symbols of an oppressive history neither changes what happened then, nor helps us make changes for the better now.

Furthermore, I think the choice these two sides present—to tear down or turn away—is a dangerous one.

To me, we shouldn't get caught in these limited binaries because on either side is a destructive act. Either we destroy history by removing the name or we destroy it by ignoring the whole truth. In many ways, these are two sides of the same coin—because both actions are based in a fear of engaging with the uncomfortable parts of our past.

And yet, our uncomfortable history is essential to our very being. Because in a larger sense, the contradictions present in the character of Woodrow Wilson are the contradictions present in the character of America.

Our founders gambled their lives, honor, and fortunes to expand rights to life and liberty and full citizenship, while counting African Americans as three-fifths of a human being—and, by the way, without mentioning women at all.

We aspire to a common good, built on collaboration and compromise, while our politics have become course, debased, and degraded—often devoid of facts and evidence.

Graduates: This is us—the good, the bad, the ugly.

Don't get me wrong, I love my country and I believe fervently that the righteous still prevail over the unjust. But my point is: No matter the outward complexity or contradiction—or the controversy that may follow—the truth is not something to shy away from, or bury deep.

One other example makes the case. For years, Thomas Jefferson's legacy was unassailable. Even scholars succumbed to the temptation to see the romance of Jefferson, not the reality. The truth, however, is that he was a man, not a marble statue—replete with foibles and flaws.

Jefferson authored the Declaration of Independence, affirming that "all men are created equal." He was a prophetic voice, advocating for religious liberty and public education. He founded the Library of Congress and established the University of Virginia.

But Jefferson also fathered children with a woman he held in bondage, Sally Hemings. He wrote some of the most racist and odious things about Black people in *Notes on the State of Virginia*.

Needless to say, the former doesn't somehow justify the latter. Quite the contrary.

At the same time, Jefferson's contradictions don't nullify his contributions, either.

What's most remarkable about Jefferson is that he embodies what actually makes us exceptional: Not the fact of perfection but the act of perfecting.

What makes us exceptional as Americans is a shared quest, from the moment of our founding, to expand the circle of promise and possibility. Inch by inch. Step by step. Bridge by bridge. Sometimes, blow by blow.

What makes us exceptional is that we have the strength to acknowledge our own flaws and failures—and the courage to make what's wrong into what's right.

This is why we must demand an accounting of the past that is not over-idealized—but inclusive and honest. Why we must embrace our past—in context, completely. And why we must not allow ourselves to settle for false choices instead of hard-earned understanding.

Some already have begun this fight.

Right now, throughout the American South, countless monuments honor Confederate history and racial hierarchy—statues, plaques, faces carved into a mountain. But there is another side of this story.

My friend Bryan Stevenson, founder of the Equal Justice Initiative, has been working to elevate this other side: Building a movement to construct markers at slave markets and lynching sites across the South, where that history of terror is all but invisible, but also at the homes and workplaces of Southern, white abolitionists. These people were heroes—risking their lives, time and again—though their stories have been lost to history. Until now, anyway.

Bryan Stevenson is helping us recover and uncover the suppressed and distorted—revealing a multifaceted history that illuminates and broadens the American narrative. He is helping us to remember a fuller, fairer story of the past—in tragedy and in triumph. He is making history by marking history, as we do, in a different sense, this afternoon.

And so, today—as you go off to make history—I ask you: What kind of history will you make?

Will you write our full history, with your words and deeds?

Will you right the wrongs of history with your actions, in a future that will be only as just as you make it?

And I'm not just talking with the history majors. We all have a part to play. Because when I look into your faces, I see the wider, broader history of America. A more perfect, more colorful history of America.

What's more, as Hunter graduates, you are uniquely suited to the task of making a better, more inclusive history—because of who you are and where you come from; and because, as an institution, Hunter has strived for inclusion through its 146 years.

Hunter College, as you know, began as a school for women back in 1870, long before women had the right to vote. It became a center for women of all racial, economic, and religious backgrounds. And throughout its own history, Hunter has produced many historymakers: Historymakers from communities that might otherwise have been excluded, otherwise not written into the story.

Historymakers like Dr. Antonia Pantoja, who worked during the day and took classes here at night, became a vital advocate for her Puerto Rican sisters and brothers, and earned the Presidential Medal of Freedom. She made history.

Or Rosalyn Sussman Yalow, the second American woman to win the Nobel Prize in Medicine, who graduated from Hunter seventy-five years ago this month. She made history.

Or Lew Frankfort, son of the Bronx who became a titan of commerce—the CEO of Coach who reinvented retail for a generation. He made history.

Or Audre Lorde, the genius poet and activist, who once wrote: "It is not our differences that divide us. It is our inability to recognize, accept, and celebrate those differences." She also wrote: "We cannot allow our fear of anger to deflect us nor seduce us into settling for anything less than the hard work of excavating honesty."

Think about that. The "hard work of excavating honesty"—this is the heavy lifting in which I know you will participate.

Hunter Class of 2016: I'm not asking you to rewrite history; none of us can do that. I am asking that you engage in "excavating honesty"—and to engage in the act of excavation honestly.

I am asking you to write our American history so that it more accurately reflects change over time. I'm asking you to *right* it—to make new history—and contribute to change in our time.

I know that you, because you come from Hunter, are up to the task. And for this reason—because of you—my faith in the future has never been stronger.

THE POWER OF PRIVILEGE

Address to the Bowdoin College Class of 2016
Brunswick, Maine
May 27, 2016

Sometimes, when we live in a place for a while—as you have here—we can take our surroundings for granted. But as I walked this campus today, as someone relatively new to Bowdoin, I found myself struck not just by its beauty, but also by its powerful sense of history. And so, on an occasion designed to cheer you on into your future, I find myself reflecting on the past.

As you no doubt know, come tomorrow morning, you will join the great American poet Henry Wadsworth Longfellow as a Bowdoin alumnus. What you may not know is that on the fiftieth anniversary of his own graduation—in 1875—Longfellow returned to this campus to read a poem he had composed for the special occasion. To invoke a line from that poem: *What passing generations fill these halls, / What passing voices echo from these walls.*

And if these walls could talk, they might tell you about the scratches of Harriet Beecher Stowe's pen. Or the determined footsteps of Olympian marathoner Joan Benoit Samuelson. These walls might tell you about

Ken Chenault cramming for an econ test—or Geoffrey Canada writing a sociology paper.

Of course, the history of this place is not the only thing that we can take for granted. We can also take for granted the privilege of being here.

Think for a moment about how you got here—how you reached this milestone in your life, on the verge of graduating from one of the best colleges in the country.

Each of us has our unique stories—no two paths are the same—though I'm sure if we took a poll, we would find many commonalities among us.

You all excelled as students and athletes and artists and musicians. You all studied hard and worked hard and played hard.

And yet, there is a temptation to believe that your hard work is the only thing that got you here, which isn't exactly the case.

Tonight, all around you, there are family and friends: People who worked hard to provide for you and support you and open doors for you. We applaud them. This weekend belongs as much to them as it does to you.

But the further and further away you get from moments like these, the easier and easier it becomes to forget how other people set us on course for success. Because in America, there's a story we like to tell ourselves about success—that it's an individual achievement, alone.

We celebrate the self-made man and woman, pulling himself or herself up by the bootstraps. But when I think about my own story—as I'd like you to think about your own story—I find this larger cultural narrative really doesn't hold up. Because I have learned that we rarely get anywhere on our own.

I was very fortunate that my mother moved me out of the poor town in Louisiana where I was born. I was equally fortunate that, in the spring of 1965, a young woman with a clipboard came up to our little shotgun house in Ames, Texas, and asked my mother to sign me up for the inaugural class of Head Start. I was fortunate to attend good public schools, to learn from teachers who urged me on, to secure Pell grants and private scholarships from generous philanthropists to pay for my education. So I always felt like my community, my country, were cheering me on. I never once thought I did it all by myself.

My point is that we are all very fortunate. None of us is here by our own initiative in isolation. Our individual achievement—determination, hard work, grit—all of this was essential to getting here, but it was not sufficient.

I point this out for two reasons: First, just because you earned this extraordinary degree doesn't mean you will suddenly, magically be able to succeed on your own. And second, because if you are here in this room tonight, you are the beneficiary of enormous privilege. We all are.

I know, privilege can be a very difficult thing to talk about in our culture. There are those who think that naming it means disparaging or discounting the hard work of individuals, or the sacrifices of families. That is certainly not my intention.

There are those who think acknowledging privilege takes something away from your accomplishments, and it does not.

Meanwhile, there are those who think just naming privilege is enough, but, believe me, it is not.

I'm sure many of you saw activist and Bowdoin alum DeRay Mckesson, Class of '07, explaining privilege to Stephen Colbert. But he also spoke to that reputable periodical *The Bowdoin Orient*, saying, and I quote: "The common good is this understanding that you are to use your privilege and your gifts for causes greater than you are."

Think about that for a moment: "Use your privilege for causes greater than you are."

What DeRay reminds us is that privilege is not something to feel guilty about or burdened by. It's something for us to embrace and extend. In many ways, privilege can be liberating.

All of these great privileges you have—these gifts of which you've made the most—use them, earn them, expand them. And acknowledging this privilege—being grateful for this privilege—is the first step in harnessing and directing that privilege to make a better world.

Last month, the journalist Robert Frank wrote a wonderful article in *The Atlantic,* titled, "Why Luck Matters More than You Think." In it, he highlights research that shows how acknowledging our own good fortune can help us improve the lives of others.

In one study, researchers found that people who feel grateful are more likely to be generous to strangers. In another study, people who credited good things in their lives to outside help—including supportive families and financial aid—were more charitable than people who chalked up their good fortune to themselves alone.

In other words, understanding how we got where we are helps us become more generous and charitable—and more thoughtful, moral, and fair. And becoming all of these things allows us to extend our privilege, to actively make our world more just for those around us.

Simply put, being aware of and grateful for the way we got ahead can help us pull others along with us.

But it doesn't happen on its own.

I hope you will actively participate in "bending the arc of the moral universe toward justice," as Dr. King said. And given the state of inequality in the world, we need every one of you to assist in the bending. To do so, you will need to immerse yourselves in the lives of others, and find a way to serve. Understanding and empathy will be your greatest tools to lift up those around you.

Graduates: A closing story about extending one's privilege.

I'm slightly obsessed with Lin-Manuel Miranda's brilliant hit musical *Hamilton.* I've seen it six times, including on opening night. Talk about privilege.

My friends are tired of hearing me talk about it. And don't worry, I'm not going to sing.

I just want to share the feeling of inspiration I have derived from Hamilton's story. Like many of you, Miranda's Hamilton was "a self-starter" and worked "a lot harder." But he also was afforded an opportunity by someone with far more privilege than he: George Washington.

As Miranda writes it, this "model of a modern major general," this "venerated Virginian," sees himself in the young Hamilton. And he lifts him up, making Hamilton his aide in the Continental Army. And then he gives him his first command. And later he appoints Hamilton as the first Secretary of the Treasury.

My point is: In a story about Alexander Hamilton rising up, and refusing to "throw away his shot," it was the most privileged member of the Virginia aristocracy who put Hamilton in position to climb.

Yes, Hamilton fought and worked and ultimately died defending his notion of our nation. But as he stretched for that first foothold, someone offered him a hand. And that made all the difference in the world.

Class of 2016: You, too, have been extended a hand up, by all of the people who helped you reach this moment. And with this privilege, comes your opportunity. Your chance. Your shot.

Do not throw it away.

I implore you: Do not throw away your shot to make a difference; your shot to fight for justice; and, most of all, your shot to give others a shot, in turn.

It has been my privilege to speak with you all today, and I cannot wait to see what you do with yours.

LET AMERICA BE AMERICA AGAIN

2017 New Year's Message
January 4, 2017

In moments of uncertainty, we often return to familiar touchstones. For me, one such anchor of comfort and clarity is the poetry of Langston Hughes, icon of the Harlem Renaissance.

During recent weeks, I've found myself ruminating on Hughes's "Let America Be America Again," especially its astonishing opening stanzas. In these ten lines, Hughes evokes the power of the American promise, coupled with the pain of indignity and inequality. He speaks to the complex mix of rage and hope, of anxiety and optimism, that characterizes the Black experience in America—and that I would argue has characterized the experience of many Americans at some point, white, Brown, Black, Indigenous, and immigrant.

Over the past year, it has become clear that the noxious swill of rage and anxiety remains as potent as ever. Regardless of which side of the US election each of us was on, we all find ourselves living with a public discourse that has become increasingly callous, contemptuous, and polarizing.

So, as we launch ourselves into a new year, I find myself reflecting on where we go from here—how we counterbalance anger and hopelessness with radical hope and optimism, and how we create, in Hughes's perfectly chosen words, "that great strong land of love" and dignity for all.

TWO REACTIONS TO OUR CURRENT MOMENT

Hughes's poem captures a tension I've noticed in many of my daily interactions over the past several weeks, in all kinds of settings and among all kinds of people, including within myself: A tension between a sense that our times are dangerously unprecedented and a sense that while dangerous, they are all too familiar.

On the one hand, many of us feel that the world has been turned upside down. To read the headlines is to see an unfamiliar landscape in which several unsettling trends have converged. The proliferation of fake news and the prevalence of brazen falsehoods on air and online are undermining faith in basic facts. The burgeoning democratic institutions that captured the imagination of Alexis de Tocqueville nearly two hundred years ago—our civil society, our free press, our universities—are increasingly beleaguered and besieged. Rising hate speech and violence across the country has rightfully frightened many people. All this constitutes an assault on what we thought were well-established societal norms.

On the other hand, some of us look to history and recognize that our current moment is not without precedent. To me, one clear parallel is America's post-Reconstruction era in the South, when some Americans worked to roll back and repeal the hard-won voting rights and educational and economic opportunities that brought freedom and dignity to the lives of so many of their fellow citizens.

Indeed, racism, sexism, xenophobia, and all kinds of othering are not new. Identity politics has always been a part of American life. Our founding fathers codified identity politics into our earliest documents, valuing the voices and contributions of white men above all others: Women were denied the right to vote; enslaved African Americans counted as three-fifths of a person; Indigenous peoples were exploited and marginalized. And throughout our history, waves of immigrants from Europe and elsewhere were initially met with suspicion and often discrimination. It's important to remember that over the course of our long, messy march toward justice, women and men—not just our predecessors, but we, the people, of every generation—have endured prejudice and persecution. We have seen it with our own eyes, and lived it in our own lives.

I'll never forget coming of age as a gay man in the 1980s—watching AIDS ravage our community as politicians stayed silent. I'll never forget the brutality of apartheid, and how our own American government condemned Nelson Mandela, Oliver Tambo, and the other freedom fighters seeking to end that unconscionable regime. I'll never forget watching as the marches and protests unfolded in Ferguson in August 2014, or standing with John Lewis on the Edmund Pettus Bridge a few months later, awestruck as he recounted the Bloody Sunday in Selma fifty years earlier.

America's rich and inspiring history has taught us that progress is not linear. As the dazzling Zadie Smith recently wrote, "Progress is never permanent, will always be threatened, must be redoubled, restated, and *reimagined* if it is to survive." So while these twin reactions—the sense that our moment is either *unprecedented* or has *clear precedent*—may seem at odds, they actually reaffirm a deeper understanding of the persistence of injustice in our world. They also remind us of the strength we must continue to find within ourselves to persevere and fight for our democratic institutions and ideals.

CONFRONTING DIVISIONS, AFFIRMING DIGNITY

Over the past three years, I've written about the ways inequality creates and exacerbates divisions. These include divisions of class, race, gender, identity, and ability, as well as differences in how we make sense of injustice in our lives.

There is no better illustration of this last category than the political binary of an election year, when our two-party system induces us to spend months defining our collective future in terms of *us* versus *them*, *this* stark choice versus *that* one. This rhetoric reinforces the notion of zero-sum outcomes, and encourages us to believe that the gains of one happen at the expense of another.

We must resist this impulse. It is easy to lose sight of what we have in common, but the fact is that *all of us* share a fundamental human aspiration: To live in dignity. This is true no matter what we look like, where we live, how we worship, whom we love, or what our abilities are. Whether by holding a decent-paying job, having agency in the decisions that affect us, or freely expressing our thoughts and creativity, we spend our lives in pursuit of dignity for ourselves and our families. Recognizing this universal quest for dignity is a prerequisite for any meaningful work toward social justice.

I am not suggesting that dignity is guaranteed. There are people and systems that seek to rob people of their innate dignity. They advance narratives that pit communities against one another—that permit some to falsely claim that the only way to ensure dignity for yourself is to strip it from others.

Of course, the dignity of one person does not preclude that of another. We can lift a poor Latina out of poverty *and* save a rural white man's factory job. We can fight to protect Black lives *and* the lives of the law enforcement officers who protect us. We can hold up a beacon of light for the "tempest-tost" refugees who seek safety and opportunity on our shores, *and* feel safe and secure in our neighborhoods and gathering places.

I'm not simply saying that we *can* do all these things; I'm saying we must.

Our current context demands that we question our assumptions and expand our understanding of who is vulnerable and excluded. If inequality fuels the fault lines of division, then our shared pursuit of dignity must help bridge the gaps. To borrow a phrase from the brilliant artist Lilla Watson, our liberation is bound up together.

THE PATH FORWARD: "AMERICA WILL BE!"

It might be tempting to ignore or abandon the mutual obligation that ties us together, to embrace a kind of nihilism of indifference or, worse, to retreat into anxiety or rage. But we can choose a better path forward. With history as our guide, we can follow a path of hope—*radical* hope.

For Langston Hughes, born in 1902, the gap between America's promise and its practices was wide. The great-grandchild of slaves on one side and slaveholders on the other—the child of educators and organizers—Hughes lived a life that demonstrated that the overwhelming *fact* of injustice does not obviate or relieve in any way our responsibility to *act* against it. He showed that a person can simultaneously feel righteous anger *about* the world and radical optimism *for* it. We must affirm the creed to which he gave voice, that the work of creating the America we envision requires optimism and resolve.

"America never was America to me," Hughes wrote in the penultimate stanza of his masterpiece. "And yet I swear this oath—America will be!"

For as much progress as we have made, America has yet to fully live up to its promise and founding aspiration to be a nation of liberty, dignity, and justice for all. Yet this noble vision remains as profound as ever.

At the Ford Foundation, our commitment to achieving this vision will not change. We resolve to continue fostering a fairer, more just America and world. We remain steadfast and unyielding in our support of the institutions and leaders fighting injustice and addressing inequality of every kind and category. And we are grateful for your leadership—and partnership—during the critical months and years ahead.

JUSTICE OVER GREATNESS: A NEW YEAR'S REFLECTION

2018 New Year's Message
January 17, 2018

During the spring of 1816, four decades after Thomas Jefferson drafted the United States' Declaration of Independence, he exchanged letters with an old colleague and companion from his days as minister to France's court of Louis XVI. This friend, Pierre Samuel du Pont de Nemours, had written to Jefferson to share a treatise he had composed about the purpose and virtues of republican government. And with characteristic eloquence—and the wisdom of an extraordinary seventy-three years behind him—Jefferson responded boldly to du Pont's manuscript: "Justice," he penned, "is the fundamental law of society."

From the very inception of the United States, this "fundamental law" has guided our grand experiment in self-determination and global leadership. In our Constitution's preamble, the framers made clear their ambition "to establish justice." In our courtrooms, we call for "equal justice under the law." In our classrooms, we pledge allegiance to a republic "with liberty and justice for all."

No question, the ideal of justice has faced all varieties of tests and trials—contests and contradictions—during these last two and one-third centuries. Each generation of Americans has, in turn, been called to reimagine, reaffirm, and renew its commitment to justice.

And still, we see justice's uneven march forward all around us. I see it—and feel it—in the humbling fact that my semiliterate grandfather's education ended in the third grade, while I am privileged to serve as the president of the Ford Foundation.

Today, however, the institutions designed to protect and promote justice in our society—to serve and strengthen our democracy—are beleaguered and besieged.

In a just society, people are guaranteed a voice—and vote—to influence the decisions that affect them. In our society, access to the levers of power is heavily skewed in favor of the wealthy and privileged.

In a just society, journalists hold the powerful to account. In our society, the powerful are waging a concerted campaign to degrade and delegitimize the free press.

In a just society, the rule of law is applied equally, regardless of identity, ability, or income. In our society, the justice system favors the privileged and powerful over the poor and vulnerable. In our society, women are too often hindered by a culture that tolerates harassment and abuse.

In these ways and many others, we have seen the United States abdicate its responsibility, legitimacy, and integrity as a leader for justice in the world. The consequence is an American society riven by and reeling from inequality, and a global community devoid of America's best example.

THE IMPERATIVE OF ACTION

Recently, the health-care expert Donald M. Berwick set the imperative of action in stark relief. In the *Journal of the American Medical Association*—a periodical not normally on my reading list—he wrote: "It is chilling to see the great institutions of health care, hospitals, physician groups, scientific bodies assume that the seat of bystander is available. That seat is gone. To try to avoid the political fray through silence is impossible, because silence is now political. Either engage, or assist the harm. There is no third choice."

While addressed to the medical community, the trustees and leaders of American foundations would be well served to hear and heed this message: In the struggle between justice and injustice, between equality and inequality, there is no third choice.

Now is decidedly not the time to wring our hands, stand on the sidelines, or quibble over whether 2018 payouts should be at 5 or 5.5 percent. Now is the time to provide general support to our grantees so they can be more resilient. After all, the organizations we support and the communities they serve are depending on us amidst swirling, disorienting winds. Paraphrasing the iconic Shirley Chisholm, we must not perpetuate injustice through inaction.

This is why I am heartened by the actions of so many foundation colleagues—by the Knight Foundation's courageous grantmaking to promote independent media and journalism; by the Open Society Foundations' redoubled determination to protect the rule of law; by the work of the Ballmer Group and the Raikes Foundation on poverty and education; by the MacArthur Foundation's 100&Change, helping the International Rescue Committee and Sesame Workshop to collaborate and bring opportunity to children and families in refugee camps; by the Chan Zuckerberg Initiative's efforts to bring tech to philanthropy, and its focus on long-term, systemic change; and many more.

I am inspired, too, by the work of the extraordinary people and organizations on the front lines—by the Committee to Protect Journalists and the International Women's Media Foundation as they promote the Fourth Estate; by the ACLU's and NAACP Legal Defense Fund's victories for immigrants' rights and voter protections. Global Witness has exposed corruption by powerful interests, and the Alliance for Safety and Justice is making impressive progress domestically to address policies that reflect racial and class bias in our criminal justice system, like the discriminatory cash-bail system. The list goes on and on.

There can be no shortage of courage in a time of injustice—and I see enormous courage in the work of thousands of groups like these across the country and world.

WHAT THE FORD FOUNDATION IS DOING

In the face of so many mounting threats to justice around the world—and informed by the resilience and resolve of our partners and grantees—we have been reconsidering our own priorities.

Beginning immediately, we will consolidate our work in some areas, while dedicating more attention and resources to others. We will integrate our programs more thoughtfully, while reducing our overall number of grantmaking areas, in order to emphasize our most essential work and maximize our flexibility.

Much of what we do *will not* change. When I became president, we focused our programs and resources to address inequality, in part, because we foresaw its cascading consequences. And as we continue to work to disrupt inequality, we will continue promoting its antidote: Justice.

To that end, we have identified several broad areas of intervention where we will deploy additional resources during the year ahead, and beyond.

DEMOCRACY, RIGHTS, AND FREE EXPRESSION

The prerequisite for a just society has always been the engagement of its people. If "establish justice" was among the first priorities of the framers of the Constitution, the role of "we the people"—as active participants in and creators of the republic—was the very first. Before there was government, there was an understanding that "we the people," together, are responsible for our collective fate.

Instead, widening inequality severs the relationship between people and democratic institutions, and unravels the fabric of a society. Our common goals and aspirations have been replaced by gaps—in incomes, in influence, in power.

Meanwhile, the space for civil society has been shrinking as governments around the world restrict citizens from organizing. Basic rights—to vote, to speak, to assemble—have been curtailed by those who hope to keep their hold on power.

Fewer people have a meaningful voice in the decisions that affect their lives—and, in turn, those decisions are increasingly unjust. Without the ability, agency, and access to participate in our society, some people have tuned out entirely.

Philanthropy can and should help restore the commitment to justice that drives a society to care for itself. For us, this means increasing support to groups that fight to strengthen democratic institutions. This includes grants that help people organize in pursuit of common ground and common good, especially young leaders, to whom we are making a strengthened commitment. We will also increase support to organizations working to champion journalism as foundational to a healthy and vibrant democracy.

DIGNITY AND WORK IN THE AGE OF AUTOMATION

Just as inequality robs civil society of its voice, the so-called fourth industrial revolution of technological change—our new digital age—threatens to rob many people of their livelihoods and their dignity.

Work is fundamental to any individual's sense of place and purpose in society. Yet wage stagnation, loss of benefits, and the feeling that the economic system is rigged have contributed to widespread insecurity among workers. As technological innovation upends more sectors of the economy, that anxiety will only continue to grow. A recent report from the McKinsey Global Institute estimated that as many as "30 percent of the hours worked globally could be automated by 2030."

We are not yet prepared for the extent to which technological revolution will alter our society. Instead, our current discourse on the issue has been reduced to an oversimplified binary: On one side, many entrepreneurs have blind faith that technology and innovation are always good for society; on the other, critics say it will render so many people unable to earn a living that we will need a system of universal basic income for millions of unemployed and underemployed workers. In our view, neither of these outcomes is desirable, and both would have potentially explosive political consequences.

Philanthropy can help chart a course between these two extremes. At Ford, building on years of work to strengthen job quality and labor standards, we will collaborate with private employers, labor economists, technologists, workforce activists, and other funders as we consider how to ensure that all people experience the dignity of meaningful work in the future.

THE INTERNET AS A PLATFORM FOR JUSTICE

Automation—or artificial intelligence, for that matter—is not the only theater in which rapid technological change will shape the future of justice. Today, the Internet is how we find employment and housing, consume media, purchase goods, start businesses, collect ideas, connect, engage, and organize with one another.

Of course, injustices in the analog world are often accelerated and exacerbated in the digital one. Algorithms are encoded with human biases. Concern about surveillance, data privacy, and security contributes to the public's growing anxiety about technology. Social media provides a platform for an anonymous culture of harassment. Access to the Internet remains unequal, while governments and corporations chip away at the freedom and neutrality on which the Internet was constructed.

A society that depends on the Internet cannot be just unless the Internet is a just platform. So we will continue supporting organizations that are working to harness this public utility for justice, and we will more actively advocate for funding and action in this space by tech philanthropists, tech-focused universities, and corporate actors who recognize the enormity of what's at stake.

EXPLORATIONS AND ELEVATIONS

As we devote more time and energy to these three areas, we're also aware that other manifestations of inequality persist around them.

The rise of the #MeToo movement has revealed pervasive gender inequality across every industry. The alarming stories coming to light are indicative of an entrenched sexism that women have known for centuries. None of our aspirations for a more just society will be achieved if we do not address these patriarchal imbalances of power—and that shift cannot happen until we invest more in the power of women and girls as unrivaled agents of change that is long overdue. Throughout this year we'll be exploring how we can expand our existing grantmaking in this area.

Finally, at a moment when forging new networks and relationships has taken on increased importance, our external partnerships require a greater portion of my time and energy—as does the management of our programs. To improve the effectiveness of our program operations, I have elevated Hilary Pennington to the new role of executive vice president for program. In this position, Hilary will lead and integrate the foundation's programmatic work, guiding it as we refocus on the demands of our current moment. Martín Abregú and Xav Briggs will continue in their critical roles as program vice presidents, working with Hilary to harmonize two program divisions from what were previously three.

JUSTICE IS THE BETTER PART OF GREATNESS

As we embark on this new year and the next stage of Ford*Forward*, I cannot help reflecting on the forces that might hold us back. Among them, in the United States, is the idea that we ought to pursue a misguided facsimile of American "greatness."

Lately, we have been told that this romanticized form of greatness should be our highest ambition. Yet this narrow-minded, small-hearted kind of greatness is not "the fundamental law of society" that Jefferson described. It is not the value the founders fought to establish—nor the ideal that our forebearers fought to extend.

That is because the distance between a so-called great America and a just America is vast.

In a great America, military might is vaunted as the only kind of strength, while in a *just* America, diplomacy and soft power are wielded to defend not only our interests, but human rights around the world.

In a great America, huge sections of the country don't vote, or are prevented from voting. In a just America, everyone is encouraged to exercise the franchise, and ensure that their voices and interests are represented.

A great America leaves too many people out. In a just America, opportunity is not a function of one's gender, race, ability, or identity; it is available to all those with talent and drive.

In a great America, patriarchy and white supremacy poison our culture. In a just America, we celebrate and honor diverse leaders and voices, and embrace and welcome people seeking freedom and opportunity from all regions and countries of the world.

A half century ago, Fannie Lou Hamer—a Mississippi sharecropper with a sixth-grade education—confronted President Lyndon Baines Johnson on his rhetoric about America's greatness. "If this is a 'Great Society,'" she said then, "God knows I'd hate to live in a bad one."

Imagine what this took. Imagine what it must have felt like for a poor Black woman, with little formal education, to challenge the president of the United States.

For 241 years and counting, Americans have done exactly this: We've strived and struggled—stood up and sat in and spoken out—all in pursuit of justice, our founding promise. We've embraced the teaching of Dr. Martin Luther King Jr. that "I can never be what I ought to be until you are what you ought to be." And our hard-fought victories—affirmations of and advances for justice, all—explain why I remain optimistic.

This week, as we celebrate Dr. King's life and legacy, let us recommit ourselves to his ennobling values—and the enduring vision that connects Jefferson, Chisolm, and Hamer. Let us demand and defend societies that are more than one man's, or one group's, definition of great. And let us do it together, with resolve for and faith in the future that we share.

WITH FOUR FREEDOMS, FOUR RESPONSIBILITIES: A DEFENSE OF DEMOCRATIC VALUES

Expanded from Addresses to the Classes of 2017
at Michigan State University, Simmons College, Oberlin College,
and Johns Hopkins School of Advanced International Studies
February 2018

In the United States and around the world, our democratic values and institutions face direct and dire threats.

Untold millions fear persecution for their religious beliefs, their sexual orientations, their gender identities. Others simply fear for their lives. In some countries, authoritarian governments seek to stamp out democratic freedoms, like the rights to protest or to a free press. Even democratically elected governments are acting to restrict these freedoms amidst a rise of tribalism and xenophobia. The moral leadership of the United States has all but disappeared from view.

Given the grueling pace of the news during the past eighteen months—amidst constant chaos—the windows for slow and steady reflection feel few and far between. Indeed, these days, chaos has become a kind of ambient noise, and it feels hard to make sense of it all—hard to know how to move forward. After all, we are charging full steam ahead into the unknown. It is not frivolous, or naive, to stop and contemplate the fact that democracy itself is imperiled for the first time in at least a generation.

As I write this, I am acutely aware that all these coalescing crises share a single, protean cause: Inequality. They claim for themselves similar, often related victims, too: Civility, empathy, and justice. And it's not only economic inequality or racial inequality, but also geographic and cultural inequality that causes whole communities and regions to feel ignored and abandoned, if not outright persecuted.

Subject to countless historical examples, we know that the greatest danger to democracy is not terrorism, nor environmental crisis, nor nuclear proliferation, nor the results of any one election. The greatest danger to democracy is hopelessness: The hopelessness of many millions who express themselves with their ballots, and the hopelessness of many millions more who express themselves by not voting at all. This hopelessness is yet another symptom of the inequality that has eaten away at our norms and eroded the bridges of common cause—the very bonds of goodwill that ought to bring us together and help us confront our shared challenges.

Despite what feel like wholly unprecedented circumstances, however, democracy is no stranger to trials from within and without. And so, of late, I have felt reassured by how another great American generation responded to the greatest threat to democracy of the previous century: The Second World War.

WISDOM FROM THE PAST

Imagine the early days of 1941, another moment when chaos abounded.

The effects of financial crisis a decade earlier continued to reverberate around the United States and afflict the American people. Across the Atlantic, a hateful demagogue came to power by democratic means, and his rise and racist policies threatened the safety of his people. The United States turned inward—many of its citizens unwilling to recognize what was happening in the world. In some corners of our nation, factions called for isolation, while others supported more virulent strains of nationalism—all as allies pleaded for American leadership and assistance.

Amid these somewhat familiar circumstances, President Franklin D. Roosevelt crafted his annual message to the US Congress. In this address, he laid out the Four Freedoms, which read:

> In the future days, which we seek to make secure, we look forward to a world founded upon four essential human freedoms. The first is freedom of speech and expression—everywhere in the world. The second is freedom of every person to worship God in his own way—everywhere in the world. The third is freedom from want—which, translated into world terms, means economic understandings which will secure to every nation a healthy peacetime life for its inhabitants—everywhere in the world. The fourth is freedom from fear—which, translated into world terms, means a world-wide reduction of armaments to such a point and in such a thorough fashion that no nation will be in a position to commit an act of physical aggression against any neighbor—anywhere in the world.

With this idea, President Roosevelt did something that, at the time, was rather remarkable—he asked Americans to implicate themselves in the struggles of their fellow human beings.

During the decades since, these Four Freedoms—and this formulation of essential democratic values—have become iconic. They inspired four of Norman Rockwell's most famous paintings. Their influence also stretches far beyond the United States or American culture; these same freedoms open the United Nations' Universal Declaration of Human Rights. These Four Freedoms reflect the urgency of their particular moment in history as well as the timeless values and aspirations our society should pursue.

WHY NOW?

While January 2016 marked the seventy-fifth anniversary of President Roosevelt's Four Freedoms speech, the events between January 2017 and January 2018 have occasioned my reconsideration of it, in part because the chasm between this hopeful vision and our reality seems particularly vast.

What appears to be implicit in Roosevelt's Four Freedoms, and necessary for our democracy today, is an understanding of our responsibilities to protect and extend these freedoms—everywhere in the world and for one another.

We know that these freedoms do not happen by themselves. In the United States, they are the product of revolution and protest, of conversation and compromise, of constant stumbling progress toward an exceptional ideal. And as citizens and participants in our society, we all have a role to play in not just exercising our own freedom, but also creating the conditions—and the country—where everyone can exercise those freedoms equally.

In other words, "we the people" means that my freedom depends on your freedom. Similarly, if freedom for one of us is removed or restricted, it jeopardizes freedom for us all—and for the larger democratic principles we all hold dear. That's why, when we live in a free society, we are charged with protecting freedom for one another through our responsibilities to one another.

OUR FOUR RESPONSIBILITIES

In the case of the Four Freedoms, therefore, I argue that each freedom contains within it a corresponding responsibility—an action demanded of us as creators and stewards of our democratic society. These can be summarized simply:

> With the freedom of speech comes the responsibility to listen.
> With the freedom of belief comes the responsibility to accept.
> With the freedom from want comes the responsibility to serve.
> And with the freedom from fear comes the responsibility to act.

What's more, these four responsibilities do not exist in a vacuum or independently of one another. Just as each of the Four Freedoms has its complement, so do each of our responsibilities complement the others. If we commit ourselves to listening, we will be more likely to accept others. If we commit ourselves to accepting others, we will be more likely to serve those who need us. And if we commit ourselves to service, we will understand how we should act.

And if we're going to act, we must act now.

WHAT FOLLOWS

During the spring of 2017, as I was reflecting on our freedoms and their corresponding responsibilities, I was privileged to deliver commencement addresses at four venerable institutions of higher learning: Michigan State University, Simmons College, Oberlin College, and the Johns Hopkins School of Advanced International Studies.

It seemed particularly appropriate to deliver a message about democratic values on these four great campuses because colleges and universities are essential institutions for our democracy—places that manifest our highest aspirations and ideals. What better audience to engage with these ideas, rise to this occasion, and defend our democratic values and institutions than these new graduates?

Of course, this duty is not restricted to the young. Far from it. It is incumbent upon each of us, as willing and humble participants in our democratic system, to maintain and expand the freedoms that enable the world's longest-standing liberal democracy, and to ensure its success both now and in the future.

In turn, I wrote this for everyone: To encourage each of us to reflect on our responsibilities—the fulfillment of which our freedoms require and our democracy demands.

I. WITH THE FREEDOM OF SPEECH, THE RESPONSIBILITY TO LISTEN

In December 1860, the great American orator and former slave Frederick Douglass delivered one of his finest speeches, "A Plea for Free Speech in Boston." In it, he boldly declared that "liberty is meaningless where the right to utter one's thoughts and opinions has ceased to exist."

That line—and that speech—emerged from a rather unfortunate incident.

The week before Douglass issued his plea, a meeting was scheduled in Boston to discuss what was, in 1860, a controversial question: How shall slavery be abolished? But before the meeting could make any progress, it was "invaded, insulted, [and] captured" by an unruly mob, who sought to silence the abolitionists.

As Douglass explained, the mayor "refused to protect" the meeting—or the free speech of the abolitionists—and instead, simply canceled it.

But Frederick Douglass knew the real danger the mob posed was not in their disorder, but in denying their fellow citizens the right to free speech. So he did what anyone who seeks to defend free speech should do: He spoke up.

In Boston's storied Music Hall, Douglass delivered his iconic, timeless oration about the incident, and about the importance of the freedom of speech. He said: "No right was deemed by the fathers of the Government more sacred than the right of speech. It was in their eyes, as in the eyes of all thoughtful men, the great moral renovator of society and government."

"Moral Renovator": The Power of Free Speech

As the phrase "moral renovator" suggests, free speech gives us the tools to repair, update, and improve our society and its principles, the way one might consider rebuilding a home. We can address damages, tear down harmful walls, open new doors, and even restore a crumbling foundation.

This power to remake ourselves is partially why the freedom of speech is enshrined in the very first amendment to the US Constitution, and why it is the first freedom that President Roosevelt asserted in his iconic speech. It must come first because our right to speak freely is a prerequisite for all of our other freedoms—and for living in a free society.

Without freedom of speech, there is no preacher in the pulpit, no defense at a trial. Without freedom of speech, we cannot cast our vote or call our representatives. Without freedom of speech, there is no women's suffrage or March on Washington, no marriage equality or Black Lives Matter or #MeToo movement.

It's no wonder that Frederick Douglass called free speech the "dread of tyrants." He knew that, as he put it, "Thrones, dominions, principalities, and powers, founded in injustice and wrong, are sure to tremble, if men are allowed to reason of righteousness, temperance and of a judgment to come in their presence." Speech and reason are bulwarks against an unjust society.

Of course, free speech is not a panacea; and while some speech allows us to confront injustice, there are plenty of instances when our speech can perpetuate injustice and harm. For example, on many college campuses today, students are testing and contesting where free speech ends and hate speech begins. It's a question worth asking—and one, from my perspective, with no easy answer.

But what amazes me is that more than 240 years after our founding, and more than 150 years after Frederick Douglass's stirring defense of the First Amendment, the freedom of speech is still vital to the functioning of our democracy.

Free Speech in Our Time

When Frederick Douglass spoke in Boston, or when President Roosevelt outlined his Four Freedoms, neither could have imagined the extent to which free expression would change. We now have more ways to exercise this freedom than ever before. The Internet allows us to transmit our ideas to an unknowably large audience of Facebook friends and Twitter followers, devoted readers and disgruntled trolls alike. Our smartphones let us make this connection anywhere, anytime. If, after reading this sentence, you wanted to express your reaction to it with a large audience, it would take just a couple taps of your fingers.

Technology also has enabled speech around the world, allowing access to information and giving people of every kind and category new avenues to organize. In some countries ruled by an authoritarian political regime, the ability to speak anonymously on the Internet has been a boon. In places where expressing your opinion under your own name can be dangerous, the anonymity of the Internet has allowed free opinion and expression to survive.

But this amazing technology has simultaneously accelerated a few unsettling trends. According to the Pew Research Center, more than two in every five Americans has been harassed on the Internet. A sickening one-half of young women have received an explicit image that they never asked for. One in four Americans has had completely false information about them posted online.

The very same anonymity that protects some on the Internet allows others to spew vitriol with relative impunity. They are emboldened by the fact that their comments do not have consequences for their lives outside the Internet. And time and again, when confronted, these trolls admit that in the heat of the moment, they forget that they are attacking real people. Speech, no longer paired with reason or respect, becomes a tool of our disintegration rather than our renovation.

The Problem of Disconnection

This phenomenon speaks to larger problems that the Internet exacerbates, but is not fully responsible for—a deepening disconnection between people, and a lack of empathy for one another.

And not only are we actively disconnecting from one another's humanity—even as we become more connected than ever before—but we also seem more willing and able to disconnect from certain kinds of information.

We tend to curate the information that comes our way, while social and commercial media try to give us what they think we want. We engage with stories that confirm our assumptions and biases, that do not challenge or expand our view of the world. Online monologues allow their writers to dig deeper and deeper into their own thoughts without considering the views of others. We become more entrenched in our own views. In some cases, it is almost as if we're just talking to ourselves.

As this happens, the algorithms figure out what we want, what is comfortable, and they just keep feeding us more of the same. Our confirmation bias compounds on itself. Meanwhile, alternative media outlets sow doubt and confusion based on what they want us to believe—even if it is not true.

In the process, our common ground gets eroded, and one of free speech's most potent uses—as a check on power, often in the form of journalism—becomes undervalued.

The Responsibility to Listen

For our freedom of speech to work—to have meaning or the power to improve our democracy—we need to listen to one another.

In fact, we have a responsibility to listen, because listening allows us to extend the freedom of speech to others. This is why the right to assemble is so closely linked to the right to free speech. They share an amendment because speech is meaningless without an audience.

Without a congregation of listeners, there's no difference between the preacher on a Sunday morning and the subway platform. Without a jury of open-minded and engaged listeners, or an attentive judge, or proper accountability, a trial becomes less just. If our elected officials do not consider the opinions of their constituents, then our political speech does little to advance our interests. Without the backing of a country or a congress, women's suffrage does not achieve the Nineteenth Amendment, the Civil Rights Movement does not pass necessary legislation or change minds and hearts, and the movement for marriage equality is stymied. Today, without people willing to listen to the legitimate grievances of a movement like Black Lives Matter—if the country chooses only to look away or to reflexively argue—people of color will continue to die at the hands of police while the deeper structural problems remain unaddressed.

So, when we listen to each other, we do more than extend a common courtesy; we give credence and power to that first and sacred right. We say, "You are a human, too, and deserve to be heard." We give dignity to others when we enable their voices, consider their perspectives, and thoughtfully grapple with their ideas. We participate in the ongoing exchange between people that defines our democracy, and allow ideas and actions to ripple through, even renovate, our society.

A Model Listener

Sometimes I worry that this kind of listening is a lost art—that we have forgotten how to look someone in the eye and hear what they are saying without being distracted by what we plan to say next.

This was one of my chief concerns as I prepared for commencement at Simmons College. Whom could I point to, as an aspirational example, for how we ought to embrace our responsibility to listen? Then I remembered that Simmons College was the alma mater of my dear friend, the late Gwen Ifill. Even though we lost her too soon, she left behind a lesson in—and a legacy of—listening.

Gwen was a giant of journalism. She covered politics for *The Washington Post*, *The New York Times*, and NBC, and was the anchor of *PBS NewsHour*. Throughout her storied career, she received numerous accolades and acknowledgments for her talent, professionalism, and poise. Thanks to her decades in the field, Gwen understood the problems our world faces better than anybody. But above all else, I believe what made her such a talented reporter was not her intellect (though it was sharp) and not her experience (though it was deep). It was her special ability to listen to others and amplify their voices.

The week Gwen passed away, her colleagues aired a powerful tribute to her. They said many great things about Gwen, but one comment from a fellow reporter struck me: "No matter how complicated and how fraught the conversations I have with people, Gwen taught me how to listen."

I saw this extraordinary talent of Gwen's in person, on many occasions. One incident that comes to mind was when we were together in Selma, Alabama, commemorating the fiftieth anniversary of the march on Bloody Sunday.

That night, we had dinner with our shared hero: Congressman John Lewis. Congressman Lewis was only twenty-five years old when he was beaten on the Edmund Pettus Bridge, but you can still see his scars from that awful day. Now imagine being Congressman Lewis. He's a civil rights legend who literally walked side by side with Dr. Martin Luther King Jr. But he is perhaps most famous for his defiance during what must have been one of the most terrible days of his life. It must be so frustrating to be asked, over and over, to recall a nightmare.

Gwen understood this. And she knew that on this night—on this sacred anniversary—the congressman must have had a lot on his mind. We both wanted to hear what the congressman was thinking—but I, personally, didn't know how to coax it out of him.

Then Gwen did what Gwen did best. She asked a couple of well-placed, thoughtful questions—and then she listened. She looked him in the eyes, smiled, and gave him her full attention. It worked. Congressman Lewis shared story after story. By the end of the night, we all had tears in our eyes.

But here's the thing: That night wasn't the exception for Gwen. And it wasn't just because Congressman Lewis is a famous civil rights leader.

Gwen wanted to listen to everyone, all the time.

Over and over again, I watched Gwen work *hard* to listen. Whether you were rich or poor, young or old, powerful or powerless—Gwen wanted to know your story. She did her research and asked questions, but above all else, she showed that she cared about people and wanted to make their voices heard. That was true even if she didn't agree with you. She always stayed resolute in her capacity to hear you out.

Of course, Gwen wasn't just listening for herself or her own edification, though she might have listened anyway. As a journalist, she was listening *to* others and *for* others, and for the sake of finding the truth and fulfilling our highest ideals. It's what made Gwen so great at her job. It's also what made her such a good friend, person, and citizen.

Being Better Listeners

We should all hope and aspire to live by Gwen's example. In our own lives, we must try to seek out stories we may not want to hear and opinions we may not completely agree with. As I've found through many of these conversations in my own life, you don't have to change your position to change your perspective. I've never regretted giving listening a chance. Every time, I've learned something new.

Listening in this way is, of course, quite difficult. Some people may hear "listen" as synonymous with "stop talking." But listening is not a passive act of staying quiet; it's an active choice to engage with others, and to be critical and compassionate in equal measure.

While it is important for members of our media, like Gwen, to listen, it is even more essential that we all embrace our own individual responsibility for listening. As citizens, this is our first and primary charge. It's not something you do only once—and again, it isn't easy. But listening to others is the kind of daily civic work that makes our democracy stronger, improves our society, and maintains our valued and essential rights. Listening gives meaning to speech, gives purpose to voice, and gives dignity to people. Otherwise, it's just talk.

Only when we listen can we find common ground. Only when we listen can we forge compromise and a common future. And only when we listen can we begin to heal the divides and build the bridges that our democracy so desperately needs.

II. WITH THE FREEDOM OF BELIEF, THE RESPONSIBILITY TO ACCEPT

In 1634, Anne Hutchinson and her husband migrated from England to the Massachusetts Bay Colony, following the religious dissident Reverend John Cotton. They believed their beliefs would be more accepted in the new world.

Anne was a forty-three-year-old housewife with no formal education, but she was also a ferocious reader and thinker. And soon after they arrived in Massachusetts, Anne started holding meetings with women in the area to discuss Reverend Cotton's sermons. She, like Cotton, argued against the Puritan belief that good works were the path to salvation. Instead, she insisted that God's grace alone was sufficient. Her meetings grew in popularity; men, some of them prominent, began to join. And religious authorities felt threatened—both by her beliefs and, more important, because she was a woman who defied authority.

Just four years after arriving in America, Hutchinson was tried for heresy, betrayed by her mentor Reverend Cotton, and excommunicated from Massachusetts. Hutchinson, her family, and around seventy of her followers fled to Rhode Island, thinking they would find safe harbor in Roger Williams's more religiously tolerant settlement. But when the Massachusetts Puritans threatened to take over Rhode Island, too, she moved once again, this time to the Dutch colony of New Netherland, later called New York, where she could finally live in peace—and lead her people.

Three generations later, her great-great-grandson returned to Massachusetts and became its governor. Her other descendants include three presidents, two governors, and a Supreme Court justice. Today, if you drive north of New York City, you'll likely take the Hutchinson River Parkway—and look out on the river that also bears her name.

Freedom of Belief: An Early Tension

Hutchinson's story shows us that freedom of belief, the second of President Roosevelt's Four Freedoms, was one of the very earliest ideals that drew Europeans to the Americas. It also reveals and reminds us that the people of this place have always struggled to accept differences in belief—despite our ideals.

Indeed, in the days before the American Revolution, when our American experiment was scarcely a germ of an idea, the freedom of belief wasn't just present; it was necessary to bring our quarreling, disparate nation together.

Remember, Pennsylvania was founded by Quakers. Maryland was founded by Catholics. New York and New England were home to Shakers and Evangelicals. Jewish families settled in Rhode Island.

And beyond religious differences, there was ethnic, economic, and social diversity as well. There were rich elites and indentured servants, city merchants and country farmers. Hundreds of thousands of Africans arrived here as slaves—stolen from their families and homes and sold into bondage. Before they were evicted from their lands, untold numbers of Indigenous peoples remained part of North America's seventeenth- and eighteenth-century social fabric.

In its early days, America needed a way to bring all these diverse threads together. At least, that was what Thomas Jefferson argued.

Our Complicated History

Thirteen years before the First Amendment was added to the Constitution, Britain's North American colonies had to fight for their freedom. Just six months after writing the Declaration of Independence, Jefferson held a meeting to discuss what he called the Virginia Statute. He believed that religious tolerance wasn't just a nice or moral idea, but a necessary tool. To have even a fighting chance at defeating the world's most powerful empire, the Baptists, the Presbyterians, and the Methodists would have to come together. A soldier was a soldier, and they needed every soldier they could get.

Of course, not everyone was on board with Jefferson's new law. Critics argued in letters to the *Virginia Gazette* that such an inclusive, wide-reaching statute would allow heathens like atheists, Jews, and even Muslims to hold office. According to the historian John Ragosta, the Evangelicals' response was, quite simply, "That's right."

Virginia's legislature ratified the statute. And Jefferson was so proud of this accomplishment that in a document laying out instructions for his tombstone, he wrote:

> On the faces of the Obelisk the following inscription, & not a word more:
> Here was buried
> Thomas Jefferson
> Author of the Declaration of American Independence of the Statute of Virginia for religious freedom & Father of the University of Virginia

Note that being our nation's third president didn't make the cut.

This is our history. It's one that should inspire awe and pride. The arguments were unprecedented, and the results uplifting.

But it is not a *complete* recounting of our history.

For while fifty-six men signed a declaration in 1776 that "all men are created equal," they built a country in which all people were not. Our forebearers' capacity to enslave our fellow human beings should stir shame and sobriety. Women would not be allowed to participate in the political process for nearly another 150 years. Early settlers—many of them immigrants, one might add—attacked, tortured, and pillaged the lands of innocent Indigenous people. Even white men who didn't own land were seen as beneath, and were barred from the political process.

And as a country, we have never reckoned with these original sins, either. America has made no reparations to its Black citizens—the "forty acres and a mule" that were promised never came. We have not reconciled with the subjugation of women or even begun to deal with the sustained economic inequality that has persisted throughout our nation's past to our present day.

Other countries, like Germany and South Africa, have taken clear steps to at least acknowledge the atrocities of their ancestors. But America has never convened its version of a Truth and Reconciliation Committee. Instead, we remain trapped by the shackles of history.

The premise of our American experiment was, and remains, both a radical idea and a contradiction. Our founding generation teed up profound questions that we are still resolving: Can we form a great nation with people from different backgrounds, beliefs, and geographies who share only an aspiration of freedom? Can we become a nation where, despite our differences, we truly believe all people are created equal?

Over the past two centuries, more people from more places have been captivated by these questions and inspired by this ideal, and have joined in this American endeavor.

Through the service and sacrifice of each successive generation, the circle of freedom has grown wider and wider, to include Irish and Italians and Jews, East Asians and West Africans, South Asians and South and Central Americans.

That promise has grown and evolved to the point where no matter your color or creed, your sexual orientation or country of origin, your accent or ability or age—you should be accepted here. The mix of beliefs and experiences represented in this country is more diverse than the founders could ever have imagined. Today, white Christians are a minority in this country. And according to the US Census Bureau, by midcentury, white people will be a minority outright.

Nevertheless, it perhaps goes without saying that the work of building our pluralistic democracy has not been easy. Nor is it finished.

How Our Differences Divide: Our Current Crises

We need not look far to understand how the American aspiration for freedom of belief—the freedom to be yourself—still falls short. To this day, we are continually tempted to mobilize around otherness rather than around our common humanity. We are still fighting against basic human tendencies and biases, against the reflexive push toward exclusion rather than inclusion. As a society, we still struggle against racism and sexism, homophobia, ableism, Islamophobia, and transphobia. The list goes on.

Sometimes it feels as though we are winning that fight and advancing in the struggle toward equality. Right now, frankly, it does not. And the numbers show that it's more than a bad feeling.

According to the Southern Poverty Law Center, in 2015 and again in 2016, the number of hate groups operating in this country actually grew. The number of anti-Muslim hate groups nearly tripled. And these hate groups aren't just spewing hate. They are taking terrible action. The FBI's data shows that hate crimes against Muslims were up by 67 percent in 2015 from the year before.

Meanwhile, women working full-time jobs still get paid, on average, $10,470 less than men per year. Or consider one of the most grotesque statistics of all: One in every five undergraduate women are sexually assaulted in college. So many more are harassed or worse on a daily basis, as the #MeToo movement has highlighted.

Similarly, people of color are continually discriminated against when applying to jobs—a resume showing a stereotypically white name is 50 percent more likely to get called back compared with an identical resume with a stereotypically Black name. The same kind of blatant discrimination has been demonstrated in scenarios as diverse as doctor's offices and eBay auctions, law firms and state legislatures, Craigslist ads and research labs.

Perhaps even more shocking are the prison statistics. In eleven states, at least one in every twenty adult Black men are behind bars. It's not a coincidence that in state prisons, Black men are incarcerated at an average rate of more than five times that of white men.

Although LGBT rights have gained ground, we still have a long way to go. In at least eight states, laws prevent schools from discussing LGBT topics, keep students from learning about their health and their rights, and discourage teachers from offering support or stopping bullying. In thirty-two states, there are no laws on the books that clearly defend transgender people against discrimination. According to the *National Transgender Discrimination Survey*, a dismaying 90 percent of respondents reported "experiencing harassment, mistreatment or discrimination on the job or taking actions like hiding who they are to avoid it."

Rising inequality makes discrimination along certain lines even easier to exert—be it based on class or race or other ways of experiencing the world. So it is understandable that many see our future as bleak. After all, we are a nation of immigrants, with a statue in New York harbor calling out to poor, huddled masses around the world, but we're also a nation that, as I write this, is considering putting up walls on our borders and deporting innocent young people who have known no other country as home.

Not all of these failures are directly a result of our differences in beliefs, but they are often reinforced by groups formed around a shared belief—by the echo chambers in which we seek affirmation. In each instance, this fracturing of our society makes it much harder to engage with one another, to establish our shared freedom, and to enlarge it and extend it to one another.

Accepting Our Differences: A False Contradiction

This runs us into a seeming contradiction. If our different beliefs are driving us apart, how will our shared beliefs bring us together? How can we accept one another if some of us do not believe in acceptance at all?

But this supposed contradiction is actually just a misrepresentation. For when we talk about the responsibility to accept that comes with our freedom of belief, we are saying something very specific.

We have to accept that we *have* different beliefs. This is decidedly different from accepting the beliefs themselves. Our task is narrower, though perhaps more difficult: We just need to accept that the differences are *real*—and a source of strength, not weakness.

What does that look like?

It means appreciating the perspectives of immigrants and Indigenous peoples, and respecting the grievances of poor people regardless of their color. It means understanding the effects of inequality on our society, the pain and anger of people who feel vulnerable—or who feel as though the world has left them behind. But it also means putting in the time to understand people who see the world through different eyes, whether that means they grew up Christian or Muslim, Republican or Democrat, in a big city or a tiny town.

It *also* means never shutting anyone out or shutting them down. That is a form of giving up, or giving in to the idea that America can't succeed. If we rejected people every time we disagreed, our democracy would not—and could not—sustain itself.

Again, let me be clear: Accepting others doesn't mean denying our differences. It actually means the opposite. We know it is never solely our differences that are the problem. As one of my sheroes, the poet Audre Lorde, once wrote: "Certainly, there are very real differences between us, of race, age, and sex. But it is not those differences between us that are separating us. It is rather our refusal to recognize those differences, and to examine the distortions that result from our misnaming them and their effects upon human behavior and expectation."

Recognizing Difference: Demanding the Impossible

We need to accept that difference has always been a part of our American experiment—for better and for worse. We must make an effort to accept and understand that difference, not ignore it.

Sometimes this work comes naturally. Sometimes it is hard. Sometimes we feel that we are learning and moving in the right direction. Sometimes it is tough to stomach that people can believe something so hateful—that they can seriously wish to divide us based on difference.

But if our nation's history includes chapters when we have mobilized against each other, it also includes chapters when we mobilized with each other and for each other. For as Dr. King reminds us in his "Letter from a Birmingham Jail," "We are caught in an inescapable network of mutuality, tied in a single garment of destiny."

I believe Dr. King's words—in part because of all the progress I've seen in my lifetime. I grew up Black and gay in small, working-class towns in the American South. I've known the sting of racism, the indignity of classism, the hatred of homophobia.

But I've also seen the impact of social movements, and the courageous women and men who have fought not just for the freedom of belief, but the right to vote and the right to marry—who have fought to be seen and heard.

No doubt, our history—and our present moment—is replete with ideas that fracture and fragment. But it contains just as many, if not more, ideas that bring us together.

From Anne Hutchinson's era to today, Americans have maintained the world's longest-lasting liberal, pluralistic democracy. And over the long arc of history, we have grown more accepting, more open, more loving, and more just. We have begun to recognize, embrace, and even celebrate difference. The freedom of belief is enjoyed by more people than our founders ever could have dreamed.

We are endowed with this freedom of belief, but we must work to make sure that we accept one another; to empathize with others without normalizing the act of "othering"; to protect the dignity of all, including and especially the people we disagree with; to walk in one another's shoes; and to be part of an American story that binds us together rather than breaks us apart.

As the iconic author James Baldwin—another of my heroes—wrote, "I know what I am asking is impossible. But in our time, as in every time, the impossible is the least one can demand."

This is what we should demand of each other: Making the impossible, the possible; making the imperfect, more perfect. After all, our democracy depends on it.

III. WITH THE FREEDOM FROM WANT, THE RESPONSIBILITY TO SERVE

When Detroit, Michigan, filed for Chapter 9 bankruptcy in 2013, it became the largest American municipality ever to do so. The city had more than $18 billion in liabilities. Thousands of retired city workers faced the unsettling prospect of having their pensions and health-care benefits cut. The options looked bleak.

In response to this unprecedented financial distress, some wanted to liquidate the city's assets, including the collection at the Detroit Institute of Arts (DIA). In order to salvage city workers' pensions while safeguarding the DIA's world-renowned art collection, a group of foundations—including the Ford Foundation—joined together and worked with the museum, the governor, the city, and the state legislature to strike a deal. This Grand Bargain, as it became known, enabled Detroit to swiftly emerge from bankruptcy just seventeen months after its historic filing.

As of this writing, nearly five years on, Detroit is no longer on the brink of financial collapse. Many of its residents, however, are still struggling to stay financially afloat and build healthy, comfortable lives for themselves and their families. Detroit—once America's wealthiest city by income per capita—has a 39.8 percent poverty rate, with the median household income a mere $26,000 per year.

Detroit is also one of the most segregated metro areas in the country, with 55.3 percent of the city's Black residents living in majority-Black neighborhoods. In these neighborhoods and others, far too many are struggling to secure gainful employment, access quality education, and enjoy freedom from want—the third of President Roosevelt's iconic Four Freedoms.

What Do We Mean by Freedom from Want?

At first glance, freedom from want is an odd phrase.

We all want something: Successful careers, flourishing relationships, healthy and happy families. And no doubt, we live in a country—and at a time—where if you want any material thing, you can get it pretty quickly. Just go online and you can get almost anything in two days, delivered right to your door.

This freedom, perhaps more than any of the other four, is clearly informed by its circumstances. When President Roosevelt first articulated this idea in 1941, the United States had just begun to emerge from the Great Depression, the worst financial and economic crisis in its history. So one can imagine just how distant the promise of this ideal was from the lived reality of many Americans at the time.

Similarly, when we think about freedom from want today, it can be equally hard for us to imagine a world where this freedom is universally experienced by all, especially when so many people feel economically vulnerable in communities like Detroit.

The reason is clear. Freedom from want isn't just about material possessions. It goes far deeper than that.

When President Roosevelt defined freedom from want, he included, in part, the ability to achieve what he called "a healthy peacetime life." That "healthy peacetime life" means security and contentment—which is precisely why so many people from around the world are drawn to live and work in the United States.

Freedom from want is beautifully depicted in Norman Rockwell's famous painting by the same name. It shows a family gathered around a dinner table, ready to eat. Toward the center of the painting is a turkey, the staple of a traditional Thanksgiving feast. But it's not the food that's striking; it's the faces. Every one of them is glowing, happy, and content.

This is the lived experience of freedom from want: Sitting with friends and loved ones, celebrating all we have and all we can be grateful for.

In the end, freedom from want not only inspires feelings of contentment and joy, but also frees us to follow our passions, discover our talents, and cultivate our skills. No longer bound by the burden of want—of making ends meet or meeting basic needs—we have the freedom to enjoy our lives, find fulfillment, better our communities, and increase our collective understanding of one another and the world. We are liberated to reach our highest potential as individuals and as members of society. That is why it remains such a compelling and desirable ideal even today.

A Responsibility to Serve

I have been fortunate enough to enjoy the benefits of this freedom, despite the forms of inequality I experienced in my own life. I was born in a poor Louisiana town, and started life in a little shotgun house in rural Texas, raised by a single mom. Needless to say, growing up wasn't easy. We didn't have a lot. And there have been times in my life when, as a gay, Black man, I felt I did not belong at that Norman Rockwell dinner table.

And yet I, too, have been lucky to enjoy freedom from want, because of the generosity and service of other people.

I was very fortunate that my mother moved my sister and me out of that poor town in Louisiana to a place where my mother had more economic opportunity and was able to study to be a nurse—and I was fortunate that, even though we were by no means wealthy, my mother worked hard to ensure my sister and I never wanted for love. I also was fortunate that, in 1965, a young woman asked my mother to sign me up for the first class of the Head Start program. I was fortunate to attend good public schools, to learn from good teachers, to receive Pell grants and private scholarships to pay for college. In other words, at every step in my journey, I was fortunate because people in my life—and my community—took the initiative to sacrifice and serve, which benefited me and many others in the process.

While we all have very different experiences, I do not believe it is too great a leap to assume that if you, too, are privileged to experience freedom from want, it's because people in your life served you and your community. We all feel grateful for those people in our lives and communities—from parents and grandparents, to teachers and peers, to friends and coworkers and employers, to doctors and nurses, to public officials and unsung heroes—who, through their service, have made our opportunities possible, our livelihoods safer or more secure.

And if this is true, then just as people have served on our behalf, or created the conditions for our success, we have an obligation to serve others in return and extend this freedom from want, especially to those who do not have those privileges we enjoy.

This is true in our own lives and immediate circles. It also extends to our communities and cities and countries as a whole. When Detroit was navigating its financial crisis back in 2013 and 2014, I traveled to the city on behalf of the Ford Foundation. We did our part to help our organization's hometown, a community that had supplied the Ford Foundation and our progenitors with the components for success. But for all the headlines heralding this historic deal, there was another side of the story that didn't get much press.

One June afternoon in 2014, I found myself sitting in the Rivera Court of the Detroit Institute of Arts, filled with awe. I was there for a reception, a celebration of new commitments to the Grand Bargain, surrounded by leaders from government and philanthropy, and CEOs of businesses—and I happened to notice two retirees sitting quietly at the front of the room: Shirley Lightsey and Don Taylor.

Shirley and Don's names were not printed in the program. Reporters and photographers weren't swarming them for interviews before and after the ceremony. They were representatives of the city's workers who, along with their fellow retirees, ultimately voted to cut their own benefits for the sake of Detroit. And because of their service and their sacrifice—and the sacrifice of tens of thousands of hardworking municipal retirees like them—Detroit was given a second chance. These public servants chose to do what they could to make the city—the same city that had given them their opportunities and their pensions—a place where the next generation could succeed.

When we think about the freedom from want, and what we must do to extend this freedom to all people in the twenty-first century, we should remember what Shirley and Don did for Detroit. Along with countless other retired city workers, they made a choice that was not in service of themselves, but in service of others. They recognized the opportunity they had to improve their communities, and they seized it. Now, more than ever, we all are being asked to do the same.

Inequality and the Persistence of Want

Just as many people in Detroit do not yet experience freedom from want, there are plenty of people across this country and around the world who do not enjoy the "healthy peacetime life" that flows out of the freedom from want. On the streets of Chicago, people yearn for an end to violence and for economic opportunity. In the mountains of Appalachia, poverty keeps families trapped, generation after generation. On tribal lands across the American West, freedom from want remains another unfulfilled promise.

Expand our view, and the same is true in places across the world—from the Kibera areas of Nairobi to the favelas of São Paulo—and for too many people forced to flee their homes throughout Latin America and Syria.

In these places, and many others, we all have the responsibility to serve. Otherwise, that grander bargain we made with one another—the social contract that lives in America's founding documents and holds us all together—starts to unravel. As inequality grows, our agreement with ourselves and one another comes undone.

This inequality not only incites animosity and strife within communities; it threatens the very institutions of our democracy. A democratic society cannot truly flourish if the people, or any subset of the people, do not believe they have equal access to its freedoms, opportunities, and resources. To create the conditions for our democracy to be healthy and vibrant—to continue and thrive—we must root out the inequality that undermines our success. And to do that, we must first accept and embrace the responsibility we have to serve one another, to reach across society's many gaps and aid those who are grappling with the debilitating consequences of inequity.

Forms of Service and the Role of Philanthropy

Given the many kinds of want and the many forms of inequality that exist in our communities, we must be prepared to remedy them with different types of service. Each of us has a responsibility to determine how we can best serve each other.

For some, this may mean volunteering in local schools and community centers, or mentoring young, at-risk children in desperate need of encouragement and inspiration. For others, it may mean directly engaging with the philanthropic work being done by countless organizations throughout the country and around the world. The service we can contribute is often directly proportional to the amount of privilege we have—be that the time, the talent, or the treasure we have to give.

As the president of a legacy foundation, I often find myself pondering what it means for organizations like ours to make a concerted effort to eliminate the structural inequalities that prevent millions of people from experiencing true freedom from want. More specifically, what does it mean for philanthropy—especially those institutions founded by individuals who enjoyed extreme freedom from want and immense privilege—to commit themselves to rooting out the very inequalities that allowed them to exist in the first place?

In some ways, philanthropy is the best example of this relationship between service and want. Foundations like ours are the product of a freedom from want enjoyed by too few; and because of that, we have the ability—and the obligation—to extend that freedom to others.

I often return to an insight of Dr. King's. He wrote: "Philanthropy is commendable, but it must not cause the philanthropist to overlook the circumstances of economic injustice which make philanthropy necessary." And while philanthropy's role is not only to address economic injustice, I do believe that Dr. King gets to the heart of philanthropy's relationship to the freedom from want, and to our responsibility to serve.

As philanthropic organizations, especially those birthed out of great privilege, we can't simply concern ourselves with meeting the immediate needs of those we serve. In order to enact true and lasting change, we must address the root causes of injustice and the underlying sources of human suffering. We must disrupt the systems and structures that have conspired, throughout history, to rob individuals of their right to enjoy freedom from want. And we must use our privileges, and exercise the freedom we have, in order to extend those privileges and freedoms to other people. That is what we must demand of our service.

This Fight Belongs to All of Us

Ultimately, the condition of our lives is intimately interconnected with that of others. When those around us lack equal rights, the quality of all our livelihoods comes under threat.

As long as income inequality, racial inequality, gender inequality, religious inequality, or any other form of inequity exists among us, the social bonds holding us together in what Dr. King called an "inescapable network of mutuality" will continue to be strained. We will continue to be divided on the basis of race, gender, class, sexuality, religion, and physical ability, while the "beloved community" of Dr. King's vision remains no more than a dream. That is why we must root out inequality in our society. If we don't, we will continue to see large subsets of our communities struggle to live safe and healthy lives.

But if we commit ourselves to mitigating inequality through acts of service toward others—to viewing the well-being of others as an extension of our own security—we will make "we the people" stronger than before. We will affirm that "self-evident" truth that all people are created equal, and are deserving of the same opportunities to succeed and flourish in this life.

So let us come together in the spirit of service, and implicate ourselves in the struggles of those in need, and truly become our neighbor's keeper. Let us do the work necessary to ensure all people—regardless of age, race, gender, sexuality, religion, or ability—have the opportunity to live a "healthy peacetime life" that is brimming with the promise of freedom: Freedom from injustice, freedom from inequality, freedom from want.

IV. WITH THE FREEDOM FROM FEAR, THE RESPONSIBILITY TO ACT

If a "healthy peacetime life" captured President Roosevelt's hope for the future, it did not reflect what loomed just over the horizon. In 1941, when he first envisioned the Four Freedoms, he understood that the United States faced a singular threat: World war. France had recently surrendered to Nazi forces. Europe seemed poised to fall against the combined might of Germany, Italy, and ultimately Japan. Only a few weeks before introducing the Four Freedoms into the American lexicon, while discussing the prospect of the United States lending munitions and equipment to Great Britain, President Roosevelt offered the image of a "neighbor's home catch[ing] fire." Europe was burning, and Roosevelt feared that fire would spread.

In this context, the freedom from fear has a very specific meaning. At the time, the idea was that no one should live in fear of military aggression from other countries—a peace which, ironically, might require military action to achieve. In the long term, Roosevelt imagined "a world-wide reduction of armaments" as part of his Four Freedoms message, and presumably envisioned a world where the instruments of global conflict would not exist on such a massive scale.

Fear and Present Dangers

When we consider the world today, it's easy to see the varied threats to "healthy peacetime life," and the advance of fear on many fronts. Some of these threats still fall into the military category, but others are environmental, ideological, or political. One is reminded of Norman Rockwell's depiction of freedom from fear—two parents putting their children to sleep. There's a newspaper in the father's hand. Of the headline, you can just make out the words "bombings" and "horror."

Scanning the headlines each morning, there are specters of danger on every page. Climate change and its impending consequences. The rise of nationalism in Europe and white nationalism in the United States. Political instability in South America and the Middle East. Famine in the horn of Africa. Mass shootings seem to be at least a monthly occurrence, while cyberattacks and terrorism remain an ever-present threat.

Of course, bombings and horror remain top of mind, as the possibility of nuclear conflict with North Korea is irresponsibly edged into the realm of probability and the proliferation of these weapons continues. Indeed, many things should keep us awake at night.

Fear is a product of—and sometimes a cause of—vulnerability. And inequality, in all its forms, makes us feel ever more vulnerable.

On an individual level, there's fear about not being able to pay the bills or put food on the table. Every day, people fear how they will be treated based on their ability or skin color, their faith or sexual orientation, their gender identity or caste identity. There's fear that you will be denied the right to determine your own future—to rise as high as your talent and hard work will take you.

How Fear Threatens Our Democratic Values

It should not surprise us, then, that fear itself—to echo President Roosevelt—can be wielded as a weapon and even as a threat to democratic values.

Often, we associate weaponized fear with terrorism. Indeed, this is where terrorism gets its name, and how terrorists believe they will come to power or prominence. Either through fear during and after specific instances, or by creating a looming, constant threat, violent extremists try to manipulate a larger narrative and influence the action—or reaction—of others.

Terrorists are far from the only actors who have deployed fear to deliver a desired outcome. Fear has long been harnessed by those in power to suppress political participation and curb civic action. Consider the Alabama state troopers waiting on the other side of the Edmund Pettus Bridge—waiting to assault Congressman Lewis and his fellow marchers as they began their journey from Selma to Montgomery. Recall the many ways in which protestors have been intimidated or suppressed in fighting for justice across history—including the mobs described in Frederick Douglass's "A Plea for Free Speech in Boston."

Then and now, fear of imprisonment or physical harm is intended to keep people from organizing and speaking out, from being themselves, from fighting for what's right. And these threats continue to mount.

For example, in Honduras, more than 120 environmental activists have been killed over the past eight years as they attempt to fight for their rights and their land. Meanwhile, around the world, authoritarian governments trample on essential human rights and democratic freedoms—whether by shutting down protestors or the press—and even some democracies have begun to follow their lead.

While fear constrains social movements, it also can paralyze well-intentioned leaders. Too often, it keeps those with power and privilege from doing what's right when that means taking risks that might imperil their organizations or businesses or individual careers. Sometimes, it may tempt them to make rash decisions that, in the name of protecting democratic rights and freedoms for some of us, erode those same freedoms for all of us.

In these cases, fear is used to justify certain actions—such as the increase of government surveillance, or tough-on-crime policy reforms that serve mostly to criminalize people of color. Meanwhile, the underlying causes of that fear—be they racism, sexism, ableism, the effective use of propaganda, or a persistent cultural narrative—go without being examined, let alone addressed.

This is because fear seizes upon our differences and exaggerates them, and almost always compels society to divide along lines of "us" versus "them." It entices the desperate or the frustrated or the furious. It empowers demagogues and strongmen who exploit the very real anxieties of ordinary people while amassing power for themselves and their cronies. It drives governments—even elected ones—to make decisions that seek to preserve "law and order" at the expense of freedom and dignity.

In other words, fear is toxic to our society because it discourages people from taking the actions that might help us feel safer, or make us freer, or allow us to heal—and instead it drives us apart.

Fear in Action, or Acting on Fear

Even President Roosevelt, the man who sought freedom from fear for every person around the world, succumbed to its temptations. Only a year after Roosevelt introduced the Four Freedoms, he authorized the relocation of 120,000 Americans of Japanese descent—over two-thirds of whom were US citizens—into concentration camps.

Thousands of human beings in this country—women, men, and children—were forced to leave their homes and submit to forced imprisonment, all because of their fellow citizens' fear.

In the 1980s, the United States finally apologized for this atrocity and acknowledged the extent of its faults—an apology that sadly, as we know, is a rare occurrence. According to a congressional report by the Commission on Wartime Relocation and Internment of Civilians titled *Personal Justice Denied*:

> The promulgation of Executive Order 9066 was not justified by military necessity, and the decisions which followed from it—detention, ending detention, and ending exclusion—were not driven by analysis of military conditions. The broad historical causes which shaped these decisions were race prejudice, war hysteria, and a failure of political leadership. Widespread ignorance of Japanese Americans contributed to a policy conceived in haste and executed in an atmosphere of fear and anger at Japan. A grave injustice was done to American citizens and resident aliens of Japanese ancestry who, without individual review or any probative evidence against them, were excluded, removed, and detained by the United States during World War II.

That President Roosevelt—and the American people—gave in to fear is a useful reminder of the power of fear to shift societies, even those that claim to be paragons of freedom. This reality forces us to acknowledge our difficult history and to recognize that even these Four Freedoms—important ideals to be sure—are not without their blemishes or shortcomings.

And this struggle against fear, and its corrosive impact on freedom and democracy, is just as relevant now as it was in 1942. If only that were the last time an executive order based in "fear and anger" or tinged with "race prejudice, war hysteria and a failure of political leadership" made waves in our society.

That's why, most importantly, this failure to protect freedom in the face of fear reminds us that our words in defense of freedom mean nothing—and will mean nothing—if we do not act.

The Imperative of Action

If one of the intended effects of fear is that it stifles action, then to oppose fear, we must be willing to act. This is particularly true when the action required is inconvenient or uncomfortable or risky—when taking action might be considered hazardous for our reputations or even dangerous for our careers.

More than just acting for ourselves, we must be willing to act on behalf of others—especially those who live in fear. Our actions can bolster those who might otherwise be vulnerable, and can provide cover to those often targeted because of their identity or affiliation.

Indeed, if a white person does not fear that police brutality or violent white supremacists will affect him—but knows how this fear affects his fellow human beings—then that white person can act on behalf of Black lives and against fear. If a natural-born citizen does not fear the persecution of a so-called travel ban or feel the threat of deportation, her actions on behalf of those affected have an enormous impact. In these cases and others, we can stand with and support those who know fear and oppression, while standing up for our own freedom.

Of course, this responsibility to act does not require that we act irresponsibly. Our safety and self-care remain paramount, especially in these dangerous times. But if we have the privilege to act, or if our privilege grants us some respite from fear, we must do what we can to create for others those feelings of safety and of being seen.

The Need for Civil Society

Throughout history, there has been no better guardian of the freedom from fear—no better defender of the vulnerable—than civil society: Groups of compassionate, engaged citizens who continue to organize themselves and mobilize others to work on behalf of the community. They are the immune system of our democratic society against the plague of injustice.

Among the most troubling trends in the world today is the outright assault and ongoing onslaught against civil society. It is an epidemic. In the countries where the Ford Foundation works, we have seen laws that restrict NGO funding and freedom of assembly, and learned of activists and peaceful protestors being assaulted and worse.

Still, around the world, civil-society organizations continue to act against fear, and fight to protect the rights and freedoms of those in need.

In the favelas of Brazil, where Black men are routinely killed by police, organizations like Redes da Maré are bringing the community together to denounce the violence and raise their collective voice.

In the courtrooms of Zimbabwe, where unjustly incarcerated demonstrators face persecution and prosecution, Zimbabwe Lawyers for Human Rights is providing emergency legal support.

In the streets of Uganda, where the LGBT community has been oppressed by the government, organizations like Sexual Minorities Uganda have risen to challenge unjust laws and defend human rights, despite personal risk. It is the same with Planned Parenthood right here at home.

And after a year of increasing nuclear threats, and in the spirit of President Roosevelt's original intention—the "world-wide reduction of armaments"—the 2017 Nobel Peace Prize was awarded to the International Campaign to Abolish Nuclear Weapons, a group of more than one hundred civil-society organizations acting against fear.

All these brave men and women speak truth to power. They forge relationships with local communities and understand their concerns. By taking action, they make people feel less vulnerable. Instead of succumbing to fear, they act in spite of it, and create the conditions so that others might be free from it.

OUR CHOICE: ACTION OR THE ALTERNATIVE

Without protection, our freedoms and rights will face contraction rather than expansion.

Of course, one problem with the erosion of our freedoms is that it happens gradually—or these days, almost constantly, in an unceasing, chaotic blur.

As certain democratic norms and values fall away, it becomes harder to motivate oneself to act. We get exhausted by, even acclimated to, the daily onslaught. There's the oft-used image of the frog in the pot of boiling water, who doesn't know to save itself because the problem—the temperature—increases slowly over time. The lethal moment comes both unexpectedly and inevitably, met not with active resistance but with passive acceptance.

That, as ever, is our choice: To act or to be passive. And to be passive in this moment is to invite catastrophes similarly unanticipated but no longer unthinkable.

In 1933, Martin Niemöller was happy to see Adolf Hitler rise to power. As a Lutheran pastor and a national conservative, Niemöller believed that Hitler would help put an end to the growing atheist movement in Germany.

Under Hitler's rule, Niemöller saw his country heading in a dark direction. But he believed he and the church were safe. Then, the Nazi government started issuing laws that directly concerned the church. Only after he came under personal threat did Niemöller decide to protest. He was quickly arrested and tried for crimes against the state.

His experience is encapsulated by his timeless confession:

> First they came for the socialists, and I did not
> speak out—because I was not a socialist.
> Then they came for the trade unionists, and I did
> not speak out—because I was not a trade unionist.
> Then they came for the Jews, and I did not speak out—
> because I was not a Jew.
> Then they came for me—and there was no one
> left to speak for me.

Niemöller spent eight years imprisoned in Sachsenhausen and Dachau. Afterward, he dedicated his life to warning future generations of our obligation to act, even and especially when we feel the matter does not concern us.

History reminds us that the only way to ensure all of our freedoms—our freedom to speak and believe, and to live a "healthy peacetime life"—is to take action on behalf of others. And to do that, we must have the moral courage to face not just our fears, but fear itself.

DEMOCRACY IS A THREAT TO WHITE SUPREMACY

January 7, 2021

I have long believed that inequality is the greatest threat to justice—and, the corollary, that white supremacy is the greatest threat to democracy. But what has become clear during recent weeks—and all the more apparent yesterday—is that the converse is also true: *Democracy is the greatest threat to white supremacy.*

This explains the backlash that has plagued American politics from its beginnings and throughout these last four years. It also casts a light on what we witnessed yesterday: A failed coup—an insurrection at the United States Capitol.

Like so many others, I watched, aghast, as a mob stormed our revered temple of representative democracy—and on a day when another 3,865 Americans fell victim to the raging coronavirus pandemic.

The world was shaken by a shocking, odious sight: Confederate battle flags inside the National Statuary Hall; gallows with nooses on the National Mall outside. With glee, two rioters reenacted the murder of George Floyd on the steps of the National City Christian Church—one kneeling on the neck of the other, fully aware of the cameras capturing their laughter. Four people lost their lives.

There is no misunderstanding the message, nor the mission.

And make no mistake: If these had been peaceful protestors for racial justice rather than violent combatants for white pride and grievance, law enforcement would have used extreme force, if not live bullets, to keep the building secure. We know for sure because this is exactly what happened only a few months ago, as federal forces tear-gassed the peaceably assembled outside the White House to clear the area for a photo op. As the inimitable, incisive Isabel Wilkerson tweeted in real time, "We have seen caste in action."

I, too, cannot see yesterday's insurrection as anything other than the latest chapter in a long, dispiriting, exhausting history. And yet, from this very same history, I also—perhaps, paradoxically—draw hope.

I'm hopeful because, from our founding contradiction, we have emerged a freer, fairer nation. All too slowly, all too unevenly, all too imperfectly—and at far too high a cost—we, the people, have struggled to root out the strand of white supremacy in our country's DNA.

Our founding aspirations were just that: Aspirations. It's been the work of generations—from Frederick Douglass and Fannie Lou Hamer to Harriet Tubman and Bayard Rustin—to realize these aspirations. And while much remains to be done, and *undone*, I believe we can emerge— and are emerging—a more unified, more equal, more just, more *American* America.

Yes, the ideal of democracy is the greatest threat to the ideology of white supremacy; neither can long endure in the presence of the other. That is why today—and every day—we must renew our commitment to protect our democratic values and institutions from all enemies, foreign and domestic, especially those falsely disguised as patriots.

THE DAWN IS OURS

January 22, 2021

Nearly three decades ago, on the pulse of a different dawn, the iconic Maya Angelou welcomed a new day—inviting us to "say simply … with hope, good morning."

On Tuesday, the radiant Amanda Gorman, the poet's phenomenal protégé, echoed Angelou's call for a nation "bruised, but whole." For me, as for so many of us, Amanda's words—and the moment they mark— herald the reappearance of light, both on us and within us, light that feels akin to liberation.

To be sure, with this new morning comes mourning: Mourning for what has been bruised and battered, for hopes deferred and dreams denied, for all those lost and laid to rest.

We grieve, too, for our democratic institutions buffeted—the infrastructure of our republic stripped and laid bare. We have only begun to assess the full extent of the damage, though the toll, without question, is higher than any of us can tolerate.

And yet, for the first time in a long time, we can exhale.

We can release that deep sigh of grief and relief, mindful that after years of desecration, we, the people, endure. Our democracy may be wearied and wounded, but it is still alive. "Not broken," as Amanda perfectly put it, "but simply unfinished."

With the night thinning, we can begin to see the path from what "just is" to "justice."

For my Ford Foundation colleagues and me, the work ahead is clear: After a season of suffering comes an opportunity to heal. After a season of destruction, a responsibility to build anew—not to restore the world as it was, but to reimagine it, fairer and better, as it should and must be.

On the pulse of our dawn, let us recommit to this work, together. We are not yet free of the hardship and heartache. But the sun glances over the horizon—and, with hope, at last, we say, good morning.

INCLUSION IS PATRIOTISM OF THE HIGHEST ORDER

The Washington Post
July 2, 2021

Exactly 245 years ago, America's founders brought forth a new nation dedicated to a radical idea: Representative democracy. As Thomas Jefferson wrote to a friend while drafting his declaration, representation "is the whole object of the present controversy."

Ever since, Americans have engaged in pitched battles over the meaning of representation—over its definition and reach; over who gets included and excluded.

And this Independence Day, representation is the "whole object" of our current controversy over voters' rights and women's rights and migrants' rights—and of that new dog whistle, critical race theory, which lawmakers across the country are suddenly banning, without bothering to understand it.

If, like me, you participate in or follow our public debates, you are no stranger to this heat. At the institution I lead, our critics on one side call us conservative bulwarks of capitalism, who cannot be trusted to repair the irreparably broken system that created us. From another direction, we are accused of promoting a divisive, subversive, even an anti-white agenda.

Most of us have some version of that experience in our own lives now. But our business—and everyone's business in my view—is hope, because hope is the oxygen of democracy. Everything we try should be aimed at helping to ensure that all people can live with dignity, participate in the systems that give order and meaning to their lives, and rise as high as their talent will take them. Because we have all benefited from America.

One element of this effort is recovering a more representative story of our past. We all should be astounded, for instance, that less than 2 percent of the commemorative sites in our national registry honor the contributions of Black Americans. So, we support initiatives such as the African American Cultural Heritage Action Fund, among others, which are writing Black accomplishment into the story of American achievement.

This is not "cultural Marxism," or "anti-American," or any of the other buzzwords that critics have levied. In fact, it is just the opposite. Inclusion is patriotism of the highest order. It informs our answers to that fundamental, founding question of representation and whether we, the people, will truly extend representation to each other—then, now, and into the future.

And so, the American story we should celebrate this Fourth of July is one of *expanding* representation—however slowly, unevenly, and imperfectly. It's the story of a small circle of white, property-owning men in Philadelphia that, generation by generation, continues to grow wider, *precisely* because of the patriotic struggle and sacrifice of the people who were once excluded—above all, Black and Brown people, and women.

To be sure, some abuse their megaphones on social media and cable news to dismiss all of this as "identity politics." The truth is, one's identity has *always* determined, at least in part, one's access to opportunity in America. Identity-based policies and privileges were codified in the Constitution itself.

Others may conflate our work to dismantle discrimination with destruction or division. But in my own life, I have seen the way that acknowledging identity can be a force for unity, for a common good, for each of us to help expand that circle for all.

I grew up Black in the still-segregated South, at a time when my mother was denied the right to vote. And yet, throughout my life, I have benefited, in ways seen and unseen, from Americans, Black and white, who challenged their nation to fulfill its promise, inch by inch, ballot by ballot, law by law.

I grew up poor in a small, rural town. And yet, in my lifetime, I benefited from the American people's investments in Head Start and public schools and Pell grants that made my journey possible.

I grew up gay, at a time when many people saw my sexuality as a psychological disorder, or a crime. And yet, in my lifetime, I have seen Americans embrace love and compassion—and marriage equality become the law of the land.

This progress came to pass not by ignoring complex issues of identity—nor by shrinking from the fact that the past, often, remains all too present. The only path to justice runs through truth.

And while each of my identities has shaped my experience of America, no identity has had a greater impact on my life or its trajectory than my identity as an American, with all that it entails.

I love my country. I'm grateful to and for it. And I believe, now more than ever, in the promise of 1776—in the radicalism of representation.

In their flawed genius, the founders entrusted us with the tools to fix what they were unwilling to repair. They left us the capacity to build something that had never existed: A multiracial, multiethnic, pluralist democracy that extends the blessings of representation to all.

This is a legacy worth fighting for, preserving, and passing forward—today and always.

JEFFERSON'S REPUBLIC, 246 YEARS ON

Rededication of the Burial Ground for Enslaved People
Monticello, Virginia
June 17, 2022

I must begin in gratitude: To the Reverend Carolyn Dillard, whose invocation lifts our sights and our souls; to Leslie Greene Bowman and Cinder Stanton, brilliant historians both, whose moral leadership and fortitude brings us to this moment; and—invoking the great Julian Bond, a generation later—to the descendants of the human beings buried as *property* whom we remember and sanctify as *people*.

Today, we honor your inheritance. We rededicate this space to you—and for you, and with you—in recognition of your ancestors, and all of our ancestors.

Across the nearly four million square miles of Jefferson's republic, 246 years on, there is no place more American than this—Jefferson's Monticello.

It is quite literally both a monument to our noblest ideals and the very blood-stained earth where Jefferson enslaved some four hundred human beings, in direct contradiction to those ideals. It, at once, gives testimony to American genius and American ignominy. It embodies American pride and American patriotism and our American promise—and, in the same breath, the searing, uniquely American pain of generations. The shame of our history—a past that is all too present.

Like Jefferson himself, these grounds are a paradox—defined by a perverse dissonance.

Less than half a mile from here, Mr. Jefferson lies beneath a granite obelisk. At his request, that monument of coarse stone lists the three accomplishments for which he wished to be remembered: The Declaration of American Independence; the Virginia religious freedom statute; the University of Virginia.

These institutions—the ideals they encompass—they became a beacon to the world. They matter still—now, perhaps, more than ever: Jefferson's declaration, our founding affirmation of equality and representation; Jefferson's religious freedom statute, of tolerance and inclusion; Jefferson's university, of reason and science and truth, of public education as the means to good citizenship.

But there is, of course, a fourth cornerstone of Jefferson's legacy, one he omitted from his self-curated account: The institution of slavery, which begat the institution of white supremacy with which we still reckon today—from lynching to Jim Crow to redlining to mass incarceration to police brutality and beyond.

In so many ways, Jefferson ensured that the republic he wrote into being would break through from an old world to a new—that it would be the vanguard of a new age. But in at least this one way, Jefferson allowed the barbaric, the callous and the cruel, to carry through from the old into the new. He and the founding generation left it to others to fix what they lacked the courage to face themselves.

And so, it is appropriate—necessary—that we recognize this fourth cornerstone, even and especially on this auspicious day and Juneteenth weekend, when we celebrate the fullness of American freedom, the jubilee of liberation.

We do so not to diminish equality and tolerance and reason—triumphs of human achievement—but to illuminate how we have failed to live up to them from the beginning; to illuminate how we got from there to here; to illuminate who we are, unequal at our creation, unequal still, but becoming more equal thanks to the sacrifice of our ancestors, our elders, and so many of you on the front lines of the fight for justice today.

In fact, to illuminate this legacy—as you all have in preserving and restoring this space—is to understand something profoundly important about the American story and about American inequality.

Look no further than these graves themselves, and you will see the evidence.

In life, Mr. Jefferson accomplished the three momentous achievements on his headstone, and many beyond them. And in life, he also enslaved more than six hundred human beings, two score of whom rest here.

In death, Jefferson was afforded the dignity and respect to define his own legacy. And in death, as in life, the people he enslaved were deprived of that right, among countless others.

For decades, the forty graves here were considered lost to history, a secret hiding in plain sight. In whispered words and inherited wisdom, it was the descendant community—you, your parents, your grandparents—who remembered them and who returned to them.

Today, some of these graves are marked with uninscribed stones; the vast majority are not marked at all. Hundreds more elude us yet. The remains of many ancestors may never be found.

We convene with them today—all of them. Those who are lost and those who have been found. Those whose names escape us, and those whose names we say with pride.

We gather to help tell an indispensable story, too long left out. To pick up the chisel. And as best we can, to carve our ancestors' epitaphs into the negative space.

It was one of Jefferson's successors—Abraham Lincoln—at the dedication of a different burial ground, in Gettysburg, who defined the challenge of his time, and of ours: The burden and privilege of being American.

We are engaged, Lincoln said, in a test of whether Jefferson's vision could triumph—whether government of, by, and for the people could long endure. Indeed, we remain engaged in a great conflict between authoritarianism and autocracy on one side and the American idea, our democratic values, on the other.

Here and now, like for Lincoln in Gettysburg, we cannot consecrate or hallow this sacred burial ground. For it was the people—the enslaved people, who led dynamic, complicated, meaningful lives here—who have long since venerated it. It was the enslaved people—who loved and celebrated and laughed here, who were sold into bondage here, who were torn away from their families here, who endured and persisted here, who lived here and who died here—these human beings made Monticello. They consecrated this place centuries ago.

And yet, in marking this burial ground anew—by marking it for the descendants of the ancestors who lie here; for the descendants of the enslaved across this land and around the world; for all freedom-seeking, freedom-loving people everywhere—we all move a little closer, together, toward realizing our inalienable American birthright, toward what Frederick Douglass would call "absolute equality."

We all move a little closer to the multiethnic, multiracial, pluralist democracy that Mr. Jefferson, paradoxically, both impeded and made possible.

Thank you, all, for joining in the shared effort to make it so—in this most solemn occasion in this most American of places.

THESE TRUTHS WE HOLD

The New York Times
July 4, 2022

The heart does not exactly swell with patriotic pride this Independence Day, as the gut absorbs one dizzying, disorienting blow after the next. Our sense of who we are, our very identity as Americans, feels assaulted and violated. Amid profound, painful regression on issue after issue, we are left gasping for breath.

Our nation seems more irreparably divided than ever before in my lifetime, barreling down a parallel path, perhaps, to the one our forebearers traveled in the 1850s.

What we do now matters urgently. And the American identity that we still share matters, too, not least because it must inform and inspire a common effort, across our differences, to find our way out and forward. I believe we still can agree on a set of ideas—values and aspirations— enshrined in our Declaration of Independence, 246 years on.

In our founding, I see flawed genius. In the declaration we celebrate, I see a statement of purpose. In our Constitution, I see our founders entrusting each generation to fix what the preceding one was unwilling to repair.

To me, the callous cruelty of our founders—at least thirty-four of the fifty-six men who signed the declaration also enslaved human beings—is less remarkable than what they set in motion, however contradictory. They initiated a grand, complicated experiment with self-government that made possible abolition and suffrage, worker's rights and civil rights and women's rights, however slowly and unevenly. More astounding still, Black people and Brown people, the Indigenous and the immigrant, LGBTQ people and people with disabilities, all claimed the American project as our own and expanded the circle of inclusion and opportunity.

Our founders bequeathed to us something radical, something unprecedented: The tools with which to build a multiracial, multiethnic, pluralist democracy that extends the privilege of American identity to all.

My love of America—of the American idea—is unwavering. This laboratory of liberty is worth saving, worth improving.

But I fear we are mired in a culture of absolutism and tearing ourselves apart at the seams.

Everything right now, it seems, is black or white, all or nothing, perfect or unacceptable. Every venue has become a theater for performatively asserting our own virtue or righteousness, or for denying someone else's. The so-called microaggressions keep getting smaller, the disproportionate penalties bigger. Nuance and complexity, let alone compromise, are nowhere to be found. In their place is a pervasive, paralyzing cynicism. And in turn, our extreme challenges remain extremely unsolved.

Even among those with whom we largely agree, we've normalized intolerance and incivility. Among those with whom we disagree, we shame and cancel. We dehumanize and demonize.

Certainly, not everyone is equally culpable or complicit. To suggest that the people and groups denigrating human rights and human dignity are somehow on equal footing with those of us defending them is wrong. This would imply a false moral equivalence.

And make no mistake about my own view: The advocacy of those working to reimagine our society is of a different category from—asymmetrical to—the backlash of those rolling back our rights and fighting to restore an unequal past. The former is challenging us to be better, more inclusive, more equitable. The latter too often is daring us to be worse.

At the same time, at least one outcome of the breakdown is clear and present for us all: A toxicity that threatens to asphyxiate our democracy. Across our country, a foul spirit of nihilism has displaced a forgiving spirit of grace.

In our distorted media, the few loudest voices garner the most coverage and clicks while the conglomerates and social networks reap the rewards. These extremes beget more extremes, coarsening our discourse.

In our politics, we delineate districts and finance campaigns and decide elections in a way that favors purity over persuasion, thus further dividing our national community. Worse, a minoritarian stranglehold—a tyranny of the minority—is suffocating both our democracy and our trust in its institutions.

Finally, inequalities of all kinds both aggravate our challenges and prevent us from joining together in common cause to solve them. For too many Americans—of every color and creed, in red states and blue—the mobility escalator has ground to a halt, setting in place an inescapable, insidious hopelessness. When so many millions live on an economic precipice, they respond with anxiety, resentment, and grievance; the forces exploiting them, with ongoing mendacity and impunity.

To break the vicious cycle in which we have trapped ourselves, we must define and agree on new rules of engagement for the commons, online and off.

First, we must make new, *open* space: Places where people of good will, operating in good faith, can speak and listen, with authenticity and vulnerability, without fear that they're using the wrong word or phrase, without self-censorship. Perhaps this is how we begin to reject the zero-sum thinking that says, "If the other side wins on anything, my side loses on everything"—how we begin to turn toward each other, at a time when it's so easy to turn away or simply turn off.

We also must embrace one another's shared humanity—across the breach, to heal the breach—which means we must at least tolerate the expression of views with which we disagree.

Among all the Enlightenment Age ideals that informed our founders, tolerance—that stuffy, unsatisfying triumph of classical liberalism—predicated the civil rights and civil liberties we cherish.

Our founders knew from experience: The alternative to tolerance was violence, the religious and ethnic strife that had bloodied centuries of European history. Make no mistake: The future could hold the same in store for us.

How do we forestall this tragedy? By rediscovering and recommitting to our American identity, to these truths we still hold: Out of many, we are one—because we believe in what Frederick Douglass called "absolute equality." We believe in equal representation, equal rights, and equal justice; that happiness is a pursuit, not an achievement, realized through self-determination, but also tolerance, generosity, and reason.

To be sure, some dismiss this tradition as fruit from a poisoned tree, and the facts are undeniable. The United States' history as a functioning democracy only began in 1965, when President Lyndon Johnson signed legislation to guarantee the franchise—and even the Voting Rights Act's protections are now imperiled in many states, as other fundamental rights are thrown into new jeopardy.

And yet what makes America great is not the fact of our perfection but our act of becoming more perfect. What makes the American people exceptional is that we have the strength to acknowledge our failings—moral, structural, personal—and the courage to make wrong into right.

Anger and grief are not unreasonable. I share the outrage and despair that many appropriately feel about America's backsliding. But this cannot be a reason to cede our patriotism. Our ancestors and elders, today's social-justice leaders on the front lines, all have sacrificed too much for us to give up on America now.

And patriotism can take as many forms as there are perspectives. Love of country can mean placing your hand on your heart during the national anthem or kneeling on one knee. It can mean serving as a police officer or a first responder to keep our neighborhoods safe, or protesting in those very same streets. The declaration itself was an act of defiant resistance.

However we give voice to our patriotism, let's step away from the extremes and from the edge, away from the sanctimony and certitude. Let's build longer bridges, not higher walls. The cost of the alternative is greater than any of us can bear.

Let's resolve to listen with humility, curiosity, and empathy—with open hearts and minds. Let's resolve to extend the presumption of grace and the benefit of the doubt.

The road to enduring justice runs through reconciliation, and the road to reconciliation runs through truth.

One of our hard truths is that, as the poet says, America has never been America. Another truth is that it can be still, and it must be, and it will be—if we renew our fidelity to the values that bind us, both despite and because of our differences.

PART X

IN CELEBRATION: PROFILES IN LOVE AND LEADERSHIP

For each of us, if we had only one wish—if only one of our prayers was answered—would it not be to live well, and fully, with joy and purpose and grace?… Let us resolve, then, to … know love and to give it freely. To be righteous in our cause, but never self-righteous in our character. To advance the slow and steady march of progress. To bend the arc of the moral universe, with our own hands, in our own way, toward justice.

New York, New York
January 9, 2022

MY DAVID: A LOVE STORY

Read by Anna Deavere Smith
New York, New York
February 23, 2019

The first thing I learned about David was how—and how well—he listened. Because he heard me, from across the room.

We met on a sunny, Sunday afternoon, almost twenty-seven years ago, at a party hosted by our friend Justin Spring—a birthday party. The way David would tell it, he walked into Justin's apartment and heard my laugh, and just knew that he should meet me. He found me behind the bar, making margaritas. And he heard in my voice, and saw in me, things I could not have articulated about myself.

Of course, this is only half the story. I saw him, too.

Right away, I could tell he was kind and gentle and thoughtful—and he was so handsome. He cared about people and art, and had a curiosity in the world. The kind of curiosity that would draw him to others, and others to him.

I'm so lucky, so grateful, it drew him to me.

We met at a birthday party. We say farewell at one, too. We gather together on David's birthday, to celebrate David's life. Grateful for everything he gave to us. Devastated because he's been taken from us.

Our friend Elizabeth Alexander opens her memoir with this: "The story seems to begin with catastrophe but in fact began earlier and is not a tragedy but rather a love story. Perhaps tragedies are only tragedies in the presence of love, which confers meaning to loss."

And so, this? This is a love story.

After that party, David called me, and my world was forever changed. Our first date revolved around art: We saw the Basquiat show at the Brooklyn Museum. It's appropriate that we gather at MoMA because David worked here after college—and if he were here now, he'd excitedly show me his favorites in the MoMA collection: The freedom and colorful feelings of Joan Mitchell; the collage and comfort of Rauschenberg's *Bed*; Jacob Lawrence's astonishing, powerful *Migration Series*.

Before David, these were artists about whom I knew very little. Falling in love with David, I fell in love with them as well.

Over the years, he taught me to see into the depths of a Rothko—to delight in Hans Hofmann. To feel the emotional truth expressed in the abstract. To understand the context around each piece. His sensibility—his sensitivity—opened up my world.

And as he gave me painters, I gave him dancers. He brought color, I brought movement. Martha Graham, Paul Taylor, and Merce Cunningham. Evenings at City Ballet.

And there are countless exhibitions, countless performances, countless experiences of the arts that we shared together.

These bright bursts of beauty illuminated our life: Kandinsky at the Guggenheim. The Whitney Biennials. Trips to artists' studios in Brooklyn and the Studio Museum in Harlem. And, of course, there was David's stunning gallery on Prince Street, with its stable of talented and diverse artists.

In so many ways, our life was not just indistinguishable from art, but inseparable from it. And David gave that love of art to others—at Bennington or the Fleming Museum in Vermont or the Skowhegan School of Art and Painting.

And in other ways, we were very different.

This boy from Chappaqua, who spent his college days in Vermont, could sit for hours in his easy chair with our dogs Beulah and later Mary Lou—named for our mothers. He read voraciously: *The New York Review of Books*, *National Geographic*, the latest novel. He relished travel magazines in general, and ski magazines in particular.

He could watch hour upon hour of nature shows on cable. I never understood how he could watch a show about crickets—yes, crickets—but he loved these nature shows, and the wild, wider world of which they were a part.

David also deeply loved his family. His beloved father, Spike, was a formidable influence on his character. He cherished his mother, Mary Lou, a talented artist herself who nurtured his love of art.

He so looked up to big brother and sister, Skip and Tish, and their spouses Michaela and Bob. He loved his niece and five nephews and took great pleasure in watching them grow up to be thriving, happy adults. He was thrilled we could join all of the Beitzels in Stowe, Vermont, last fall, to revel at the wedding of his nephew Mac to his beautiful bride, Mary. And he adored his cousins, who in the summers descended on Ocean City, where—for four generations—the family gathered every year.

And my mother, Beulah, and sister Renee brought him much happiness and hilarity in their regular phone calls and their visits to New York City. I'm so grateful they joined us in December for what would be David's last Christmas.

David found tremendous pleasure in the athletic pursuits he had mastered: Elegantly, easily breezing down the mountain on his skis, the way he had since he was a boy; gliding through the ocean on his surfboard, awaiting the next crash of his next wave; hiking to the top of the Grand Tetons or fishing with Spike in Alaska and Norway.

And yet, for all this action, he also was my anchor. He taught me to slow. Down.

It was true of the magical week we spent in the British Virgin Islands for his fortieth birthday, where I snapped the photo on the cover of today's program.

And the same was true at home. He was patient with my peripatetic intensity, constant in his caring as I could be constantly on the go. Especially in recent years, as my travel, daily schedule, and pace accelerated, David reminded me that *we* had to make room for *us*.

"You can go mad during the week," he'd say. "But weekends are ours."

Our weekend schedules were diverse and slightly incongruent: We might see a European painting exhibition at the Met, Kehinde Wiley at the Jewish Museum, and then the latest Tyler Perry movie, because David *loved* Medea!

Or we'd just go out to dinner. He'd look down the menu, and when the waiter approached the table, David would ask questions. About one entrée. About a second. A third, a fourth, a fifth. I got so accustomed to this, I would say to the waiter, "You're going to earn your tip tonight."

Eventually, David would order something entirely different—nothing he had asked about. It was both adorable and maddening. And I'd say to the waiter, "Welcome to my world."

Because David was my world.

I would say, "This is what love looks like." Because this is what David's love looks like. The attention. The curiosity. The deliberateness.

(The patience. "Darren, slow down.")

He made us make time. He made us make time for us, and he made us better for it.

I remember, after we'd been together for a few years, but before we'd moved in together, we hit a rough patch. We hadn't talked for a few days, which was unusual. David called my office in Harlem and said, "I've been thinking. We should go to couples counseling."

And I said, "Why—would we do that?"

And he said to me, "Because I think this relationship is worth saving."

And it was. It was worth saving and serving for twenty-six years, in every day and every way. Growing and evolving, challenging and changing, living and loving together.

Even that last day—that ominous Sunday—started much like the Sunday I met him almost twenty-seven years ago: Sunny and bright. The light streamed in the windows. The love poured out.

We spent the morning talking and planning.

More art: In March, we'd go to Paris for the opening of Denise Murrell's brilliant show *Posing Modernity* at the Orsay. In May, Venice for the Biennale.

More travel: Aspen for the Ideas Festival in June. Ibiza for Pierre's and Ebs's wedding in July.

And more time for us: Our annual Presidents' Day stay in Miami with Fred and Tom.

We were always looking forward and moving forward—delighting in the idea that we would keep looking and moving forward, living until the end of our lives, together.

And then, everything turned to darkness.

Yet, in darkness, David has helped me find light, and grace—in part, because he gave me enough love and laughter and joy to last a lifetime. He made room for all of me in his heart. He never forced me to change.

But he did change me. And changed my life. Because he taught me how to see the world through his eyes.

Those eyes that saw me—like those ears that heard me—fully and completely. That loved me, unconditionally.

I am so grateful that he was my partner, my teacher, my cheerleader, my counselor, my anchor, my best friend, my soulmate, my love.

So, while David is gone, I still see him. I see what he would have loved everywhere I look. I see his sensibility in the way he taught me to understand art, and life, and the deep, abiding connections between them.

I see him in the faces of his sister and brother and nephews and niece, his many loving cousins, and in the friends and family we made together. I see him in all of you.

And I see the beauty, the beauty of David—the beauty he loved, and taught me, and taught me to love. A beauty, and love, that has no end.

JOHN LEWIS:
A LEGACY OF GOOD
TROUBLE

July 18, 2020

I could not have known at the time but, when I was five years old, some five hundred miles northeast of my rural Texas home, a young man named John Lewis crossed a bridge for me. That historic day, like many others in his extraordinary life, Congressman Lewis endured the unconscionable to challenge and change the conscience of the nation he loved—to make our union more perfect, to bring us closer to our founding ideals, so that little Black children, like me, could pursue our American dreams.

On a number of occasions, I had the profound privilege to talk with the congressman, to learn from him, to absorb his wisdom and warmth—both the resolve he inspired from afar and the joy he radiated up close. My Ford Foundation colleagues and I were honored to host him for a conversation and were moved deeply by his presence and perspicacity.

Five years ago, he invited me and others to join him on a fiftieth anniversary pilgrimage across that modest, Selma bridge—to affirm a sacred conviction, in his words, that "love will conquer hate" and "hope will conquer fear," that "our struggle is not the struggle of a day, a week, a month, or a year," but "the struggle of a lifetime." That moment was among the most powerful and meaningful of my time on this earth.

Late last night, Congressman John Lewis, my hero, crossed another bridge, from elder to ancestor, with characteristic courage and grace. In marking this passage, we need not idealize Congressman Lewis beyond who he was: A founder of—a righteous force for—a more *American* United States and a fairer, better world.

Upon President Abraham Lincoln's passing, a colleague noted, "He belongs to the ages now." So, too, does Congressman Lewis, whose life of good troublemaking bequests a legacy of justice across division, and distance, and generations.

THE RESOLVE AND RIGHTEOUSNESS OF RUTH BADER GINSBURG

September 19, 2020

I had long admired Justice Ginsburg, but my first real interaction with her was this past February—so long ago, it seems—when she helped present my friend Aggie Gund with the Justice Ruth Bader Ginsburg Woman of Leadership Award.

That evening, her *notorious* passions were on display: Her love of the law and of the arts. Her testimony from the podium that night lifted our sights—and a surprise performance from a favorite mezzo-soprano lifted her spirits, in turn.

The bridge that spanned these twin loves—what made her such an exemplary lawyer, advocate, and judge—rested on the bedrock of empathy. She cared deeply, and was deeply concerned, about the rights of all people. She fought for women (and men, she might add) of every color and creed and circumstance—for the equal protection of the most vulnerable and marginalized in our society. She understood the heavy burden that persistent inequality placed on them most of all.

Justice Ginsburg once commented that she aspired "to make life a little better for people less fortunate." She defined a meaningful existence as "[lived] not just for oneself, but for one's community." She embodied this commitment with every ounce and instant of her being.

Ancient Jewish teaching suggests that God chooses those who pass on Rosh Hashanah, the transition from the old year to the new, because they are the most righteous—because their service, their *tzedakah*, is the most sorely needed for the full duration. It is somehow fitting, then, that during this high holiday season—this period of reflection, and repentance, and reconciliation, and renewal—we honor and grieve a giant of justice.

Justice Ginsburg's walk on this earth ended at sundown, in the twilight of a difficult year for all humanity. But her extraordinary life's journey affirms that when the sun rises, our march must continue, and our work, for equality, shall endure.

STANDING ON THE BROAD SHOULDERS OF VERNON JORDAN

March 2, 2021

I was blessed and fortunate to know Vernon Jordan as a mentor and a friend. He played an instrumental role in my life.

Vernon spoke often about standing on the shoulders of others—and during the decades that I counted on his counsel, often across the lunch table, I was always proud to stand on his.

As a civil rights lawyer, in his work with the NAACP, the Voter Education Project, and later as President of the National Urban League, he fought on the front lines of social change. Then he carried the cause of justice with him to the boardroom, opening the door for countless others, like me, behind him. While no one can fill his chair, he added seats to the table—inviting new voices to crucial conversations about the righteous responsibility of necessary change.

Vernon said that "we exist temporarily through what we take, but live forever through what we give." Through all that he gave, he not only led a uniquely American life, but leaves an extraordinary legacy—in all of us who stand on his shoulders.

We mourn Vernon's passing. We grieve with Ann, Vickee, Toni, Janice, Mercer, and their families. But he lives forever, with the ancestors, through the work that we carry forward.

CELEBRATING THE REMARKABLE LEGACY OF FRANKLIN THOMAS

December 23, 2021

Franklin Thomas was a giant—an American original; a singular leader; an iconic figure in the history of the Ford Foundation and philanthropy, our city and all cities, our nation, and the world. And just as Frank shaped a half century of human progress in our neighborhoods and around the globe, he shaped the course of my life, as a mentor, counselor, and friend.

I first met Frank many years ago in Harlem when I, a fledgling nonprofit executive at Abyssinian, hoped to emulate his astounding work with the Bedford Stuyvesant Restoration Corporation, the granddaddy of community development corporations.

To me, Frank was the consummate New Yorker. The son of immigrants from Barbados and Antigua, he made a life in Bed-Stuy and never left it behind. But he was also the quintessential leader of a new school of urbanism—a philosophy of revitalization that put people and communities at the center.

This philosophy found expression in the many institutions that Frank served and strengthened—at the agency that later became the Department of Housing and Urban Development, the United States Attorney's Office for the Southern District of New York, the New York City Police Department, and, of course, in Brooklyn, where Frank's profound legacy endures street by street, block by block.

At the Ford Foundation, Frank's perspicacious voice still echoes and his long shadow still looms. During his tenure as president from 1979 to 1996, Frank presided over the groundbreaking Study Commission on US Policy Toward South Africa, an indispensable ally of the anti-apartheid movement—and forged a fateful partnership with Nelson Mandela, championing South Africa's constitution and opening the first foundation office in the country. He also helped to establish the Local Initiative Support Corporation, which has supported countless neighborhood revitalization efforts.

And in our own institution's most perilous hour, after a 90 percent depletion in our endowment's real value during the 1970s, Frank courageously rescued us from insolvency. He made painful, unpopular decisions that set us on a path to long-term sustainability and made possible two generations of impact to follow.

While Frank surely changed the world, perhaps equally remarkable is what never changed about Frank: His humility, his generosity, his equanimity. Long after his tenure at the Ford Foundation, he made time to dispense wisdom and perspective from a small office in the Chanin Building on East 42nd Street, guiding me through good times and bad.

He taught us all to do the right things in the right way—to act with righteousness, not self-righteousness. To be in Frank's presence was to feel awe, reverence, and gratitude. I miss him, and appreciate every word and every moment we shared.

Today, my thoughts are with Frank's beloved wife Kate, his four children, Kyle, Keith, Hillary, and Kerrie, and the entire Thomas family.

Let us all strive anew for the equanimity that Frank so graciously, gracefully embodied.

FRANKLIN THOMAS, GIANT OF JUSTICE AND GENEROSITY

Remarks in Remembrance
New York, New York
January 9, 2022

To Kate; to Kyle, Keith, Hilary, and Kerrie; to Franklin's family and friends: Today, we celebrate a life lived well, and fully, with joy and purpose and grace—and a legacy that reaches around the world.

We celebrate a giant of a man: This devoted husband. This proud and doting father. This modest son of immigrants, who cast a long shadow on a basketball court, as a young man—and with his best friend Vernon beside him, later in life. This brother in arms, who wrapped his long arms around all of his brothers and sisters.

We also celebrate a giant of justice: This force of righteousness, without a trace of self-righteousness. This American original, who inherited and embodied and passed on a generational pursuit of the more perfect, for all. This singular leader, who uprooted inequality and apartheid, in his neighborhood and around the narrow world he bestrode like a quiet colossus.

And, for me, as for countless others, we celebrate a giant of generosity: This intrepid trailblazer. This cool, collected, courageous pioneer who opened countless doors—and whose life's work guaranteed that an entire generation could follow him through those doors and make a difference inside; an entire generation that stands on his slender but strong shoulders.

One of my life's great privileges was visiting regularly with Franklin in his office at the Chanin Building, on East 42nd Street.

On clear days, I would walk the few blocks from the foundation that Frank stewarded and saved—excited to see him, grateful for his perspicacity.

Ever since I first met him in Harlem, I relished our time together. I luxuriated in these opportunities to bask in his glow—to wallow in his wisdom. He gave me the gift of clarity—but also confidence.

Through the years, Frank counseled me on dealing with colleagues and grantees, on managing a board, and, later, on joining boards myself. I felt comfort in the knowledge that he had walked a path before me—or at least one like it. That he could help me see the ways I might contribute to the good of the world.

Frank challenged my thinking, sharpened my ideas, warned me against the entitlement and ego that naturally accrete in any high office, including the office we shared.

Even now, I marvel at his discretion, his humility, his equanimity in all things. He could pull me back or lift me up or keep me on track—knowing always what I needed to hear, even if I didn't want to hear it.

Frank believed in the human capacity to transform, evolve, and build bridges across lines of ideology and difference. And he fully embraced me and David for the people we were and the life we shared.

In short, Frank made an indelible impact on my life. He changed its trajectory. And I was hardly the only one.

Countless individuals and institutions, even nations, owe a debt to Frank Thomas.

At home: The United States Attorney's Office for the Southern District of New York; the New York City Police Department; the Bed-Stuy

Restoration Corporation, the granddaddy of the community-development movement; the September 11th Fund.

Across the nation: Early in his career, at the agency that later became the Department of Housing and Urban Development; the Local Initiative Support Corporation—LISC—which he helped create; and later, on the boards of companies and universities.

And around the world: Where Frank's partnership with Nelson Mandela modeled the power of truth and reconciliation; where Frank championed the rule of law and values of democracy in South Africa's new constitution; and, of course, through the Ford Foundation—which he boldly served and strengthened.

Dare I say, no Frank? No Ford.

So, what are we to make of a world without Frank, now that he has left us? How are we to inhabit this world that he shaped and improved for us, knowing we feel his absence and miss his voice?

It is difficult to consider our own mortality—our finite, limited time on this earth. We humans tend to have a problem with such things. But we learn from Frank that the measure of our lives is not how big we are, but how bighearted we are. That significance, meaning, comes from how we love, not just what we lead.

For each of us, if we had only one wish—if only one of our prayers was answered—would it not be to live well, and fully, with joy and purpose and grace? Would it not be to live—to leave a legacy—like Frank's?

Let us resolve, then, to continue as Frank did: To know love and to give it freely. To be righteous in our cause, but never self-righteous in our character. To advance the slow and steady march of progress. To bend the arc of the moral universe, with our own hands, in our own way, toward justice.

Yes, Franklin Thomas changed the trajectory of my life—of all our lives. He changed the trajectory of our world. And while we must carry on without him, we carry his influence with us—and we pass his legacy on to those who follow us. For there is more work to do. And Frank showed how to do it.

VARTAN GREGORIAN: THE PHILANTHROPIST'S PHILANTHROPIST

Tribute at Carnegie Hall
New York, New York
April 13, 2022

To Dareh, Vahé, Raffi, and Vartan's and Clare's wonderful grandchildren; to the Carnegie Corporation trustees and staff, past and present, who commanded VG's loyalty and affection; and to all of our colleagues and comrades, gathered to celebrate a life of meaning and consequence: Vartan Gregorian was an icon. A marvel, and a mensch. The oxygen and light of every room, and the life of every party. The author—the protagonist—of a most improbable, most extraordinary American story.

I remember, a few years ago, meeting VG for tea in his beautiful office, high above Madison Avenue—the books piled from floor to ceiling. We got to talking about Andrew Carnegie, widely regarded as the founding father of American philanthropy.

I said to Vartan, teasing only slightly: "Could you imagine what Andrew Carnegie—the steel baron, the titan of industry—would say about you, the Armenian immigrant, running his storied foundation?"

Without missing a beat, VG countered: "I prefer to imagine what Henry Ford would say about you."

Helene Kaplan, the former Chair of Carnegie Corporation, once noted that VG was a teacher's teacher, a scholar's scholar, and a philanthropist's philanthropist. But here at Carnegie Hall, one can't help but note that VG was the original American philanthropist's philanthropist.

Standing in this great hall today, one might note that the juxtaposition of AC and VG represents the noblest evolution of American philanthropy.

In so many ways, Vartan walked in Carnegie's footsteps. He led from Carnegie's chair. And to the very end, he remained a stalwart champion of Carnegie's values, applied to the times—and a gracious steward of his legacy for all time.

Of course, by legacy I don't just mean the Carnegie Corporation, I mean the very idea, and practice, and evolution of our work and its promise.

And in the field of philanthropy, I can add to Helene's list: VG was a mentor's mentor.

He was a mentor to some of the most generous and prolific philanthropists of our times: Mike Bloomberg, Bill Gates, Melinda French Gates, Walter H. Annenberg, Agnes Gund—and so many more. And he mentored the leaders of many of our nation's legacy foundations. I count myself proudly (and appreciatively) among this group.

I'll never forget his coaching as I prepared for my interviews with the Ford Foundation trustees. And when I became president, he offered sage, candid, and frank advice—in, and for, a sector where there are no shareholders, customers, or other market forces to ensure accountability.

He said: *Be humble. Extend dignity to all those you encounter. Remember, it's not your money.*

Don't be intoxicated by the unearned praise and accolades. Appreciate the people who make the foundation run.

And finally: *Ignorance is the first philanthropic sin. Arrogance is its twin.*

These were the words of a man who loved philanthropy and its power for good in the world.

Of course, VG was also the ultimate connector—in part, I think, because he knew what it was like to be an outsider. He led a life he could only have imagined, growing up in Tabriz—in Soviet-occupied Iran.

When VG was a boy, his family couldn't afford to buy books—or even rent them from the local stationery store. But his passion for books became a passion for education, and his passion for education became a ticket to America—the nation he loved so fully and served so capably.

As VG wrote so beautifully, he said each book "transported him to a realm of possibilities" and "to a life of beauty." When I think about all the books in his office—his own Gregorian Library—or even at his cherished Brown University or New York Public Library, I can't help but feel that it was VG who opened up that realm of possibilities. It was VG who helped people in his charge, in his orbit, and all around the world to feel welcome, to understand one another, and to imagine what could and should be. It was VG who showed all of us—with his wit and his warmth and his wisdom—what it means to build a life of beauty.

I see that beauty now, in the legacy he leaves. In the grand institutions he built, and sustained. In the family who adored and revered him, as do we all.

Each of our lives—and the realm of possibilities we see for this world, however darkly through the glass—all have more oxygen and light thanks to VG. That is more valuable than any philanthropist's gift. And knowing Vartan—and his example—was a gift to all philanthropy.

UNAFRAID, UNBOWED, AND UNAPOLOGETIC: THE LIFE AND LEGACY OF JUDY HEUMANN

March 6, 2023

Judy Heumann taught me—and the world—a seventy-five-year lesson in the power of humanity and dignity. She taught us how to live and lead with it, how to fight for it, how to embody and represent it fully and completely.

Judy's time with us was defined by joy, purpose, and consequence—not despite the fact that she had a disability but because, as she famously declared, "I never wished I didn't." She was unafraid, unbowed, and unapologetic. She demanded respect for the rights of her community and marshaled a movement to secure them.

When I first met Judy, I had much to learn, far more than I knew. She was among the courageous advocates who, in 2014, rightly called me out for the Ford Foundation's omission of people with disabilities from our strategy to address inequalities of all kinds—an unintended, but damning, embarrassing reification of the very inequalities we aspired to disrupt and dismantle.

The way Judy engaged then was both remarkable and remarkably characteristic. I remember her justifiable frustration, vividly, but also her grace and her kindness. Indeed, she was far more generous than I had any right to expect, ultimately agreeing to give her time, testimony, and tenacity as a Ford Foundation Senior Fellow, and bringing insight and nuance to our institution's approach to one of the most significant (and ongoing) civil rights and human rights issues of our time.

Judy was at once relentless and compassionate, full of urgency and full of patience—a transcendent figure. She was somehow capable of recognizing the best, even in those of us unaware of our ignorance, focused always on our potential for transformation.

She informed my understanding of the challenges facing people with disabilities, and she invited others along on the journey as well. She helped to establish the Presidents' Council on Disability Inclusion in Philanthropy and inspired the entire social-justice sector to reimagine how to collaborate with the disability rights community. At Ford, she introduced us to the brilliant, late Marca Bristo, whom we elected to our board of trustees. And she helped build a professional home for visionary colleagues like Rebecca Cokley and Catherine Hyde Townsend.

This is how Judy changed the world: Person by person, from the corridors of New York City's public schools to the streets of Berkeley to the halls of power around the globe.

She displayed her superpowers from youth, even before she confronted government officials on a makeshift congressional panel organized in response to the occupation that she and other activists staged in a San Francisco federal building. I will forever hear her voice in that 1977 hearing, shaking with emotion, reverberating in its clarion conviction: "We will no longer allow the government to oppress disabled individuals."

A promise and a prophecy—one she helped fulfill through a lifetime of service and the sacrifice it required.

From Judy's work in President Clinton's and President Obama's administrations to her position with the World Bank and beyond, Judy championed the rights of people with disabilities. Her ideas, her initiative, and her persistent insistence have lifted lives on every continent, in every country, and in every community on this planet.

In 2020, Judy's groundbreaking activism reached a new generation through the Oscar-nominated documentary *Crip Camp*, which we were proud to support. The story captured the essential Judy—her fundamental decency, her unrelenting character, and her enduring spirit.

For every one of us, life is terribly fleeting. We each have precious little time on this earth; incalculably much time to be gone from it. This recognition should embolden and ennoble our efforts, as it did for Judy and her beloved Jorge. And when we go, as each of us will, we can only hope to leave a legacy as profound as hers. She was a dear friend and revered hero—an extraordinary teacher who became a mentor and partner.

Judy's life was a blessing to countless millions. May her memory be, too.

HARRY BELAFONTE: FIREFIGHTER FOR JUSTICE

April 25, 2023

During the final days of Dr. Martin Luther King Jr.'s life, he confided in his dear friend Harry Belafonte. He said then that he feared America was like a burning house, Belafonte recounted in his memoir—and he challenged all of us "to become the firemen."

For ninety-six years, Harry Belafonte—to me and many others, "Mr. B."—embraced this responsibility with graceful, joyful strength. He was the quintessential, indispensable firefighter for justice.

To be sure, this stunning, captivating man could set one's heart ablaze, as he did mine, vicariously via the pages of *EBONY*, when I was a young boy in rural East Texas. But Mr. B.'s voice also helped to douse raging flames of withering injustice, across our nation and around the world. As an artist, he moved our feet, our pulses, our minds, our spirits. As an activist, he stirred our collective conscience, mobilizing many millions to righteous indignation and intervention.

A few years ago, I helped to commemorate Mr. B.'s singular influence and impact, presenting him with the Roosevelt Institute's Four Freedoms

Award. I still hear his admonition from late that evening, as he leaned over to me and cautioned, "Do not waste any time."

This was characteristic of a man defined by strategic impatience. Time and again, Mr. B. put everything on the line—his career, his livelihood, his safety—to fight America's many converging fires with a fierce urgency.

Throughout his life, he struck a precarious balance—beloved by audiences of all colors and creeds but constrained within the Hollywood establishment. He was a target of McCarthyism in the 1950s and later risked condemnation from industry leaders and peers. Nonetheless, he forged ahead in the front line of the long Civil Rights Movement, without reservation, guided by his belief in the dignity and humanity of all.

For some, growing older can mean succumbing to the temptations of comfort—becoming numb to ongoing inequality. Not for Mr. B. Through the years, he became ever more radical—more dedicated to the causes to which he devoted his life, at home and abroad.

Today, Mr. B.'s legacy endures, in those who learned from him and those who loved him. I mourn with his beloved wife, Pamela, and his children, Adrienne, Shari, David, and Gina, who continue to advance his crucial work. Gina leads Sankofa, which the Ford Foundation is proud to support.

Through his century of life, Harry Belafonte shaped the century in which he lived—a century of imperfect, uneven progress that would have been implausible, if not outright impossible without him. He did not waste a moment. And he earned his place in that vanguard of the march—among the founders of a more *American* United States of America.

THE GIFT AND THE GRACE OF ALMA POWELL

Tribute at the Kennedy Center
Washington, DC
October 25, 2024

To Michael, Linda, Annemarie, and your families; to the extended Powell and Johnson families; to the community gathered in this American cathedral, this monument to the American spirit: I feel humbled to help celebrate the gift and the grace of Alma Powell. And I feel honored to help fete the courage and character of this extraordinary woman—a historic figure, a transcendent figure, but also a human in full, a beacon of light and laughter for all of us who adored her.

I counted Alma as a confidante and companion—this giant of the wider world, and my own—and let me tell you: This woman had a bullshit detector like none other.

I first met Alma a quarter century ago, at a gathering hosted by our dear, mutual friends Ronald and Jo Carole Lauder. I knew, immediately, this is the person with whom you want to sit at a party.

She was discerning, unsparing, delightful—clever and cunning. She did not suffer fools. And she possessed a singular ability to size someone up, without putting them down.

Everyone would say, "Oh, I'm friends with Alma!" And everyone wanted to be friends with Alma. But that didn't always mean it was reciprocated.

And I must say, that made our friendship—one of the most meaningful of my life—feel all the more special, delicious, like she had invited me to join a secret club. It was my great fortune that our club could convene and reconvene—whether at a fancy dinner party in New York or at the National Gallery of Art or on her beautiful terrace in Alexandria—and immediately pick up where we left off.

When I reflect on her journey, it occurs to me that her life story was a love story: A love story in three parts.

First, of course, there was the reluctant blind date with a handsome young soldier, the instant spark, the chance connection that swept her off her feet—and on to a rich and wonderful and complicated American odyssey.

By the time I met Alma, that young lieutenant had long since earned his fourth star, but I can imagine what that moment must have been like: The energy, the thrill, like two supernovas colliding, creating something entirely new, with physics all its own.

About ten years ago, we all descended upon a large Hamptons estate for an Apollo Theater fundraiser. Pharrell, Ariana Grande, and others performed on stage—and then, all of a sudden, they started calling on members of the audience to join them. One after another, they called up singers, and actresses, and then Jamie Foxx said, "I see the great General Powell in the audience."

Colin Powell didn't hesitate. He bounded up the stairs—and he immediately started dancing and singing. Somehow, he knew the words to the "Happy" song—and sang in a duo with Pharrell and Robin Thicke.

I was sitting next to Alma and the look on her face was priceless. She leaned within earshot and said simply: "Welcome to my world."

This was the man Alma loved—and this, among countless other reasons, is why she loved him. She was singularly devoted to him—and he to her.

Of course, the second part of her love story proved perhaps more powerful than the first: Her love for her family.

Alma was a fiercely private woman—uncompromising and unyielding in her efforts to protect her family from all that accompanied Colin's notoriety. But she carried that pressure like everything else, with ease and finesse. Even in the crucible of a life with one of the most celebrated, respected, and admired husbands and fathers on the planet, she always kept her cool. She raised Michael, Linda, and Annemarie—also the loves of her life—to do the right thing, and to do things right.

The last time I visited with Alma in person was almost exactly a year ago. We sat in her apartment in Alexandria reflecting on our many blessings. We remarked on the changing leaves—the changing seasons of our lives.

We talked about many things, but she spoke of nothing with greater joy than her children, her grandchildren, and her first great-grandchild, recently arrived. She scrolled through photo after photo—beaming, radiating with wonder and awe—sharing every detail of news from every grandchild's latest adventure.

I couldn't help but think: To move one's family twenty-some times, as Alma did, requires a certain kind of love. To raise young children alone, often for up to a year at a time, requires a certain kind of love. To sacrifice so much? To give so fully, with such devotion? To do so without losing her own identity? To feel such accomplishment for it—in her children and grandchildren and great-grandchildren? This love story defined her life, too.

As did a third love story: Alma loved her country. Alma Powell believed in the promise of America—because Alma Powell lived the promise of America.

One thread that tied Alma and me together, I think, was our shared experience as children and expatriates of the American South.

As you all know, she was born in Birmingham—the heart of Dixie. Her father was the revered principal of a segregated school. She attended Pratt City Negro School herself.

Alma knew Jim Crow. She knew American apartheid. But she defiantly refused to be confined or limited by it—to let it subsume her dignity or the elegance with which she would soar though the world.

Alma rarely returned to Alabama—nor was she sentimental about it. She harbored an ambivalence about the American South with which I can identify.

But she never forgot where she came from, either. She never lost sight of the many pernicious ways—as James Baldwin said—that "history ... does not refer merely ... to the past. History is literally present in all that we do." She never relinquished her profound feeling of responsibility—her feeling of obligation—to help make possible more American stories like her own.

This was why she was singularly committed to America's promise and its mission—why she gave so much of herself to children, especially disadvantaged children, from families and communities left behind.

Alma Powell broke bread with queens and kings, presidents and prime ministers, but she was never intoxicated by it. She never equated wealth with virtue.

She never allowed her own privilege to dull her righteous sense of wrong and right—her awareness of inequality and injustice—nor her conviction about America's sacred mission to advance the democratic values that we still share, to protect and promote the American idea.

Alma understood better than anyone that what makes America great— what makes America exceptional—is not that we are inherently perfect, but rather that we become more perfect through a labor of love. This love story shaped Alma Powell's life as well.

I loved Alma Powell. And I feel overwhelmed with gratitude that I was Alma's friend—and that she was mine—that we all are the beneficiaries of the way she perfectly embodied dignity and decency, integrity and intellect, pluck and perspicacity and patriotism.

The human heart is an astounding thing. I marvel at the ways a full heart can be broken—a broken heart, full.

Alma led a life of love—replete with love—for her husband, for her family, for her country. May we all lead lives of such meaning. And may we carry forward her memory—and her legacy—in our own hearts forever.

CECILE RICHARDS, CHAMPION FOR JUSTICE, FOREVER UNDAUNTED

Tribute at the Ford Foundation
New York, New York
February 1, 2025

To Kirk; to Daniel, Hannah, and Lilly, and your families; to Secretary Clinton and our many honored guests; to everyone who loved and revered Cecile (and to love her was to revere her): Thank you for joining us.

In Cecile's and Kirk's beloved New Orleans, tradition dictates that, as we mourn, the dirges and hymns give way to a swinging, soulful celebration—and you heard the Crescent City jazz as we congregated.

Well, look around: The saints are all here. We gather in grief. We gather in gratitude. We gather in this house of justice to send home a giant of justice: A giant of our time, and of all time; a self-proclaimed troublemaker *for good*; a steel magnolia, as comfortable in white gloves as brass knuckles.

I first met Cecile a lifetime ago and a world away. I was a college fresh-man in Austin, finding my way in Democratic student politics. And Cecile's inimitable mother—then the Travis County Commissioner—was shaking up Texas government.

During the summer of 1978, I trekked over to a local event, hoping to meet her, when in walked this tall, radiant, twenty-one-year-old—Ann's brilliant daughter Cecile—spending her summer break from Brown organizing workers and migrants in rural Texas.

Cecile was born organizing. Organizing was coded into her DNA.

And everything that came to define her? It was all on full display, right from the very beginning: The fire in her belly. The indignation—and impatience—with inequality. The courage and kindness in equal measure.

Through the years, Cecile's and my paths occasionally would cross. And then, when I joined the Ford Foundation as a vice president, there she was again, the shining star of Margaret Hempel's and my portfolio: A Ford Foundation grantee.

From the day I arrived, she was a teacher: About movements, and how to mobilize them. About pluralist democracy—*feminist democracy*—and how to advance it. About the idea of America—the promise of America—and how we realize it, together.

She spoke truth to power. She commanded respect. And she could put you in your place with just a glance or a shrug.

She would not be diminished or dismissed. In perpetual efflorescence, she refused to wilt, or to wither.

Of course, Cecile was also my boss—a Ford Foundation trustee for a dozen years. In this capacity, she gave generously of her wisdom, her per-spicacity, her grace. From this platform, she served our mission with excellence and aplomb. She was a champion for democratic values and democratic institutions, human dignity and human rights during this era of deconstruction as some are working to tear down the scaffolding from which our mothers' and grandmothers' generations built the fullest measure of American democracy.

Cecile was often the first colleague to whom I turned for counsel, to guide us, to keep us moving forward. She was collaborative, collegial, always ensuring that every voice was heard and perspective represented. I am bereft at the idea of a world without Cecile Richards—especially this world, especially now.

The last time I saw Cecile she was organizing—perhaps little surprise. She visited the foundation to gather support for her effort to share the stories of the countless American women whose lives have been upended by abortion bans. Here she was, enduring extraordinary personal hardship, without indulging—for one instant—in self-pity. She was undaunted, undeterred, defiant—as ever, as always—for there was no time to waste, not a moment to lose.

In short, Cecile was the quintessential visionary on the front lines. And, today, we—all of us—we are the second line.

So as we fete her—as we celebrate her—let us resolve to embrace as our own the urgency with which she lived and led and loved. Let us draw joy from her joy, strength from her strength, hope from her hope.

PART XI

A CALL FOR COURAGEOUS, MORAL LEADERSHIP

Leadership is an action, not a title. And many of our leaders are paralyzed by broken, perverse incentives that impair their abilities to fulfill institutional missions and mandates....

Those in positions of leadership fear they will say the wrong thing, or what they believe to be the right thing in the wrong way. They fear risk, recrimination, and reprisal. They fear a coarsening culture—our collective instinct to shame and shun, our collective intolerance for nuance and complexity—that squeezes them from all sides, corralling them toward the straightest, narrowest path....

Courageous, moral leadership demands more. Because it challenges us to recognize that bringing light is often worth enduring the heat, especially in moments of profound challenge for our democracy, our communities, and our world....

We need leaders who manifest a moral capacity to embrace the nuance and complexity to which we've become allergic, come what may—to take a stand for progress, even if incremental or imperfect.

Indeed, effective leadership requires managing nuance and complexity, seeing all sides of an issue from the perspective of every stakeholder, and then setting a course, and communicating with clarity, consistent with common values.

After all, no courage? No leadership. We cannot move forward, however unevenly, without courageous visionaries blazing new paths that illuminate the way for all of us to follow.

The New York Times
October 20, 2024

A CALL FOR MORAL COURAGE IN AMERICA

2017 Annual Message
September 6, 2017

When I was first appointed president of the Ford Foundation, I felt joy and excitement about the work to come. Every year since then, I have offered a September message in this same spirit—to share my perspective, to honestly engage with issues facing philanthropy and the world, and to illuminate my sources of hope.

As I begin my fifth year, however, my sense of optimism has been tested like never before. For the first time I can remember, I am troubled by a deep sense of anxiety and anguish for my country.

As a native Texan, I have been pained by Hurricane Harvey's devastating impact on the Texas Gulf Coast. I grew up in two small towns, between Beaumont and Houston, that were ravaged by the storm. My heart breaks for the people and families who, but for fate, would have been my neighbors, and for the community that nurtured and supported me. The news from Texas has only compounded the worry I have for America and clarified the need—especially during such troubled times—for compassionate, competent, and courageous leadership.

Like so many of you, I am bewildered, almost daily, by the onslaught of dispiriting, sometimes debilitating news. Just this week, a new, politicized (and heartless) assault on young, mostly Latino immigrants—the cancellation of DACA—has left me reeling. When I travel to visit the organizations we work with in Africa, Asia, and Latin America, friends and colleagues express shock about America's leadership and standing in the global community.

While we've endured challenging times before, I have always maintained an unwavering faith in America's promise and, more broadly, in our democratic values—and I still do. I have always believed that progress is cumulative—that, as more people and communities win their place in the circle of American equality and opportunity, this circle will continue expanding, in a virtuous cycle.

At the same time, I recall James Baldwin's words during the height of the Civil Rights Movement in 1965: "History ... does not refer merely ... to the past ... History is literally present in all that we do." And so I am mindful that just like the leaders who came before us, we are caught between the history from which we emerge and the history to which we aspire.

A RUMBLE OF HATE, A MOMENT OF CLARITY

A few weeks ago, the most insidious elements of our history—as much a part of our national character as the Constitution itself—announced themselves anew, and in the most disgusting and frightening ways. In Charlottesville, Virginia, racist, anti-Semitic, white nationalists marched without hoods, shame, or stigma. As I watched the images emerging from Charlottesville, aghast, I worried that hate was being normalized in America.

I was not alone, of course. In recent weeks, the American people affirmed, as they have so often, that from darkness comes light. By the thousands, and in cities across the country, they expressed that, in Fannie Lou Hamer's perfect phrasing, "righteousness exalts a nation; hate just makes people miserable."

To me, it seems clear, not just in this alarming episode, but in the deeper history it has laid bare: America has reached another defining moment. We face a crisis—the next battle for the soul of this country, one that will play out on the battlefield of our collective consciousness.

HOW WE GOT HERE

Even though only one month has passed since the terror and tragedy of Charlottesville, our news cycle has moved on. After far too many elected officials offered perfunctory or unsatisfactory disavowals, after blame was cast, this conversation—like so many difficult conversations—has already begun to lose its urgency, and perhaps even our attention.

This should not surprise us. Americans have been trying and failing to have a conversation about race and justice for the whole of American history. Indeed, what happened in Charlottesville was merely the latest tremor along fault lines that have been present in the American story since its founding, a reopening of wounds that have barely been treated, and never healed.

It bears repeating that at the same instant that fifty-six men signed the Declaration of Independence, swearing that "all men are created equal," they founded a nation in which all people were not. And because we have never sufficiently acknowledged this fact, America's original sin has never left us. Indeed, it has fueled inequalities that persist to this day—whether in the form of mass incarceration or wealth inequality, housing discrimination or education and health disparities.

All of these very *current* crises stem from our complicated, difficult, unaddressed history. The time has come for our nation to reckon with its past.

RECKONING WITH OUR HISTORY AND REALITY

The United States is not alone in the need to evolve—and emerge stronger—from history marred by injustice and hate. Countries like South Africa and Germany have worked deliberately to address the evils in their own national histories, but America has been neither willing nor able to take comparable steps.

As emancipation and reconstruction in the 1860s gave way to a restoration of the antebellum order in the 1870s and 1880s, America made no sustained effort toward what some today might call transitional justice. The nation paid no reparations to freed slaves; the "forty acres and a mule" promised to most freed Blacks never materialized. Our country never convened a Truth and Reconciliation Commission nor engaged in an officially sanctioned public interrogation of our shared history, North and South.

As a Southerner, I grew up immersed in the romanticized memory of the "Lost Cause." I knew people in college who hung Confederate flags on their dormitory walls, fraternities that held parties where men wore Confederate uniforms. To them, it was a source of Southern pride, and while I found these symbols problematic, I understood their intentions on some level. We each put the best face on our history, as a way to reinforce our notions of our communities, our families, and ourselves. For all Americans—indeed, for all human beings—history is identity.

Nevertheless, we have failed to reconcile the airbrushed, heroic narrative with the searing reality. In this instance, the truth is that the Confederacy was founded—and its soldiers fought—to *destroy* the United States of America. Their cause was to defend and make permanent the brutal practice of slavery, the underpinning of the Southern economy (and a significant component of the Northern economy, too); their aim, to keep millions of Black Americans in bondage. The Confederate position was not morally ambiguous; the intent to uphold and expand slavery was the Confederacy's foremost objective. There is simply no way around these facts.

Despite this, astonishingly, it was not until 2008 that the US House of Representatives could muster the votes to offer an official apology for slavery and Jim Crow injustices. That it took more than 150 years to pass this resolution reminds us that America's failure to deal with its history is also a failure of its leadership and of collective will.

THE SYSTEMS THAT CONSTRAIN US

That is why last month's events in Charlottesville were so revealing. Too many of our leaders remain uninterested in healing the wounds of discrimination and prejudice, injustice, and inequality. Our ideals have been hijacked at the highest levels, perverted by narcissism and selfishness. At the ballot box and in our digital public square, too often, our leaders are rewarded for practicing the divide-and-conquer, dog-whistle politics endemic to our modern era.

In the not-too-distant past, the American people would turn to their elected leaders—especially the president—for guidance and moral clarity. Today, in a vacuum of such moral leadership, fear tempts many Americans to hunker down, protect themselves and their interests, and withdraw for the purposes of safety and self-preservation.

To make matters worse, even our most honorable leaders are neither incentivized nor encouraged to make decisions based on what they know is right. Rather, they operate in—and are constrained by—systems that reinforce historical inequalities and perpetuate the status quo. Our entrenched structures push leaders to be averse to precisely the moral leadership they should embrace.

The most obvious example is in government.

It's not controversial to say that our elected officials often are discouraged from putting nation ahead of party. In gerrymandered districts, they face retribution and primary challenges. With post-Watergate campaign finance norms obliterated, they are forced to spend far too much time fundraising, fearful of money pouring in to oppose them. The result is a broken set of incentives—all of which discourage bipartisanship and deter them from tackling the real problems facing the people they represent.

In the private sector, meanwhile, corporate CEOs are mired in a system that compels them to subordinate their personal values and beliefs.

Yes, some have raised their voices—and this is progress—but too many feel pressured to focus on quarterly earnings and share prices, at all costs, rather than enter moral debates or consider the human costs of their silence or support. Why risk offending consumers, analysts, or stockholders by taking a stand, especially when the stock market is riding high?

The obsession with, and American addiction to, short-term gain—at the expense of long-term good—is the most obvious example of a larger phenomenon: Leaders who make the trivial into the important and the important into the trivial.

In philanthropy and civil society, we have also been slow to recognize the ways our systems discourage moral leadership. We foundations often hide behind the particulars of our missions, rather than standing up for the deeper values our missions embody. We keep our heads down to avoid making our organizations targets for criticism, especially in the era of social media warfare.

Neither the Ford Foundation, nor I, are immune to these trends, and I know we must do better. I often wonder whether the foundation uses its voice in the most effective way. I question whether I have inadvertently contributed to these problems, or reinforced these entrenched systems.

I know many nonprofit leaders and university presidents face similar challenges. They worry about offending their wealthy donors. Some feel constrained in their ability to speak out. They have my empathy, because every day these leaders walk a tightrope to address the diverse and often conflicting perspectives of the constituencies they serve.

Even though these problems feel particularly acute in the United States, my Ford colleagues and I see these trends on every continent where we work. From exclusionary populist movements to attacks on public institutions, the media, and the very idea of knowable facts, the challenges we face are global—and so is our crisis of leadership.

PROFILES IN COURAGE: THE LEADERSHIP WE NEED

While systems conspire to constrain our leaders, the only acceptable response is courage—the moral courage to reject and rewrite the old rules. It was from the steps of the United States Capitol, in the presence of presidents, and with hope for the future, that Maya Angelou proclaimed, "History, despite its wrenching pain, cannot be unlived, but if faced with courage, need not be lived again."

Already, I have been heartened by the many people practicing such moral courage, on the ground and in local communities, across every sector.

In spite of the disincentives facing CEOs—the pressures from consumers, shareholders, and boards—we've seen many industry leaders stand up and use their power, like Kenneth Frazier of Merck and Tim Cook of Apple (who himself frames the obligations of corporations as a "moral responsibility").

In spite of criticism from other public officials, many elected leaders and university presidents have acted swiftly and courageously to remove Confederate monuments and address the uncomfortable truths of our history. In 2015, when South Carolina's then-governor Nikki Haley removed the Confederate flag from the statehouse grounds, she noted that "this is a moment in which we can say that that flag, while an integral part of our past, does not represent the future of our great state"; Mayor Mitch Landrieu of New Orleans reminded us, in his speech on the removal of similar monuments, that "now is the time to come together and heal and focus on our larger task." Others, like Mayor Catherine Pugh of Baltimore and President Greg Fenves at my alma mater, The University of Texas, have done away with their communities' own monuments to our country's racist past.

In spite of the risk-averse cultures of many foundations, leaders like Jim Canales of the Barr Foundation and Grant Oliphant of the Heinz Endowments, among others, have offered powerful words rebuking the hate we saw in Charlottesville. Their admirable responses inspire me as important examples of how we can speak truthfully and forcefully.

And in spite of many personal risks, leaders around the world are organizing and advocating for human rights for those who have been rendered invisible, exploited, and silenced by history. I'm talking about the moral courage of people like Cecile Richards, president of Planned Parenthood, and Sherrilyn Ifill, president of the NAACP Legal Defense Fund. I'm talking about Farhana Khera, president of Muslim Advocates, and Reverend William Barber, leader of a powerful moral movement for justice. I'm talking about the courageous young people known as the DREAMers, numbering in the hundreds of thousands, who contribute every day to the only country they have ever known.

These leaders are my reason for hope in this time of peril. They demonstrate how we might fill the moral void at the top of our government and dismantle the systems that stifle progress on the ground. They remind us what is possible when our political leaders, corporations, nonprofit organizations, foundations, and fellow citizens and neighbors take up the mantle and *choose* to lead.

We need more like them.

We need leaders who build bridges, not walls. We need leaders who work across party lines and bring us together, not politicians who degrade our discourse and drive us apart. We need leaders who transcend the politics of division, who reject the language of exclusion even though it has proved to be a powerful political tactic.

It is up to each and every one of us to stand up for what is right—to our boards and shareholders and political parties, to our friends and colleagues, if necessary—even when it is not in our immediate interest. And we cannot wait; we must be the leaders our countries need and the world deserves. After all, what is the point of leadership, if not to lead in times like these? What could we possibly be holding on to, or out for, when everything— *everything*—is at stake?

Soon, it may be too late for courage, too late to take the necessary steps to mend our society. We risk reaching a day when whatever ability we had to influence change or protect our democratic values will have been squandered.

Instead, I am hopeful that we can—and will—realize the urgency of now. I am hopeful because I see every day that we, together, are ready and eager and impatient to lead the way toward a more righteous world defined by its commitment to justice and fairness.

Now is the time for courage. Maya Angelou famously said, "When someone shows you who they are, believe them the first time." And so this year, my message is simple: Like the poet says, let us show each other—and the world—who *we* are.

IN DEFENSE OF NUANCE

2019 Annual Message
September 9, 2019

As I begin my seventh year as president of the Ford Foundation, I find myself reflecting on all that has changed in our world since 2013. If asked to encapsulate this tumultuous period in a single word, a reasonable observer might rattle off a list of possibilities—aberrant or abhorrent, appalling or inhumane—or they might reject the question entirely. Too much has happened, too quickly, for one term to perfectly capture it all.

If pushed, however, one might gravitate toward a telling adjective: Extreme.

This is the age of extreme weather and extreme inequality. The age of extreme hate groups, extreme nationalism, and extreme populism around the world. The list goes on.

The business case for the extreme is well documented. The loudest voices garner the most coverage and clicks, while media companies and social networks reap the rewards. And these extremes beget more extremes, coarsening our discourse and dividing our societies.

The problem is that "extreme" is not just a descriptor of gathering crises for our planet—or the political personalities most breathlessly covered in the news and amplified in the echo chambers of our newsfeeds. Extreme opposition seems to have entered the playbook of leaders in every category. In this worldview, it's all or nothing, good or evil, the best or worst.

Nuance and complexity, meanwhile, are nowhere to be found. And our extreme challenges remain *extremely* unsolved.

In the boardrooms of businesses and museums, on committees and campuses—and everywhere in between—seeking common ground has been replaced by a retreat to our corners. Like fighting fire with fire, the fiery is met with fiery, and no one seems willing to turn down the temperature. Nuance is a concession no one seems willing to make.

And yet, while nuance and complexity are clear victims of this new normal, they are hardly the *only* victims.

Our ability to solve our collective problems—especially, but not only, in our politics—is called into question. Common goals are framed as coercive demands; potential partners and experts unnecessarily cast as victims or enemies.

Rather than building bridges and relationships based on mutual understanding or shared respect, this oppositional, nuance-averse posture rewards ideological purity and public shame—the very things that scuttle strong working relationships and incentivize people to dig in their heels.

To be sure, there are cases where ineffective incremental progress has contributed to the frustration and anger that many in our society rightly feel. Now is no time for small steps or half measures—especially when it comes to extreme inequality and injustice.

And yet, ambition and animosity need not be linked; in fact, the latter impedes the former.

We must recognize that what has nuance on the run are distorted incentives, which in turn create more destructive behaviors.

This same flywheel drives every category of inequality—from economic disparity to racial injustice—and pits selfishness against social welfare, when the latter is in everyone's self-interest.

One powerful example comes from our collective response—or lack thereof—to the global climate crisis. Too often, the debate about climate change is dominated by an extreme form of denial—by the voices who refuse to acknowledge its very existence and who denigrate the efforts of the people, communities, and organizations working to address it. The solution, of course, is not just in the middle but on the ground—with the Indigenous communities who face the most immediate and dire consequences of our climate catastrophe. Yet, these are the same groups that are dismissed as antidevelopment.

We at Ford have learned the impact that comes from honoring and amplifying the voices and experiences of the communities most directly affected by injustice. So, we support individuals and institutions that understand a simple idea: Averting a climate catastrophe cannot mean displacing, disassembling, or ignoring Indigenous communities. And, for their part, Indigenous leaders have proven time and again that they are in fact open to development—providing that it is done with their input and creates opportunities and benefits for their communities.

Another example is closer to home: New York City's effort to close Rikers Island, a complex of eight separate Department of Correction facilities on 413 acres in the middle of the East River. For decades, Rikers has represented the very worst of America's criminal justice system. It is infamous for barbaric conditions, insidious corruption, and unrelenting brutality. And, as a consequence of America's broken for-profit bail system, some 80 percent of the incarcerated at Rikers have not yet been tried for any crime. Instead, many thousands of innocent-until-proven-guilty people are waiting for their trials—sometimes for years.

Rikers has been in desperate need of reform—if not a wrecking ball—for longer than any of us can remember. And yet, it was only in 2016 that the Independent Commission on New York City Criminal Justice and Incarceration Reform was established—a group of judges and lawyers, activists and educators, nonprofit leaders and justice advocates—to finally devise a plan to shut it down.

As a member of the commission, I am proud of our work to propose reasonable, workable solutions to shutter this warehouse of inhumanity and to end its long history of abuse and injustice. This was heavy lifting, full of competing interests and complexity—of nuance.

Meanwhile, some advocates—including some community leaders who have moved the needle on criminal justice reform—oppose the construction of smaller replacement jails, which will make the shuttering of Rikers feasible. No doubt, some simply are NIMBYs who don't want these facilities in their neighborhoods. Many more—courageous visionaries whom I admire and respect—argue that these new jails will fuel the forces that lead to mass incarceration.

Without question, as a community, we will need to hold replacement jails to account, especially in light of the negligent affronts to human dignity at other New York City jails. And, more broadly, we must work together to address the root causes of mass incarceration—to develop and deploy a more just approach to criminal justice.

But we cannot let the perfect be the enemy of progress. If we skip steps, we risk creating a new kind of gap—a gap of missed opportunities and lost alliances.

Indeed, these examples help inform the path forward—a journey away from the extremes.

To begin with, we need to reestablish incentives that encourage our leaders to seek more nuanced solutions and reject unproductive extremes. For instance, the way we measure value has lifted up quarterly earnings without fully accounting for environmental or social costs. The way we delineate political districts and decide elections favors ideological purity over persuasion. And the way we practice philanthropy too often allows for the obscenely wealthy to whitewash or greenwash their reputations through charity, rather than dismantling the systems that make their charity necessary in the first place.

We must also recognize the ways in which a patient, inclusive, and nuanced approach already has resulted in more productive conversations and constructive solutions.

We can see how our capitalist systems have broken down, *while also* appreciating that markets have helped reduce the number of people around the globe who live in poverty. Indeed, we can and should acknowledge the positive step forward by the Business Roundtable and a group of 181 global CEOs who, this summer, committed to redefining the purpose of a corporation in order to benefit all stakeholders, not just shareholders. Now, let's ensure that BRT members follow through on the changes in corporate behavior reflected in the lofty principles in their manifesto.

We can see the historical failures of our own republic on fault lines of race and gender and sexual orientation and class—as *The New York Times* has illustrated with deft, delicate care in its 1619 Project—*while also* protecting and promoting our democratic values and institutions, and participating fully in democratic processes, around the globe.

We can be critical of ill-gotten fortunes, *while also* appreciating the current need for private capital to fund certain valuable public goods, and encouraging wealthy individuals to understand their own privilege and support institutional reforms.

Of course, even the need for nuance is not without its nuances. Some cases are so morally odious and corrupt that no nuance is required: We can disagree about immigration policy without accepting that a government separates parents from their children, or warehouses babies in cages. We can disagree about tax rates and the reach of regulation without accepting white supremacists marching in our streets. We can disagree about the exact scope of the United States Constitution's Second Amendment without accepting violence and terror as an inevitable fact of American life.

Within this kind of rationality—within this kind of complexity—I believe we can find reason for hope: Hope that we can reclaim the commons and common ground; hope that we can join in common cause for a common good; hope that we can extend our hands, and our good faith, and, occasionally, even the benefit of the doubt.

THE IMPERATIVE OF MORAL LEADERSHIP

2020 Annual Message
October 7, 2020

In the late fall of 1863, President Abraham Lincoln traveled to a small town in Pennsylvania, the site of the American Civil War's bloodiest battle. On that sunny, November day—the war still raging—Lincoln addressed the ages. The republic, he said, was engaged in a great battle, testing whether democracy can long endure.

Nearly 157 years on, we, too, are engaged in a test of whether democratic values and institutions can endure. And the test is happening everywhere, all at once.

It's become commonplace to note that America faces a pandemic of pandemics: Fear and fire and fury that betray corruption and climate catastrophe and callous indifference to four hundred years of a racialized caste system; a lethal virus and subsequent economic fallout that lay bare the profoundly unequal ways in which we survive or succumb—in which we live and die. America has lost as many people to the coronavirus during the last eight months as during the two-plus years of battle leading up to that decisive conflict in Gettysburg.

In this context—in *any* context—the passing of icons Justice Ruth Bader Ginsburg and Congressman John Lewis felt like heavy blows. And, in addition to the lives we mourn, we grieve countless other losses: Visits with family or meals with friends. A first day of school. Plans canceled, and dreams deferred. Birthdays, graduations, and holidays—all those rites of passage, stolen. Lost forever, a precious moment to sit with a loved one in their final days, or a memorial service to say goodbye.

In these cases, some of us might say, "thank goodness for technology"—for the video calls and Internet service that keep us connected. But I grieve for those children without tablets and laptops and high-speed connections at home, in urban communities and rural ones alike. Shame on us for asking students—some twelve million kids across the United States—to click into classrooms from the parking lots of fast-food restaurants.

This is hardly the only way inequality has announced itself, or amplified our anguish. The statistics and stories abound.

A couple of weeks ago, clicking through the channels late at night, I landed on C-SPAN's *Washington Journal*. The producers had opened the phone lines and invited Americans to share how the pandemic had affected them. Some people had lost their jobs, but not received the unemployment checks promised to them. Others were staring down an eviction or a foreclosure. Thea, from South Carolina, openly wept as she described her situation—her desperation and anxiety about merely caring for herself.

As she spoke, I found myself weeping with her. Her story was a gut punch—a visceral reminder of how much people are hurting.

Our converging crises—these unceasing traumas—continue to exact a physical and mental toll from each of us. The road here has been exhausting; the road forward seems daunting, especially when it feels we are careening out of control or teetering on the edge of a cliff.

This is a season of suffering—in the United States and around the world. The sum of all this suffering, of all this mourning, of all this daily grief, can be a crushing burden to carry, especially when it feels as though we must carry it on our own. We're all grappling with our own version of what Michelle Obama rightly called "some form of low-grade depression."

And as we bear all of these trials, there is another test—a test akin to the one Lincoln described—that will determine whether and how democracy can long endure: A test of moral leadership.

A TEST OF MORAL LEADERSHIP

We know what effective leadership looks like. When faced with any crisis, with any kind of uncertainty or upheaval, we instinctively look to our leaders—to the people we respect and admire, who call on us to be and do better. As children, it starts with the parents, teachers, and coaches, and other adults in our lives. As students, we pore over those profiles in courage: The stories of statespeople who attended to our ancestors through adversity. At work, we look to the executives in charge or generals in command. We look to authority figures in their various disciplines—the doctor at the hospital, the principal of the school—to exercise their expertise; to organize and orchestrate; to challenge, encourage, or inspire. To tell the truth.

We should expect no less of our elected officials and the institutions they steward, especially in times of local, national, and global crisis. At minimum, we expect some basic level of competence and compassion.

We also know what the downfall of leadership looks like. We have seen the perils associated with immoral leadership. We've seen firsthand how quickly democracies can decay into autocracies—whether in Europe, Africa or Asia, the Americas or the Middle East.

The patterns are consistent, and all too familiar. Truths dismissed as falsehoods. Propaganda and gaslighting embraced as truth. Peaceful protestors attacked. Journalists vilified. Experts undermined. Justice systems politicized as tools of autocracy rather than equality. Human rights jeopardized. The voices and votes of too many suppressed or, simply, uncounted.

All of these egregious violations not only foment inequality, but share a common factor: Impunity.

Through eight decades of work around the world, we at the Ford Foundation have seen how impunity—unjust action without consequence—erodes institutions, and permits and perpetuates corruption, all while exacerbating inequality. We've borne witness to the ways in which a lack of accountability undermines the rule of law.

For years, scholars and experts have warned that American institutions are not immune. Many have sounded—and are sounding—the alarm about the impunity with which norms have been pushed aside in the pursuit of unchecked power and the dangers of "democratic backsliding."

To be sure, American history is rife with injustice. But I have always believed that we were pushing toward progress—however unevenly and incrementally. As an avowed optimist, I never quite grasped—until recently—what it could mean for extreme impunity to become a wrecking ball to the America I love. At the time, perhaps, it was my shortfall of empathy or imagination; now, to not recognize our vulnerability is simply delusion.

For when we look to our leaders in challenging times, we assume they will rise to those challenges. We expect that given the responsibility and opportunity, a person's character and values prevail. We hope that some sense of common good or decency, honor or shame, might awake their better angels, compel them to look past their cynicism or self-interest, even shake them from their silence.

To me, that we have fallen this far points to a failure of moral leadership.

And by moral leadership, I do not mean the kind that *moralizes*; we don't need self-righteousness, but selflessness. I don't claim any special access to moral principles, nor mean to suggest the primacy of any kind or class of individual. I do believe, however, that in every theater of our lives, we need more people focused on the bigger, broader objective beyond the next earnings call or election: A long-term vision for a more just society. We need leaders who are motivated by values and incentives and outcomes that transcend those offered by the systems which, by design or neglect, have widened inequality to an untenable degree. We need new profiles in courage—more business leaders who serve the interests of all their stakeholders, not only their shareholders; more elected officials who serve a common good, not only the donors and partisans who comprise their base of support.

We need these leaders not only for ourselves but for others. After all, right now, the world watches and wonders whether America can live up to its promise as a champion of human rights and a beacon of liberty and justice for all.

To be sure, America's leadership crisis is far from new; like inequality, it has only been made excruciatingly plain during recent months and years. It is not even the first time I have spoken about moral leadership. It will likely not be the last because this crisis of moral leadership cuts across every issue.

Every one of our ongoing crises has been compounded by choices made and not made. Choices that deny humanity and dignity and justice to others on a daily basis, whether they take the form of active harm or passive neglect. Choices that, in an era of impunity and inequality, yield no consequences for the powerful, and too many for everyone else.

In this way, moral leadership—of all kinds, in every movement and institution, organization and community—is a prerequisite for positive change. And my continued hope comes from my faith that we can turn the tide, as we have before. To paraphrase Gwen Carr, the mother of Eric Garner, we can channel our mourning into a movement, our pain into purpose.

If our heroes could step up to meet their moments, so can we. If John Lewis and Ruth Bader Ginsburg could—if Fannie Lou Hamer and Shirley Chisholm could—we can too. And we must.

A VISION OF ABSOLUTE EQUALITY

Six years after Lincoln asked whether democracy can long endure, four years after the test at Appomattox, Frederick Douglass offered a vision for not just endurance but transformation. As historian David Blight writes in his Pulitzer-Prize-winning biography of Douglass, in 1869, he traveled the country, delivering perhaps the most remarkable of his orations, "Composite Nation."

Douglass proposed the terms and tenets of a multiracial, pluralist democracy that would feel familiar, if still aspirational today: An antidote and antithesis to the division of the last several years; a more perfect, more inclusive, more hopeful future.

Douglass said: "We have for a long time hesitated to adopt and carry out the only principle which can ... give peace, strength and security to the Republic, and that is the principle of *absolute equality*."

That principle—and his vision—must inspire us now to act.

The future may feel uncertain. But the only real certainty is that, if we do nothing, we lose the fight for "absolute equality." And when the world feels out of control, we must remember that we control whether or not we act.

That starts with voting. For as Douglass himself once put it, failing to vote is "as great a crime as an open violation of the law itself."

And while voting is necessary and imperative, it, alone, is not sufficient. No matter the outcome of any election, our work remains clear.

We must hold our leaders accountable, and we must hold each other accountable as well. We must break the vicious cycle of corruption, impunity, and cynicism—and demand better incentives for better leadership. We must continue to participate and engage, to show up and take action, because the fate of democracy is not decided any one day.

As Justice Ginsburg once wrote of Dr. Martin Luther King Jr.'s moral arc of the universe, it will only bend toward justice with "a steadfast national commitment to see the task through to completion."

We must constantly renew our steadfast commitment. We must see the task of justice through to completion, knowing that for our most vexing problems, the reward of our work may come for the next generation, or the one after that.

Once again, we are, as Lincoln suggested at Gettysburg, facing a great test. But with moral leadership, we can and will pass it. With moral leadership, this can and will be a moment, in Lincoln's words, for "a new birth of freedom"; an opportunity to rebuild, more perfect.

DEMOCRACY AT A CROSSROADS: A CALL FOR COURAGEOUS LEADERSHIP

Benjamin Menschel Distinguished Lecture at Cooper Union
New York, New York
March 4, 2024

For some 165 years, Cooper Union, this great hall, has served as a great American crossroads—an intersection of people and ideas; an intersection of past, and present, and future. For generations, this is where we, collectively, hold up history's compass—to orient and reorient ourselves; to find our way forward.

I must confess, I feel overwhelmed with awe and humility as I reflect on my moment at this podium, on our moment together here: To imagine what Abraham Lincoln might have observed from this vantage; what Frederick Douglass might have discerned looking out from this dais; what Susan B. Anthony and Elizabeth Cady Stanton might have beheld. To see in your faces, the faces of our forebearers, who could not know how history would unfold. To see in our great city on edge, their great city on edge—in our great republic on the brink, their great republic on the brink.

At every consequential juncture, this great hall is where we, the people, come to deliberate and to decide. And for us, as for those who came before us, we are staring straight, unavoidably, into a crossroads of our own—into a hard set of choices.

These are choices about what kind of nation we are and will be; about what kind of leaders we will be; about what kind of citizens we will be. These are choices between hope and fear; between courage and despair; between one worldview that tells us "might makes right" and another that insists, as Lincoln affirmed for the ages here, that "right makes might"— that our shared values, our democratic values, remain our greatest strength.

These days, one might reasonably wonder whether America's many multitudes are even reading the same compass. We are pulled hither and yon, in so many different directions.

Tonight, though, I would propose that we still do share what Frederick Douglass called "True North": A set of ideas—aspirations—enshrined in Thomas Jefferson's declaration, to which Lincoln appealed time and again during the tumultuous, transformative years that followed his visit here:

We all are created equal. We all are endowed with inalienable rights.

Our American identity emerges not from "blood and soil," but from fidelity to these truths we hold self-evident even still. Out of many, we are one.

We believe in equal representation, equal rights, and equal justice—in what Douglass called "absolute equality."

We believe in freedom, with fairness—in free expression, free exercise, and a free press.

We believe in our moral responsibilities, in empathy and generosity.

We believe in liberty and justice—and in striking the balance between the two, between the rights of the individual and our responsibilities to the collective.

To be sure, some say, these are "hollow words, at best." The facts are undeniable. America has functioned as a democracy for less than one human lifetime—and an imperfect democracy at that. When you think about it, our democracy is only as old as I am.

I was born in 1959, into a nation riven by American apartheid. When I was a child, the adults in my life could not vote in our Louisiana and Texas towns. I was six years old when President Lyndon Johnson enacted legislation to guarantee the franchise. And even these protections are imperiled now, as are so many of our fundamental rights.

And yet, for my part, I believe that our American compass is still true. I see flawed genius in our founders and their legacy—and in Lincoln's determination to preserve that legacy at the greatest cost.

To me, the contradiction—the hypocrisy—of our founders is less remarkable than what they set in motion. They initiated a grand, complicated experiment in self-government. It led to abolition and suffrage and workers' rights and civil rights and women's rights—however slowly, however unevenly.

More astounding still, generation by generation, Black people and Brown people, the Indigenous and the immigrant, Jews and Muslims, queer people and people with disabilities—we all claimed the American project as our birthright. We expanded the circle of inclusion and opportunity, making real the American promise, step by step, crossroads by crossroads, now 250 years on.

Jefferson and the others passed to us something unprecedented, something radical: That true compass—the tools with which to navigate our course toward a multiracial, multiethnic, pluralist democracy that extends the privilege of American identity to all.

I love my country. I am grateful to my country. We should be proud of our country.

Instead, a sense of nihilism has taken hold, all across America. We are tearing each other down, tearing ourselves apart at the seams, and tearing our nation asunder.

It is almost banal to note, America is more irreparably divided than ever before in our lifetimes. We may well be barreling down a parallel path to the one that Lincoln and his contemporaries traveled in the 1850s. The sustainability, the durability, the survival of our democratic republic is in jeopardy.

What's different, today, are the trends that have converged and carried us here.

The primary current carving a great chasm across our land—across our national soul and psyche—is inequality: Inequality in access and agency, in resources and respect, in voice and value; inequalities of all kinds and categories, the consequence of a market system that is wildly out of balance.

I am a proud capitalist. I believe in the market system's unique power to lift lives and livelihoods when abetted by public policy that ensures the market is fair and inclusive. But in a democratic-capitalist society, democracy must come first, or the whole enterprise collapses.

Today, for too many Americans of every color and creed—in red states and blue—the mobility escalator has sputtered to a stop. Millions live on the brink—their lives defined by trauma, by pain, by an inescapable and insidious hopelessness. And hope? Hope is the oxygen of democracy.

The poet asks, "What happens to a dream deferred?" Well, what happens to the American dream betrayed?

One can understand why so many people respond to a world that feels completely out of control—a world turned completely against them—with fear, with resentment, with grievance, with vitriol.

One also must acknowledge how the forces of narrow self-interest in our society exploit these disaffected, disillusioned people and communities—how they prey on them for their own gain, with impunity.

One can also see, then, how our broken, for-profit media system aggravates our inequality crisis.

If America's founders agreed on anything, it was that democracy would depend on a free and fact-based press; that, through the free press, facts would precede opinion, not the other way around; and that through "enlightenment," as Jefferson said, "tyranny ... [would] vanish like evil spirits at the dawn of day."

Of course, what we see today—the media conglomerates' current operating model—is exactly the opposite.

Audiences respond to the most prurient and pernicious content. So, the content and programming algorithms deliver hour after hour of it, monetizing the degradation of our democracy.

On cable, we see hate and hostility, misinformation and disinformation, sometimes outright falsehoods, pumped into the bloodstream of the body politic. And online, the most obnoxious, odious voices garner the most clicks, and likes, and shares—truth be damned—training the algorithms to feed us ever-increasing doses of poison.

This formula may provide a healthy return on capital, but it does so at the cost of an information cancer, now metastasizing throughout our democracy.

And then into the torrent converges another defining, destabilizing trend, too: We are mired in a culture of absolutism.

If I asked you to encapsulate the last decade of American life in a single word, you might offer up a few possibilities: Aberrant? Abhorrent?

I might suggest another: Extreme.

Everything right now, it seems, is black or white, all or nothing, perfect or unacceptable. Every venue has become a theater for affirming our own virtue or righteousness—or for denying someone else's.

The purpose of the public square has become completely perverted. Only a generation ago, we used the commons as the infrastructure through which to negotiate diversity and difference—to find common ground, sometimes more effectively than others. But now, we treat the public square as merely another platform on which to perform; another platform on which to take a side and to prove our piety to it.

Nuance and complexity are nowhere to be found. In their place is a pervasive, paralyzing cynicism. And so, our extreme challenges remain extremely unsolved.

Certainly, not everyone is equally complicit. To be clear, I am not suggesting that the people and groups that denigrate our long-shared American values are somehow on equal footing with those of us defending them. This is a false moral equivalence.

Make no mistake about my own convictions: I believe that the advocacy of those women and men with their hands on that long moral arc, bending it inch by inch toward justice—they are of a different category than those whose hands are tearing it all down. The former are challenging us to be better. The latter too often are daring us to be worse.

Nevertheless, as a result, we have normalized mendacity and malice—bizarrely enough, even among those with whom we mostly agree.

And among those with whom we disagree? We shame. We cancel. We dehumanize. We demonize.

These are the facts—the painful facts. As Americans, we are increasingly intolerant of each other. Intolerant.

Lincoln's admonition—"a house divided against itself cannot stand"—feels truer, realer, rawer than ever. And we must decide what matters most: The America we love? The America we are, at our best? The democratic values to which we aspire? Or the self-satisfaction of our self-certainty, and the self-destruction that follows?

So, what are we to do? At this hour of choosing, what are we to decide?

For starters, let's choose to lead. And let's choose to make things easier on the people who are courageous enough to lead, and courageous enough to tell the truth.

Effective leadership, moral leadership, demands that we listen with more humility, and curiosity, and empathy, even if we don't agree with 100 percent of what we assume we are hearing. It requires that we build longer bridges—among communities that look, speak, work, worship, or vote differently than we do. It challenges us to recognize that within all of this rolling crisis, there is opportunity—if we are brave enough to see it, and to seize it.

We—all of us—have made it too difficult for good leaders to do the work of holding up that compass and finding the way out and through. We are discouraging courage.

Honestly, there never has been a more difficult time to lead anything, global or local, public or private, big or small.

And the new prevailing attitude says: Just keep your head down. Protect yourself—and your reputation. Speaking out will cost you more than it buys.

We must reject this way of operating. For goodness' sake, what is the point of calling ourselves leaders if we are afraid to actually lead?

I don't claim any special access to moral principles. I do believe, however, that we need more leaders focused on something bigger than the next earnings call—or living in fear of the next reporter to call. We need new profiles in courage—leaders who recognize that bringing light is always worth the heat.

We also need leaders with a moral compass and the courage to embrace the nuance and complexity to which we have become allergic. Indeed, the very definition of effective leadership is managing nuance, managing complexity, seeing all sides of an issue from the perspectives of every stakeholder, and then setting a course and communicating with clarity, consistent with a core set of values.

This is true in government and business and civil society alike. And it is not easy.

We struggle with this in reconciling with and rectifying the past—which was never all sin or all salvation. We struggle with this in the present—given the pain and grief and despair of this moment; given widening deficits of trust and empathy and faith in our shared humanity; given the inequality that desensitizes us to the suffering of others, preventing us from joining together in common cause to solve shared challenges.

And yet, we know, the road to reconciliation—to shared healing and shared hope—runs through precisely these things: Trust and empathy and faith in each other; grace and love for each other; collective action for a common good.

And progress down that road requires that we rediscover and recommit to our shared American identity.

From my own life's journey, I understand how, and how much, our identities matter. I understand how the intersecting elements of our identities too often determine what doors are open to us, and what doors remain closed. And yet, from more than six decades on this earth, I believe that none of my identities matters more than my American identity.

The truth is, I have lived on both sides of American inequality.

I grew up Black in the "Lost Cause," Jim Crow South. In college, I knew people who proudly hung Confederate flags on their dormitory walls, who attended fraternity parties in their Confederate greys. And yet, throughout my life, I have benefited, in ways visible and invisible, from Americans, Black and white, who challenged our nation to fulfill its promise.

I grew up poor—the son of a single mother, in a small shotgun house. And yet, throughout my life, I benefited from the American people's investments in Head Start, and public schools, and Pell grants.

I grew up gay at a time when many people saw my sexuality as a psychological disorder, or a crime. And yet, throughout my life, I have seen Americans choose equality.

This is not to deny that I sometimes feel exhausted and demoralized, too. I feel the impatience. I feel the frustration. And I worry deeply about the ubiquitous sense of unfairness that has consumed so many of us. Too many people sense that others are gaining an advantage or an edge, while they are falling behind.

No doubt, by virtue of good fortune, our system has made me a winner. It has lifted me out of poverty—and given me the opportunities to realize my dreams. Yet, too many feel that this same system is working against them—that it is rigged against them. So, I also worry deeply about the rage that tears away at our patriotism.

We cannot allow this kind of anger to fester, not any longer. We cannot surrender our patriotism, neither our love of country nor our service to country, because the only way to ensure that America works for everyone is for everyone to put in the work for America—not just giving something back, but giving something of ourselves; sacrificing to be part of something greater.

Which brings us back to that snowy evening, 164 years ago last week, when a lanky, young Illinois congressman stepped onto this very stage in his wrinkled suit. At that moment, Lincoln's opponents were demanding that the federal government permit slavery's spread to the West. But more than that, they were threatening to destroy the republic itself, unless, as Lincoln said here, they be allowed to "rule or ruin" as they pleased, without regard to the Constitution.

This kind of all-or-nothing government—this kind of asymmetrical autocracy—may well sound familiar. We hear the echoes almost daily.

But what Lincoln wisely knew then—what we would be well served to remember now—was that democracy is no permanent condition. He knew that the only way to protect democracy, to preserve democracy, is through the give and take—through the slow, sometimes-frustrating, consensus-building machinery that our founders engineered.

In a word, through compromise.

After all, if and when we lose our ability to disagree without destroying one another, then everything is jeopardized, everything is imperiled—because where compromise ends, where the basic value of tolerance ends, this is where violence begins.

For too long, we have accepted the zero-sum thinking that says, "If the other side wins on anything, my side loses on everything." Enough.

Compromise is often undesirable. It is frustrating, distasteful, by definition. Worse, it can perpetuate the very harm that we most fervently yearn to heal.

But the work of justice is much bigger than any one compromise. It is the work of a lifetime, the work of generations, the work of the American project itself.

And so, together, at this time of choosing, let us recommit ourselves to the grandest project of all: The American experiment, the American idea. Let's step away from the extremes and from the edge—away from the sanctimony and certitude.

At this profound crossroads for our democracy, let's, once again, hold up history's compass and take measure—of the road we have traveled, of the journey ahead. There is no map; there never was. But with leadership, with open minds and open hearts, with vigilance, with hope, we can and will find our way back to "True North," together.

THERE IS NO LEADERSHIP WITHOUT RISK

The New York Times
October 20, 2024

There has never been a more difficult time to lead anything—whether a publicly traded corporation or a nonprofit nongovernmental organization; whether a global university or a local, public school or classroom.

Indeed, many of the best would-be leaders I know are asking, *Why would I even want to be a leader?*

As I prepare to step down from the Ford Foundation, having served through the years on more than a dozen boards of directors across sectors and industries, I see a gathering crisis of leadership.

The consequences for our shared democratic values and institutions are clear and present. The cycle that causes America's leadership crisis ought to be as well.

Hardly a day passes without a fellow leader lamenting—in sidebar or green room or private-lunch conversations—the myriad ways in which our culture actively *discourages* the *courage* that is essential to effective leadership.

Leadership is an action, not a title. And many of our leaders are paralyzed by broken, perverse incentives that impair their abilities to fulfill institutional missions and mandates. Paradoxically, many leaders feel that any reduction in their visibility brings with it a promise of reward.

Increasingly, I worry that well-intentioned boards of directors are selecting rising leaders for safety, appointing executives who have assiduously avoided controversy rather than those most adept at managing it. Then, they counsel toward caution, not conscience.

Around too many board tables, trustees and directors tell their executives: *Just keep your head down.* The prevailing attitude says: *Speaking out will cost you more than it buys. Better to say as little as possible, to protect yourself and your reputation, to exhibit neutrality for the purpose of self-preservation.*

Those in positions of leadership fear they will say the wrong thing, or what they believe to be the right thing in the wrong way. They fear risk, recrimination, and reprisal. They fear a coarsening culture—our collective instinct to shame and shun, our collective intolerance for nuance and complexity—that squeezes them from all sides, corralling them toward the straightest, narrowest path.

To be sure, some argue that leaders should stay in their respective lanes: Better not to risk offending one constituency or another, especially with a policy or perspective that might be construed as political. Sometimes, discretion is well advised and appropriate.

But courageous, moral leadership demands more. Because it challenges us to recognize that bringing light is often worth enduring the heat, especially in moments of profound challenge for our democracy, our communities, and our world.

We penalize bold leadership when we should be rewarding it. Inequalities of all kinds have eroded the very foundation of our American community—because inequality has created the conditions in which the American people are both desperate for leadership and programmed for corrosive cynicism about seemingly anyone who offers it.

Many millions of people feel completely out of control—as if the world has turned against them—and they respond with distrust and resentment and grievance and vitriol, reflections of deep hopelessness.

We have become, simply put, antisocialized. As the political scientist Robert Putnam has demonstrated, we engage less in community activities and organizations, and as the journalist Bill Bishop has documented, we self-sort into homogeneous geographic clusters more. The US surgeon general has even declared an epidemic of loneliness. Leadership—a communal exercise by definition—is relentlessly undermined.

At the same time, in a divided and often lonely nation, our society's forces of narrow self-interest prey on disaffected, disillusioned people and communities, for their own gain, with impunity, and they do so in part through our distorted media system.

Polarizing content drives engagement and profit: Hour after hour, post after post, content is monetized to further degrade our discourse and democracy. This has an effect on our leaders, in turn.

This formula may provide a healthy return on capital, but it does so at the cost of an information cancer.

Only a generation ago, leaders used the commons as the place in which to negotiate diversity and difference—to find common ground—sometimes more effectively than others. But now, we treat the public square as merely another platform on which to take a side and to prove our piety to it. And all of this renders us, in a word, ungovernable.

One indispensable solution is the thing contemporary culture deters and disparages: Bold, undaunted, audacious leaders.

Fearless leaders have been essential to the survival of America's grand experiment from the very beginning. On scales large and small, the vision of our leaders has always changed the ways we see ourselves and one another.

Heroes of each successive generation attended to our ancestors through adversity—against reactionary resistance—not only from the top down, but also from the bottom up; from the community, civic, and civil-society organizations that give shape and structure to our lives; from the people we respect and admire, who call on us to be and do better.

To be clear, I do not claim any special moral principles. Far from it. I do believe, however, that we need leaders focused on something bigger than the next earnings call or living in fear of the next journalist to call.

We need leaders who manifest a moral capacity to embrace the nuance and complexity to which we've become allergic, come what may—to take a stand for progress, even if incremental or imperfect.

Indeed, effective leadership requires managing nuance and complexity, seeing all sides of an issue from the perspective of every stakeholder, and then setting a course, and communicating with clarity, consistent with common values.

After all, no courage? No leadership. We cannot move forward, however unevenly, without courageous visionaries blazing new paths that illuminate the way for all of us to follow.

The responsibility rests on all of our shoulders—in the ways we lead, in the ways we choose our leaders, and in the ways we allow ourselves to be led.

ACKNOWLEDGMENTS

The "idea of America" remains contested, as does the provenance of the phrase.

The transcendentalist, abolitionist, Unitarian minister Theodore Parker first popularized the expression in 1850—and the founders of *The Atlantic*, led by James Russell Lowell, made "the American idea" their new publication's shibboleth in 1857, on the eve of the Civil War.

Horace Meyer Kallen, who coined the term *pluralism*, infused the American idea into his thinking and writing throughout the first half of the twentieth century—as did Nobel laureate Gunnar Myrdal, whose 1944 *An American Dilemma* notably captured the contradiction at the heart of the American experience as the Civil Rights Movement first began to stir.

One of my heroes, Barbara Jordan, invoked the American idea in her iconic keynote address at the 1976 Democratic National Convention: "Though it is shared by all of us, it is realized in each one of us." A decade later, the celebrated journalist Theodore White wrote of the American idea in a final essay published posthumously in 1986: "Englishmen are English, Frenchmen are French, Chinese are Chinese.... But Americans are a nation born of an idea."

Peggy Noonan, author of the 2024 book *A Certain Idea of America*, channeled this same ethos with elegance and consequence in much of her work with and for President Ronald Reagan, as the American idea was central to his concept of American exceptionalism, a parallel precept that reaches back to Alexis de Tocqueville, if not further. Indeed, in a 2011 collection under the same title, distinguished historian Gordon S. Wood traced the idea of America to our founding with incisive rigor.

Of course, Pulitzer laureate Nikole Hannah-Jones reminds us through her *The 1619 Project* that the idea of America always has been an aspiration: An echo of the poet Langston Hughes, who affirmed the most *American* of American ideas—that America *will* be.

* * *

To me, in its simplest formulation, the idea of America is that from many we are one, united by our shared values.

On the grandest scale, this is true of our pluralist democracy. On a smaller one, this idea has found expression in my own American journey—and my own leadership journey in and through philanthropy (also an American idea)—the last dozen years of which are represented in these pages.

To *many*, then, I am humbled by the debt that I owe and by the profound gratitude that I feel. And I am especially thankful to all who have given so much to my term of stewardship at the Ford Foundation.

First, thank you to our prodigious board of trustees, past and present: Since 2013, this includes Sir Tim Berners-Lee, Afsaneh Beschloss, Ursula Burns, Catalina Devandas, Martin A. Eakes, Amy C. Falls, Henry Ford III, Juliet V. García, J. Clifford Hudson, Laurene Powell Jobs, Robert S. Kaplan, Thomas Kempner Jr., Lourdes Lopez, Thurgood Marshall Jr., Paula Moreno, N.R. Narayana Murthy, Peter A. Nadosy, Gbenga Oyebode, Ai-jen Poo, Samantha Power, Chuck Robbins, Bryan Stevenson, Gabrielle Sulzberger, Richard R. Verma, George H. Walker IV—and, forever with us in memory, Marca Bristo and Cecile Richards. You have been a wellspring of wisdom, strength, and stability, especially board chairs Irene Hirano Inouye (whom we miss dearly), Kofi Appenteng, and Francisco G. Cigarroa.

Thank you, also, to my exceptional leadership team, including officers Martín Abregú, Nishka Chandrasoma, Eric Doppstadt, Sarita Gupta, Diane Headley, Depelsha McGruder, and Michele Moore, who valiantly oversaw the project that produced this book. I am indebted to many of their predecessors, as well, foremost among them John Bernstein, Maya Harris, Hilary Pennington, Maria Torres-Springer, and communications leaders Marta L. Tellado and Alfred Ironside, whose unmistakable fingerprints grace and improve the compositions memorialized here.

In this same spirit, thank you Nick Gabriel and Barron (Buzz) Tenny for blazing the trail before me.

To my team, brilliantly led by my indefatigable Chief of Staff Taara Rangarajan—and before her, Kristen Jarvis West and Deesha Dyer—thank you for making possible my peripatetic life and leadership, and for juggling the large and small with joy and aplomb. To Noorain Khan and Juliet Mureriwa, thank you for translating our ambition into action through our grantmaking. Robyn Gibbons was with me since our days in Harlem; I am forever appreciative. And I extend fervent thanks to Azrial Greene-Pina, Juliana Woodley, Carly Machado, Saranna Nabirali, Jeffrey Hernandez, and Giselle Blanco-Santana.

My thanks, as well, to the advisers who provided invaluable perspective along the way: Jeff Bradach, Tom Tierney, and the Bridgespan team; Tom Freedman and Freedman Consulting; Holly Sidford and the Helicon Collaborative; Maurice Obeid, Linda Liu, Kurt Strovink, Dom Williams, and their McKinsey colleagues; and Kathryn Williams, my executive coach.

For this project's success, I am grateful to all who contributed: To President Bill Clinton for the generous foreword and extraordinary example across a lifetime of exceptional leadership; to Annie Leibovitz for her masterful photography (I've never been a fan of my own photo, until I encountered Annie's genius in action); to Matthew Creegan and Archie Bell, who expertly coordinated our efforts from the foundation's office of communications; and to the team at Wiley, led by Bill Falloon.

I also owe singular thanks to the incomparable Jonas Kieffer and his team at West Wing Writers (including, through the years, Christopher Fox, Laurence Pevsner, Marcus Allen-Granderson, Leah Abrams, Caitlyn Jordan, Julia Ishiyama, Annabelle Long, and Veronica Bean). Jonas and I were colleagues at the Rockefeller Foundation—and in the summer of 2013, I asked if we might pick up where we left off. We have been partners in thought and prose ever since, collaborators in the truest and fullest sense. He curated and edited this collection, with an able assist from Kris Pauls and Pam Harcourt, who provided both expertise and a heroic effort to secure permissions. Thank you, Jonas, for helping me to impose some order on the voices in my head—and to develop, strengthen, and amplify a powerful voice in the world.

To the Ford family, thank you for your open hand, open arms, and open door—especially to matriarch Martha Firestone Ford and Henry Ford III, the first Ford to serve as a foundation trustee in forty years; to Edsel II and Cynthia (Henry's proud parents); to Anne, Charlotte, and their families, including Alessandro Uzielli, all of whom are descendants of Henry Ford II; and to William Clay Ford Jr., Sheila and Steve Hamp, and the wider Ford-Firestone family.

Maya Angelou said, "We are who we are because they were who they were"—and I thank the intrepid leaders who showed me and shared with me the way: Ned O'Gorman and Elsie V. Aidinoff at the Children's Storefront School; Karen Phillips at the Abyssinian Development Corporation; the late Sir Gordon Conway and Julia Lopez, who hired me, and then Judith Rodin, who elevated and encouraged me at the Rockefeller Foundation; my Ford Foundation predecessor, Luis Ubiñas, who persuaded me to leave Rockefeller and join his leadership team; Ligia Cravo, Sharon King, Geri Mannion, Adam Meyerson, Mary Jo Mullan, Nancy Roob, Karen Rosa, Hildy Simmons, Jon Stryker, and the late Urvashi Vaid, who tutored me in the art and science of philanthropy.

To my peer foundation executives who have taught me much on my journey, thank you—especially Ellen Alberding, Elizabeth Alexander, Tonya Allen, Richard Besser, Deepak Bhargava, Jim Canales, Don Chen, Heather Templeton Dill, Patrick Gaspard, Sam Gill, Patti Harris, Stephen Heintz, Brian Hooks, Alberto, Ibargüen, Cinny Kennard, Larry Kramer, Risa Lavizzo-Mourey, Gara LaMarche, Nancy Lindborg, Grant Oliphant, John Palfrey, George Pavlov, Barbara Picower, Angelique Power, Rip Rapson, Sigrid Rausing, Chris Stone, Mark Suzman, La June Montgomery Tabron, and Nicole Taylor.

To the courageous, phenomenal women who transformed philanthropy, a special thank you for your inspiration, innovation, and determined resilience: Laurene Powell Jobs, Alice Walton, Melinda French Gates, MacKenzie Scott, Agnes Gund, and Barbara Hostetter.

And thank you to three other venerable counselors and teachers: Susan Berresford, another Ford Foundation predecessor and matron saint of courage, decency, and integrity; Michael Bloomberg, whose unrivaled pace of personal giving has earned him the title "Most Generous American"; and Ken Chenault, dear friend and standard bearer of excellence for the next generation of business and civic leaders.

These last few years have brought immense challenge for our national and global communities. They also have brought painful loss to my own community—and I thank the countless friends (too many to name here) who nourished and sustained me with love and support, none more so than my dear Holly Peterson, who has been at my side for three decades.

I think every day of the mentors who made my journey possible, especially the late Rev. Calvin O. Butts III, Joel Fleishman, Vartan Gregorian,

Vernon Jordan, and Franklin Thomas, whose legacies we carry forward; these are the giants on whose shoulders I stand. And I live every day with gratitude for my David, forever my light and my love.

* * *

During the summer of 2013, as I prepared for my final interviews with the Ford Foundation's board, I sketched out a set of guiding principles, a credo, for *how* I promised to lead: *Be ambitious, but humble—bold, not reckless. Seek to inspire, not impress. Pursue collaboration, not credit. Act with righteousness, not self-righteousness.*

A dozen years later, as I take my leave with a heart full of gratitude, I return to this refrain and to the energizing, ennobling feeling of hope, *radical hope*, with which I began. For hope, too, is indispensable to the American idea.

From 250 years of history, we learn that the single greatest threat to our democracy is not economic collapse or environmental crisis; not disease, disorder, disinformation, or demagogy; not who holds (or abuses) power between elections, nor the impunity with which they wield it. The greatest threat to democracy is hopelessness.

And so, if *we the people* are to fend off inequality's progeny—grievance, mendacity, nihilism, and the rest—then we might start by recommitting to our common values and common good, with the unwavering, unyielding, unfaltering hope that has fueled our most *uncommon* story of progress.

To all engaged in this grand American project—in *keeping* this republic of ours, this democracy with which our founders entrusted us—thank you. To the ambitious, the bold, the inspiring, the righteous—to all who serve the idea of America—you have my admiration and appreciation always. To you, I dedicate this volume.

CREDITS

"Repeal of Affirmative Action Is Only the Beginning" originally appeared in *The New York Times* on June 30, 2023.

"Work in Detroit Doesn't End with Grand Bargain" originally appeared in *Detroit Free Press* on November 19, 2014.

"All In on Detroit" originally appeared in *Detroit Free Press* on June 15, 2015.

"Unleashing the Power of Endowments: The Next Great Challenge for Philanthropy" originally appeared in *Stanford Social Innovation Review* on April 5, 2017.

"A $1 Billion Experiment in Philanthropic Investing" is reprinted with permission of *Wall Street Journal*, Copyright © 2017 Dow Jones & Company, Inc. All Rights Reserved Worldwide. License number 5999411284103.

"Healing the Breach: The Ford Family and Ford Foundation" originally appeared in *Fortune* on December 5, 2024.

"Rejecting the Tyranny of Strategy" is based on a contribution to "Strategic Philanthropy for a Complex World," a debate that appeared in the Summer 2014 issue of *Stanford Social Innovation Review*.

"Why Giving Back Isn't Enough" originally appeared in *The New York Times* on December 18, 2015.

"Philanthropy Is an American Idea and Birthright" is from TIME. © 2016 TIME USA LLC. All rights reserved. Used under license.

"In Support of Philanthropic Pluralism" is used with permission of *The Chronicle of Philanthropy*, volume 35, issue 7, May 2023; permission conveyed through Copyright Clearance Center, Inc.

ABOUT THE AUTHOR

Darren Walker serves as the tenth president of the Ford Foundation—established in 1936 and endowed with more than $16 billion in assets—among the largest and most influential philanthropic institutions in the world. Since 2013, Darren has overseen more than $7 billion in grantmaking, while transforming the foundation and philanthropy and promoting democratic values around the globe.

Previously, Darren was vice president at the Rockefeller Foundation, where he led all program work. In the 1990s, he was COO of the Abyssinian Development Corporation, Harlem's flagship community-development organization. He began his career in international law at Cleary Gottlieb Steen & Hamilton and then in capital markets at UBS.

Darren cofounded both the US Impact Investing Alliance and the Presidents' Council on Disability Inclusion in Philanthropy. He serves on many boards, including the Art Bridges Foundation, Bloomberg, Inc., the Clooney Foundation for Justice, the High Line, Lincoln Center for the Performing Arts, the National Gallery of Art, PepsiCo, Ralph Lauren, and the Waverly Street Foundation.

He has been recognized among *TIME*'s 100 Most Influential People, *Rolling Stone*'s 25 People Shaping the Future, and as *The Wall Street Journal*'s 2020 Philanthropy Innovator of the Year. He has received twenty honorary degrees, including Harvard University's W. E. B. Du Bois Medal.

In 2022, Darren was awarded France's highest cultural honor, *Commandeur de L'ordre des Arts et des Lettres*, for leadership in the arts. In 2023, Her Majesty Queen Elizabeth II appointed Darren to the Order of the British Empire for services to UK–US relations. And in 2024, President Joseph R. Biden awarded him the National Humanities Medal.

A proud product of public schools, Darren was a member of the first Head Start class in 1965 and earned BA, BS, and JD degrees from The University of Texas at Austin.